T0293753

Feminism, Republicanism, Egalitarianism, Environmentalism

This book addresses hegemonic ruling class masculinity and emphasized femininity within renewables organisational governance, and critiques Anglo-Celtic male privilege as a barrier to women's leadership participation.

Primarily using the Australian socio-political context, the author considers the patriarchal control of organisations and renewables governance, and argues that women-led emphasized femininity-resistance strategies can challenge the hegemonic status of ruling elites to create a leadership that is less power oriented, more collaborative and open to change. Utilising detailed interviews with Australian women environmentalists, together with feminist, sociological and social movement theory, whilst considering the historic context of Red Vienna and contemporary political challenges (Brexit, Monarchism, etc.), it puts forward an innovative policy framework for an Australian Bill of Rights Act and Republican Constitutional change.

Written for academics, activists and policymakers alike, this book offers a unique insight into women's inequity within patriarchal institutionalist governance. It will be engaging and inspiring reading for feminist and environmental activists and practitioners, in addition to professional associations focussing on gender, justice and environmental change. Academics and postgraduates in Gender Studies, Ecofeminism, Sociology and Organisational Studies will also find the book of key interest in its interdisciplinary discussions of Sustainable Scientific-Technological Development Initiatives (SSTDI) and feminism in an Australian political context.

Yulia Maleta's research addresses gender identity, sustainable technological development and qualitative methodologies within the frame of sociopolitical NSMs. She has a PhD in social sciences and has contributed to reputable interdisciplinary peer-reviewed publications, including *Journal of Sociology*, *Third Sector Review* and *Journal of International Women's Studies*.

Feminism, Republicanism, Egalitarianism, Environmentalism

Bill of Rights and Gendered Sustainable Initiatives

Yulia Maleta

Routledge
Taylor & Francis Group

LONDON AND NEW YORK

First published 2020
by Routledge
2 Park Square, Milton Park, Abingdon, Oxon OX14 4RN

and by Routledge
52 Vanderbilt Avenue, New York, NY 10017

Routledge is an imprint of the Taylor & Francis Group, an informa business

First issued in paperback 2021

British Library Cataloguing-in-Publication Data
A catalogue record for this book is available from the British Library

Library of Congress Cataloging-in-Publication Data
A catalog record has been requested for this book

ISBN: 978-1-138-58594-2 (hbk)
ISBN: 978-1-03-208968-3 (pbk)
ISBN: 978-0-429-50495-2 (ebk)

Typeset in Goudy
by Newgen Publishing UK

Contents

Acknowledgements

I acknowledge the valued, voluntary participation of women advocates/activists of the Australian Greens party, eNGOs, grassroots and academia to my research study.

I thank the following individuals: Professor Rodney Smith, Dr Peter Chen, Assoc. Prof. Catriona Elder, Dr. Elisabeth Valiente-Riedl and David Bray (academics from the University of Sydney).

This book is based on some material from my PhD, completed at Western Sydney University. Western Sydney University approved the research component of my study.

Part I

Feminism: A Precursor for Republicanism

1   Introduction

Envisioning an Australian Republican-Constitutional Change and Bill of Rights Act

Introduction

Utilising my interviews with Australian women environmentalists, this book addresses hegemonic (ruling class) masculinity and emphasized femininity along with intersections of constructivism/essentialism within global renewables governance. My study is framed by a feminist-constructivist-sociocultural qualitative approach centred on: 1. women's *agentic performative multiple skills-set*; and, 2. an emphasized femininity approach that is 'resistant' to patriarchy (Cockburn 1988, 2013; Plumwood 1997; Gaard 2001; Butler 2007, 2013; Culley and Angelique 2010). My Republican-Bill of Rights modelling of Sustainable Scientific-Technological Development Initiatives (SSTDI) is supported by Women-Led Wind, Wave and Solar Energy (WW & SE) solutions. Applying Connell's (1995, 2005, 2009) theorisation of hegemony and Cockburn's (1988) gendering of competence plus patriarchal critique of Social Movements (Cockburn 2012, 2013), and Butler's (2007, 2009, 2013) insight to gender performativity and political agency, I critique Anglo-Celtic male middle class privilege and 'the boys club' as patriarchal barriers, affecting working and middle class women's renewables leadership (Donaldson and Poynting 2013; Buechler and Hanson 2015; DAWN 2015; AHRC 2016b; Canty 2017; WIE 2018). I develop an *emphasized femininity-constructivist-resistant approach to patriarchy*, arguing that women-led agentic competence in environmental science is an empowered gender performance, challenging the ruling power of elites (Gerulis-Darcy 2010; Staggenborg 2016; Maleta 2018b; STEMM 2018).

Australia is one of the few Western democracies without a Bill of Rights (Thampapillai 2005; Anderson 2010; Martin 2011; Commonwealth of Australia Constitution Act [1977] 2013; Hickman 2018). My book provides an innovative framework for: 1. an Australian Bill of Rights Act; and, 2. a Republican Federal Constitutional change. Such change is an opportunity to challenge patriarchal institutionalisation, and a culture of privileged elitist envy, replicated through a monarchist polity. My articulation of a Bill is supported by key Sections, aiming to: legislate on women's renewable technological leadership; reinvigorate governance; revise conservative, dated policies with new policies; replace the Westminster Constitution; challenge hereditary elitism and patriarchal privilege;

enable the electorate to vote for an Australian Head of State, thereby envisioning a more inclusive Social Egalitarian Democracy. Although the 1999 Republican referendum was unsuccessful, there is growing momentum for a Republic (MacSmith 2016; Veri 2016). Egalitarianism is associated with Australian identity; and Republicanism is an opportunity to realise such a vision.

In addition, I source the historic era of Red Vienna (1919–34), as a landmark egalitarian example of Republican governance (Blau 1999). With the fall of the Habsburg Monarchy, middle class and working class citizenry gained more power, whereby patriarchal ruling elites were dually challenged (Gruber 1991; Rentetzi 2004, 2010). My appraisal of Red Vienna is supported by a compelling case study of women's scientific competence in radium research (Rentetzi 2004, 2010). Following Austrian suffrage (1918), women experienced greater civic and civil rights; enabled by Red Vienna's intellectual and creative scope plus social policies (Blau 1999; Mattl 2009). In my global monarchist critique, I also assess contemporary politics, contending that Brexit (Britain's exit from the European Union) will neither erode sociocultural inequality, nor achieve an ideal social democratic model. Whereas a 'British Republic' is an opportunity to challenge hierarchical elites and to reinvigorate governance as well as British sovereign identity.

1.1 Aspirations for an Australian Republic and Bill of Rights Initiatives

In the development of my Bill of Rights Act, I focus on four Sections/articles. **Section 1. *Women's Renewables Technological Leadership Initiative*.** This Initiative legislates on women's renewables leadership in Wind, Wave and Solar Energy (WW & SE) solutions, supported by diverse sector financial investment (Alston 2011; McFarland 2014; Carnegie Clean Energy 2018; WIE 2018). **Section 2. *Minority Women's Leadership in Renewables Organisational Governance Initiative*.** This Section legislates on leadership quotas for my six conceptual groups of women: CALD (Culturally and Linguistically Diverse), socioeconomically disadvantaged, disability status, mature age, Indigenous and Anglo-Celtic women (McFarland 2014; Canty 2017). I include Anglo women as Minority Women, for Anglo men dominate renewables management (Bombora Wave Power 2018; Carnegie Clean Energy 2018). **Section 3. *Women's Leadership Equality in Male-dominated Work Sectors Initiative*.** This Section targets leadership quotas in under-represented sectors, as politics and science, in order to counter glass ceilings and structural barriers (Maleta 2011b; Farr et al. 2017; STEMM 2018). **Section 4. *Indigenous Treaty*.** Recently, Indigenous Constitutional recognition was rejected by the ruling establishment (Jacks 2017). Yet a Republican Constitutional change would recognise Indigenous sovereignty, with a formalised Treaty (Brennan 2015; Prokhovnik 2015; Gaard 2017; Nagy 2017; Patel 2018). Hence, my conceptual application of a *Human Rights* frame, supported by key sub-frames of *Inequity-Injustice* plus methodological intersections of *Feminism, Constructivism, Egalitarianism, Republicanism* and *Environmentalism*, aspires to achieve gender equity, to spur on sustainable technological investment, and ideally, enable Indigenous to non-Indigenous reconciliation plus Indigenous sovereignty. It is an ideal model for a more egalitarian socially just, vibrant participatory democracy.

This sociopolitical change is aligned with the conceptual modelling of *my six women groups* (CALD, Indigenous, mature/older, socioeconomically disadvantaged, disabled status and Anglo-Celtic), *agentic performative multiple skills-set*, whereby I envision women's greater technological leadership of Wind, Wave and Solar Energy (WW & SE) solutions. An overarching human-rights framework, and sub-frames of (in)equity and (in)justice, support my methodological approach. My constructivist framework is supported by my conceptual modelling of feminism, egalitarianism, environmentalism and republicanism, whereby I identify core thematic insights, relative to my women participants (members of the Australian Greens party, International [I]eNGOs, grassroots organisations and academic institutions) experiences of gender-organisational barriers/enablers. My 31 interviews with women environmentalists support this framework. Notably, *my six groups* are a futuristic, conceptual modelling, relative to my Act. When I discuss these groups, I source my interviews – but am referring more broadly to women (whom may not be participants). Hence, I propose a futuristic Republican model, aspiring to address women's greater participatory inclusion through frames of equity/justice within renewables governance.

Gender performativity entails an active negotiation of hegemonic masculinity/ emphasized femininity, in which participants negotiate their agency (power relations), competence (intellectual skill) and the 'I' in their identities, entailing feminist empowerment and environmental change goals (Butler 2007, 2013; MacGregor 2014). In relation to my interviews with salaried and voluntary women participants of the eNSM (environmental New Social Movement) and its eSMOs (environmental Social Movement Organisations), I aim to improve women's equity, belonging and empowerment, relative to egalitarian frames (Diani 1992; Snow 2013; Staggenborg 2016; Maleta 2018b). My interviews highlight participants' *agentic performative multiple skills-set* and emphasized femininity resistance to 'the [Parliamentary] boys club' and 'executive arm' of the eNSM. In light of my critique of hegemonic masculinity, women tend to define masculinist approaches as 'aggressive', 'adversarial' and 'domineering' whilst women-led strategies are seen to be 'conciliatory', 'consensus-based', 'no ego', 'no power' and 'less hierarchy'.

Thus far, my Bill provides an innovative framework for a national policy initiative that legislates on women's workplace inequity, whilst addressing gender barriers and shortfalls in EEO outcomes (Connell 2009; STEMM 2018). In relation to my **Women's Renewables Technological Leadership Initiative** (Section 1), I propose 75% of women in WW & SE – an ambitious figure, yet necessary to redress women's historic to contemporary under-representation in environmental science (Cuomo 2011; McFarland 2014; BWE 2018; EREF 2018; EU ETS 2018; EUREC 2018; SolarPower Europe 2018). This Initiative extends to Section 2, focussing on my six Minority Women groups' scientific leadership engagement. My Initiatives should contribute to women's greater economic independence, elevated career and sociocultural status, thereby challenging the prevailing notion of a patriarch, plus institutionalised patriarchy (Walby 2013, 2015). In support, I source European, British and Australian modes of renewables governance, such as equity programmes, targeting women's leadership in technological development (RenewableUK 2017; Clean Energy Council 2018; WIE 2018). My legislation of an Indigenous Treaty aims to achieve Indigenous sovereignty and reconciliation of non-Indigenous and Indigenous communities, relative to frames of peace and justice (Brennan 2015; Nagy 2017; Pemberton 2017; Kawharu 2018; Patel 2018).

1.2 My Research Project: Qualitative Design and a Snapshot of Participants

My forthcoming interview-driven chapters are conceptually and methodologically framed by a feminist-constructivist-sociocultural qualitative approach, centred on: 1. women's *agentic performative multiple skills-set*; and 2. an emphasized femininity 'resistant' approach to patriarchy (MacLeod 1992; Plumwood 1997; Butler 2007, 2013; Culley and Angelique 2010; Cockburn 2013). Hence, the epistemology is constructivist, the theoretical perspective is feminist, and the method is sample-based interview research (Berg and Lie 1995; Crary 2001; Gaard 2001, 2011; Delanty 2005; Wibben 2016). In my interview analysis, I utilise theme identification, plus data, content and conversation analysis (Delanty 2005; Punch 2005; Gaard 2014). This enables me to construe knowledge, framed by participants' agentic prowess, plus their emphasized femininity leadership resistance to patriarchy (Gaard 2001, 2017; Leahy 2003; Connell 2005; Ruane 2005; Butler 2013; Staggenborg 2016; Nagy 2017).

Considering agentic competent-based interaction, I argue that women members of eNSMs/eSMOs may challenge oppressive patriarchal hierarchies plus ruling class masculinity (Poynting and Donaldson 2005; Donaldson and Poynting 2013; DAWN 2015). My methodological-methods-based approach is supported by feminist, ecological, sociological, socio-legal and movement theory (Connell 1995; Gaard 2001; Butler 2004, 2007, 2009, 2013, 2015; Maddison 2004; Culley and Angelique 2010; Cockburn 2012). Also, I source government reports and legislative Acts; third sector reports; and the demographical composition of global renewable energy organisations and political parties (Commonwealth of Australia Constitution Act [1977] 2013; Disability Discrimination Act [1992] 2013; ABS 2016b; AHRC 2016a, 2017b; EEO Act [1987] 2016; Greenpeace International, Annual Report, 2016; RenewableUK 2017; Australian Greens, Our Policies, 2018; BWE 2018; Clean Energy Council 2018; SolarPower Europe 2018; WIE 2018).

Drawing upon supporting material and my interviews, I investigate how women in the eNSM experience their activism in relation to gender identity and work relations, and the extent to which their experiences justify my Republican-Bill of Rights. My human-rights frame, supported by sub-frames of (in)justice/

(in)equity, enable me to argue for greater women-led direction in renewables technological development. My goal is to achieve a more sustainable, safer, healthier world, framed by my anti-war ethos and peaceful modelling of social and environmental change (Warren 1997, 1999; Butler 2009, 2017; Cockburn 2012, 2013; Wibben 2016; Nagy 2017). Thus, women's emphasized feminine performativity, in science and technology, questions the patriarchal control of environmental politics and resource-based approaches (Maleta 2015, 2018a).

1.2.1 *Conceptualising* My Six Groups

My proposed Republican Constitutional sociopolitical change model, is aligned with the conceptual modelling of *my six groups* (CALD, Indigenous, mature/older, socioeconomically disadvantaged, disabled status, Anglo), leadership of WW & SE technological solutions and participation in male-dominated work sectors. This is legislated through my Initiatives/Sections. My 31 interview accounts support this framework; I should add that *my six groups* entail a futuristic, conceptual modelling, relative to my proposed Act. When I discuss these groups, I source my interviews – but am also referring more broadly to women (whom may not be my participants). The interview data, in my empirical chapters, was collected while I was a PhD student, and provide authentic context to my emphasized femininity and gender performativity framework. Relative to my human-rights-(in)equity/(in)justice frames and feminist-constructivist approach, my Bill of Rights, strives to integrate feminism, republicanism, environmentalism and egalitarianism, so as to envision greater women's leadership in a male-dominated world.

1.2.2 *Research Procedure and Design*

As Chief Qualitative Investigator, I led a research project (as part of my PhD study), whereby I interviewed 31 Australian women members of renewables organisational governance: the Australian Greens party, International eNGOs, grassroots organisations and academic institutions. The research study was approved by Western Sydney University. As a former PhD Candidate of Western Sydney University's School of Social Sciences and Psychology, I officially graduated with a PhD testamur in 2015. My book sources the interview data collected whilst I was a PhD student. This book utilises some material from my PhD thesis. Interview data provides a primary source of knowledge for this book, thereby contributing to the global gender studies field.

Each participant received an information sheet about my study and a consent form – signed on the day of interview. The interview was in a semi-structured format, and qualitatively interpreted, enabling me to draw upon rich, meaningful accounts (Punch 2005; Ruane 2005; Wibben 2016). Ruane adds that qualitative data empowers researchers to 'walk a mile' in subjects' shoes (2005: 12). Also, interviews provide evidence to one's sociocultural environs. Each interview was tape-recorded with a digital recorder and manual tape recorder. I transcribed some interviews and outsourced the remainder to a professional agency, due to time constraints. Pseudonyms or code names were used, ensuring the privacy of individuals and their organisations. The duration of each interview was approximately 90–120 minutes. One limitation, from my research, is that my sample of 31 is somewhat small, whereby, it is challenging, to represent an overall frame of society. Nonetheless, my research sample represents a sub-frame or snapshot of society, and my empirical evidence connects and/or contradicts with supporting theory and studies (Gaard 2001; Butler 2004, 2009; Connell 2005). My sample, relative to the voices, concerns and struggles plus achievement of women, frames the constructivist development of my Act.

I interviewed Australian women activists/advocates partaking in paid and unpaid capacities of the eNSM and its eSMOs. The initial target was 30 women, with an estimated 50/50 split, for example, fifteen salaried and fifteen volunteers. The interview period was extended, as I required an extra participant. The first interview was conducted in late 2009, and the last interview achieved in 2011 – with a grand total of 31 interviews. Although the academic category has fewer participants, their data is detailed and descriptive, and of immeasurable worth to my intellectual scope. Most academics recognise that EEO laws have enabled women in universities, but they still struggle with gender barriers and glass ceilings, framed by 'the boys club' and women as token members on climate panels.

What each participant revealed about themselves and environs was collated in my qualitative analysis, and organised into key and sub-themes. I recognise the subjective element of interviews. As Chief Researcher, one should be careful not to misconstrue opinions or retrospections with facts. Nonetheless, data frames my thematic insights. Chapter headings are based on themes, such as 'the boys club' and 'token women'.

As women volunteers also partake in paid work and salaried women often perform volunteer work, this enables me to compare social relations and work sectors within environmentalism. The rationale of an anti-nuclear activist, for example, may contrast with that of a salaried woman politician. I contend though that participants' share a common ground sustainable-justice mission, unifying their social and environmental change agendas. While I compare diverse work roles, I avoid casting judgement on whether one is more valued than the other. Rather it is the work experience and subjective satisfaction/dissatisfaction of women, that is of relevance.

1.2.3 Demographics: A Sociological Snapshot of Participants

Of the 31 participants, ten are members of the Australian Greens party, nine of eNGOs/IeNGOs (international environmental nongovernmental organisations), seven of grassroots organisations, and another five are academic activists/advocates. The majority work in salaried environmentalism. The Greens group has eight salaried politicians and two volunteers. In the eNGO group, eight are salaried and one voluntary; whilst, in the academic group, all five are salaried academics. Nevertheless, these academics also perform public (unpaid) advocacy/activism, such as public, community talks. Most salaried participants perform voluntary work. Environmentalism is not a nine to five job, evident by women's afterhours work, showcasing their passion and determination for the cause. All the grassroots women (total of seven) are volunteers, but had paid jobs, such as in government departments or in public sector roles. Overall, an exact, statistical breakdown of paid versus unpaid is difficult to quantify. What is characteristic about environmental work is that it is community centric and reflective of modern 24/7 schedules.

I have a mix of Anglo-Celtic, CALD, and Indigenous women in my sample. Most are mature/older women. Most participants are White, middle class, well-educated and work in the professions. Six were from CALD backgrounds, including one participant of South American heritage, another of Indian stock, another of Ashkenazi Jewish background, and another three of comparative Dutch, German and Irish migrant parents. I did not identify any linguistic challenges, as most women were born in Australia.

Some participants identify as having a disability, and being socioeconomically disadvantaged. Greens woman Tanya identified as having a disability, and spoke of how being of a socioeconomically background framed her struggle. But Tanya's competence as a politician transformed experiences of disadvantage:

> I believe in the old saying, power corrupts and absolute power corrupts absolutely, but I am in a position that has some power. Having been one of the powerless, a disability pensioner living in housing commission... whether I like it or not, I do not like dealing in power, but I have some power.
>
> (Tanya [audio] 2010)

The Greens sample is dominated by Anglo women. My Greens data illuminates a shared standpoint on gender, social and environmental justice issues plus Indigenous rights and advocating for migrant women. Markedly, one participant, Barbara, identified as an Indigenous Tasmanian with mixed European heritage. Barbara's identity was relayed through spiritual and maternal understandings of environmentalism. In turn, I am privileged to have a participant of Indigenous Tasmanian ancestry in my sample (an extreme rarity within Australian demography). Some participants comment on their CALD identity relative to their activism. For instance, Wendy, of an Asian background, contends that being an activist is breaking away from family expectations, as this is an unusual role for a young Asian woman. Despite this conservative sociocultural assessment, Wendy was committed to social change-climate-sustainable leadership within CALD communities.

Most participants are in the age group of 35+, either married or living with partners. A good representation of older women enables me to draw upon an extensive, historical to contemporary, involvement in the eNSM along with rich data and thematic insights (Punch 2005; Ruane 2005; Wibben 2016). Most women 35+ have one or more children. To a significant extent, being a mother guides women's social and environmental responsibility plus their outlook for future generations (Maleta 2015). Those considered to be 'non-mothers', such as women without children and younger women (in the age group of 18–34), shared this commitment. Hence, a nurturing identity can be applied to mothers with children and non-mothers. Younger women had less experience; however, this was not a barrier, for all my women participants (see my forthcoming chapters), are dedicated campaigners, whom diligently and passionately perform advocacy. Although I did not find age to be a barrier due to my participants' competent gender performances, my analysis reveals that women struggle with ageism within the eNSM and its eSMOs/eNGOs. Hence, ageism, framed by patriarchy and ruling class masculinity, is a shared barrier for my younger and older participants. Through a feminist lens, I apply an overarching human-rights frame and sub-frames of (in)equity/(in)justice to my qualitative empirical-thematic analysis.

One finding from my analysis is that labels of activism, age and ethnicity can be more of a barrier than gender (Maleta 2012). Also, hierarchy, in relation to patriarchal structures, may be contrasted to egalitarianism, for most women prefer to work in flatter, less hierarchical, grassroots-framed eSMOs. All women struggled with degrees of gender differences, stereotypes and stigmas (Culley and Angelique 2003, 2010). But for some, being differentiated as a woman was starker. This 'othering' was framed by competence, in how politicians and scientists struggled to be taken seriously. Also, this otherness was conceptually framed by women's struggle with 'the boys club' and gender tokenism. Despite women's struggle with labels of incompetence, participants' knowledge, akin to their multiple-agentic performative skills-set, framed their rising social statuses (Cockburn 1988; Culley and Angelique 2010; Farr et al. 2017; Maleta 2018b). Some participants did not have tertiary qualifications; yet status was elevated through merit and prowess.

Regarding residence, most participants resided in urban metropolitan areas of a large Australian city; including (progressive) inner-city and some suburban areas (of the city). Another three resided in regional areas, and another in the peri urban fringe. This reflects a proportionate urban versus rural representation.

On the topic of sexual identity, two participants identified as lesbian or gay. One participant had separated from her husband, and identified as a lesbian, living with a female partner for a number of years. The other participant was in a younger age group, and resided in a progressive urban area with her female partner.

1.2.4 My Groups

1.2.4.1 Group 1 – The Australian Greens

The Australian Greens constitute the largest group in my study. This was due to their quick response to my recruitment drive, and passion for ecological justice and gender rights. Although I am not a member of the Greens, the party were a key source due to their policies on a Bill of Rights, gender equality, Indigenous rights, renewables and egalitarian democracy (Australian Greens, Constitutional

Reform and Democracy, 2018, Gender Equality and Empowerment of Women, 2018). Most Greens participants hold salaried positions. My eight salaried women include: two Parliamentarians, four Locally Government Authority (LGA) elected Councillors and two administrative staff. The other two are volunteers, involved in grassroots campaigns. My ten Greens women are grouped as such:

> Group 1.a – Greens – Politicians (Salaried): Jennifer, Maxine, Amy, Margaret
> Group 1.b – Greens – Councillors (LGA) (Salaried): Jacquie, Stacey, Kate, Tanya
> Group 1.c – Greens – Volunteers: Joan, Ruth.

1.2.4.2 *Group 2 – eNGOs*

The eNGO category includes eight salaried employees and one volunteer. As mentioned, most employees perform voluntary after-hours work – indicative of the 24/7 scope of environmentalism. My nine eNGO participants are categorised into these two groups:

> Group 2.a – eNGOs (Salaried): Deborah, Linda, Juliet, Heidi, Penny, Mara, Stephanie, Barbara
> Group 2.b – eNGOs (Volunteer): Eileen.

1.2.4.3 *Group 3 – Grassroots Organisations*

In the grassroots group, all seven activists are volunteers. In my interviews, women discuss their other salaried roles, representative of diverse sectors. The organisational aspect of my study is strengthened by assessing women's performative skills-set in paid and unpaid capacities for a comparative inter-disciplinarian scope. Initially, I predicted that grassroots participants were more likely to identify as activists, yet biographies reveal that the term 'activism' is fraught by degrees of complexity and even stigmas, as with gender:

> Group 3.a – Grassroots (Volunteers): Dion, Jessica, Shelley, Gillian, Wendy, Catherine, Abigail.

1.2.4.4 *Group 4 – Academic Activists/Advocates*

My five academic women activists/advocates work in a salaried environmentalist capacity in an academic institution. Most perform voluntary unpaid work, such as, community advocacy. Yvonne conducts free talks on climate change, and lawyer Rachel provides free pro bono services to clients. Helen, a former eNGO Director, works in a scientific advisory capacity within a government/research institution. All are committed to the eNSM, and reflect upon gender dynamics in their work. All have PhDs, whereas, Maggie, is a medical doctor by profession, who incorporates her professional background to climatic and sustainably advocacy, including talks. What is notable about my academics is the way education is tool, linking professional and grassroots environmental advocacy.

> Group 4.a – Academic activists (salaried): Anna, Yvonne, Rachel, Maggie, Helen.

1.3 Discussion

My 31 interview accounts (and six groups) captures my feminist constructivist methodological approach and qualitative analytical framework, striving for women's leadership of renewables organisational governance and a Republican change. Also, this frames my conceptual insight to participants' emphasized femininity performativity (as discussed in my interview-driven-data chapters). As Chief Qualitative Researcher, in-depth interviews enabled me to identify core themes, along with insights to 'a boys club', 'gender tokenism' and a 'maternal activist identity'. Such thematic insights enable me to deduce powerful power-based interplays of constructivism/essentialism and emphasized femininity/hegemonic masculinity. Notably, my emphasized femininity-qualitative approach, focussing on 1. women's agentic multiple-performative skills-set, and 2. resistance to patriarchy, relative to my proposed Bill of Rights Act plus Constitutional framework, is innovative, in its social (Republican) and environmental (women-led sustainable technological development) change ambitions. This model is not limited to Australian governance, but ideally is a model of social democratic action for other nations and sustainable leaders around the world, aspiring for women's greater equity/justice.

Through my Act's legislative drive on Initiatives/Sections addressing women's leadership in environmental science and inequity in male-dominated work sectors, I aim to contribute cutting-edge knowledge to the global field, of which there is no research. My research fills a pressing gap: illuminating conceptual-methodological applications of feminism, republicanism, egalitarianism and environmentalism relative to the eNSM/eSMOs. This gap is further cemented through a robust Bill of Rights Act and its key Initiatives. Of note, my participants may not all share a Republican viewpoint; nonetheless, women's struggle with 'a boys club', is authenticated by insights to the gendered nature of the elite and ruling class masculinity, as a barrier (see Chapter 5). In support to Plumwood's (1997), Connell's (1995, 2005, 2009), Gaard's (2001), Culley and Angelique's (2003, 2010), Butler's (2007, 2009, 2013), Cockburn's (1988, 2012, 2013), Staggenborg's (2016) and Wibben's (2016) works, my constructivist framing of gender performativity is strengthened by an anti-war ethos and peacemaking model and frames of human-rights-(in)equity-(in)justice, informing the Initiatives of my Act. This is authenticated by participants empowering emphasized femininity resistance to masculinist elites, whereby women-led strategies are defined as: 'conciliatory', 'consensus-based', 'less hierarchy', 'less aggression' and 'no egos… or power to protect'. Through a Republican Constitutional framework, I aim to challenge the hereditary elitism of Monarchism, indicative of Anglo male middle class privilege, whilst striving for working and middle class women's equity/justice in renewables work. Thus, I aspire to legislate/advocate on women's scientific-technical leadership in WW & SE solutions, relative to women's agentic performative skills-set as well as a much sought after egalitarian-socio-ecological change.

1.4 An Introductory Insight to Empirical Themes

Women members of the Australian Greens party, eNGOs, grassroots organisations and academic institutions contextualise the focal point of my empirical themes. I contend that participants may not necessarily be of a Republican or anti-monarchist persuasion; nevertheless, my ambition for a Republican-Bill is plausible through participant's struggle with ruling class masculinity and patriarchal institutionalisation. Arguably, the hereditary elitism of monarchism and male-dominated elitist privilege, is replicated within social hierarchies of power hierarchical cultural-structures (Otnes and Maclaran 2018). Arguably, Anglo male middle class privilege, is a core example of ruling class hegemonic masculinity within Australian organisational governance, whilst representing a barrier to women's greater leadership (Donaldson and Poynting 2007, 2013; DAWN 2015; ABS 2016a). Although Anglo middle class males, are not necessarily peers of the realm or members of the aristocracy, as are sovereign monarchs (for Australia rejected rigid class-based establishments in its postcolonial development), their elevated hegemonic status has evolved from cultural, social and ethnic privileges, whereby such privilege is dually simulated in the rule of patriarchal elites (Otnes and Maclaran 2018). Along gender lines, misogyny and chauvinism are points of contention, framing women's otherness in the global organisation of work, governance and politics (Arendt 1945, 1959; Arendt and Kohn 2005; Maleta 2011b; Summers 2013; Manne 2017).

In my Greens interviews, participant, Jennifer (pseudonym) similarly claimed that women politicians are judged more harshly than men, in terms of image, dress and what they say. Men's resistance to women's leadership, therefore, signifies that 'a boys club' operates in Parliament. By men resisting women's political leadership, particularly those from conservative or right-wing-aligned neoliberal parties, this suggests that the masculine paradigm is, in turn, threatened (Connell 2006, 2009; Walby 2011, 2012; Butler 2013; MacGregor 2014). Yet men politicians do not experience the same degree of stigmatisation from other men. Regarding gender performativity as an exercise of agency, women politicians can choose to resist (Gillard) or accommodate (Thatcher) ruling class masculinity. The choice to resist patriarchy is not without consequences, as with Greer's stigmatisation (Greer 1999, 2010a; Petherbridge 2014; Wright and Holland 2014).

Considering gender as a performance, some Greens participants critique the way women, from opposing conservative parties, adopt masculine performances, rather than challenging 'male-dominated' practices. In Parliament, critiqued as 'a boys club', Greens women resist masculinist forms of 'aggression', 'adversity' and androcentrism. My Greens women do not identity sexism or misogyny as an issue with fellow Greens men (Mellor 1993, 1997; MacGregor 2001, 2006, 2009; Maleta 2011b). Rather its (male and female) members accommodate/ accept feminism and ecological justice viewpoints, which is accentuated by the party's policies on gender equity and grassroots democracy (Australian Greens, Constitutional Reform and Democracy, 2018, Gender Equality and Empowerment of Women, 2018, Participatory Democracy, 2018). One participant, Jacquie, commented that she worked well with a male Independent politician, although other men, particularly from conservative neoliberal parties, were prone to treat her differently, in terms of 'the outer'. The processing of 'othering' is consequently specific to 'non-Greens' men akin to conservative neoliberal or indeed right-wing politics/polity.

Connell identified the resistance of Australian men green political activists to hegemonic masculinity, in favour of feminism and egalitarianism (2005: 120). In the context of environmental politics, participant, Barry Ryan, learned about feminism and how the term 'sexism' accounted for men's personal, if not biased attitudes towards women (Connell 2005: 129). Yet Barry endeavoured to adopt more supportive attitudes towards women whilst criticising men's sexism. Comparatively, these 'green political men activists' were labelled 'soft', 'unmanly' and 'feminine' by the dominant hegemonic male order (Connell 2005: 127–29). This shows that men who do not ascribe to the machoism of hegemonic masculinity are subject to othering by men, as are women. Through interviews with men green activists, four movement themes symbolised an alternative to hegemonic masculine norms: a practice of ideology of equality; an emphasis on 'collectivity' and solidarity; a practice and ideology of personal growth; and, an ideology of organic wholeness (Connell 2005: 127–28). Connell argues that these themes constitute the subversion within Green politics and cultural practices resistant to hegemonic masculinity (2005: 128). Dominance is contested by a commitment to equality and participatory democracy, while competitive individualism is contested through collective ways of working. An emphasis on personal growth undermines the defensive style of hegemonic masculinity, especially its control over emotions (Connell 2005: 128). In summary, green men's embracement of feminism, reworked masculinity through a resistant egalitarian lens, centred on a progressive counter-culture, radicalism and opposition to hierarchy and authoritarianism (Connell 2005: 120).

Grassroots eNGOs enable feminism and women-led strategies; nonetheless, the executive arm of the movement is hierarchically organised, meaning that men's hegemony contrasts with emphasized femininity strategies. According to Stephanie, women's leadership is defined by 'collaboration' and 'consensus-building', in how women-led meetings were framed by 'less hierarchy', 'no power to protect' and 'no ego'. Chauvinism, pertaining to her boss's attitude, was perceived to be a barrier for Stephanie; nonetheless, compared to corporate finance, her eNGO was 'progressive' and less of 'a boys club' ([audio] 2010). Thus, corporate finance was more indicative of 'a boys club' than the eNSM and its eSMOs. Moreover, Barbara ([audio] 2010) contended that the 'executive arm of the environmental movement' was dominated by chauvinistic and misogynist males. Despite merit and competence, Barbara was bullied by men executives in the Sydney 2000 Green Games. Undoubtedly, her expert competence compelled men's hostility and ostracisation. Bullying even led to a loss of job. Maxine assessed conservation-based eNGOs as male-dominated and conservative, whereby gender rights and social justice were not topical issues. Although Deborah rejected that being a woman differentiated her, she identified dualist gender campaigns, in how women dominated the 'soft sciences of biodiversity' and volunteer 'home care' projects, whereas men dominated 'the hard sciences', namely climate change. On one level, women are included in the professional arm of the eNSM; alternatively, their merit and skill, is not fully enabled, and curtailed by gendered-organisational barriers; thus, men do not let women achieve their full potential by resisting their leadership (Cockburn 1991; Marshall 2011; Cook and Glass 2014).

My findings on men's dominance in environmental science confirms their privileged sociocultural status, thereby disputing assumptions of equity (Pollack 2015; Watts et al. 2015; Cohen 2016; Farr et al. 2017). I found that women perform gender by adopting 'feminine' or emphasized femininity women-led strategies, whereby masculine hegemony and patriarchy is susceptible to change. Participants' recognition of/resistance to 'a boys club' in turn symbolises resistance to ruling class masculinity, and that my participants are not acting like men, nor ascribing to masculine performativity. For the most part, women do not accept nor conform to patriarchy. They are adopting empowering subjective women-led approaches, whilst critiquing chauvinism, misogyny and sexism in their strategic engagement (Summers 2013; Manne 2017; STEMM 2018). This is not to say that women are soft, docile or passive, but rather that their competence is comparatively situated in approaches that reject aggression and androcentrism, and are equally resistant to rigid hierarchy and patriarchal privilege (Mellor 1997; Buckingham-Hatfield 2000; Segal 2007; Walby 2011, 2013; Mattl 2016). Also, I reject the notion that women are not as ambitious as men; but rather that their struggle is discursive to paradigms framed by men's/masculinist dominance. Despite barriers, women's career mobility is accentuated by an *agentic performative multiple skills-set*, rather than a competitive 'fight' to the top.

Emphasized femininity is, consequently, situated in women's prowess and resistance to patriarchy, while constructivism is actualised through performativity, resulting in empowered gendered identities. In my constructivist approach, I consider the way participants exercise agency (social relations of power) and negotiate subjectivity (empowerment) (Giddens 1991; Gaard 2001; MacGregor 2010; Cudworth and Hobden 2013). Essentialist assumptions of women: 'not being born leaders' or that 'men are ideal rulers' are being subverted through women's agentic performativity in similar positions to men (Leahy 2003; Gaard 2011). Also, I source Cockburn's (1988) historic critique of the gendering of competence, framed by assumptions based on sex, whereby sex-segregation sustains men's hegemonic leadership dominance within organisational hierarchies. Even in the most feminine of occupations, the higher the rank, the more masculine the occupation becomes (Cockburn 1988: 234). For instance, Cockburn highlights the blue/masculine and pink/feminine colour-coded distinctions that define sex segregation in occupations:

> An over-arching dichotomy, of course, that men everywhere and always are able to deploy to their advantage is quite simply: masculine equals superior, active and powerful; feminine equals subordinate, submissive and directed. Lowly jobs may be pink or blue, and men manage to establish a compensatory advantage for masculinity even here in the 'heroisms' of heavy manual labour. Top jobs in any field, however, are blue, through and through.
>
> (1988: 235)

Although organisational hierarchies privilege men/masculinities, when women work in the same or similar roles, they often out-perform men. Participants also comment that women are less likely to engage in conflict at work and their approach is more conducive to harmonious social relations, thereby reflective of a productive work environment (Mellor 1993, 1997; Buckingham-Hatfield 2000; Buckingham and Kulcur 2010; Butler 2011; Gaard 2011; Kemp 2011). My focus on 1. women-led agentic prowess and 2. women-led resistance to patriarchy is framed by a methodological accommodation of emphasized femininity. Through feminist subversion, I contend that the 'I' in women's identity is enabled along with social and environmental change aspirations (Butler 2007, 2013, 2015). Women's competent resistance frames a futuristic Republican change, whereby a feminist-Act challenges patriarchal hierarchies.

1.5 Emphasized Femininity Resistance to Patriarchal Institutionalisation

1.5.1 *Feminist Agentic Leadership Competence Within Environmentalism*

My research study is framed by a feminist-constructivist-sociocultural qualitative approach centred on 1. women's *agentic performative multiple skills-set* and 2. an emphasized femininity approach that is 'resistant' to patriarchy (Cockburn 1988, 2013; Plumwood 1997; Gaard 2001; Butler 2007, 2013; Culley and Angelique 2010). Hence, my methodological critique of patriarchy focusses on emphasized femininity resistance to ruling class masculinity and masculine hegemony, in how women's agentic leadership competence, strategically challenges the ruling power of men within renewables governance. I refer to Connell's (1995, 2002, 2005, 2009; Nascimento and Connell 2017) conceptualisation of hegemonic masculinity/femininity, whilst Butler's (1997, 2009, 2011, 2013, 2015) theory of gender performativity and political agency enables me to assess participants 'performative' agency, along with strategies of resistance and accommodation (MacLeod 1992; Butler 2004, 2007, 2017).

The late ecofeminist Plumwood (1997, 2002, 2006) framed a resistant femininity in her critique of patriarchal hegemony, whilst contemplating women's position as the insider/outsider of the eNSM: 'Women have played a major role, largely unacknowledged, in the male-dominated environment movement, in resisting the assault on nature' (1997: 9–10). In turn, women's resistance to the patriarchal control of the eNSM points to an emphasized femininity constructivist strategy, that is agentic and competent; nonetheless, this interaction is dynamically framed by hegemonic masculinity as a barrier (Connell 1995, 2005; Donaldson 2009). But a Republican change would challenge patriarchal privilege, or, as in my argument, Anglo male middle class privilege – an overarching barrier to working and middle class women's leadership in sustainable technological development. My Bill of Rights Act, hence, legislates on women's equity within the eNSM and eSMOs whilst challenging women's historic replicated experience as the dualist insider/outsider.

Concerning a feminist resistance strategy, I aim to subvert the discourse surrounding patriarchy into a type of 'resistant femininity' (Connell 1995; Leahy 2003: 109). Emphasized femininity leadership resistance is evidenced by my participants' *agentic performative multiple skills-set* – representing a compelling challenge to patriarchal institutionalised power (Plumwood 1997; Gaard 2001; Donaldson and Poynting 2013). In support, Plumwood argued: 'For women, the real task of liberation is not equal participation or absorption into a masculine culture, but rather subversion, resistance and replacement' (1997: 30). In my subversive approach to patriarchy, I incorporate *human-rights-(in)equity-(in)justice frames*, supported by my conceptual *emphasized femininity-egalitarian-ecological resistant model*. This model enables me to frame women's agentic leadership competence in renewables technological development, relative to a desired social (Republican) and environmental (sustainable) change (Staggenborg 2016; Wibben 2016; Canty 2017; RenewableUK 2017; Clean Energy Council 2018).

Donaldson and Poynting's (2007, 2013) critique of ruling class masculinity within Australian organisational governance, provides context to my censuring of Anglo male middle class privilege, framing working class and middle class women's struggle with (in)equity/(in)justice. Arendt's (1945, 1973) Republican critique of imperial chauvinism, centring on European pre-World War I monarchies, foregrounds my articulation of Red Vienna, as an egalitarian social democratic model, relative to Suffrage and Austrian women's elevated political, civic and scientific prowess (Rentetzi 2004, 2010; Mattl 2013).

Women's agency is framed by resistance, protest and challenge (MacLeod 1992). MacLeod's study on agentic power within an Egyptian context frames the way women exercise agency, and subvert hegemony and patriarchy (1992: 537). MacLeod considered the verbs: 'accept, accommodate, ignore, resist, or protest in terms of dichotomies of patriarchal power relations' in her exploration of Cairo women's use of the veil (1992: 533–34). MacLeod argues that women are active subjects and subjects of domination:

> I argue that women, even as subordinate players, always play an active part that goes beyond the dichotomy of victimization/acceptance, a dichotomy that flattens out a complex and ambiguous agency in which women accept,

accommodate, ignore, resist, or protest – sometimes all at the same time. Power relationships should be viewed as an ongoing relationship of struggle, a struggle complicated by women's own contradictory subjectivity and ambiguous purposes.

(1992: 534)

My emphasized femininity appraisal of women-led strategies, and Republican critique of patriarchal chauvinism, is situated through an anti-war ethos and peacemaking model of social (Republican) and environmental (sustainable technological) change (Warren 1999; Cockburn 2010, 2012, 2013; Wibben 2016; Butler 2017). Cockburn's (2012) critique of patriarchal militarism and appraisal of British women's anti-atomic activism, in the landmark 1983 Greenham Common Peace Camp, frames the power of the grassroots as an agentic peacemaking sociopolitical model, resistant to atomic energy and nuclear technologies. In my legislative stand on a Republican Bill of Rights, I source themes from my interviews, critiquing aggression, androcentrism, chauvinism and misogyny, along with resource-based (war) versus renewables (peace) methods (Warren 1999; Butler 2017). My aspiration for global peace incorporates women-led grassroots Initiatives and robust political strategies (Wibben 2016). In support, Warren's (1997, 1999) peacemaking model of ecological-ethics justice, and Shiva's (2005, 2008, 2014) focus on earth democracy and sustainable agriculture, centring on goals of justice, peace and harmony, foregrounds my ethical and human-rights approach to a sustainable-technological anti-war legislative Act.

Culley and Angelique's (2003, 2010) research with long-term Three Mile Island (TMI) anti-nuclear campaigners (as a consequence to the partial nuclear meltdown, at Three Mile Island, Pennsylvania, in 1979) identified gender barriers and enablers, affecting women's social change goals. A core barrier was stereotypes of grassroots women's technical incompetence, whilst a core enabler was women's acquired knowledge of nuclear technology and applying this, in a resistant framework, in their negotiations with governing and industry executives (Culley and Angelique 2010; Maleta 2012). Such themes conceptualise my focus on women's technical competence as agentic and empowering; and that professional and grassroots women possess the skills to challenge the hegemony of resource-based environmental industries (including nuclear and even nuclear arms proliferation), whilst striving for a safer, sustainable world (Maleta 2011a, 2018b).

Sustainable technological development is the crux of my peacemaking model and social change ambitions (Wibben 2016; Maleta 2018b). Continued reliance on nuclear energy, in particular, represents the ultimate barrier to an equilibrium that is sustainable plus peaceful (Caldicott 2014). My focus on women's emphasized femininity leadership of sustainable technologies frames my Bill of Rights, relayed through a resistant framework, challenging patriarchy and the ruling power of social (industrial) and governing elites (Plumwood 1997; Gaard 2001; Gerulis-Darcy 2010). Although a gender-specific lens is 'invisible' within global governance, my insight to emphasized femininity women-led prowess, challenges tags of technical incompetency, gender biases and injustice/inequity

(Culley and Angelique 2010; MacGregor 2010, 2014; Canty 2017; AHRC 2017a).

Juxtaposed to barriers, I focus on enablers, in how women's performative scientific prowess, along with economic independence and career mobility, empowers their subjective identities, whilst challenging patriarchy. In addition, nature/the natural environment, is a source of empowerment for future sustainable solutions and the role of women. Cudworth and Hobden state that 'it is possible to conceive of agency beyond the human' (2013: 430). Regarding this statement on agentic power, I add that a greater emphasis on renewable technological development, such as solar, wind and wave energy, framed through women's leadership, highlights human intellectual ingenuity whilst enabling alternative development and less reliance on the extrapolation/exploitation of nature for capitalist, economic gains (Mellor 2002, 2010, 2012; Shiva 2014, 2016).

In addition, Gaard's (2001, 2011) critique of environmental sexism, classism and racism, plus Stein's (2004) intersections of race, class and health with environmental ills, represents the multiple sociological barriers, that constitute women activists' struggle for sustainable-social change and women's empowerment within the global spheres of the eNSM. Using Canadian and U.S. examples, Gaard exposes corporate exploitations of water and power in regional communities, in which ecofeminism is appropriated as an empowering resistance strategy: 'ecofeminism illuminates the way in which gendered, cultural assumptions about water, power and human relations have led to creating a water-power infrastructure that perpetuates environmental sexism, environmental racism and environmental classism' (2001: 157). Alternatively, Gaard advocates 'ecological democracy and ecological economics' and 'a partnership culture', whereby 'water and energy flow freely' (Gaard 2001: 157; Buechler and Hanson 2015). This sustainable model enables me to incorporate the agentic power of women-led democratic participatory action and ecologically economics, as a framework to aspire for sociopolitical change.

The work of Buechler and Hanson (2015) on *Women, Water and Global Environmental Change*, links political ecology and feminism with social change. I contribute to this model by focussing on environmental change through women's WW & SE leadership. My work also appeals to an interdisciplinary audience, interested in women's rights and environmental justice, in which emphasized femininity leadership (centred on *my six groups* of women) challenges the masculine hegemony of global environmental politics. My model addresses gender and ecological reformative measures. In relation to Canty (2017), I strive to illuminate multicultural women's voices, focussing on CALD and Indigenous women's multiple performative agentic competencies, whilst critiquing their leadership under-representation. Certainly, in the Australian context, Anglo-Celtic men and Anglo women are privileged in executive posts (Donaldson and Poynting 2013; DAWN 2015; ABS 2016a). Additionally, I aim to improve feminist networks between diverse women, along with their social and work relations with men. Hence, my modelling of emphasized femininity-agentic competence contributes to Canty's (2017) socio-ecological model.

Mellor (2013) contends that feminist and green movements constitute the basis for a new radical social movement. My empirical data on professional and grassroots women's radical and conservative strategies illuminates the vitality of feminist, environmentalist and Indigenous New Social Movements (NSM)s; downplaying assumptions that SMs are in a state of abeyance or have hibernated (Taylor 1989; Maddison 2004; Doyle 2005; Grey and Sawer 2008; McLellan 2009). In relation to Mellor (2013), I assess intersections of feminism and political ecology through women's radical and *seemingly* passive strategies. Although radicalism may be viewed as an example of constructivism, whilst conservatism exemplifies essentialism, I consider that women's radical and conservative techniques are viable sociopolitical change strategies, framed by agentic environmental competence.

In relation to my interview-driven thematic insights, it is intriguing that women MPs are members of Parliament, yet also engage in civil disobedience. One Greens politician was part of a group that was arrested outside Federal Parliament House. Similarly, across my interviews, women working in eNGOs, academia and grassroots organisations comment on radical and passive strategies, thereby showcasing resistant and conservative femininities. Some Greens and grassroots activists partake in civil disobedience, while others engage in peace marches. Such approaches contextualise my anti-war ethos (Warren 1999; Cockburn 2012; Wibben 2016). Feminism in relation to ecology is evidenced through political resistance to the establishment – unequal gender power relations that privilege men within patriarchal governance. It is evidenced by women's WW & SE leadership through emphasized femininity resistance to patriarchy.

MacGregor (2001, 2006, 2009, 2010, 2014) argued that patriarchy pervades green political theory along with sustainability and climate change debates, whereby women are 'invisible' from rational dialogue. Across the global North and South, women's needs are absent from policy reforms on climate change along with water and food security (Alston 2011, 2013; Shiva 2014, 2016). Concerning 'visibility', I found that women are often placed on climate science panels as 'token women', in order to fill a gender gap. Participants also comment that men scientists, on climate panels, often take credit for the work of women, initially performed by women in a grassroots (activist) and/or professional (scientific) capacity. I found that volunteer and professional advocates demonstrate technical-intellectual prowess in climate science and diverse problems affecting the social and natural world. This knowledge is learned (activists) or through expert training (scientists/academics). While professional and voluntary women are competent political actors, whom understand the environment and its challenges, their deliberate placement on panels, confirms that environmental science is defined by male-dominated structures relations of power. Consequently, it is challenging for women to acquire status, when cultural structures are conducive to patriarchy plus men's decision-making capacity.

The 'otherness' of women in executive leadership is a gendered-organisational barrier (Cockburn 1991; Maleta 2012; Cook and Glass 2014; Haynes et al. 2015). Within a global context, an interrelated feminist barrier is the numerical superiority of men in renewable boards, plus in the executive hierarchy; whilst women are better represented in not-for-profit-based renewables organisations (RenewableUK 2017; BWE 2018; Clean Energy Council 2018; EREF 2018; EUREC 2018; REA 2018; SolarPower Europe 2018). Hence, grassroots-based renewables eSMOs are conducive to egalitarianism and feminism, encompassing my Republican agenda of emphasized femininity social change.

Leading global International eNGOs, like Greenpeace International are hierarchically organised; nevertheless, the organisation's headquarters has two women in supreme positions of International Executive Directors (Greenpeace International, Annual Report, 2016, International Executive Directors, 2018, Management Structure, 2018). This insight frames two issues: 1. women's leadership acquisition is framed by their *agentic performative multiple skills-set*; and 2. an egalitarian-organisational ethos frames women's inclusion, even in hierarchical eSMOs. The second point does not deter from women's merit and prowess, but suggests that egalitarianism and hierarchy can operate cohesively, enabling women's inclusion, without delineating their competence. Nonetheless, global renewable energy boards are male-dominated, reflecting the problem of the patriarchal control of global environmental politics (Maleta 2011b; Bombora Wave Power 2018; Carnegie Clean Energy 2018; EREF 2018; EUREC 2018; REA 2018).

1.6 Gender Performativity, Political Agency and the Identity of the Subject

Utilising Butler's (2007, 2011, 2013, 2015) theory of gender performativity and political agency, plus Connell's (1995, 2005, 2009) patriarchal critique of hegemonic masculinity/femininity, I add that women's strategic performance in renewables advocacy, entails 'repeated, stylized corporeal' acts (Butler 2007: 191). My argument is that emphasized femininity leadership, is akin to women's *agentic performative multiple skills-set*; whereby women-led leadership is equally resistant to patriarchy. The connection of oneself to the social and natural world, or human and nonhuman dimensions, entails 'doing gender', whereby activists negotiate the 'I' in their identity and social change ambitions. This performative act is a ritual that is repeated and enacted in sociopolitical contexts (Butler 2007). Butler's landmark text, *Gender Trouble: Feminism and the Subversion of Identity*, elaborates on gender as an act, requiring a repeated performance; intersecting public action and corporeality with the agentic identity of the subject:

> the action of gender requires a performance that is repeated. This repetition is at once a re-enactment and re-experiencing of a set of meanings already socially established; and it is the mundane and ritualized form of their legitimation... gender ought not to be construed as a stable identity or locus of agency from which various acts follow; rather, gender is an identity tenuously constituted in time, instituted in an exterior space through a stylized repetition of acts. The effect of gender is produced through the

stylization of the body and, hence, must be understood as the mundane
way in which bodily gestures, movements… This formulation moves the
conception of gender off the ground of a substantial model of identity to one
that requires a conception of gender as a constituted social temporality.

(2007: 191)

Gender is constituted through repeated actions, but also framed through social
and bodily interactions. Gender identity is realised through internal and external
premises of self (Butler 2007, 2015). Thus, it is a corporeal and intellectual self-
reflexion. Gender involves a subjective recollection of one's internal (psyche) self
to one's natural (external) environment. Gender identity is not fixed nor stable,
in that one's recognition of self, is changing and mobile – it is constituted through
individual actions that are repeated but these have an external dependency or
social locus of time and space (Butler 2007). This points to Connell's (1995: 77)
point that hegemony is not fixed or static, but representative of changing, mobile
social relations of power. Agency, thus, is measurable by one's exercise of power,
and subjective identification of self with society and environs. The 'bodily gestures,
movements' identified in Butler's (2007: 191) assessment situate corporeal agency,
whereby one's physical and intellectual action frames resistance and subversion.
Butler's (2007: 191) emphasis on 'bodily gestures, movements' and 'stylized
repetition of acts', enables me to contextualise women's corporeal-intellectual
WW & SE leadership, plus a sociopolitical NSM, informed by republicanism,
feminism, egalitarianism and environmentalism. Yet as 'essentialized', 'hetero-
sexualized' gender subjects, Butler's (2007, 2011, 2013) critique further frames
the way women are subject to dispossession.

In the context of the neoliberal expropriation of labour, Butler (2013)
contemplates how dispossession is politically performative, relative to lower and
higher degrees of agency. The context of war or being a victim of war arguably
places women in a position of subjected agency, for agency has lessened, relative
to dispossession and destabilised senses of national and civic identity (Butler
2009, 2013, 2017). Women in war situations or as war victims experience less
agency and higher degrees of dispossession than men (Butler 2009, 2013).
Such possession is discursive to militant forms of patriarchy, whereby women
are 'othered'. Butler's (2013) conceptualisation of the performative as political
is developed in my critique of 'women's dispossession' within patriarchal
hierarchies. Yet emphasized femininity-women-led strategies elevate feminist
agency (Leahy 2003; Butler 2004, 2007; Maleta 2015). Feminist agency, as a
form of possession versus dispossession, is actualised by women's resistance to
ruling class governing and industrial elites. Participants' performativity as skilled
agents, accompanying robust social and environmental change goals, challenges
patriarchal institutionalisation in how, through subversion, women realise the 'I'
in their identity (Plumwood 1997; MacGregor 2001; Butler 2004, 2007, 2011; Di
Chiro 2011; Merchant 2013; Walby 2013, 2015; WIE 2018).

Feminist advocacy encompasses human and nonhuman dimensions, in how
women's agentic competence within ecological leadership of sustainability and

climate justice reforms – integrates the social (human) and natural (scientific) world (Merchant 1994, 2013; Cudworth 2002; Horton 2006; Canty 2017). Contemplating human and nonhuman dichotomies, more women in power, aligned with my egalitarian-peace-renewables-technological vision, frames an urgency to fix 'the fragility' of the natural world (Culley and Angelique 2010; Di Chiro 2011; Cudworth 2012; Merchant 2016). More women in power, entails less danger, less disasters and more sustainable, safer, healthier social change outcomes. My emphasized femininity-women-led model is one in which, ideally and practically, the social and natural world operate in cohesion rather than disharmony (Merchant 1994, 2013; Cudworth 2002; Cudworth and Hobden 2013). Markedly, women's greater leadership of WW & SE represents the ultimate challenge to the patriarchal control of global resource-based polities (Mies 1986; Merchant 1994; Maleta 2011a; Cockburn 2012). Concurrently, my Republican-Act model legislates on targeted quotas for women's leadership, whilst hopefully inspiring nations and global leaders towards the pursuit of greater sustainably around the world (Maleta 2011b; Hickman 2018; Patel 2018).

Through an active negotiation of gender power relations, women are partaking in a subjective sociocultural process of agency, realising the 'I' in their identity and social change ambitions (Giddens 1991; Butler 2007, 2015). This performative reckoning of self to society, plus the human to nonhuman, involves a dualist recognition/resistance to hegemonic masculinity, and recognition/accommodation of emphasized femininity (MacLeod 1992; Leahy 2003; Doyle 2005; MacGregor 2006; Butler 2015). The latter, represents a compelling form of dichotomous resistance to masculinist hegemony. By engaging in active performative subversiveness, women experience higher degrees of agentic empowerment (Connell 1995, 2002, 2005; Nascimento and Connell 2017). As Connell contends, hegemony is not fixed, enabling resistance from 'subordinate groups':

> Hegemonic masculinity can be defined as the configuration of gender practice which embodies the currently accepted answer to the problem of the legitimacy of patriarchy, which guarantees... the dominant position of men and the subordination of women... hegemonic masculinity embodies a 'currently accepted' strategy. When conditions for the defence of patriarchy change, the bases for the dominance of a particular masculinity are eroded. New groups may challenge old solutions and construct a new hegemony. The dominance of any group of men may be challenged by women. Hegemony, then, is a historically mobile relation.
>
> (1995: 77)

From this empowering premise, women can resist hegemony, or indeed the cultural-structures, that privilege men. As patriarchy is embedded in organisational governance, a Republican-Bill of Rights, aspiring to replace the Constitutional Monarchy, is the ultimate legislative framework from which to challenge hereditary privilege and ruling class masculinity (Bogdanor 1995; Palmer 2014). Although dominant notions of masculinity are replicated through *uneven* and *unequal* social hierarchies of power, a Republican change should challenge the ruling power of social (industrial) and political (governing) elites, whilst legislating on women-led sustainable technological development. Arguably, CALD, Indigenous, mature, socioeconomically disadvantaged, disabled status and Anglo women (*my six groups*) – subject to historic forms of workplace exclusion – remain trapped in a system that privileges Anglo middle class males (Kaufmann 2004; Donaldson 2009; Cuomo 2011; DAWN 2015; ABS 2016a; AHRC 2017b). My patriarchal critique of monarchist governance, plus insights to chauvinism and misogyny, hence views Republicanism as a strategic challenge to ruling class privilege (Arendt 1945; Kaufmann 2004; Fenster 2007; Canty 2017; Manne 2017). It is also an opportunity to improve gender, renewables and EEO policies.

Masculine hegemony is dually replicated in the executive arm of the renewables eNSM, whereby dominant power relations, evidenced through 'a [patriarchal] boys club', reveal that the sexual division of labour, gender differentiation, plus privilege, encompasses female marginalisation in the 21st century (Bombora Wave Power 2018; Carnegie Clean Energy 2018; EREF 2018; EUREC 2018; REA 2018; SolarPower Europe 2018). My research findings show that participants' inclusion is heightened in grassroots organisations and the Greens party, dually informed by egalitarianism and feminism, along with policies on gender equity plus ecological and social justice (Australian Greens, Our Policies, 2018). Although I am not a member of the Greens, I draw inspiration from their position on a Bill of Rights, framed by grassroots democratic ecological egalitarianism (Maleta 2011b; Australian Greens, Constitutional Reform and Democracy, 2018, Participatory Democracy, 2018). My feminist-environmentalist Republican-Bill, in turn, legislates on women's WW & SE leadership, thus, enabling ecological and gender justice. My Bill is also aligned with Red Vienna's social egalitarian democratic mode of governance, enabling equality for working and middle class women. Republicanism, thus, aligns with my emphasized femininity resistance to ruling class masculinist privilege.

Drawing upon my interview material, plus supporting materialist and idealist studies, I evaluate the extent to which women: resist and challenge patriarchy, or, alternatively, accommodate and even 'accept' masculine hegemony (MacLeod 1992; Connell 1995, 2002). Arguably, gender performativity involves a comparative recognition/resistance to cultural structures that reproduce men's dominance, whereby a social (Republican) change and environmental (sustainable technological development) change is the goal. In relation to Connell (1995, 2002) and MacLeod (1992), women possess the choice to resist hegemony, suggesting that 'femininity' and 'masculinity' are not fixed. Women, thus, possess the agentic power to challenge masculine hegemony.

Nonetheless, women Parliamentarians may also be criticised for performing masculinity by accommodating towards patriarchy. The first female Prime Minister (PM) of Great Britain, the late Dame Margaret Thatcher, appeared manlier than her male colleagues within cabinet (Greer 1999; Segal 2007; Connell 2009; Maleta 2011b). Her masculine, and somewhat 'hard' performance contributed to the label of 'Iron Lady' (Fraser 1989; Skard 2014). This was further evidenced in her leadership of the Falklands-Argentine military campaign of 1982, in which the invasion of the Islands was viewed as necessary to protect British civilians along with geopolitical territorial interests (Taylor 1997). In the frame of gender performativity, chauvinism, nationalism and imperialism intersected uncomfortably through Thatcher's conservative neoliberal leadership.

The former first (and only) female Prime Minister of Australia, Julia Gillard, resisted 'the boys club' of Parliament (Donaghue 2015). In her landmark 'Misogyny Speech', Gillard (2012) accused the former conservative Liberal party Opposition Leader Tony Abbott (also former PM) of sexism and misogyny, drawing upon his chauvinism and resistance to her leadership, framed by commentary on women's 'appropriate role' as housewives (Greer 2010a; Hall 2013; Murphy 2013; Wright and Holland 2014). Abbott also mocked Gillard in public community actions, holding up placards depicting her as 'a witch' (Petherbridge 2014; Wright and Holland 2014). In retrospect, Greer (2010) elaborated that Gillard was mocked for her clothes, morals, 'deliberate childlessness' and unmarried defacto status. Such moralist judgements place women as the dualist insider/outsider within politics (Plumwood 1997, 2006; Greer 1999, 2010b; Maddison 2004; Maleta 2011b).

1.7 Gendered Representations and Renewable Energy Equity Programmes

Privilege is defined by sociological dimensions of gender/sex, class/social status and race/ethnicity, in how the Anglo-Celtic middle class, affluent male, represents the most privileged category (Gaard 2001; Stein 2004; Connell 2009; Maleta 2011a; Grusky 2014). Such privilege is replicated in the upper echelons or executive hierarchy of global environmentalist new social movements (eNSMs). In this section, I highlight Australian, E.U. and British examples of White male privilege. In the state of Western Australia (W.A.), Anglo male middle class privilege pervades the patriarchal executive hierarchy of renewable energy boards (Bombora Wave Power 2018; Carnegie Clean Energy 2018). As W.A. has a high Indigenous population, I stress their greater representation in renewables governance, as in my Bill. Within the context of the European Union (E.U.), women are increasingly acquiring executive posts; but men still dominate renewable energy boards and renewables associations (EREF 2018; EUREC 2018; SolarPower Europe 2018).

Comparatively, the U.K.'s Renewable Energy Association's board has degrees of gender diversity, along with five males and three females (REA 2018). A feminist argument is that women are 'deliberately' placed on male-dominated boards to fill a gender gap (Gupta 2007; Terjesen et al. 2009; Yoder et al. 2011; Gheaus 2015). This is a somewhat pessimistic viewpoint; nonetheless, I do not intend to delineate women's competence nor merit in acquiring executive roles. Moreover, my research findings also point to gender tokenism on climate panels, despite women's proven scientific and intellectual prowess. If women dominate executive boards, the question of competence or gender tokenism inadvertently comes into play. Nonetheless, with more women in positions of power, such as in male-dominated industries, like environmental science; this is a compelling framework from which to test and resist hegemony (Cadaret et al. 2017; Farr et al. 2017; STEMM 2018). Patriarchy is not fixed; as with hegemony – its paradigms are culturally-structurally discursive by complex power relations within existing social hierarchies (Connell 1995; Leahy 2003). Such power is subject to altered horizons, new ways of working and empowered identities – framed by women-led resistance (Connell 1995, 2002, 2005; Segal 2007). Thus, women's agency is testing the structures that privilege men/masculinities.

Within a global environmental framework, not-for-profit-based renewables organisations tend to have better gender equity. In Britain, for example, RenewableUK has a progressive 'Women in Wind' programme, encouraging more women to work in wind farm technological development (RenewableUK 2017). Such programmes inspire my WW & SE technology Initiative (Bill of Rights). Regarding female recruitment drives, in Australia the Clean Energy Council, has a female Board Chair (the General Manager), plus the Council offers scholarships: the '2018 Women in Renewables Scholarship' (Clean Energy Council 2018). Hence, the goal to recruit more women to renewables energy highlights a global gender gap; yet this is being resisted through proactive campaigns. As women are not entirely included in renewables scientific leadership, programmes targeting their equity signifies two goals: 1. to improve their equal employment opportunity, and 2. to recognise their merit and prowess. My Bill of Rights, however, cements this in legislation, ensuring that EEO outcomes are achieved, rather than an aspirational goal (STEMM 2018).

One viewpoint is that renewables energy is conducive to emphasized femininity ways of working (in contrast to the 'hard sciences'). My participants outlined that they prefer to work in organisations characterised by 'conciliatory approaches', 'consensus-building', 'less power' and 'less hierarchy'. They also demonstrate an ethos of egalitarianism, fairness and justice in their work. This is evidenced in campaigns advocating for sustainable technology versus uranium and fossil fuels extrapolation. As participants criticised 'male-dominated' strategies, in terms of: 'misogyny', 'chauvinism', 'androcentrism' and 'aggression', they also criticised some men for not knowing 'how to control their emotions' and being 'less rational'. Such findings dispute essentialist dualist assumptions of women/femininities, in terms of heightened emotion and irrationality (Mackenzie and Stoljar 2000; Pease 2002; Meynell 2009; Wright and Holland 2014; Butler 2015; Manne 2017). My accounts also reveal that women often out-perform men, which challenges the dichotomy of masculinity/femininity, pertaining to the notion that men possess superior skill, intellect and strength (Cockburn 1988; Buckingham-Hatfield 2000).

Grassroots-based organisations and the Greens party, experience progressive gender and work relations, and are a fertile ground for egalitarian-based social democracy (Maleta 2012; Carter 2013; Gauja and Jackson 2016). As a grassroots-based party, Greens members tend to reject rigid hierarchy, whereby patriarchy is also resisted (Maleta 2011b; Gauja and Jackson 2016). Such resistance is replicated through party policies (Carter 2007; Raunio 2015; Australian Greens, Participatory Democracy, 2018). My findings on unified gender relations here disputes prior research that Leftist greens politics is patriarchal and not conducive to feminism nor women (Mellor 1993, 1997; MacGregor 2006).

Along with egalitarian democratic principles, I draw inspiration from the Greens policy on a Bill of Rights (Australian Greens, Constitutional Reform and Democracy, 2018, Gender Equality, 2018, Our Policies, 2018, Participatory Democracy, 2018). From a comparative standpoint, the integration of feminism and women's empowerment plus social egalitarianism and grassroots ecological democracy, inspires my Act: to replace the Constitutional Monarchy and Westminster Constitution (Commonwealth of Australia Constitution Act [1977] 2013). The leaders of grassroots eNSMs and eSMOs represent a powerful force for an egalitarian-informed Social Democratic Republican change vision.

I also draw inspiration from the framing of *my six groups*' agentic prowess, as a point from which to revitalise the women's, enivronmentalist and Indigenous NSMs; downplaying assumptions that such SMs are in a state of abeyance or have hibernated (Taylor 1989; Havemann 1999; Maddison 2004; Doyle 2005; Grey and Sawer 2008; McLellan 2009). The greater inclusion of my six 'dispossessed' groups is a standpoint from which to advocate for a Republican change. CALD and Indigenous women *should empathise* with 'an Australian republic', whilst acknowledging their contentious status in the hegemonic ruling order (Mellor 1997; Brown 2011; DAWN 2015; Kermoal et al. 2016; Kawharu 2018).

1.8 Conceptualising a Patriarch Within Patriarchy: Women's Economic Independence

A patriarch is traditionally a male figure, who is situated in a position of authority and responsibility. This conceptualisation can refer to men in public and private domains/spheres, such as a male CEO of a company, or even one's father in a domestic situation. Patriarchy is endemic to cultural structures that privilege men and masculinities (Walby 1990, 2011, 2013; Buckingham-Hatfield 2000). However, women's economic independence, whereby they are not reliant on men or partners for an income, challenges patriarchy. In most occupations, across advanced OECD nations, men earn considerably more than women (Walby and Armstrong 2010; ABS 2016b; AHRC 2017b). Women's unequal pay, and career (in)equity, is a rationale to state that patriarchy is a pressing gender-organisational barrier, even in the 21st century (Walby 1990, 2013; AHRC 2016b). However, in my Act, I strive for women's greater economic independence, as leaders in sustainable technological development. Women's economic independence, represents feminist empowerment, whilst challenging the traditional conceptualisation of a patriarch within patriarchy – relative to unequal systems of organisational governance.

The notion of women as 'the other' or being 'othered', relates to the 'logic of domination', prevalent within patriarchy (Glazebrook 2005: 77). On this point, Glazebrook acknowledges the principles of domination in the work of de Beauvoir – whom identified within patriarchal frames how both women and nature appear as 'the other' (1952: 144, cited in 2005: 80). Similarly, Warren contends that modernity is contextualised by a patriarchal logic of domination and proposes a 'transformative feminism', that makes 'a central place for values (e.g., care, friendship, diversity)' (1987: 19, cited in Glazebrook 2005: 80). Hence, ecofeminists, like de Beauvoir and Warren, identify the oppressive logic of domination within modernity, and offer alternate feminist frames to patriarchy (Glazebrook 2005: 80).

The otherness of women is replicated through the domineering role of the male patriarch within institutionalised systems of patriarchal organisational governance. Dualist dichotomies of men/masculinities as dominate and women/femininities as subordinate are being disrupted though; for women are asserting their careers and economic output (Cockburn 1988; Plumwood 1997; Buckingham-Hatfield 2000; Cadaret et al. 2017). As economic providers, it is not feasible to perceive women as subordinate or 'the other' to the male. As a patriarch is a chauvinistic, misogynistic figure, women-led economic independence challenges the dominant/subordinate dichotomy of men/women as polar yet mutual opposites (MacGregor 2006; Maleta 2012, 2015; Pollack 2015). Economic independence, thus, empowers women, whilst representing resistance to patriarchy, chauvinism and misogyny. Nonetheless, my empirical insights to 'a boys club' underlies gender-organisational barriers, framing women's otherness. Contentiously, EEO laws and meritocracy have not fully enabled women's career mobility and economic independence.

1.9 EEO Gaps and Meritocracy

Concerning my emphasized femininity-egalitarian framework, I contend that shortfalls in EEO outcomes and meritocracy, along with privileged executive hierarchies, frame women's struggle of (in)equity/(in)justice within patriarchal organisational governance. A Bill of Rights, is, however, an opportunity to resist the cultural-structures that advantage men and masculinities (Probert 2005; Commonwealth of Australia Constitution Act [1977] 2013; Public Service Commission 2015; DAWN 2015; EEO Act [1987] 2016). Although meritocracy (in which we supposedly live in) along with EEO measures, aspire to address women's workplace marginalisation, one could add that meritocracy and EEO are susceptible to patriarchy (Pocock 2003; Pocock et al. 2013). As such, women may be expected to conform to masculine ideals and practices in order to achieve status and elevation in their careers. Direct challenge to men executives, or feminist activist resistance to patriarchy, may place women even more as outsiders or 'the other' in their organisations. This accounts for why some women may accommodate patriarchy, by performing/accommodating masculinist discourses, without apparent resistance. Evidently, women's performative accommodation of masculinity does not challenge the ruling power of men. Moreover, as a gendered performance, agentic competence, situated in emphasized femininity resistance, is conducive to women's empowerment (Cockburn 1988; Butler 2004, 2007; Maleta 2009). Hence, women may choose to resist or alternatively accommodate patriarchy (MacLeod 1992; Plumwood 1997; Meynell 2009). Resistance, in my argument, is aligned with emphasized femininity, enabling social change outcomes.

Through resistance, women acquire an empowering sense of self, identity and purpose. Such action undermines the power relations that privilege men and their sociocultural 'hegemonic' dominance of organisational governance (Butler 2015). Hence, agentic competence, or the performance of agency (negotiation of power) and competence (skilled work performances), enables women to realise the 'I' in their identities and social change ambitions (Cockburn 1988; Probert and Wilson 1993; Butler 2013; Gheaus 2015).

My conceptual articulation of *my six groups'* greater WW & SE leadership aspires to redress historical to contemporary gender gaps (Tatchley et al. 2016). Ultimately, my constructivist-feminist-egalitarian-environmentalist Act challenges the shortfalls in current EEO-framed meritocracies, whilst aspiring to achieve women's leadership equity (McFarland 2014; Ajani 2015; BWE 2018; STEMM 2018; WIE 2018). One criticism of current EEO legislation is that it represents a formality of organisational governance (EEO Act [1987] 2016). An assumption of gender equality is created in law, but this is somewhat an allusion; for gender legislation does not adequately account for women's struggle with structural and cultural inequality, particularly in leadership.

Executive and board positions within renewables governance, are dominated by Anglo middle class men (ABS 2016a; Bombora Wave Power 2018; Carnegie Clean Energy 2018). Male dominance is prevalent in Parliament, International eNGOs and corporations, whereby ruling class masculinity evokes a counterpoint to women-led emphasized femininity strategic engagement (Donaldson and Poynting 2013; Maleta 2015, 2018b). Women are articulate political negotiators and environmental performers; but existing EEO laws need to be challenged in order to achieve women's greater leadership in sustainable technological development (EPBC Act 1999; EEO Act [1987] 2016; RenewableUK 2017; BWE 2018; Clean Energy Council 2018; WIE 2018).

Sourcing my interview data, empirical themes and supporting studies in the global interdisciplinary field, I strive to construct women's transformative gendered roles and empowered work-based identities, along with their negotiation of gendered-organisational enablers/barriers (Culley and Angelique 2003, 2010; Maleta 2012). Undoubtedly, women experience enablers (agentic competence) and barriers (the male-dominated control of their organisations, patriarchal institutionalisation, masculine hegemony) across renewables governance. Women's enablement and empowerment is evidenced through their active negotiation of gendered power relations and agentic performance of emphasized femininity. Emphasized femininity, in theory and praxis, aspires to subvert ruling class masculinity whilst framing women's greater leadership in WW & SE technological development, akin to my social (Republican) and sustainable (Bill of Rights) framework.

1.10 Women with Disabilities at Work

The formation of nations into republics does not necessarily resolve gender inequity or glass ceilings (Irving and Murray 2001; Sharp et al. 2008; Cook and Glass 2014; AHRC 2016a, 2017b; Veri 2016). The proposed idea to replace monarchist-based governance with republicanism is an opportunity to address heredity privilege, gender justice and sociocultural disadvantage (pertaining to my core six groups). Although positions of employment are ideally based on merit, women and minority groups endure perpetual sociocultural inequality (Walby 2011; Butler 2013; Cooper 2013; Disability Discrimination Act [1992] 2013; AHRC 2016b; Lipenga 2018). Concerning equity, I propose legislated federal policies in my Republican Constitutional framed Bill. In particular, I target women's 75% leadership, in which CALD, Indigenous, Anglo, older, low SES and disabled women are proportionately represented in sustainable technological leadership positions (Cooper 2013; DAWN 2015; AHRC 2016b; Lipenga 2018). This is an ambitious target; nonetheless, with more women leaders, patriarchal privilege should lessen (Sharp et al. 2008; Gillard 2012; Summers 2013; Donaghue 2015; ABS 2016a; AHRC 2017a).

Although the Disability Discrimination Act ([1992] 2013), addresses the discrimination of disabled peoples in the workforce, this does not account for disabled women's marginalisation within governmental and corporate leadership positions (AHRC 2016b; Evans 2016; Edge et al. 2017; Lipenga 2018). A woman, for example, of a Non-English Speaking Background (NESB), in her fifties, of a socioeconomically disadvantaged status, along with linguistic challenges, would endure multiple barriers and stigmas, or indeed otherness (Cooper 2013; AHRC 2016b). Her 'acceptance' and sense of belonging is complicated by cultural-structures that are conducive to Anglo middle class men (DAWN 2015; Donaldson and Poynting 2013). Hence, women/femininities' potential for inclusion is discursive to one's class/social status, ethnicity, age and disability status.

Instead, diverse sector recruitment drives should target 'disabled' women for their potential to offer significant skills in the workforce (Pocock et al. 2013; Haynes et al. 2015). It is not to say that *my six groups* are less skilled, but that disabled, older and ethnic women face unfair barriers (Barry 2008; Donaldson 2009; Cooper 2013). These barriers are of a social, cultural, economic and political dimension. Nonetheless, if one is disabled, it is reasonable to expect that 'she' would endure more challenges in having her competence realised, not because of her skill, but because of certain physical or intellectual challenges (AHRC 2016b). Contentiously, EEO laws and policies fall short in addressing diversity and the equal representation of women with physical and intellectual disabilities.

Conclusion

Patriarchy is arguably replicated in meritocracy. Although EEO policies and practices ascribe to gender equity, the cultural structures in place – that is the system itself – in work, society and governance, is somewhat framed by patriarchal hierarchies that uphold men's dominance. Hence, current cultures of meritocracy do not fully enable women's leadership equity/justice. My methodological approach though is framed by two core points of contention: 1. women's *agentic performative multiple skills-set* and 2. women's resistance to patriarchy and masculine hegemony. My modelling of Sustainable Scientific-Technological Development Initiatives (SSTDI) is supported by an emphasis on women-led Wind, Wave and Solar Energy (WW & SE) solutions, akin to a Republican sociopolitical change. Relative to my Bill of Rights, I legislate on quotas to redress women's workplace under-representation, whereby prowess and merit in renewables technological-scientific development are criteria for further career advancement. Quotas are necessary to ensure that women are not continually marginalised in the workplace; nonetheless, career elevation depends upon proven competence. Within executive social hierarchies, discursive to hegemony – the male, or as in my argument, the Anglo, middle class, affluent male, is the most privilege category (Poynting and Donaldson 2007, 2013; DAWN 2015). In order to challenge patriarchal privilege, my emphasis is on the agentic leadership of CALD, Indigenous, disabled, older, low SES and Anglo women. Such groups' greater participation in renewable governance is achievable by a Republican-Constitutional-framed Act, whereby quotas aspire towards gender equity, sustainability reforms, plus an Indigenous Treaty, in turn, strengthened by Indigenous women's leadership input.

Hence, I emphasise emphasized femininity resistance to patriarchal institutionalisation, supported by progressive Sections/articles within a Bill of Rights. Such an Act addresses (in)justices centred on one's (dis)ability, under-privileged socioeconomic status, age, ethnicity and essential othering, as a woman. In my constructivist framing of gender performativity, I aspire to achieve feminist empowerment and elevated women-led identities, enabling women to realise the 'agentic I' in their identity and social change-sustainable ambitions (MacLeod 1992; Connell 1995; Gaard 2001; Butler 2007, 2013). Gender performativity, entailing accommodation towards emphasized femininity (and resistance to hegemonic masculinity), thus, highlights my critique of ruling class elitist privilege (Connell 2002; Butler 2004; Poynting and Donaldson 2005; Donaldson and Poynting 2007, 2013). Nonetheless, empirical thematic insights to 'a boys club', glass ceilings and tokenism reveal that women's equity will not be achieved without sociopolitical change. A Republic-Bill of Rights is the framework for such change.

2   What a Bill of Rights Should Achieve

Introduction

My proposed Republican Constitutional Bill of Rights Act, aligned with the conceptual modelling of *my six groups'* (CALD, Indigenous, Mature/Older, Socioeconomically disadvantaged, Disabled status, Anglo-Celtic) multiple agentic performative competencies, challenges patriarchy. My Act envisions women's 75% leadership of Wind, Wave and Solar Energy (WW & SE) technological solutions. My 31 interviews with women environmentalists support this framework. Notably though, *my six groups* are also a futuristic, conceptual modelling, relative to my Act. When I discuss these groups, I source my interviews – but am referring broadly to women (whom may not be participants). Hence, I propose a futuristic Republican model, aspiring to address women's participatory inclusion through frames of equity/justice within renewables governance.

My Bill of Rights is centred on egalitarianism, and aims to subvert patriarchal institutionalisation and the Westminster Constitution, whereby a Republican Constitutional change would ideally replace the Constitutional Monarchy (Bogdanor 1995; Selway 2003; Anderson 2010; Commonwealth of Australia Constitution Act [1977] 2013; Veri 2016). My egalitarian model, aligned with emphasized femininity-women-led resistance, therefore represents a rigorous challenge to the ruling power of social (industrial) and political (governing) elites.

2.1 A Human-Rights Framework and (In)equity/(In)justice Initiatives

A Bill of Rights serves as a human-rights template, focussing on four key sections: 1. *Women's Renewables Technological Leadership Initiative*; 2. *Minority Women's Leadership in Renewables Organisational Governance Initiative*; 3. *Women's Leadership Equality in Male-dominated Work Sectors Initiative*; and 4. *An Indigenous Treaty*. In Section 2, my articulation of *Minority Women*, is relative to *my six groups*. I include Anglo women as minority women, for Anglo men dominate renewables management (Bombora Wave Power 2018; Carnegie Clean

Energy 2018). These four Sections address gender barriers, women's leadership (in)equity, and shortfalls in EEO legislation plus meritocracy. Women's greater renewables leadership strives to redress women's historic to contemporary workplace imbalance (Gaard 2001; McFarland 2014; RenewableUK 2017; BWE 2018; STEMM 2018; WIE 2018). As my emphasis is on gender equity plus technological development; this Act is a model for nations and global leaders aspiring towards greater women-led inclusion. This model is not limited to Australian governance.

2.2 Women's Renewables Technological Leadership Initiative and Indigenous Treaty

A Republican change would contribute to a higher participation rate of my six conceptual groups in renewables governance, in particular, CALD and Indigenous. A Treaty, supported by a Bill of Rights, would legislate on Indigenous sovereignty and ideally achieve reconciliation between Indigenous and non-Indigenous communities (Pemberton 2017; Australian Greens, Constitutional Reform and Democracy, 2018). Also, a Treaty is an opportunity to address Native land entitlements, more so to the needs of the Indigenous peoples, rather than ultimately through the lens of White middle-upper class judges, presiding over the High Court (Smith et al. 2012). Currently, the Australian High Court is where Constitutional amendments are contested (Smith et al. 2012). In relation to Jacks (2017), former Prime Minister Turnbull's assessment of Indigenous Constitutional recognition as 'too hard' and that the Australian electorate are 'conservative' about change cements the way in which the neoliberal hegemonic ruling establishment is not willing to address greater Indigenous rights or sovereignty (Doyle 2005; Connell 2006; Brennan 2015; Prokhovnik 2015; Nagy 2017). Without sovereignty, reconciliation is not possible.

Whilst a Treaty, supported by a Bill of Rights Act, addressees Indigenous sovereignty, it should also challenge the myth of 'terra nullius' (Plumwood 1997; Brennan 2015; Prokhovnik 2015). The term 'terra nullius' means 'empty land' and was appropriated by the British to colonise the Australian continent (Havemann 1999; Doyle 2005). Regarding resistance to 'terra nullius', I source inspiration from Indigenous women, in the development of such a Treaty. Markedly, Indigenous women possess a bold history in anti-nuclear-toxic waste activism (Mellor 1997; Cockburn 2013; Kermoal et al. 2016; Gaard 2017; Maleta 2018b). Hence, Indigenous women's mission inspires my conceptual ambitions for social change and environmental justice whilst strengthening my anti-war ethos and peacemaking model (Warren 1999; Cockburn 2000, 2012; Gaard 2017; Nagy 2017).

2.3 Critique of Conservatism Within Australian Sociopolitical Contexts

Former Prime Minister Turnbull's assessment of the Australian electorate as conservative contrasts with the electorates vote for marriage equality in 2017

(ABS 2017; Tomazin and Koziol 2017). Same-sex marriage legislation was passed in December 2017 and enacted officially in early 2018; since Commonwealth conception, only eight of the proposed 44 referendum amendments to the Constitution have been successful (Smith et al. 2012; ABS 2017). However, marriage equity shows change is indeed feasible; extending perhaps even to an Indigenous treaty (Prokhovnik 2015; ABS 2017; Pemberton 2017; Tomazin and Koziol 2017; Australian Greens, Constitutional Reform and Democracy, 2018). The historic lack of successful Constitutional amendments, nonetheless, points to the lack of clear Parliamentary leadership, especially by conservative neoliberal parties (Walby 2012; Butler 2013; Cornish 2017; Jones 2017). As former leader of the Australian Republican Movement, Turnbull commented on Republicanism whilst Prime Minister (Snow 2016). But his leadership here was passive; not inspiring the nation to Republicanism. As former Prime Minister, Turnbull possessed major influence to drive such a change – within a Parliamentary context and through engagement with the electorate. News polls reveal increasing support for a Republic (MacSmith 2016; Newspoll 2018). The same-sex marriage debate and proposed Indigenous Constitutional recognition require engaged political leadership (MacSmith 2016; Jacks 2017). The electorate decided on the former, revealing the power of grassroots-led change, and the lacklustre leadership of conservative Parliamentarians (Connell 2007; Grady et al. 2012; Butler 2013; Jones 2017).

CALD and Indigenous women's greater leadership should enable Australian Republicanism. The upholding of the Constitutional Monarchy, moreover shows that the nation is not independent; reminiscent of postcolonial chauvinism (Arendt 1945; Australia Act 1986). As a middle power in the Asia-Pacific region, with China one of Australia's main trading partners, governance is dominated by Anglo-Celtic men, whereby cultural ties to Britain are replicated through the Monarchy (Taylor 2007; Donaldson and Poynting 2013; Albinski 2016). Minority groups will remain marginalised under this system. Australia's Westminster model of governance is dated, whilst a Republican change, plus policy and polity reform, would reinvigorate governance. My approach to egalitarianism, akin to emphasized femininity-agentic leadership, accompanies such a grassroots-driven change.

My integration of feminism and environmentalism with republicanism is an opportunity to challenge patriarchal institutionalisation, and to address gender gaps, whilst advocating women's scientific and technical leadership of WW & SE solutions (RenewableUK 2017; BWE 2018; Clean Energy Council 2018; EREF 2018; EUREC 2018; REA 2018; SolarPower Europe 2018; WIE 2018). Women's renewables decision-making encompasses a compelling skills-set. In my interviews, grassroots and professional women demonstrate confidence, passion and dedication in their social and work relations. Republicanism, framed by a Bill of Rights and women-led quotas, is an opportunity to achieve women's leadership equity and sustainable solutions, whilst undermining patriarchal privilege (Gow and Leahy 2005; Baruah 2016; AHRC 2017a; Bombora Wave Power 2018; Carnegie Clean Energy 2018; Clean Energy Council 2018; WIE 2018).

Although the neoliberal conservative leadership is not susceptible to a 'radical sociopolitical change', Republicanism, is thereby mandatory, in order to challenge the dinosaurs within governance (Connell 2006; Mellor 2013; Shiva 2014; Philpott et al. 2016). The grassroots are a powerful force for change, especially the role of grassroots women leaders in an anticipated Republican change. Egalitarian change is led by the voice of (Australian) everyday people. Nonetheless, the role of a politician is one of critical engaged responsibility: to respond to the concerns of constituents, and to advocate on behalf of the greater good of citizens. Separation from a Monarchist form of governance entails independent modes of operation that are intrinsically reworked, revitalised and improved. Undoubtedly, 'our' Westminster Constitution is 'dated' (Hudson and Kane 2000; Irving and Murray 2001; Thampapillai 2005; Anderson 2010; Commonwealth of Australia Constitution Act [1977] 2013; Jones and McKenna 2013; ARM 2018).

Republicanism challenges imperialism, along with chauvinistic and paternalistic views of nationhood, foregrounding patriarchal hierarchies of organisational governance (Arendt 1945, 1959, 1973; Bolton 2005; Veri 2016). Continued reliance on the Monarchy suggests the notion of Australia as a colony or outpost of Britain – in a social, cultural, economic and political sense. Despite increased cultural diversity since World War II, Australia is predominantly an Anglo-Celtic country; evidenced by Anglo male middle class privilege within governance and business (Greer 1999; McGregor 2009; DAWN 2015; ABS 2016b; AHRC 2017a). On the other hand, social inequity, in Australia is not as profound as Britain or the U.S. (Kaufmann 2004; Grusky 2014; ABS 2016a; Glencross 2016; Britton 2017). Nonetheless, the divorce from Monarchy to Republic should challenge ruling class elites (Donaldson and Poynting 2013; Grusky 2014). Republicanism thus challenges colonialism and sociocultural privilege along gender, ethnic and class lines (Arendt 1945, 1973; Healey 1998; Arendt and Kohn 2005; Walby and Armstrong 2010; Veri 2016).

My model invokes an Australian Head of State replacing the Monarch as figurehead (Jones and McKenna 2013; Veri 2016). This model is driven by grassroots consensus and egalitarian ideals, relative to *my six groups'* greater inclusion. The public, namely the Australian electorate, vote for the Leader, invoking egalitarianism and equitable grassroots engagement (Hudson and Kane 2000; Irving and Murray 2001; Marshall 2002; Jones and McKenna 2013). This model is an opportunity to revise and improve the nation's laws, especially EEO-merit based laws, which do not adequately address gender (in)equity and women's uneven workplace participation (Connell 2009; Public Service Commission 2015; EEO Act [1987] 2016; AHRC 2017b). The replacement of the current Constitution with a Republican (Australian) Bill of Rights, is an opportunity to address my gender, renewables and sociocultural goals. Further, my qualitative findings, integrating feminism, republicanism, egalitarianism and environmentalism, contributes cutting-edge knowledge to interdisciplinary gender research, sociopolitical NSMs and legal studies. Such a Bill, plus EEO reforms, should enable *my six groups'* workforce participation (DAWN 2015; ABS 2016a; AHRC 2016b).

2.4 An Anti-war Ethos and Peacemaking Model: WW & SE Solutions

My articulation of emphasized femininity is aligned with an anti-war ethos and peacemaking model, engrained in my Bill of Rights, emphasising women's greater leadership of WW & SE technological solutions (Warren 1997, 1999; Butler 2009; Anderson 2010; Cockburn 2012; Wibben 2016). Although resource-rich nations, like Australia, export much of their coal, iron ore and uranium to nations like China and India; global governments and corporations should focus on greater investment and technological development of renewables as a realistic option for the future. This would diversify the market and provide consumers with more options, plus less reliance on corporates for energy sources (AGL 2018). The continental climate of Australia (extreme sun, extensive coastline), make it viable for wind farms, thermal wave power and solar development (Alston 2003, 2013; Love and Garwood 2011; Bombora Wave Power 2018; Maleta 2018b). This futuristic investment, frames the sustainability of the planet, and move away from resource extrapolation. Renewables is a viable economic market; but requires more scientific development and recruitment, whereby women leaders, in urban and rural areas, play a vital role (Alston 2003, 2011; Johnson and Gurung 2011; McFarland 2014).

Women environmental activists have been instrumental in global anti-nuclear-toxic-waste campaigns, striving for peace and justice within the human and nonhuman world (Warren 1999; Doyle 2005; Brown 2011; Burn 2011). Indigenous women activists have long fought against their traditional lands being used as toxic waste dumping grounds (Gaard 2001, 2017; Caldicott 2014; Maleta 2018b; World Nuclear Organisation 2018). Doyle (2005) elaborates on how Indigenous Australian campaigns in rural areas were strategically supported by urban third sector eNGOs. Regional and urban collaborative efforts were unified towards social and environmental justice outcomes. Additionally, environmental justice is driven by a nurturing ethos of care, whereby mothers as activists, demonstrate concern for the future health and well-being of their children and communities (Maleta 2015). Sustainably action initiatives, thereby, contribute to safer, healthier, resilient communities, inclusive of the human and nonhuman (Gaard 2001; Stein 2004; MacGregor 2006, 2014).

My interpretation of feminism, as an anti-war ethos and peacemaking model, is supported by research on women's peace actions in an international context. Women in Britain, Australia and New Zealand have played a strong part in anti-war and anti-nuclear framed eNSMs and eSMOs, particularly from the 1970s to 1990s (Rankin and Gale 2003; Cockburn 2012; Maleta 2018b). Women's agentic competence was demonstrated in the landmark peace eNSM at Greenham Common RAF base in 1983, whereby women formed a 'human chain' in their protest against atomic weapons (Cockburn 2012: 41). In particular, women activists' organised 'a 70,000-person, fourteen-mile human chain linking Greenham to the atomic weapons establishments…' (Cockburn 2012: 41). As an example of women-led resistance to industrial and military elites, the Greenham

Common Peace Camp imagined 'new forms of protest' (Cockburn 2012: 41). Cockburn's (2000, 2012) insight to peace advocacy enables me to emphasise the power of women-led social change acts, and subversive approach towards ruling class masculinity. Women's skilled leadership and collective resistance to atomic energy and nuclear weapons, exemplified by the Greenham Peace chain, represents a strategic emphasized femininity approach, in its resistance to ruling social and industrial elites. Hence, I draw inspiration from how the Greenham Peace Camp challenged patriarchal forms of war and militant symbolism.

During the 1980s, Australian women activists, supported by an Indigenous female contingent and eSMOs, organised a peace protest camp at Pine Gap – a U.S. military base – in the Northern Territory. This camp brought global attention to Australia and the U.S.'s military alliance, along with the power of women-led resistance to war and military androcentrism. Pine Gap was a site also criticised for nuclear experimentation (Rankin and Gale 2003). On the other hand, New Zealand women were active in the anti-nuclear NSM of the 1980s, helping to stop French nuclear testing in the South Pacific (Doyle 2005; Maleta 2018b). This was a strategic attempt to resist war and nuclear technology or indeed the proliferation of nuclear weapons in the Asia-Pacific region (Maleta 2018b). The anti-nuclear activism of Australian, New Zealand and British women, and many others in the global North and South, shows the power of global resistance to men-led aggression, or even war versus peace (Shiva 2005, 2008, 2016). These structures are already in place, due to patriarchy, but are unlikely to change or alter, without active resistance and challenge (Connell 1995, 2005; Butler 2007, 2013). Women play a vital role, therefore, in challenging patriarchal systems.

The extrapolation of the natural environment, or exploitation of it, for capitalist economic profit, counters with my anti-war ethos, rooted in peaceful renewables development (Warren 1997, 1999; Butler 2009; Cockburn and Enloe 2012). It is up to women, as a matter of survival, to resist the patriarchal control of global institutionalised governance. Women-led WW & SE strategies, relative to emphasized femininity resistance, frame a duty of care and peace, encompassing responsibility towards the human and nonhuman. An emphasized femininity-led peacemaking model should save the social and natural world from an impending (nuclear) resource-based climatic disaster.

Gender as a performance, consequently, is evidenced by the way women resist male-dominated (resource-based, nuclear) approaches, and advocate renewable technology (McFarland 2014; Ajani 2015; RenewableUK 2017; BWE 2018). Drawing on Butler (2007), in my forthcoming empirical chapters, I aim to articulate the 'I' in women's identity, relative to their negotiation of hegemonic masculinity/femininity, framed by emphasized femininity and social change ambitions – inspired by care and respect for the social and natural world – thereby integrating gender with the environment (Merchant 1994, 2013; Connell 1995, 2005; Eder 1996; Ahern and Hendryx 2008; Johnson and Gurung 2011; Cudworth and Hobden 2013; Maleta 2018a). In this framework, I draw upon Connell's (1995) point that hegemony is not fixed nor stationary, but mobile and fluid. Fluidity foregrounds women's capacity to challenge the 'seeming' ruling power of men – in a cultural and structural sense. I consider the way women construct their identities, whilst resisting patriarchy and advocating sustainability; thus, realising the 'I' in their subjectivity and social change goals (Butler 2004, 2007, 2013). Identity is situated by one's self-reflexivity and action, whereby women's activist participation should elevate agency. Republicanism, in my argument, enables women's empowerment. Also, a Bill of Rights should create more jobs for women (Mellor 2013; McFarland 2014). A greater focus on my groups' skilled leadership, should revitalise environmentalist, women's and Indigenous NSMs.

Additionally, I strive to identify strengths and weaknesses between women and men, in order to improve gender and social relations. 'A boys club' is replicated through Anglo male middle class privilege in organisational governance (Greer 1999; Donaldson and Poynting 2007, 2013; DAWN 2015; ABS 2016a). My emphasized femininity goal is to redress structural-cultural barriers, emphasising an Act centred on women's equity, whilst challenging 'a boys club', endemic to hegemonic ruling class masculinity (Connell 1995, 2002; Maleta 2009; McDonald 2011). In my qualitative data analysis, 'a [patriarchal] boys club' is framed by: women politicians' struggle to have their voice heard in Parliament; the male-dominated 'executive arm' of International eNGOs; contradictory insights to career advancement versus glass ceilings; deliberate placement on climate panels in order to fill a gap, to name a few. Hence, the patriarchal control of the eNSM/eSMOs and men's 'superior' status underpins women's struggle with tokenism and labels of incompetency (Cockburn 1988; Walby 2011; Yoder et al. 2011; Pollack 2015; Cohen 2016). In contrast to 'a boys club', emphasized femininity is conceptualised by the way participants tend to resist competitiveness and adopt egalitarianism, in their social and work relations (Buckingham-Hatfield 2000; Stein 2004; MacGregor 2006; Canty 2017). Heightened forms of egalitarianism are evident within the Greens party and grassroots-based eNGOs, thereby informing the ideological plus structural development of my Bill of Rights Act (Carter 2007; Grady et al. 2012; Maleta 2012; Australian Greens, Our Policies, 2018).

Conclusion

My egalitarian-equity model is, therefore, situated in an anti-war ethos, whereby emphasized femininity, akin to women's greater leadership in renewables technological development, is the solution for a more peaceful (undoubtedly sustainable), safer, less androcentric world (Warren 1999; Shiva 2005; MacGregor 2006; Shiva 2014; Wibben 2016). In support, Cockburn and Enloe's (2012) analysis of peace movements, critiqued militarism, suggesting that patriarchy is a key barrier affecting global peace. Women's peace marches against atomic energy and atom weapons of war, in turn, highlighted collective feminist resistance to patriarchal militant models (Cockburn and Enloe 2012). Patriarchy, thus, frames women's motivation and rationale to engage in anti-war-peace actions. Emphasized femininity is aligned with women-led strategies, characterised by both competence and resistance; competence is evident by their *agentic performative multiple skills-set* whilst resistance is enacted against patriarchy: inclusive of the patriarch and patriarchal institutionalisation. Egalitarianism is heightened through grassroots, collaborative efforts, whereby men and women's shared environmental goals enable the achievement of universal, unilateral social change outcomes. In my data-driven chapters, I highlight how egalitarian women-led strategies destabilise the ruling power of men plus hegemonic masculinity and rigid hierarchical structures. Arguably, an integration of republicanism and environmentalism, aligned with women's WW & SE leadership plus egalitarianism, enables feminist equity and justice, whilst subverting gender-organisational barriers (Maleta 2012, 2018a, 2018b). Women-led subversion is, contextualised by my innovative Act, striving to legislate on equity/justice, thereby linking theory to praxis.

3 Red Vienna
A Viable Republican Model?

Introduction

My feminist modelling of Republicanism draws upon historical and contemporary political examples: Red Vienna and Brexit (see Chapter 4). Regarding successful Republican nations, I refer to the Republic of Austria, formed in 1918 (following the demise of the Austro-Hungary empire), as a leading European Social Democracy. I focus on the landmark Red Vienna (1919 to 1934) era, characterised by egalitarianism and social class diversity along with middle class and working class women's greater participatory inclusion in civic/civil and working life (Blau 1999; Mattl 2009; Kershaw 2013). During this era, egalitarian social reforms 'revolutionised' the working classes, whilst artistic creativity and scientific progress prevailed within the Viennese middle classes (Rentetzi 2004, 2008). Following on from the imperial chauvinism of the Habsburgs (Arendt 1945; Mack 1993; Barker 2012; Rauchensteiner 2014), I draw inspiration form Viennese women's suffrage (1918), and how Red Vienna enabled women's agentic performative competencies as scientists and politicians (Hannam et al. 2000; Rodriguez-Ruiz and Rubio-Marin 2012; Mattl 2016). Women were workers, academics, political activists and home-carers, representative of a diverse demographic (Rentetzi 2008; Mattl 2009).

Although women's gendered roles were changing, in terms of the social change affecting Viennese residents during the 'Red era', the patriarchal chauvinism of the Habsburgs, dually configured in the Republic state (Arendt 1945; Mack 1993; Barker 2012; Rauchensteiner 2014; Mattl 2016). Arendt's (1945) critique of the imperial chauvinism of the pre-World War I Austro-Hungarian, German and Russian Monarchies censures privileged ethnic groups and their monopoly on power. As certain groups were more privileged, this was a foreground for nationalist revolts and republicanism (Arendt 1945, 1959, 1973; Mack 1993). Such privilege was a catalyst for the declaration of independence of nations, like Czechoslovakia and Poland, whom both became Republics in 1918, after centuries of monarchist rule (Seton-Watson 1945; Crampton 1997; Prazmowska 2000).

3.1 Red Viennese Republicanism: Social Democracy for All Classes?

Red Vienna (1919–34) represents an egalitarian-social democratic model of governance, along with an innovative – even revolutionary, reactionary example of republicanism (Gruber 1991; Jeffery 1995; Mattl 2013). Austrian suffrage, challenged patriarchal institutionalisation, pertaining to men's entrenched leadership across sociocultural, economic and political contexts (Gilardi 2015; Mattl 2016). With equal voting rights, Viennese women acquired an empowering civic identity along with subjective plus political empowerment (Rentetzi 2004, 2008, 2010). Women's voting sway influenced the progressive reforms characteristic of that era, thereby improving the living standards and work–life balances of working class residents (Bader-Zaar 1996).

Following the defeat of the Austro-Hungary military in World War I, the empire dissolved, whereby the Republic of Austria (1918) replaced the centuries-old Habsburg Monarchy (Arendt 1945; Mack 1993; Barker 2012; Rauchensteiner 2014). After the Great War, Vienna was dogged by high unemployment along with housing and food shortages (Blau 1999; Kadi 2015; City of Vienna, Municipal Politics, Red Vienna, 2018). In response, the Austrian state enacted an arena of 'reactionary' social, work/industrial, health and housing reforms (Blau 1999). Over 60,000 flats were built – accommodating to the Proletariat – the most famous being Karl Marx Hof (City of Vienna, Municipal Politics, Red Vienna, 2018). Imperialism subsided to republicanism, for Red Vienna was the most successful 'leftist' social democratic mode of governance in Europe, if not the world, at this time.

This was also a progressive era for the Intelligentsia and middle classes, pertaining to creative flair within the arts and architecture, and scientific innovation in medicine and health (Gardner and Stevens 1992; Blau 1999). The rising prominence of psychoanalytical theory (Freud) and Modernist architectural design (Loos), akin to art nouveau, paralleled the rise of the state-centric state (Gardner and Stevens 1992; Blau 1999). The drafter of the Austrian Republican constitution, Hans Kelsen, was part of this revolutionary intelligentsia (Kelsen 1996, 2004; Thoma 2012). Although Red Vienna was conceptually a working-class model; the cultural intellectualism of the Intelligentsia reached unprecedented levels (Hacohen 2000; Mattl 2013). As a progressive model, the middle and working classes experienced elevated social, cultural, political and economic enlightenment.

Traditional gender roles, relative to intersections of masculinity/femininity, were also undergoing transformation. The endemic domestication of Viennese women's home life was challenged by their engagement with socialist reforms and social policies (Rentetzi 2010; Gilardi 2015). The enlightened eight-hour day was an empowering form of 'feminist' legislation, enabling women's work–life balance (Hautmann 2012; Kershaw 2013). Republicanism, in turn, challenged cultural practices of chauvinism and structures of patriarchy (Arendt 1945, 1973; Arendt and Kohn 2005). Red Vienna is, thus far, a landmark Republican example of egalitarian governance, meeting the needs of its sociocultural demography: the Proletariat and Bourgeoise (Mack 1993; Blau 1999; Mattl 2013, 2016).

3.2 Intersections of Republicanism with Feminism

In light of suffrage and Republicanism, Austrian women became more visible in civic/civil life, rather than as essentialised domestic creatures. Women's equal voting, contributed to unprecedented 'social feminist empowerment' (Rodriguez-Ruiz and Rubio-Marin 2012; Mattl 2016). Following the Great War, an emphasized femininity outlook, relative to women's performativity in voting, academic research and political activism, plus their support of 'Red' policies, strengthened the new Republican nation (Rentetzi 2004, 2008; Mattl 2009, 2013). In the frame of Red Vienna, women still dominated the role of homecarer. Such gender performativity points to an intersection of constructivism and essentialism (Berg and Lie 1995; Butler 2007, 2013; Gaard 2017; Nagy 2017). Nonetheless, the role of Viennese women gradually changed, from one as 'essentially' domestic carer, to a more constructivist one; 'an engaged active citizen', who was a political activist and even a scientific academic (Rentetzi 2004; Rodriguez-Ruiz and Rubio-Marin 2012; Mattl 2013).

Mattl (2013, 2016) presents an insight to Charlotte Glas (1873–1944), a Viennese Jewish woman and founder of the Austrian Social Democratic Party. Mattl elaborates that 'Glas was forced to confront both the repressive policies of the Habsburg state and the patriarchal practices of her society and her party' (2016: 1). Critically, Glas accommodated patriarchy, rather than engaging in emphasized femininity-agentic resistance: 'Glas chose to subordinate the fight for women's suffrage to the broader socialist campaign for universal male suffrage' (Mattl 2016: 1). In another case study of Red Vienna, Rentetzi (2004, 2010) outlines women's prowess in scientific academia. Rentetzi focussed on the Viennese Institute for Radium Research, arguing that 'the work culture of its laboratories was fairly gender equal, allowing women physicists to achieve important scientific goals' (2010: 127). Women's performativity in science was enabled by the progressive politics of Red Vienna: 'During the interwar period women accounted for the one third of the total number of the researchers thanks to the encouraging attitude of the director of the Institute, the politics of Red Vienna, and the interdisciplinarity of the field' (Rentetzi 2010: 127).

As well as scientific academic competence, women's agentic performance in civic and political life was somewhat revolutionary for the early 20th century. Women's changing role was framed by nation-states evolving from patriarchal imperialism to reactionary republicanism (Arendt 1945; Rodriguez-Ruiz and Rubio-Marin 2012; Kershaw 2013). In this landscape, essentialism (the traditional role of mother) intersected with constructivism (political advocacy) and the exercise of agentic power (Berg and Lie 1995; Crary 2001; Gaard 2011; Maleta 2015). While women were homecarers, they were also represented as scientists and politicians, thereby revealing a dynamic power-based interplay of essentialism with social constructivism. Regarding essentialism, the traditional role of women as 'a carer' of families, children and the community was upheld within Viennese society (Rodriguez-Ruiz and Rubio-Marin 2012; Kershaw 2013; Maleta 2015). Simultaneously, women were engaged workers, academics and politicians, representative of diverse social class demographics, as well as rigorous constructivist engagement (Mattl 2009, 2013, 2016; Rentetzi 2010). Constructivism, as a performance, contributes to feminist agency; for working class and middle class women's negotiation of power and assertion of their work-based identities, empowered their agency whilst challenging patriarchal privilege. During the Red Vienna era, middle and working class women's dualist public/private roles were further enabled through a progressive work–life balance. The voting power of women as equals contributed to Vienna's 'Red reactionary revolution' plus social policy reforms. Hence, an empowering sense of nationalist identity was rooted in republicanism.

Although suffrage challenged patriarchal institutionalisation, men continued to dominate the Austrian Parliamentary hierarchy (Bader-Zaar 1996; Kelsen 2004; Thoma 2012). Gendered power relations within organisational governance consequently privileged men/masculinities. Hence, women's capacity to influence civic politics and scientific academia was limited by patriarchy (Mattl 2016). Social, cultural, economic and political life was still susceptible to the ruling power of men plus male-dominated cultural structures. Hence, my critique extends to how patriarchal power continued with republicanism; a remnant of the Habsburg rule, but also conducive to the chauvinism prevalent in other European nations of the inter-war era, in transition from imperialism (Arendt 1945; Hacohen 2000; Rauchensteiner 2014). Although Red Vienna represented greater social and gender diversity, the patriarchal chauvinism of the Habsburgs was not eroded; thus revealing the limitations of an egalitarian social democratic model.

Conclusion: The Fall of Red Vienna

The Red Vienna era achieved progressive social reforms and enabled women's political and scientific competent performances (Rentetzi 2004, 2010; Mattl 2013, 2016). This era sharply eroded with the steady take-over of Austria by the Nazis, whereby the landmark 1938 Anschluss of Austria with Germany, represented the rise of dangerous fascism and convoluted nationalism (Hochman 2016). This was accompanied by notions of cultural and ethnic superiority, and simultaneously signified the end of the Austrian Republic as an inclusive social democracy (Wasserman 2012; Hochman 2016). In retrospect, it is intriguing that Red Vienna, characterised by creative flair and scientific innovation, along with successful modes of egalitarianism, succumbed to Nazism. The diverse electorate, especially the working classes, inclusive of men and women, greatly benefited from Red Vienna's progressive social reforms (Gardner and Stevens 1992; Blau 1999; Barker 2012; Mattl 2016). Hence, Red Vienna evoked greater working rights and privileges for the Proletariat and Bourgeoise. Both industry and artistic ingenuity, such as art nouveau, flourished. So why the turn to Nazism? This is a pervasive question. One rationale harks back to the Great War following Austria-Hungary's imperialist military defeat (in World War I), when the Austrian people lost much territory and, as a result, struggled with their national identity. A sense of future, purpose and meaning was left open to much criticism. Hence, the alignment with Germany, a traditional ally of Austria, along with shared language, similar culture and customs, entailed perhaps some security for the Austrians, and a defining purpose (Barker 2012; Hochman 2016). Yet, a union defined by cultural superiority threatened Republicanism (Arendt 1945; Arendt and Kohn 2005; Hochman 2016). Conclusively, Fascism/Nazism contrasts with democratic ideals and ways of life, whilst representing the most dangerous and adversarial political regime in human history (Arendt 1958, 1959). Even the Marxists or Communists did not attempt to annihilate categories of human ethnic demography from the planet. The integration of 'nationality with socialism' was therefore a dangerous mix, and not compatible with working nor middle class objectives. Rather Republicanism is the solution to equity.

4 Brexit and 'WASPishness' as the Antithesis

Introduction

My appraisal of Republicanism is developed by a critique of Brexit. This is situated in the facet of a somewhat 'revolutionary' reactionary anti-monarchist framework. Arguably, the British exit from the European Union (E.U.) community, or Brexit, does not diminish the issue of social inequality in Britain (Walby and Armstrong 2010; Walby 2015; Glencross 2016; Mount 2017). Arguably, a Republican sociopolitical change will challenge inequity and achieve more outcomes for the majority, rather than 'the privileged few' (May 2016; Perkins 2016). This change should come from within Britain rather than Brussels or the E.U. British inequity is defined by historic to contemporary factors and situations: one's class status and income level, along with the capacity to be economically independent (Leahy 2003; Mason 2003; Walby 2010, 2012; Grusky 2014). In relation to Bourdieu (1985), one's cultural (educational accruement and knowledge), social and economic capital (financial resources/savviness) defines the extent to which one holds and wields agency within neoliberal democracies (Ross-Smith and Huppatz 2010; Arthur 2012; Garrett 2013; McGovern 2017). Contentiously, one's capital and agency are limited by a Constitutional Monarchy, relative to a disproportionate command of resources and uneven spread. Those privileged, continue to yield and wield more power than the dispossessed.

4.1 Hereditary Elitism: A Counterpoint Towards Egalitarianism?

A monarchist system is related to a peerage hierarchy (Taylor 2004; Cretney 2008; Williams 2015; Schutte 2017). Historically, heredity elites are replicated through peerage, whereby the aristocracy, traditionally, are the most privileged group (Taylor 2004; Wasson 2017). Today, I would add that Anglo middle class affluent males, not peers of the realm or gentry, wield and yield status as the dominant hegemon, further curtailing working and middle class women's career aspirations (McGregor 2009; Fedorowich and Thompson 2013; DAWN 2015; Collins 2017). Simultaneously, in the Australian context, privilege is evidenced through Anglo men's executive dominance of hierarchical renewable Boards (Poynting and Donaldson 2005; Maleta 2011b; Donaldson and Poynting 2013; Bombora Wave

Power 2018; Carnegie Clean Energy 2018). One's position pertaining to degrees of inclusion, or even exclusion, is measurable by one's gender, ethnicity/race and class/ social status (Gaard 2001; Garrett 2013; Jones and McKenna 2013; McGovern 2017). Australia and New Zealand, as postcolonial British societies, inherited a Constitutional Monarchy, plus privileged demographics (Havemann 1999; Maleta 2011b; Donaldson and Poynting 2013; DAWN 2015; Godfery 2018; Kawharu 2018; Patel 2018). A monarchist polity, replicated in social and work contexts, upholds the status of privileged elites. Heredity-based Monarchism is, thus, representative of ruling class power, and is counterpoint to my conceptualisation of an ideal integration of feminist, egalitarian and republican ambitions.

One could say that Brexit will not alter hereditary or even upper-middle class privilege in Britain. Although Britain, as other neoliberal democracies, tend to define its society as a meritocracy, the fact that its government is led by a Monarch – such a figurehead represents hegemonic peerage authority (Williams 2015; Schutte 2017). The Royal Family, the Windsors, are the most privileged family in Britain (Glencross et al. 2016). Royal wealth has been accumulated over the centuries, from taxes and public monies (Sturgess and Boyfield 2013; Glencross et al. 2016). As Head of State, the Sovereign's primary role is to sign government legislation, thus formalising documents. As royal figurehead, the Monarch is somewhat removed from the electorate together with the public's particular needs or thoughts and struggles. Moreover, Parliamentarians possess expert skills, and can sign documents, whilst acting on behalf of the electorate (Savage 2017). The Monarch's rubber stamp, serves as a formality to the Constitution, but is not mandatory for effective governance.

4.2 A Replication of Anglo Male Middle Class Privilege

In Australia, the core gender barrier is the ruling sway of the Anglo middle class male through sociocultural privilege, rather than necessarily a peerage-based system of aristocrats. Hence, it is middle class males, replicated through their hegemony of organisational governance, rather than upper class males, who are the core barrier, affecting women's equity/justice. In Britain, a class-based system of hereditary privilege bears more status than in Commonwealth, postcolonial nations (Mason 2003; Donaldson 2009; Donaldson and Poynting 2013; Collins 2017). But, in English-speaking nations (including the U.S.), the Anglo middle class male's privileged status is maintained, due to a prevailing ruling order, conducive to their hegemonic dominance (Hazel 1966; Kaufmann 2004; May 2016; Sheppard 2017). Such an elitist cultural-structure is replicated through networks, framed by 'who you know', indicative of 'an [old] boys club' at play in work and society (Gregory 2009; McDonald 2011). Not to say that Australia has a rigid class-based system; but that one's sociocultural demography bears influence upon career elevation and the potential to achieve societal acceptance (Poynting and Donaldson 2005; McGregor 2009; ABS 2016b).

Brexit does not delineate from the fact that a Monarchist form of governance should prevail in the United Kingdom – unless it is challenged. Without resistance to the Monarchy, in Britain and other monarchist nations, Anglo male middle-upper class privilege will prevail. Such privilege is simulated through materialist and structural forms of ruling class masculinity, operating in overt and covert ways. It is not always obvious that one is more privileged than the other. I suggest, moreover, that the Monarchy, in the heart of its context – be it Britain – should be challenged, in order to conquer entrenched sociocultural inequality. Resistance to the Monarchy is necessary, therefore, in order to challenge the embedded foundations of patriarchal institutionalised privilege. Interestingly, the notion of 'a British Republic', and reformed Bill of Rights, is not alien, for it is an opportunity to realise PM May's vision of an inclusive Britain: 'not just the privileged few' (Bill of Rights 1688; May 2016). Brexit will not achieve this. A British Republic, or indeed an Australian one, relative to other reactionary nations, is ideally framed by a Republican-Constitutional change, addressing the divisive issues that pervade polity, whilst realising egalitarian social democratic governance with an equity/justice framed Bill of Rights (Healey 1998; Bolton 2005; Thampapillai 2005; Hiebert and Kelly 2015; Veri 2016; ARM 2018; Hickman 2018).

4.3 Divorcing the Monarchy

The notion of a British Republic, does not entirely delineate from the Royal Family maintaining their peerage status. Turning to my Red Vienna example, after the Austrian Republic formed (1918), the Habsburg Royal Family still acquired their peerage status, but no longer possessed the rule of law nor direct influence over government (Mack 1993; Barker 2012; Lagi 2012; Rauchensteiner 2014). Not that I endorse a peerage system, but stress that the link between Sovereign and State should be separated in order to achieve the desired outcome of grassroots egalitarianism, sociocultural equality as well as gender justice equity, relative to women's greater workplace leadership participation. My proposed Republican change, aligned with the key Sections of my Act, frame this vision.

As I aspire towards an Australian Republic, the notion of a British Republic, the home of the Constitutional Monarchy, is a benchmark from which to challenge ruling class masculinity and social hierarchies of power. Relative to my Act, an envisioned Republican change in Britain is an opportunity to redress 'the boys club' and glass ceilings, whilst advocating *my six groups'* greater WW & SE leadership (Connell 2009; McFarland 2014; Pollack 2015; Cohen 2016; Marfo 2017). To reiterate, this can be dually applied to the British context. As my group of six women are not equally represented in organisational governance, such a Bill, aligned with an emphasized femininity framework, centred on women's *agentic performative multiple skills-set*, strive to redress plural yet interrelated gender, social and environmentalist (in)equities/(in)justices. A monarchist form of governance privileges men/masculinities, in particular members of a superior (rather than 'subordinate') social hierarchy. Comparatively, middle class males are more privileged than working class males (Connell 1995, 2002, 2005; Maddison and Scalmer 2006; Donaldson 2009; McGregor 2009; Maleta 2011a). To sum up, a Bill of Rights, akin to Republicanism, should inspire Commonwealth nations to rework governance structures and revise legislation and Acts (Canadian Bill of Rights 1960; Hiebert and Kelly 2015; Hickman 2018; Patel 2018).

4.4 Envisioning a Peacemaking Sociopolitical Model

A Monarchist form of governance is not conducive to my anti-war ethos and peacemaking model. Although the British army does not have the royal decree in its name, unlike the Royal Navy or Royal Air Force (RAF), this does not deter from the Royal Family's involvement in the military, and armed combats around the world (Woodward and Winter 2006; Chapman 2007; Hale 2008; Dixon 2012; Woodford 2013). Most royal males served in the British army, Navy and RAF (Cowell 2013; Schutte 2017; *The Telegraph* 2019). Military service, duty and governance is linked to ruling class masculinist representations, and contrasts with my anti-militant mode of social democratic governance (Butler 1997; Greer 1999; Woodward and Winter 2006; Cowell 2013; *The Telegraph* 2019). War and military conflict should be resisted rather than engaged upon. Regarding gender performativity, women in supreme positions of leadership possess the choice to accommodate/accept or resist/protest/challenge existing patriarchal cultural structures (MacLeod 1992; Connell 1995; Butler 1997; Greer 1999; Williams 2015). Resistance to warfare, through peaceful performativity – further akin to women's greater role in sustainable technological leadership – cements my feminist-egalitarian sociocultural position, aligned with strategic resistance to ruling class elitism.

To a certain extent, Brexit represents degrees of grassroots resistance to the ruling class political elite or political establishment (Glencross 2016; Mount 2017). Nevertheless, Brexit was also complicated by issues of race/ethnicity together with nationalism, whereby exiting the E.U. was seen as necessary to reassert national sovereignty and national identity (Black 2017; Fabbrini 2017). Although Brexit was associated with nationwide dissatisfaction over high levels of immigration to Britain and threats to identity (Glencross 2016; Fabbrini 2017; Hunt and Wheeler 2018); my assessment is that social inequality is the biggest problem in Britain, and the maintenance of hierarchical elites, replicated through a monarchist polity, dually replicated in the patriarchal institutionalisation of work, society and governance, is not going to erode with Brexit. Contentiously, the Constitutional Monarchy is a core barrier for British peoples, in particular, its working class 'battlers', accounting for why the privileged remain so. On the other hand, Red Vienna achieved an impressive egalitarian equilibrium through its empowered working class and middle class citizenry, who acquired agentic power with the transition towards Social Democratic Republicanism (Gruber 1991; Gardner and Stevens 1992; Hautmann 2012; Jonsson 2013).

A Republican-framed Bill of Rights represents a proactive way forward, particularly in its rigorous challenge to conservativism. The Bill addresses gaps pertaining to the (in)equity of women of disabled, low SES, Indigenous and ethnic minority demographics (Healey 1998; Di Chiro 2011; DAWN 2015;

Prokhovnik 2015). More women in the renewables energy sector, in turn, adheres to progressive EEO outcomes as well as compelling methodological intersections of feminism with republicanism and environmentalism. Hence, the agentic power of the Anglo male is susceptible to emphasized femininity resistance. Additionally, a Republican Constitutional change is an opportunity for economic restructuring, ensuring that the public purse is extended to disadvantaged groups, or *my six groups* (McGovern 2017). My *Renewables Technological Leadership Initiative*, as such, targets women in WW & SE leadership development.

In contrast to egalitarianism, the overarching role of the Monarch, supported by the Governor General, distorts the relationship between governing authorities and the grassroots populace or electorate (Healey 1998; Howell 1998; Selway 2003; Kumarasingham and Power 2014). The link between Monarch and Governor General, relative to governing MPs and the electorate, is not transparent within governance. These figures are disjointed from the grassroots voting populace (Howell 1998; Marshall 2002; Jones and McKenna 2013; Veri 2016). Egalitarianism accompanies the voice of the people, as a stage for dissent and change. Grassroots-informed sociopolitical change leadership, particularly that of women leaders, is a frame of inspiration for nations aspiring towards republicanism (Healey 1998; Irving and Murray 2001; Veri 2016). My Bill strives for EEO reforms and an Indigenous Treaty, whereby grassroots and professional women play a strong role in its advocacy and legislative drive towards Aboriginal and Torres Strait Islander sovereignty (Gaard 2001; Cuomo 2011; Brennan 2015; Nagy 2017; Pemberton 2017; WIE 2018). Social change ideally informs leaders in Australia, New Zealand and Canada (Healey 1998; Campbell et al. 2006; Hiebert and Kelly 2015; ARM 2018; Godfery 2018; Patel 2018). Yet Britain, rooted in centuries of Monarchism – except the anti-monarchist era of Parliamentary rule, led by Oliver Cromwell (Woodford 2013; Wasson 2017) – could draw inspiration from Republicanism, challenging the notion that Monarchism is conducive to British national identity. Arguably, emphasized femininity agentic competence, together with resistant performative femininities, challenges patriarchal institutionalised elitist privilege (Connell 1995, 2005; Plumwood 1997; Leahy 2003; Butler 2007, 2013).

4.5 'WASPishness' Within Neoliberal Democracies

Hereditary privilege within patriarchal leadership, curtailed by gender, class/social status, and ethnicity/cultural agency, frames my argument for a Republican-social change. 'WASPishness' represents a historic to contemporary cultural-structural barrier, endemic to ruling class masculinity and the ruling power of privileged governing and industrial elites (Donaldson 1993, 2009; Donaldson and Poynting 2013). WASP demographic privilege, is represented through Anglo-Celtic middle class male leadership dominance of organisational governance (Kaufmann 2004; Nunlee 2016). Traditionally, WASP, stands for White Anglo-Saxon Protestant (Hazel 1966; Kaufmann 2004; Baldwin 2017). This hegemon frames *my six groups*' agentic dispossession (Connell 1995, 2002;

Butler 2013, 2015). In my argument, working and middle class women possess less agency due to the hegemony of Anglo middle class men (Connell 2005, 2009; Meynell 2009; DAWN 2015).

I do not focus on historic religious divides; but on how Anglo male middle class privilege is replicated through 'a boys club' within English-speaking neoliberal democracies (Donaldson and Poynting 2007, 2013; Sheppard 2017). 'A boys club' was identified as a core gender-organisational barrier in my thematic interview results. Established 'old boys clubs' and networks, exemplified through social bonds and economic affiliations, replicate this group's powerful status and greater degree of agentic power (more so than other demographics) (Kaufmann 2004; McDonald 2011; Davey 2012; Marfo 2017). Postcolonial rule has replicated Anglo privilege, dually reproduced in cultural structures, further simulated through patriarchy (Lobo and Morgan 2012; Bachand 2017).

Despite claims of being 'liberal', 'progressive', 'diverse' and 'open societies', neoliberal Anglo democracies experience inequity, framed by 'waspishness' plus 'the boys club' (McGregor 2009; Walby and Armstrong 2010; Walby 2011; ABS 2016a; Godfery 2018). Nonetheless, inequity is less prevalent in Australia, due to a postcolonial rejection of class-based establishments, and endorsement of egalitarianism (Donaldson 1993; Bolton 2005; Doyle 2005; McGregor 2009). An egalitarian vision, relative to my conceptual framing of human rights and sub-frames of equity/justice, has yet to be realised. Existing patriarchal cultural-structures curtail the sociocultural disadvantage of *my six groups*, and shortfalls in a meritocracy – also yet to be realised. Women's competent merit has yet to be fully recognised. A Republican change should redress this. Thus, a Bill of Rights, framed within a gender-lens, is an opportunity to review civil law and achieve egalitarianism, both in legislative theory and praxis (Campbell et al. 2006; Hickman 2018; Patel 2018).

Although the U.S. has a diverse representation of social groups in its contemporary workforce, the WASP category, as in other English-speaking nations, prevails as the leading force within governance, work and society (Davey 2012; Sheppard 2017). Whilst 'WASPishness', as a concept, has evolved to include a broader Caucasian representation (yet still White); its historical association with Anglo (White) male, middle-upper class privilege prevails (Kaufmann 2004; Baldwin 2017). This is evident, in recent times, by Trump's presidential victory, and his selection of WASP figures to the front bench; except UN representative Nikki Haley – who has since resigned (Haberman 2016; Copley 2018). Haley could be perceived to be a token woman; a female placed in governance in order to fill a gap, thereby providing an illusion to equity, which does not exist (Gutpa 2007; Gheaus 2015; Pollack 2015; Cohen 2016). In retrospect, most of the Republican leadership fits the WASP mould of 'a [privileged] boys club'.

WASPishness thereby represents a compelling predicament to Republicanism. Although the U.S. is a Republican nation, it is one of the most unequal OECD nations in the developed world (Sheppard 2017). Initially, U.S. Republicanism evolved when U.S. leaders successfully resisted the rule of Britain's King George the Third plus taxes imposed on the American colony; this culminated in the 'Boston Tea Party' resistant action, and thereafter, revolutionary war against the British Monarchy (Carp 2010). As victors, the U.S. became a Republican Federal democracy and developed a Bill of Rights (1791), as its constitutional framework (Palmer 2014; Bill of Rights Institute 2018). Such a Bill, however, has not achieved sociocultural inclusion nor egalitarianism (Burn 2011; Garry 2012; McIvor 2016; Yancy 2017). Recently, the Black Lives Matter movement provides evidence to this effect, in how young African-American women's leadership campaigning against discrimination and racism reinvigorated the social change-legislative premise of the civil rights NSM (Taylor 1989; Connell 2002; McIvor 2016; Yancy 2017).

Conclusion

Emphasized femininity resistance, in legislative theory and praxis – conducive to my Bill of Rights Act and its core Sections/Initiatives, challenges cultural structures that privilege men's hegemony. 'A boys club', or WASPishness, exemplifies ruling class masculinity in place, whereby patriarchy is dually replicated through conservative neoliberalism within organisational governance (Connell 2006; Butler 2013; Donaldson and Poynting 2013; Cornish 2017). Anglo male middle class privilege stands as a counterpoint to my egalitarian-republican model. I thereby resist CALD, Indigenous, low SES, mature, disabled and Anglo women's marginalisation through Initiatives. My *six groups' agentic performative multiple skills-set*, framing my four Initiatives on WW & SE leadership plus male-dominated sectors (within my Act), legislates on more jobs for women in environmental (renewables) science (McFarland 2014; Ajani 2015; BWE 2018; Clean Energy Council 2018; WIE 2018). This Bill challenges hereditary privilege endemic to monarchist regimes and non-inclusive forms of republican nationhood.

Republican nationhood is an opportunity to address sociocultural inequality, and for economic restructuring, supported by a Constitutional change (Irving and Murray 2001; Selway 2003; Bolton 2005; Kumarasingham and Power 2014; Veri 2016; ARM 2018). My argument is that women of CALD, Indigenous, disabled, low SES and mature age statuses, are skilled agents of change, whom can strengthen the eNSM, its institutions and ways of working (Gaard 2001; DAWN 2015; WIE 2018). I envision such groups, greater leadership in my modelling of a robust social (Republican) and environmental (sustainable technological development) change. My *six groups'* leadership is central to my feminist, republican, environmental and egalitarian conceptual-methodological ambitions. Such ambitions are modelled by my legislation on a Bill of Rights Act, supported by a Republican Constitutional change, thereby discarding the Westminster Constitution (Selway 2003; Smith et al. 2012; Hiebert and Kelly 2015; Hickman 2018). To reiterate, my model draws inspiration from the Red Viennese egalitarian example of an equitable middle and working class equilibrium, along with women's suffrage and agentic competence as scientists and politicians (Rentetzi 2004, 2008, 2010; Kershaw 2013; Mattl 2016). I do not reject a socialist or left-wing persuasion but do frame republicanism through a critique of right-wing-neoliberal 'WASPish' conservatism, and its lack of social democratic egalitarian enablement (Sheppard 2017). My constructivist framing of the Act, with women quotas on technological development, aligned with emphasized femininity 'resistant' agentic scientific competence, plus an Indigenous Treaty, should subvert elitist hierarchies, whilst envisioning an egalitarian participatory democratic change.

Part II

The 'Boys Club' and Emphasized Femininity Resistance

5 The Gendered Nature of the Elite

'The Boys Club' and Ruling Class Masculinity Within Renewables Organisational Governance

Introduction

This chapter critiques the gendered nature of the elite, pertaining to ruling class masculinity and men's leadership dominance within renewables governance. As a sociocultural constructivist feminist, utilising my interviews and supporting theory, I assess the leadership participation of women in politics, IeNGOs and academia (Buechler and Hanson 2015; ABS 2016a; AHRC 2017a; Canty 2017; WIE 2018). Arguably, renewables board positions are dominated by Anglo middle class men (Bombora Wave Power 2018; Carnegie Clean Energy 2018; EREF 2018; EUREC 2018). In my findings, patriarchy underpins women's struggle with glass ceilings, gender tokenism on climate panels and labels of incompetency (Greer 2010a; Donaldson and Poynting 2013; Pollack 2015; Cohen 2016; Cadaret et al. 2017). 'A [patriarchal] boys club' encompasses cultural-structural barriers, relayed through women's struggle in the upper echelons of Parliament, IeNGOs and academia. From a 'traditional position of subordination', I articulate enablers, framed through feminist agentic prowess. Ideally, greater women-led strategies should revitalise the women's and eNSM plus its eSMOs (Maddison 2004; McLellan 2009; Staggenborg 2016). My model aims to create more jobs for women, focussing on my six conceptual groups: CALD, Indigenous, Anglo-Celtic, older, disabled and socioeconomically disadvantaged (McFarland 2014; Ajani 2015; Clean Energy Council 2018; WIE 2018).

5.1 A Thematic Overview

In my critique of hegemonic ruling class masculinity within environmental politics, I advocate (and legislate, akin to my Bill of Rights) emphasized femininity as a compelling resistance strategy. In my interviews, 'the boys club', in terms of a male-dominated culture, is critiqued by participants as: 'androcentric', 'aggressive' and 'blokey'. Greens participants identify chauvinism and misogyny within hierarchical structures of Parliament and Local Government Authorities (LGAs), whilst eNGO participants struggle with men's resistance to their leadership in the 'executive arm' of the eNSM. Women's otherness is not entirely specific to Greens men, nor men that endorse feminism and environmental justice

(Mellor 1993; Leahy 2003; Connell 2005; Culley and Angelique 2010; Cadaret et al. 2017). Similarly, grassroots-based eNGOs, dominated by volunteers and an egalitarian ethos – that are flatter and less hierarchical, are pillars for gender equity and environmental justice. My critique of 'a boys club', in terms of ruling industrial and political elites, is evidenced through 'non-Greens' men's 'superior' and chauvinistic attitudes to women, and their dominance in the sociopolitical hierarchy (Greer 2010a; Gillard 2012; Hall 2013; Murphy 2013; Summers 2013; Australian Greens, Our Federal MPs, 2018).

Firstly, I shall highlight Greens women's recognition/resistance to ruling class masculinity within Parliament and LGAs. Secondly, I pinpoint their resistance to patriarchy through grassroots participatory democratic ecological engagement. Thirdly, I highlight eNGO and academic activists' recognition of merit, EEO polices and glass ceilings. Fourthly, while eNGO participants struggle with gender barriers, they also resist the patriarchal control of their organisations. Women-led resistance frames my emphasized femininity constructivist approach, elevated through agentic performative competencies; thus, opposing the pervasive power of ruling class masculinity and patriarchal privilege.

5.2 'The Boys Club' Within Australian Politics

Australian Greens women recognise and resist 'the boys club' and men's 'domineering' leadership styles within Parliament and Local Government Authorities (LGAs). The Greens egalitarian-ecological model, aligns with my Republican model, aspiring to address sociocultural (in)equality plus gender and environmental (in)justices. As mentioned, I am not a member of the party, yet I embrace their policies on gender equality and empowerment of women, participatory democracy and a Bill of Rights standpoint (Maleta 2011b; Gahrton 2015; Gauja and Jackson 2016; Australian Greens, Constitutional Reform and Democracy 2018, Gender Equality 2018, Our Policies, 2018). Greens participants do not identity 'a boys club' in their party – but find one when negotiating with 'non-Greens men' or men from conservative, right-wing 'non-egalitarian' parties. The 'boys club' was relayed through gender differences and policy struggle – when debating in Parliament and Councils (Mellor 1993, 1997; Carter 2007, 2013; Sundström and McCright 2014; Raunio 2015). Hence, 'a boys club' pervades 'non-Greens' political contexts.

My findings contradict some (eco)feminist analyses that Leftist-greens politics is male-centric and patriarchal (Mellor 1993, 1997; MacGregor 2001, 2014; Carter 2013; Gahrton 2015). However, recent accusations of sexual misconduct by Australian Greens women, and the party's alleged mis-handling of their assault complaints (Karp 2018; Knowles and McClymont 2018) connects to ecofeminist critiques that Leftist-socialist 'Greens' politics is hostile to women (Mellor 1993, 1997; Plumwood 1997; MacGregor 2006, 2010). But my interviews with Greens women did not reveal such findings. Nonetheless, even in a party 'framed by gender equity', it is not possible to eradicate sexism, framing women's experience as the dualist insider/outsider within environmental politics.

Moreover, Connell's (2005) research on Australian men political environmental activists, found that men and women 'green' group members collaborated successfully, akin to shared (eco)feminist ideals, egalitarian principles, and justice goals. A mutual sense of respect, akin to shared ecofeminist green ideologies and practices, enabled equity. Ecofeminism, thus, acts as an enabler – strengthening work, social and gender relations of activists (Leahy 2003; Connell 2005; Gow and Leahy 2005; MacGregor 2009; Stoddart and Tindall 2011). Nonetheless, women politicians' struggle with 'the [patriarchal] boys club' of Parliament is contextualised by neoliberalism and conservative right wing political agendas, thereby framing women's mission for sustainable policy reforms (Connell 2006, 2009; Walby 2012; Butler 2013; McFarland 2014; Ajani 2015; Bell 2016).

Although the governing Liberal-Coalition party is the ruling hegemon, led by Prime Minister Scott Morrison, Greens women are well represented in the Senate (Upper House of Parliament) (Australian Greens, Our Policies, 2018, Our Federal MPs, 2018). From within the Senate, the Greens, is, therefore, situated in a powerful legislative capacity, and can support or reject legislation, plus initiate social and environmental change-inspired actions.

My sample has a good representation of Greens women as Senators, Members of Parliament (MPs), and elected Councillors in Local Government Authorities (LGAs). Others are administrative employees and volunteer members. Whilst my Greens politicians tend to dominate urban social demographics, I also have some regional and semi-rural representatives. I have labelled Parliament as external, because it has members from different parties, aligned with competing ideologies. It is also a site to argue for one's political agenda, whilst being a difficult place for women to achieve acceptance, hence, the framing of 'the boys club' (Maleta 2011b; Raunio 2015; ABS 2016b; AHRC 2017b). Even as MPs and Senators, performing the same roles to men – plus in the same context – women struggle with marginalisation (Greer 1999, 2010b). This is further experienced through gendered tokenism and token placement on male-dominated scientific panels. Hence, dualist notions of being 'on the outside' and 'inside of politics' impact women's capacity to exercise agency and to be recognised for their competence (MacLeod 1992; McNay 2000; Cudworth 2002; Maddison 2004; Butler 2013; Cudworth and Hobden 2013).

My participants perceive ruling class masculinity through men's dominant leadership styles, defined as: 'adversarial', 'aggressive' and 'blokey'. Jennifer ([audio] 2010) and Maxine ([audio] 2010), comment on a Parliamentary culture, framed by 'the male voice' and 'men speaking'. For Jennifer, 'a boys club' is at play in the leadership hierarchy, enacted by men in suits, whereby, there is a double-standard for women:

There's still very much a boys' club in Parliament… We have women in the three major parties. The stereotypes are being broken down but not fully… Women politicians get judged more harshly than men… if you're constantly seeing one's leaders are men in suits and used to men speaking, making the announcements, giving the leadership; when women are in those positions, they're judged harshly in terms of their voice because we get used to hearing the male voice. We see today, how fussy people get about women's hair, women's clothes. Things that were virtually never discussed with male politicians. When we get more women into leadership, we will get used to hearing women, hearing their voice, seeing them give leadership and then some inconsistencies would fall away.

(Jennifer [audio] 2010)

As Jennifer suggests, women's otherness should change with more women leaders in politics (Maleta 2011b). In my assessment of sociological intersections of gender, ethnicity, age and status, women point to Anglo male middle class privilege, as a barrier (DAWN 2015). Maxine adds that 'a boys club' exists in Parliament, conservative eNGOs and corporate boards. Parliament is assessed as 'traditional', 'blokey' and composed of 'old White men' who are 'chauvinists' and 'conservative', framing their work relations:

this is ridiculous how traditional and blokey this place is. I am the only female [omit], and they are old White men; really, old White men, largely conservative. A lot of men are absolute chauvinists and they don't get challenged, they're older blokes, that could be from the country, and that's how they do that kind of thing. I was in a meeting with the opposition, and the only woman around the table. There is ten guys, and the [omit], when I asked him whether he was supporting a motion, he called me a 'bright girl.' He said, 'I'm not going to support your motion, c'mon [omit], you're a bright girl.' I challenged him on that.

(Maxine [audio] 2010)

Participants' sharp commentary adds scope to my methodological critique of masculinist privilege and men's ruling power – evidenced by deliberate exclusion and abuse – with women being labelled as 'bright girls'. Although women are fully fledged members of Parliament, conservative attitudes to women politicians and obstacles to policy reforms was found in urban and regional LGAs. Jacquie critiques being 'on the outside':

I'm close with the Independent Councillor, but everyone else, there's a pretence to chumminess. Two of them, it's like a little boys' club. They're from different parties... myself and the Independent Councillor are always on the outside, which is why we work together so much. We just help each other... they're quite Green. We work together along party lines. There can be that cross, political stuff but it depends. There's one male Councillor I work better; he's a lot more open to ideas. So, it depends on the issue but definitely I feel on the outer.

(Jacquie [audio] 2010)

Jacquie's struggle with 'a boys club' or being 'on the outer', contrasts with her good work relations with male Councillors from Independent parties, whom, evidently, share a 'green' ethos. Shared political ideologies and beliefs, thereby contribute to productive work and social relations, representative of enablers, rather than barriers (Culley and Angelique 2003, 2010; Maleta 2012). Such enablement undermines patriarchal structural relations of power and privileged hierarchies, omnipresent within 'the boys club'. Women politicians, however, endure more pronounced gender barriers in regional political contexts (Poiner 1990; Alston 2003; Gow and Leahy 2005; Barry 2008). My findings point to a conservative 'boys club' within rural LGAs, framed by men's socioeconomic competitiveness and cultural leadership dominance (Alston 2003, 2011; Maleta 2009). Regional Australian politics is overwhelmingly dominated by Anglo-Celtic males, whereby the rule of the ethnic majority prevails. Within conservative rural contexts, Margaret censures her LGA as 'a boys club', for women are still marginalised:

> the local Council [omit] is totally 'a boys club'. We had a woman Councillor for four and a half years and it was wonderful, but there were only two. That sets an example to our community, women are marginalised, women aren't that important. In metro areas, it's a different ball game. In my area, it's a long way to go.
>
> (Margaret [audio] 2010)

This commentary concerning women's marginalisation and 'a long way to go', shows that 'a boys club' is a structural and cultural barrier, framing women's leadership equity in renewables governance (Marshall 2002; Tatchley et al. 2016; Cadaret et al. 2017). Turning to an urban context, Tanya assesses Parliament as 'a huge "boys club"', characterised by 'adversarial' practices and behaviours, quite unlike that of the Greens:

> men are more adversarial and I'm more conciliatory and consensually based... I was absolutely horrified... I used to go and watch Parliament. They'd have their things they'd say about the women ones... the behaviour of the house was appalling... Our MPs, two of whom are female, did not do that... it was incredibly abusive... It's that line of men, sort of going at each other and then you look at someone like [omit], she behaves just like a man, it's horrible... The Greens try and work with them, but it's just so competitive.
>
> (Tanya [audio] 2010)

Tanya's excerpts outline men's gender performativity as 'abusive', 'going at each other' and 'just so competitive', framing a particular type of masculinity in politics. Also, Tanya's retrospection attacks some women's apparent accommodation to masculinity. She elaborates that 'non-Greens' women politicians sometimes behave 'like men' in Parliament, which is 'horrible' (Greer 1999, 2010a, 2010b; Butler 2013). Nonetheless, men's leadership performativity reflects the adversity of Australian Parliamentary politics: 'I was absolutely horrified and any normal person who watches this would lose all respect for the Parliamentary process'

(Tanya [audio] 2010). Instead, women (and men) should be unified in the similar pursuit of renewables reforms: 'We should be all working together' (Tanya [audio] 2010). On one level, masculine performativity in Parliament confirms the existence of 'a boys club'; on another level, this compels women's emphasized femininity strategic defiance (Plumwood 1997; Butler 2007, 2011; Jonnergård et al. 2010; Cook and Glass 2014). Further, Tanya debates the way in which a high-status female politician, from another party, is accommodating towards a masculine culture:

> she's in [omit] Parliament, which is a huge 'boys club'. She has to be operating in a masculine environment. I see photos of her and she's the only woman. I'm sure she would agree she operates in a fairly male-dominated culture.
>
> (Tanya [audio] 2010)

Despite women's struggle with 'a boys club' as an example of ruling class masculinity, my constructivist aim is to challenge 'dominant' notions of masculinity and 'subordinate' dichotomies of femininity (Plumwood 1997; Buckingham-Hatfield 2010). Also, in my resistance to gender stereotypes, my interview data reveals that men often behave in more emotional and irrational ways, which defies essentialist assumptions of women, relative to frames of heightened emotion and irrationality (Eder 1996; Meynell 2009; Kosny and MacEachen 2010; Maleta 2015; Canty 2017). Within LGAs, 'a boys club' is reviewed as 'a male thing', with men behaving in emotionally driven ways:

> When I first got onto Council there were three women out of 12. This time round we have five women out of 12… I think it's a male thing. There's an aggression in the way they hold the position and debate a position… if they feel that the vote is going to against them, they go manic. They don't know how to control their emotions. It's like they're more adversarial. You're with me or against me, whereas it's not so black and white for women. We see the grey and can find a way through. We don't always agree but we're respectful of each other's opinions.
>
> (Stacey [audio] 2010)

Concerning gender performativity, Stacey's excerpt captures a male-dominated aggressive debating position that pervades veto decisions, whilst hindering Greens social change agendas. Masculinity as a performance is relayed through heightened emotionality and irrationality, framed by 'aggression', 'adversarial' and 'manic' engagement. Also, this prevents the *potential* for women and men, even from competing parties, to collaborate on projects and policy agendas. Whereas 'it's not so black and white for women', for they 'see the grey and can find a way through', as Stacey concluded. Participant Kate similarly points to 'a boys club' as 'aggressive', and how masculine performances, are a barrier to women: 'diabolical', 'old school stuff', 'a very gendered culture' and 'blokeyness':

Local Government to be one of the most diabolical things, in terms of old school stuff... it's a very gendered culture in terms of the blokeyness... a totally different way of working and dealing with people; ah it's a lot more aggressive... I copped a lot of personal flak with my style, not being aggressive... but that culture of being aggressive and going to a fight and nit-pick over silly details, not being able to think about consensus building, I found shocking.

(Kate [audio] 2010)

5.3 Discussion

Greens women recognised and resisted a gendered elite, framed by 'a boys club', pertaining to men's competitive and dominant leadership styles. In support to Stacey, Kate frames 'a very gendered culture of work' within Local Government through men's 'aggressive' leadership performances along with women's leadership under-representation: 'about 3 per cent of General Managers in local Councils are women' (Kate [audio] 2010). While Kate found this 'challenging', as a transport campaign leader, she recognised the power of 'consensus building' and successfully subverted an aggressive approach: 'I copped a lot of personal flak with my style... who has managed to get the best results in the last 12 months? That would be me' (Kate [audio] 2010). Comparatively, participants' recognise/ resist ruling class masculinity within urban and regional contexts (Poiner 1990; Alston 2003, 2011; Gow and Leahy 2005; Maleta 2009, 2011b). Although women are increasingly entering Australian Parliament, as Senators and MPs, male hegemony is a barrier, framing their struggle with (in)equity/(in)justice. Concerning ruling class masculinity, Greens women identified 'the boys club' in Parliament and LGAs, in terms of: 'blokey culture', 'aggressive', 'adversarial', 'competitive', 'abusive', 'male-dominated culture', 'androcentric' practices, 'male voice', 'male dress' and 'appalling behaviour of men in Parliament'. Embedded cultural structures, informed by patriarchal hierarchies, therefore, reinforces men's dominance and women's position of 'subordination' within governing executive hierarchies. But a resistant emphasized femininity, akin to women-led strategic political environmental competence, challenges hegemony (Plumwood 1997).

The landmark 'Misogyny Speech' by former (first and only female) Australian Prime Minister Julia Gillard, directed at former conservative Liberal Opposition Leader, Tony Abbott, captured her struggle with a male-dominated culture (Gillard 2012; Summers 2013). Also, her speech pinpointed sexism and chauvinism, framed by patriarchal barriers (Greer 2010a, 2010b). In support, Arendt's (1945) historical critique of monarchist pre-World War I empires, identified paternalism and chauvinism as barriers, framing European nationalism, whereby ideologies of 'superiority', influenced two World Wars. Yet, the defeat of European Imperialism in 1918, enabled the losers (and victors) of World War I, to develop into Republican nations (Arendt 1945). Nonetheless, notions of 'cultural superiority', transcended through Fascism/Nazism, whereby Republicanism sharply eroded.

'The boys club' is endemic to patriarchal institutionalisation, accounting for why men/masculinities are privileged (Mellor 1997; Buckingham-Hatfield 2000; Gaard 2001; Carter 2007; McDonald 2011; MacGregor 2014; Gahrton 2015). In my argument, Anglo male middle class privilege, frames middle class Greens women's dichotomous struggle as the insider/outsider within political hierarchies (Maleta 2011b, 2018b). However, feminism (or ecofeminism) can strategically unite women political advocates against classist-based exploitation (Gaard 2001; Buckingham 2004; Connell 2005; Di Chiro 2008, 2011; Stoddart and Tindall 2011). On this point, using Canadian and U.S. sources, Gaard exposes corporate exploitations of water and power in regional communities, whereby ecofeminism is appropriated as an empowering resistance strategy: 'ecofeminism illuminates the way in which gendered, cultural assumptions about water, power, and human relations have led to creating a water-power infrastructure that perpetuates environmental sexism, environmental racism, and environmental classism' (2001: 157). Alternatively, Gaard advocates 'ecological democracy and ecological economics' and 'a partnership culture', whereby 'water and energy flow freely' (Gaard 2001: 157). Women-led strategies, framed by democratic-ecological-partnership, is a platform for socioeconomic change, whilst challenging environmental sexism, racism and classism (Gaard 2001; Stein 2004).

Evidently, women's leadership style is conducive to an emphasized femininity-constructivist approach, situated in agentic competence, but also resistant to 'aggressive', 'adversarial' hegemonic masculinity and essentialist stereotypes of female technical-intellectual incompetence (Cockburn 1988; Berg and Lie 1995; Culley and Angelique 2003, 2010; Cockburn 2012, 2013; Gaard 2014; Wibben 2016). Rather than accommodating 'androcentrism', Greens women endorse consensual and conciliatory approaches (MacGregor 2006; Schlembach 2011; Gaard 2014; Wibben 2016). But they also resist men who position them as 'the other'. Kate's rejection of hierarchy is validated by 'consensus' as an engagement strategy in tough negotiations. Tanya described herself as 'more conciliatory and consensually based'. Also, women engage in active and passive resistance, which suggests the power of multiple performative acts of social change. Greens women are articulate political actors, whose egalitarian leadership, is an empowering premise to envision a futuristic Republican Social Democratic mode of governance, akin to a Bill of Rights, challenging ruling class masculinity and patriarchy.

5.4 Greens Protest Voice for Change

The cultural domination of 'the male' in terms of voice, dress and authority, undermines Greens women's protest voice for change. Protest is an activist-social change strategy; nonetheless, women advocates struggle to have their voice for change heard within global political arenas (Doyle 2008; Culley and Angelique 2010; Hosey 2011; Mellor 2013; Shiva 2014; ABS 2016b; AHRC 2017b). In my Greens accounts, an obstacle to women's inclusion is men's structural-cultural dominance in Parliament, critiqued as: 'old White men' (Maxine). This supports Connell's critique of glass ceilings and 'White men in middle management'

(2009: 117–18), and that a pervasive ruling class masculinity, characterised by Anglo male privilege, is embedded across diverse sectors (Giddens 1991, 2009; Poynting and Donaldson 2005; McDonald 2011; Donaldson and Poynting 2013; Pocock et al. 2013). Such privilege, exemplified by gender-organisational barriers but also enablers (women's leadership), inspires my Republican change manifesto, aligned with an Australian Bill of Right; thus, replacing the 'dated' Westminster Constitution.

An obstacle to Greens social change agendas is male veto power in Parliament. A 'boys club' is shown by men's dominance of internal voting practices, and conservative parties' resistance to climate reforms and sustainable policies (Irwin 2010; Gahrton 2015; Haute 2016; Tatchley et al. 2016; Maleta 2018b). Chauvinistic attitudes to women pervaded urban and regional politics (Poiner 1990; Alston 2003, 2013). Alston's (2011) study on the Australian drought, in the Murray-Darling Basin region, highlighted gendered impacts of climatic changes, whilst arguing for a gender sensitive policy to address the needs of locals under stress. Additionally, Maxine ([audio] 2010) condemned the chauvinism of male politicians from the country, whilst Margaret ([audio] 2010) assessed glass ceilings in regional politics.

From my qualitative analysis, a feminist-environmentalist ethic, and prominent levels of female participation, undermines the idea that feminism is not central to 'green' or left-wing politics (Mies 1986; Mellor 1993; Shiva 1993; MacGregor 2006; Kopecek 2009; Carter 2013; Gahrton 2015). Although Mellor (1993) had criticised the lack of a central feminist agenda within leftist Greens politics, Mellor (1997) later identified a strong feminist ideology in the West German Greens party, led by Petra Kelly, in the 1980s. Carter (2007, 2013) also appraised the high female participation in North-Western European Greens parties, crediting women as educated and articulate politicians. I found that feminism is central to left-wing Greens politics, but also that emphasized femininity resistance to patriarchy is a necessary strategy to subvert the ruling power of 'non-Greens' men (Mellor 1997; Plumwood 1997). Women's resistance to hegemonic masculinity, thus, tackles structural power-based inequity, prevalent within global governance (Giddens 1991; Doyle 2008; Donaldson and Poynting 2013; Doyle et al. 2015; Gahrton 2015).

Pertaining to gender performativity, participants like Tanya contend that 'non-Greens' women sometimes behave like men in Parliament. This reflects Greer's (1999) review of the masculinist performance of the late Dame Margaret Thatcher, first female Prime Minister of the U.K., during the 1980s, who was criticised for being 'manlier' than her male colleagues. Evidently, Thatcher accommodated hegemonic masculinity in her leadership and social engagement. Also, the neoliberal conservative policies of the Tories, parallel to ruling class masculinity, influenced her leadership, and relations with others in the party (Taylor 1997; Greer 1999; Segal 2007). Resistance to patriarchal elitism was not evident in Thatcher's engagement. Hence, as a feminist, it is challenging to sympathise with Thatcher's performance – despite being the U.K.'s first female Prime Minister.

5.5 Resisting 'a Boys Club': Grassroots Participatory Socioecological Democracy

Grassroots participatory democratic socioecological engagement is a strategic approach and goal of Greens women political activists. Within governance, participants resist dominant forms of neoliberal patriarchal institutionalisation, and advocate (plus legislate) on egalitarian-sustainable models. As members of the Senate, Greens women engage and subvert the neoliberal political establishment. Greens women's leadership, consequently, challenges the ruling power of social (industrial) and political (governing) elites (Plumwood 1997; Connell 2005, 2006; Gerulis-Darcy 2010; Maleta 2011b). Such leadership contributes to elevated feminist agentic empowerment. The party's polices on gender equity, grassroots democracy, ecological and social justice, plus a Bill of Rights, also challenges patriarchy (Australian Greens, Gender Equality, 2018, Our Policies, 2018, Participatory Democracy, 2018). Additionally, the rising prominence of Independent parties, due to disenchantment from the electorate with conservative parties, subverts the neoliberal establishment, whilst representing scope for allegiances, in the cause of Republicanism.

My Republican model (although not based on the Greens party), takes inspiration from the Australian Greens' manifesto on a Bill of Rights and grassroots-based social democratic action (Shiva 2005, 2008; Faber 2008; Raunio 2015; Gauja and Jackson 2016; Australian Greens, Participatory Democracy, 2018). Such modelling is egalitarian in theory and practice. The Greens enable an intersection of voices. Jacquie ([audio] 2010) adds that Greens policies focus on: 'consensus building, environmental and conservation issues as well as women's issues, Indigenous representation and social justice'.

Women politicians, of left-wing and socially progressive parties, can collaborate successfully on legislative campaigns. Kate points out that women politicians, from different parties, formed an allegiance in maternity leave policy reform:

> We have a lot of office bearers, female staffers at Parliament, female MPs, there's a different vibe, a lot of emphasis on gender equity in the Greens and in our pre-selection processes. Even in our local groups, we actively support women to stand for the Greens. We had the Local Government Shire's Conference and there was an alliance of women across the Greens, Labor and the Independents, to knock over some draconian maternity leave proposals. We worked hard to network and come up with comprises and get decent maternity leave provisions through. That was a good active network, women who were in support of each other.
>
> (Kate [audio] 2010)

Women's collaborative networking efforts, inclusive of the Greens, Labor and Independents (largely left-wing parties), were instrumental in achieving 'decent maternity leave provisions'. This except suggests that leftist parties are conducive to feminism and women's equity, disputing assumptions that the Left is androcentric and unsympathetic to feminism or women's concerns (Mellor 1993, 1997; MacGregor 2006; Carter 2013; Raunio 2015; Haute 2016). Positively, the Greens egalitarian anti-discrimination EEO model, informs my Republican challenge to hegemony and class-based patriarchal privilege. My data provides evidence to this effect. In contrast to hierarchy, Ruth describes the Greens grassroots democratic model as: 'positive discrimination', 'dialogue', 'open communication', 'consensus decision-making', 'very democratic', 'allows everyone to have their say', 'cooperative', 'good', 'ethical' and 'transparent'. Internal positive discrimination models also promote equity. The gender policy within 'pre-selection processes' ensures women are equally represented in leadership, without men dominating. A justice-driven-EEO model is, therefore, framed by women's greater performativity, and one in which rising status depends upon a performative multiple skills-set and merit.

A goal of feminism is to integrate the positive working roles and agendas of women and men in shared goals of environmental and social change. A greater collaboration between the sexes should enable a Republican change, whereby both genders operate in unity. While the Greens has a high female membership, it attracts both genders, which emphasises its diversity, Ruth adds. Kate states that 'all members have a say on policies which ensures that it bottom-up versus top-down'. Stacey outlines that the Greens was constituted by members of political parties and environmental groups that rejected patriarchal conservativeness in favour of grassroots democratic social change. In support, Die Grünen (the German Greens) rejected patriarchy in favour of feminist frameworks (Mellor 1997; Davis 2015). The Greens, framed by an ecological-egalitarian grassroots model, is one in which women politicians and activists, play a defining leadership role:

> lots of the people that came to the Greens came out of the peace movement... They moved from the other parties because it was so patriarchal; it was a top-down approach whereas the Greens are about the grassroots. It's bottom-up, that is how our model works and how we do our decision-making.
>
> (Stacey [audio] 2010)

The Greens rejection of other parties as 'so patriarchal' and 'top-down', and alignment with the 'grassroots' and 'bottom up' approaches, subverts ruling class masculinity, whilst representing emphasized femininity resistance in action (Davis 2015; Maleta 2015; Gauja and Jackson 2016). The Greens evolution from 'the peace movement' and resistance to the nuclear age: 'it was made from the Nuclear Disarmament Party, environmental groups, social justice groups' (Stacey [audio] 2010), enlightens my anti-war ethos and peacemaking modelling of women-led Sustainable Initiatives (Doyle 2005; Shiva 2014; Merchant 2016). A future without atomic energy and nuclear arms is a serious topic of global debate; nevertheless, renewables models aligned with women's WW & SE solutions is the only solution to the endemic patriarchal control of nuclear energy power (Rankin and Gale 2003; Doyle 2008; Culley and Angelique 2010; Maleta 2018b). In relation to Stacey, my egalitarian model is framed by grassroots participatory democracy, encouraging active citizenry participation in the sociopolitical process: 'promoting grassroots democracy, everybody has a chance to be involved, particularly for me, the political process and to be an active community member' (Stacey [audio] 2010).

The high number of Greens women in the Senate contrasts with mainstream parties (Raunio 2015; Gauja and Jackson 2016; Australian Greens, Our Federal MPs, 2018). Relative to other parties, men constitute the majority in Parliament: 'there is still a strong dominance of a male outlook' (Jennifer [audio] 2010). 'A boys club' in action thereby sets women apart whilst cementing a strong gender culture in politics. Amy speaks about being 'recognised as a woman in the workplace and having different needs to your male counterparts' (Amy [audio] 2010).

Another finding is that ageism acts as a barrier and enabler. Ageism is recognised/resisted by Greens participants. Kate claimed that older men dominate LGA meetings, whilst she is often the only young woman. Her competent performativity in political negotiations, however, was an enabler. Interestingly, most leaders in the Greens campaign team are young women. The Greens is a positive EEO model for younger and older women. Agentic prowess as performative, enables women's career elevation, and subjective empowerment, realising the 'I' in their social change goals (Butler 2007, 2013).

Feminism, as an ideology and gender diversity, through women-led action, consequently, challenges structural relations of power that privilege men/masculinities (Buckingham-Hatfield 2000; Connell 2002, 2005, 2009; Nascimento and Connell 2017). Maxine argues that Greens men must respect the feminist viewpoint, while equal opportunity is 'very alive in the party' ([audio] 2010). Jennifer, who identifies as an ecofeminist, points out how as a politician 'people defer to you', but that 'the Greens commitment to grassroots democracy means people have a real say' ([audio] 2010). One may deduce that meritocracy downplays hierarchy. Tanya's account points to the Greens as a model of meritocracy, in its leadership of women-led networking, female mentoring and rejection of rigid hierarchy. Her first role in the party was voluntary; through merit, it became a salaried Councillor position. She appraises the Greens as 'warm', 'encouraging' and 'I've loved every minute of it' (Tanya [audio] 2010). Meritocracy, relative to the Green's recruitment model, enables women's roles, but also that women elevate through their *agentic performative multiple skills-set*.

5.6 Discussion

Greens women's identification with grassroots ecological democracy, as a political activist strategy, is strengthened by an egalitarian ethos. Such a grassroots-egalitarian framed model, challenges the patriarchal control of Parliament and LGAs. This model inspires my Republican vision, framed by women-led recognition/resistance to patriarchal elitism, and advocacy of emphasized femininity agentic competence. Historically, the Greens formed in protest to a patriarchal elite, and sought to improve the rights of women and the environment (Maleta 2011b). The Greens is, therefore, situated in direct contrast to traditional ideas of 'the boys club', ruling class masculinity and privileged elites (Carter 2007; Doyle 2008; McDonald 2011; Donaldson and Poynting 2013; Davis 2015).

Feminism and gender equity is crucial to social cohesion and productive work relations. My interviews reveal evidence to this effect – feminism informs the roles, identities and empowerment of women. Tanya esteemed Greens women-led networks and gender equity recruitment models, framing women's career mobility. Whilst egalitarianism challenges ruling class privilege, it is a cornerstone of emphasized femininity resistance.

A commitment to equality/justice defines the rationale of participants in the eNSM. As most participants identify with feminist principles, and endorse this through their actions, it is not mandatory to be a feminist in order to be a competent environmentalist (Barry 2008; Duncan 2010; Keller 2012). Yet the environmental cause and gender justice compel salaried and volunteer activists' social change goals. Participants' performance of resistant, protest femininities undermine assumptions that eNSMs are in abeyance or that feminist activism stalls within the frame of non-receptive political scenarios (Taylor 1989; Maddison 2004; Grey and Sawer 2008; McLellan 2009).

Resistance to the destruction of the environment and patriarchal elitism, as dichotomous intersections, is evidenced through ecofeminist actions (Buckingham-Hatfield 2000; Gaard 2001; Mellor 2013; MacGregor 2014). Resistance is situated through a power-based struggle, framed by hegemony (Connell 1995; Plumwood 1997; Unger 2008; Mellor 2012). Concerning struggle, the grassroots ecofeminist movement is fuelled by women-led: 'resistance, persistence, stubbornness, passion and outrage' (Mellor 1997: 16). Despite women's activism in global struggles, there is a perception that there is no formal ecofeminist movement (Mellor 1997; Buckingham 2004; MacGregor 2006). However, my participants' ambition for gender and ecological justice legitimises ecofeminist actions, and the validity of a 21st-century ecofeminist movement. With more women in leadership, WW & SE solutions are feasible. The grassroots principles of volunteers and professionals signify a common ground, community-centric approach towards social and environmental change. Most salaried women perform voluntary duties, stressing environmentalism as an issue of genuine concern, rather than a nine to five job (McFarland 2014). To add on Mellor's point: 'resistance, persistence, stubbornness, passion and outrage' (1997: 16); women's agentic competence, plus resistance to patriarchy, is an empowering point from which to envision a Republican change, informed by a Bill of Rights Act.

Participants' (eco)feminist actions and resistant femininities challenges ideas that leftist green politics is patriarchal and anti-feminist (Mellor 1997; Mortimer-Sandilands 2008; Gaard 2011; Haute 2016). My findings contradict some feminist analyses of the Left as unsupportive to women (Mellor 1993; MacGregor 2006). MacGregor (2006) had condemned the ecological movement for not embracing feminism in its participatory democratic framework. She observed that environmentalism, as an androcentric (male-dominated) position, lacks a feminist lens (MacGregor 2006). MacGregor (2006) adds that feminism has had a contentious relationship with leftist-green politics, relating to the failure of male-dominated perspectives to acknowledge women's concerns. I found that the Greens, as a left-wing environmentalist political party, endorse gender and ecological justice, emphasising anti-patriarchal plus anti-hierarchical standpoints. My findings point to the way the Greens resist androcentrism and sexism. However, recent reports of the Australian Greens mishandling of internal sexual misconduct allegations (Karp 2018) perhaps support MacGregor's (2006) and Mellor's (1993) critiques of Leftist-greens politics as sexist and androcentric. My data did not point to such critiques of the party.

It is intriguing that as Senators and Councillors, Greens women are exercising the laws of the land, but also challenging the ruling political establishment or indeed, neoliberal hierarchy (Connell 2006; Grady et al. 2012; Walby 2012; Butler 2013; MacGregor 2014; Cornish 2017). Women do struggle with gender differentiation and othering, because they are women. In their capacity as performative agents, encapsulating legislative change and grassroots ecological-egalitarian democracy, women defy such otherness – conducive to masculine hegemony and ruling class power (McGregor 2009; Schlembach 2011; Donaldson and Poynting 2013). Greens women are proving their worth in left-wing parties. Such competence frames the potential for an inclusive meritocracy. Emphasized femininity, framed by my Bill of Rights and Initiative on women's WW & SE leadership in sustainable technological development, envisions a new way forward for greens politics.

5.7 Resisting 'a Boys Club' and Glass Ceilings Within Academia

The gendered nature of a sociopolitical elite, pertaining to hegemonic dominance and patriarchal institutionalisation, is also recognised/resisted by Australian women in academic institutions. In this section, I consider the way my academic participants experience 'a boys club'. I also consider the strengths and weaknesses of a meritocracy. Although women are increasingly achieving Professorship posts, they struggle with glass ceilings, for the senior echelon is male-dominated, replicated through Anglo middle class men's privileged statuses (Connell 2009; Donaldson 2009; McDonald 2011; Britton 2017; Cadaret et al. 2017). Critically, EEO laws, such as the Equal Employment Opportunity Act (2016) have not fully enabled women's equal participation in the workforce. This is also due to structural gendered biases within patriarchal institutionalisation (Elsesser and Lever 2011; Kmec and Skaggs 2014; Public Service Commission 2015; EEO Act [1987] 2016).

Hegemonic masculinity, in my interviews, is evidenced by the way academic women identify 'a boys club' in executive hierarchies: the Bar (Barrister's Court), Vice-Chancellorship posts and Ivy League Universities. It is 'executive men' and 'executive hierarchies' that hinder women's career mobility. My data provides evidence to this effect. Despite gender-organisational barriers, women appropriate power and skill, which challenges men/masculinity along with patriarchy. The 'boys club' is not specific to the eNSM, but to the institutions that women partake in, through formal and informal levels of engagement. The below excerpt reveals the way 'a boys club' is evolving and changing. Rachel, an environmental barrister and academic, contemplates the Bar (Barrister's Court) as 'a boys club', dominated by older men with chauvinistic attitudes, but claims that this is gradually changing with the competency of women in leadership positions:

> the attitude was I may be a lawyer, but I'm just a woman. That attitude gets my goat, I get very antsy… when I first went to the Bar 20 years ago, it was very much 'a boys club'. Women were patronised or discounted. You had to prove your worth by winning cases against men. Today, there are more assertive women on the bench… that's done a lot to change male attitudes in the law. There are fossils, men 50+ who have a very chauvinistic view of women. It is changing slowly, because more women are receiving judicial appointments and as magistrates.
>
> (Rachel [audio] 2010)

Patronising attitudes and chauvinism, situate Rachel's struggle within the legal profession. In similarity to women Parliamentarians, women lawyers struggle with the patriarchal control of their profession. At the Bar, one 'had to prove your worth' and be better than the men. However, women have proven their prowess in the same positions to men, which has 'done a lot to change male attitudes in the law'. Nonetheless, chauvinism is a prevailing gender-organisational barrier, particularly with older men or, more so, White middle-upper class middle-aged men. But the rise of women in 'judicial appointments and as magistrates' is transforming and undermining the traditional patriarchal privilege associated with men/masculinity in law (Connell 2009; Buckingham and Kulcur 2010; Ainsworth 2012; Colson and Field 2016; ABS 2017). In the next account, Yvonne challenges the notion of 'a boys club', focussing on women's leadership:

> We have a male Vice Chancellor but [omit] of our deputy Vice Chancellors are women so there's more senior or equal numbers of senior women in the university then there are males. Other universities are very male-dominated. I think having a female Vice Chancellor helped, but our current Vice Chancellor is also very non-discriminatory and looks to hire the best people, not other males.
>
> (Yvonne [audio] 2010)

This commentary suggests that having a woman as Vice Chancellor enables other women to rise in ranks. Yvonne critiques 'other universities' for being 'very male-dominated', which contrasts with an impressive number of females at her institution: 'there's more senior or equal numbers of senior women in the university then there are males'. A positive culture of meritocracy enables women, also implying that recruitment is not based on gendered tokenism or filling a gap. As Yvonne points out 'our Vice Chancellor is very non-discriminatory and looks to hire the best people, not other males'. This points to competence, suggesting that men nor women are particularly privileged. It appears that women are treated equally and not overlooked, as often is the case in senior executive recruitment. Nonetheless, executive hierarchies, as in most academic institutions are male-dominated; consequently, patriarchal institutionalisation undermines equitable female engagement (Probert 2005; Pocock et al. 2013; Farr et al. 2017; Marfo 2017).

Participants recognise/resist the notion that being a woman sets them apart as different. This suggests gender-specific and gender-neutral insights to dualist dichotomies, representative of women/femininities and men/masculinities (Eder 1996; Buckingham-Hatfield 2000; Connell 2005; MacGregor 2006; Gupta 2007; Jonnergård et al. 2010). Gender differences evolve in transparent and subtle ways within sociocultural contexts. Rachel, downplays gender issues, pointing to an empowering culture of equality:

> I have no gender issues at all; it's a great environment to work. We have a lot of very competent, assertive women working at [omit] in a number of capacities. There is a culture of gender equality, which is great.
>
> (Rachel [audio] 2010)

In addition, Rachel contemplates the discriminatory representation of women-specific associations. She argues that if men had such an exclusive organisation, they would be subject to harsh criticism, and perhaps even anti-EEO scrutiny:

> I have issues in regard to the Women Barristers Association, I think that's discriminatory. Why should women have an exclusive club? Whereas if it was men doing, if it was a men's barrister club, there would be a hell of an outrage you know. So why should women get away with things that men can't do?
>
> (Rachel [audio] 2010)

Focussing on Rachel's questions: 'Why should women have an exclusive club?', and 'why should women get away with things that men can't do?'; this entails how performative merit-competence is critical for the fair representation of women. Nonetheless, I confer that the Women Barristers Association actually enables women; such an organisation is necessary to redress the discrimination women face in male-dominated professions, like law, science and politics. Relative to the Bar, women-led associations enable women to network and build momentum on social change, equity and improved career advancement (Sharp et al. 2008; Terjesen et al. 2009; Ainsworth 2012). Although EEO policies point to an inclusive meritocracy, gender equity has yet to be realised within most sectors, including academia (EEO Act [1987] 2016; Britton 2017).

My Republican model is instrumental in its challenge to Anglo male middle class privilege within executive hierarchies (Poynting and Donaldson 2005; McGregor 2009; DAWN 2015). A Bill of Rights, supported by robust Initiatives, redresses gender (in)equity through its emphasis on quotas, such as, 75% of women leaders in technological-scientific development, whereby merit and competence are dually recognised (McFarland 2014; Ajani 2015; BWE 2018; Clean Energy Council 2018; WIE 2018). My model is centred on targets, but also that career elevation and status is dependent upon one's performative prowess, rather than solely gender status. My model, consequently, challenges gender tokenism and women's deliberate placement on panels in order to fill a gap (Yoder and Aniakudo 1997; Terjesen et al. 2009; Yoder et al. 2011; Gheaus 2015; Irvine 2017).

As with Greens women, academics resist frames of ruling class masculinity within scientific academia (Hosey 2011; Snow 2013; Fisher and Kinsey 2014; Pollack 2015; Cadaret et al. 2017; Farr et al. 2017). Yvonne recalls aspects of 'an old boys' network, as a young academic employed in a U.S. Ivy League University, but there were other barriers:

It was an old boy's network, but there were senior women in the department, there were young women coming through the ranks. In general, the American system's very different; there are a lot more opportunities in terms of places, but a huge amount of competition… It's a hard slog. It's not easy here, but I don't think it's got anything to do with being a woman. I think being an Australian in an American institution, that's more challenging than being a woman. There's an element in a place like [omit] and in America of being patronising about the rest of the world… we're very small and not visible on the world scientific stage.

(Yvonne [audio] 2010)

Despite 'an old boy's network', 'competition' and 'patronising' attitudes to Australians were overarching obstacles. Through performativity, senior and younger women were elevating in science (Butler 2004, 2013; Pollack 2015; Cadaret et al. 2017; STEMM 2018). Yvonne's excerpt reveals intersections of gender-specificity and gender-neutrality, where the latter is emphasised: 'I don't think it's got anything to do with being a woman', but that 'being an Australian in an American institution, that's more challenging'.

Despite evidence of women's competent performativity, patronising attitudes in science situate an academic culture of superiority and privilege, in which 'outsiders' struggle to fit in (STEMM 2018). Arguably, the culture is elitist and not common ground or egalitarian, unlike the Greens and grassroots-based eNGOs. My critique, therefore, is that privileged elitism frames the patriarchal control of science (similarly claimed by Rachel in law). Whilst Yvonne contends: 'there were senior women in the department' and 'young women coming through the ranks', empirical connections to 'an old boys network' and evidence that science is male-dominated framed by glass ceilings suggests that women are entering a patriarchal culture, conducive to men's hegemony (Glazebrook 2005; Shepard and Corbin-Mark 2009; Marshall 2011; Valles 2015; Cohen 2016).

Women scientists may be expected to accommodate to patriarchy in an institutional context. Questionably, are women scientists indeed accommodating/ resisting hegemonic masculinity and ruling class elitism? In an optimistic frame, women's agentic competence showcases their accommodation to emphasized femininity and resistance to male privilege. Yvonne points to affirmative action in universities, enabling women's opportunities, but contentiously women are under-represented in senior leadership:

> I'm an ecologist and an environmentalist and a feminist – somebody who believes women should have the same opportunities as men… in academia there is very little blatant discrimination against women. There's a fair bit of affirmative action… the number of women coming through PhDs is about on par with men. Women in the upper levels of academia are still very low and lower further up the levels. Something has happened to prevent those women from advancing or they are choosing not to advance, or a combination of things. In some ways, being a woman's opened up opportunities rather than hindered me, because of the field I'm in.
>
> (Yvonne [audio] 2010)

Yvonne's assessment that 'Something has happened to prevent those women from advancing or they are choosing not to advance', points to embedded glass ceilings in scientific academia as well as women's struggle with a work–life balance (Pocock 2003; Probert 2005; Bendl and Schmidt 2010; Cook and Glass 2014; Pocock et al. 2013; Vildåsen et al. 2017). On the other hand, Yvonne's identification as an: 'ecologist', 'environmentalist' and 'feminist' parallels her appraisal of affirmative action and women's rising status within academia. Her ecofeminist identity frames a proactive EEO model: 'women should have the same opportunities'. My EEO-egalitarian democratic modelling of feminist Initiatives is framed by women's access to the same opportunities as men, whilst contending that structures have prevented women's full equity and empowerment. As such, emphasized femininity is situated in women's performative scientific-intellectual competence as well as performative agentic subversion to patriarchy. Such performativity disputes gender stereotypes and labels of female technical-scientific incompetency (Cockburn 1988; Culley and Angelique 2003, 2010; Maleta 2012; Butler 2015, 2017).

The Greens gender equity policy, relative to their pre-selection process, is a viable EEO policy for sectors to implement in their recruitment practices (Mellor 1993, 1997; Eder 1996; Carter 2007; Raunio 2015; Australian Greens, Gender Equality, 2018). What is needed, is a uniform gender equity policy across diverse sectors of organisational governance. My Republican-Bill of Rights Initiatives, legislating on 75% of women in sustainable scientific leadership, is an empowering frame from which to realise universal gender equity. My model accentuates agency and competence; women's leadership is akin to quotas on equity, yet career elevation also depends upon proven prowess – thereby conducive to emphasized femininity in action. Anna, a scientific academic, outlines her struggle to recruit women Professors, and argues for improved equal opportunity:

> I've tried to recruit women. I'm going through the lists of people in universities that I might have forgotten, but we recruited two people and the

same thing; we had over 100 applicants and one woman. That was for the Professorial level… women should have equal opportunities to men, they bring something extra to the workplace… the men are more ego driven and talk over women.

(Anna [audio] 2010)

Anna's struggle to recruit women scientists: 'we had over 100 applicants and one woman', suggests that the recruitment process is not supportive to women (Marshall 1995; Fisher and Kinsey 2014; Valles 2015; Watts et al. 2015). But women 'bring something extra to the workplace'. More women as science Professors, should be a cornerstone of progressive global academic recruitment drives (Pollack 2015; Cadaret et al. 2017; STEMM 2018). Without rigorous women-led recruitment Initiatives, as I legislate and advocate on, patriarchal privilege in science will prevail (Blackwell and Glover 2008; Haynes et al. 2015; Cohen 2016; Evans 2016). Men's performativity as 'more ego driven' who 'talk over women', reveals gender as a differentiator. This also frames a non-productive work environment, running counterpoint to women-led strategic engagement.

Anna's critique of masculine egoism frames an essentialist position (Berg and Lie 1995; Crary 2001; Wibben 2016; Gaard 2017). But by women not being egotistical, my interviews point to the power of a more conciliatory, consensus-based emphasized femininity constructivist approach. Women-led constructivist strategies contribute to less workplace conflict, and frame renewables outcomes (Shiva 1993, 2005; Maleta 2018a).

More women in scientific leadership challenges the hegemonic power of patriarchal (industrial and governing) elites and domineering men-led decisions (Leahy 2003; Gow and Leahy 2005; Unger 2008; Marshall 2011; Cook and Glass 2014). Hence, masculinity, as a cultural and structural domineering power relation, is being challenged through women-led scientific-intellectual competence. This insight harks to Connell's (1995) point that hegemony is not fixed or stationary, but rather mobile and fluid. As such, power is susceptible to resistance, in which I perceive emphasized femininity as a powerful yet poignant resistance strategy. I envision this through women's greater leadership of WW & SE solutions, relative to my Republican-Constitutional framed Bill of Rights Act.

Anna was a core figure in establishing her university's research centre, and points out how women leaders are more competent than men, even in the same positions:

We have a fantastic female Director of Research… she's an absolute dream to work with compared to the men. She gets things done. Men tend to dither a bit. One thing about women is that they multi-skill and tend to get things done more if they're good at their job. She's fantastic.

(Anna [audio] 2010)

Empowering adjectives of 'fantastic female Director', 'an absolute dream to work with' and '[she] gets things done', whilst 'men tend to dither', situates women's *agentic performative multiple skills-set*. The above excerpt intersects essentialism/constructivism (MacGregor 2001, 2010; Vildåsen et al. 2017). Arguably, constructivism is paramount (Delanty 2005; Moore 2008; Mortimer-Sandilands 2008; Nagy 2017). The fact that women are 'getting things done', enables me to frame an empowering feminist-constructivist-activist approach, as a platform for social (Republican) and women-led environmental (sustainable technological development) change (Gaard 2001; Mellor 2013; Canty 2017).

Relative to my sociocultural-constructivist-feminist framework, women's gender performances and work-based subjectivity is not entirely dependent on EEO laws, but through performativity (Walby 1990, 2011, 2013; Gaard 2001, 2011; Schlembach 2011; Tatchley et al. 2016). Anna's discernment that women scientific managers are more competent and easier to work with, suggests essentialism; yet shows that emphasized femininity, akin to agentic constructivist performativity, challenges the patriarchal control of scientific academia. The 'I' in women's identity, thus, enables feminist empowerment and transformative gender roles (MacLeod 1992; Plumwood 1997; Butler 2007, 2013).

Emphasized femininity, in relation to essentialist-constructivist-performativity is evidenced in other academic accounts. Maggie points to women's agency, but also criticises the way women are not using their power to challenge the nuclear industry:

> 53% of us are women and we lack the guts to do what is necessary… we let the men take over rather than stepping into our own power. There should be a law that 53% of every corporation, academic, Parliamentary body is women… It's across the board, because we're nurturing and understand the intrinsic value of life. We're not into power and that terribly nasty stuff that men tend to play act. I'm not talking about the Thatchers or Hillary Clinton. I'm talking about women. When there are very few women in power they behave as men to rise up the ranks and that's what those women did.
>
> (Maggie [audio] 2010)

Interplays of social constructivism and essentialised notions of women/femininities underpin Maggie's ([audio] 2010) critique of women's gender performativity (Crary 2001; Butler 2004, 2011; Gaard 2011; Nagy 2017). Maggie's additional criticism of women letting men take over: 'women tend to vote to please the males' rather than stepping into 'our own power', frames a constructivist maternal ethos for change: 'We're voting for milk for children' (Maggie [audio] 2010). The above excerpt signifies emphasized femininity approaches as empowering, for women should be aspiring to confidence through 'nurturing' qualities. For Maggie, this is not politically motivated: 'That's got nothing to do with political lines' but strengthened through women's affinity for an 'intrinsic value of life' (Maggie [audio] 2010). Essentialised notions of women/femininities, as 'nurturing' and not into 'that terribly nasty stuff that men tend to play act', point to women-led performance, conducive to environmental change. Maggie review of women's seeming compliance to men, is counterpointed, through an emphasis on women's rejection of masculinist power: women should act like women in order to enact change. Strengthening my peacemaking sociopolitical model, an anti-war ethos is framed by women's emphasized femininity-constructivist resistance to militant, androcentric aggression: 'no, you're not getting your missiles today' and 'We're not into power and that terribly nasty stuff' (Maggie [audio] 2010). Hence, women-led qualities and strategic direction reveals a powerful interplay of essentialism and constructivism. Performativity intersects through emphasized femininity, as a frame for peace, framed by Maggie's subversion to 'missiles' and aspirations for greater women-led strategies. More women in leadership and power should challenge a patriarchal war ethos from pervading geopolitical spheres.

Emphasized femininity, plus powerful interplays of essentialism and constructivism, challenges androcentrism and aggression, or indeed: 'that nasty stuff that men tend to play act' (Maggie [audio] 2010) (Connell 1995; Buckingham-Hatfield 2000; MacGregor 2006; Mellor 2013). Maggie's criticism of women politicians: 'the Thatchers or Hillary Clinton' whom 'behave as men to rise up the ranks' and 'act like men in order to achieve power', contrasts with emphasized femininity leadership strategies. Women's masculine performativity, or acting like men, upholds the hegemonic status of men and the structural relations of power conducive to patriarchal institutionalisation (Connell 1995; Greer 1999; Butler 2004, 2013). But women-led approaches, akin to emphasized femininity constructivism, represent feminist empowerment, enabling me to realise the Butlerian 'I' in one's identity and social-ecological change goals (Loizidou 2007; Jagger 2008; Butler 2013).

Maggie's excerpt links to my Republican manifesto of gender equity reforms, pertaining to a Federal Bill of Rights, targeting 75% of women in leadership. Such legislation disputes patriarchal institutional privilege, therefore ensuring that women are recognised for their multi-skills-set. Maggie's condemnation of women as lacking 'the guts to do what is necessary' was underpinned by her case for a uniform gender equity law: '53% of every corporation, academic, Parliamentary body is women' ([audio] 2010). Such laws would improve women's leadership in renewables governance and male-dominated sectors, thereby minimising glass ceilings (Probert and Wilson 1993; Probert 2005; Connell 2009; Butler 2011; Cook and Glass 2014). Undoubtedly, women need to exercise power and reject the supreme power of men and patriarchal elitism for real change to be realised. The power is in the hands of women, as Maggie argues. Social change is framed by competence.

Greens politician Maxine elaborates on how women are acquiring executive roles in corporations, but they 'are entering a culture that is male-dominated'. In Parliament, Maxine strives to influence laws, and channel a more women-led sustainable approach:

> I think the way that it does for me would be around the masculine corporate world. Women are starting to get on Boards and become CEOs, but they are coming into that corporate world, as created by men. That corporate

domination of nature, and the fact that we are using resources so unsustainably, we are looking at everything in a short-term, profit-making way, rather than long-term generations. To me, that reflects a very masculine way. My being in Parliament, trying to change laws; I am not so much an idealist that I think we are not up against it, when it comes to an overpowering corporate dominance of everything we do, in terms of the laws… Other political parties are controlled by the wishes of companies and individuals, making profits for corporations… I doubt women would have come up with something like that.

(Maxine [audio] 2010)

5.8 Discussion

This section has articulated the gendered nature of the sociopolitical elite through participants' recognition/resistance of ruling class hegemonic masculinity, framed by 'the boys club' and glass ceilings in the upper strata of academia (Forbes-Mewett and Snell 2006; McDonald 2011; Donaldson and Poynting 2013; Gheaus 2015; Pollack 2015). My interviews pinpoint the patriarchal control of universities, Parliament and corporations, as gender-organisational barriers, but also the empowering way women-led strategies challenge men's ruling power along with structural relations of power. Women's subversiveness is framed through emphasized femininity, whereby powerful interplays of constructivism and essentialism, intersect through: 1. women's *agentic performative multiple skills-set* and 2. resistance to patriarchal forms of ruling class masculinity. But women are also criticised for not using their agency and power, which is at their disposal, in order to enact social and environmental change, as Maggie contended. In likeness to my Greens' results, academics activists' scientific-intellectual leadership shows that women are proving their worth in 'masculine occupations' and often out-perform men, in the same or similar roles (Walby 2011; Valles 2015; Merchant 2016; Farr et al. 2017). Although Yvonne points to women's rising Professorship and Vice-Chancellorship status within universities, heightened through positive EEO models; men are still privileged in the upper echelons of academia (Walby 1990; Greer 2010a; Cadaret et al. 2017; STEMM 2018).

Essentialism/constructivism is relayed by the way participants reject androcentrism and aggression (Buckingham-Hatfield 2000; MacGregor 2006, 2010; Wibben 2016; Gaard 2017). Women's patriarchal subversion is underpinned by empowering essentialised approaches: 'we're voting for milk for children' and 'we're nurturing and understand the intrinsic value of life' plus 'we're not into power and that terribly nasty stuff that men tend to play act' (Maggie [audio] 2010). Women-led global empowerment, through emphasized femininity performativity, is an empowering framework aimed at environmental change (Connell 1995; Plumwood 1997; Leahy 2003; Butler 2011, 2015; Maleta 2015).

My interviews reveal insights and contradictions. Rachel identified 'a boys club' around '20 years ago', but nowadays, 'there are more assertive women on the bench' ([audio] 2010). Rachel contends though that older men 'possess a very chauvinistic view of women'. Women, consequently, struggle with otherness, prejudices and stereotypes associated with their equal competence (Jonnergård et al. 2010; Cook and Glass 2014; Cadaret et al. 2017). Even in the 21st century, a sexual division of labour, along lines of competence, positions women as the other in organisational governance (Cockburn 1988, 1991; Probert 2005; Connell 2009; Bendl and Schmidt 2010; Sullivan 2011; Sundström and McCright 2014; Bombora Wave Power 2018). Frames of (in)equity/(in)justice underpin a complex masculinist culture of work, dually informed by hierarchy, patriarchy and privilege. Nevertheless, women's rising status as Professors and Judges challenges ruling class men and ruling class masculinity (Donaldson and Poynting 2013).

In support to my Greens and academic data, glass ceilings are an issue of contention within 'the executive arm' of the eNSM (as eNGO participant Barbara points out in the next section) whilst 'the boys club' provides further context to this effect (Pocock 2003, 2005; Eriksson-Zetterquist and Styhre 2008; Jonnergård et al. 2010; Pocock et al. 2013). Similarly, Connell (2009) connected glass ceilings to gender barriers, in how the prejudice and bias of men has prevented women from achieving executive posts within multinational corporations (2009: 117–18). As women are increasingly achieving Professorships, men still dominate policy decisions across academia. Nonetheless, women are not entirely subordinated, and are making a positive difference in how their organisations and the world is run (Warren 1999; Merchant 2013, 2016; Shiva 2014).

Maggie's point that women need to 'use their power' suggests that women's future is in their hands. Women's exercise of agency is an empowering premise to challenge patriarchy (Connell 1995, 2009; Butler 2004; Cockburn 2012, 2013). Simultaneously, Maggie is critical of global women political figures who accommodated to ruling class masculinity: 'the Thatchers, Hillary Clinton'. Besides, Maggie points to gender performativity, as a feminine approach, for women need to act like women. Emphasized femininity, thus, aligned with women-led qualities and empowering intersections of constructivism/essentialism, should elevate feminist agency, whilst challenging the masculinist hegemony of global environmental politics (McNay 2003; Meynell 2009; Maleta 2011a; Shiva 2014; Sundström and McCright 2014; Doyle et al. 2015).

Within a materialist framework, a gender equity law, as argued by Maggie, is also a core policy that foregrounds my legislative Bill of Rights Act: aiming to redress historical imbalances, privileging men/masculinities at work. My Republican model is centred on equity/justice frames, as platforms for change – targeting 75% of women in sustainable scientific leadership. Status and mobility are enhanced through prowess and merit, rather than women as token members (Yoder and Aniakudo 1997; Gupta 2007; Terjesen et al. 2009; Gheaus 2015; Watts et al. 2015). Women are articulate, competent negotiators, but their skills are not reconciled in the workforce. Gender policies, targeting diversity recruitment, as with CALD women's leadership, should address glass ceilings or 'glass cliffs' (Cook and Glass 2014: 92). In support to Maggie, Maxine's objective is to influence laws affecting women and the environment. This is framed by women-led performances, resistant to patriarchy. If more women were in corporate leadership, organisations would be 'healthier', for women would not act like men: 'My being in Parliament, trying to change laws', and 'Other political parties are controlled by the wishes of companies and individuals, making profits for corporations… I doubt women would have come up with something like that' (Maxine [audio] 2010). Following on from Maggie, Maxine and Rachel's viewpoints (amongst my other participants), I argue that social change (Republicanism) and environmental change (women-led renewables solutions) frames feminist agency and subjective empowerment, enabling women to realise the 'I' in their identity (McNay 2000; Butler 2007; Meynell 2009; Cudworth and Hobden 2010, 2013). Across my interviews, dynamic intersections of essentialism/constructivism, reveal that executive hierarchies are subject to resistance, diversity and change (Connell 1995, 2002; Mortimer-Sandilands 2008; Gaard 2011).

Emphasized femininity performativity entails peace, harmony and justice for the social and natural world, whereby greater women-led direction frames my methodological aspiration for a unified world, centred on sustainable technological development. My anti-war ethos envisions that the human and nonhuman operate in cohesion rather than conflict (Shiva 2005, 2008, 2014; Di Chiro 2011; Cudworth 2012; Mellor 2013; Merchant 2016). My modelling of WW & SE Initiatives (relative to my Bill of Rights) aspires to subvert the pervasive rule of militant patriarchal elites as well as the pervasion of nuclear energy and nuclear arms proliferation (Butler 1997, 2009; Cockburn 2010, 2012, 2013; Maleta 2018b).

5.9   Resisting 'the Boys Club' and Gender Differences in eNGOs

Continuing my discussion of patriarchal elitist privilege, in this section I develop insights to ruling class elitism pertaining to participants' experiences of gender differentiation, barriers and glass ceilings within international environmentalist nongovernmental organisations (IeNGOs) (Mellor 2002, 2013; Eriksson-Zetterquist and Styhre 2008; Doherty and Doyle 2013; Doyle et al. 2015). In contrast to grassroots community-based eNGOs, men's domineering leadership, is starker in 'the executive arm of the movement' (Barbara [audio] 2010). My interviews also point to women's emphasized femininity resistance to patriarchy, and how women are breaking down gender barriers, evidenced through WW & SE leadership, women-led meetings and radical campaigns (Connell 1995, 2002, 2005; Culley and Angelique 2010; Schlembach 2011; Sundström and McCright 2014). The destabilisation of men, in the ultimate position of power, relative to women's greater leadership, therefore, contributes to greater agency for women along with feminist empowerment (MacLeod 1992; Meynell 2009; Butler 2011, 2013). In relation to my methodological focus on women's leadership, eNGOs and the third sector play a crucial role in a Republican future versus Monarchist governance.

In similarity, to Greens and academics' accounts, eNGO women recognise/resist 'a boys club', entailing an active negotiation of hegemony and competent performances, plus emphasized femininity subversion to ruling class masculinity (Donaldson 1993; Connell 1995; Leahy 2003; Gow and Leahy 2005; Mallory 2006; Nascimento and Connell 2017). I consider the way a masculinist culture of work, relative to conservatism, chauvinism, ego and misogyny, contextualise women's struggle with 'the boys club' across the eNSM (Connell 2002, 2005; McDonald 2011; Summers 2013; Staggenborg 2016). Nonetheless, this effect is not entirely specific to the eNSM and its eSMOs; but more so to the broader uneven structural relations of power, informing the 'hegemony' of patriarchal hierarchies. Maxine had previously criticised the chauvinism of men Parliamentarians and 'male corporate culture'. Here, Maxine criticises the conservative gender politics of eNGOs:

I did find after coming through uni as a feminist and Greens politics, going into the [omit NGO name], the gender politics and dynamics within the environment movement less than ideal. Particularly within some older organisations, some of the dynamics in terms of gender politics were interesting. I challenged them. I would have been seen as a full on feminist. The dynamics within the [state] environmental movement, I was the only female head of an environment group. Every other peak group other than the [omit] had no woman at the head… it is the kind of older bearded men brigade that tend to dominate the movement. That's a problem. I'm talking of traditional movements, nature based conservation. There's a male-dominated group mentality. It has been dominated by strong male individuals.

(Maxine [audio] 2010)

Ruling class masculinity, compared to 'a boys club' and older Anglo men's privilege, is pronounced in the 'traditional', executive arm of conservation-based eNGOs, described as: 'older bearded men brigade', 'a male-dominated group mentality' and 'dominated by strong male individuals'. Comparatively, ruling class elitism is framed by insights to ageist-based conservatism, chauvinism and misogyny, whereby patriarchy privileges established men/masculinities (Arendt 1945; Segal 1999, 2007; Gillard 2012; Summers 2013). Participants also comment how organisational structures are changing, thereby enabling women, and downplaying 'the boys club'. When Eileen first started in her NGO, the culture was 'male'; whereby the male management encouraged female involvement through proactive recruitment strategies and 'now there are more females and the work environment is more conducive to women' (Eileen [audio] 2010). Participant Deborah disputes 'a boys club' in her eNGO, and remarks that ageism and activist tags are more of a barrier than gender (Mallory 2006; Barry 2008; Culley and Angelique 2010; Yoder et al. 2011; Maleta 2012). The activist label of 'tree hugger' or 'radical' is a barrier when negotiating with executives and politicians, which is why formal attire is required in meetings: 'they're politicians and you know what they look like, they wear a suit you have got to wear a suit' (Deborah [audio] 2010). Although Deborah experienced an 'old boys club' in an inter-state meeting, her position as an inter-state outsider was paramount:

That was the only time I ever felt Old Boys' Club… when I was in [omit state] and I went to meet the [omit] Minister. The [omit] CEO was there with me and he was a man obviously. He introduced himself to someone and there was a little bit of old boy's thingee, oh we used to work together years ago, so, it was chummy. But I was the outer-stater, so it was possibly more of him establishing his position as, well I'm [omit state] rather than some blow in from outside the state. Maybe it wasn't Old Boys' so much as, we're [omit] and she's not.

(Deborah [audio] 2010)

Deborah's interview reveals contradictions, framing gender as a performance (Butler 1997, 1999, 2004). While she resists the notion of 'a boys club' or being treated differently as a woman, she outlines gender differences in paid/unpaid eSMO campaigns:

the climate change team, it's all men whereas the green home team, it's all women... the green home team don't do advocacy work like we do. They're not campaigners, they do the public outreach program, they do teaching.

(Deborah [audio] 2010)

This commentary intersects dichotomous performances of masculinity/ femininity with gender differentiation, framed by men's dominance of paid climate change and nuclear campaigns, and women's dominance of 'the green home team' and 'teaching' duties (Rankin and Gale 2003; Butler 2007, 2013; Jagger 2008; Unger 2008; Ainsworth 2012). Deborah ([audio] 2010) explains how men are attracted to the hard sciences: 'our two nuclear campaigners are both men... I think climate change attracts men and to the economics... it's more of a hard science as opposed to a soft science'. Comparatively, Deborah ([audio] 2010) finds 'the biodiversity side more interesting'. Such retrospection highlights women's interest in the 'soft sciences', whilst underscoring differentiated women/ men interests, but not delineating from women's 'natural leadership affinity' for greater Sustainable Initiatives. Gender differentiated campaigns and dualist representations point to essentialist notions of men/masculinities and women/ femininities (Buckingham-Hatfield 2000; Mortimer-Sandilands 2008; Donaldson 2009; Stoddart and Tindall 2011). Such differentiation evokes prejudices of women's scientific-intellectual competence (Cockburn 1988; Ahern and Hendryx 2008; Payne 2009; Culley and Angelique 2010; Gheaus 2015; Merchant 2016; STEMM 2018). However, women's performativity of 'biodiversity', 'advocacy', 'the green home team' and 'teaching', reveals empowering leadership qualities, framing the potential of greater women-led WW & SE Initiatives.

Gender performative differences framing dualist work and social relations, also encompass identity (Plumwood 1997, 2006). Men's identity is bound with paid work, thereby determining men's self-esteem and sense of worth (Pease 2002: 97; Segal 2007: 243). Psychological studies contend that men are more preoccupied with their masculinity and become anxious over the lack of it (Segal 2007: 243). When women increasingly enter male-dominated occupations, men struggle to negotiate their work identity (Cockburn 1988; Pease 2002; Segal 2007). In my study, voluntary and salaried women accrue a strong sense of identity through their performative unpaid/paid roles. Following on from Pease (2002: 97) and Segal (2007: 243), Deborah's account appears to confirm that men acquire esteem from paid work, as with their dominance of 'hard versus soft sciences'. Although I do not intend to position essentialism as a frame of otherness for women, my empirical insights suggest that essentialism, relative to participants' maternal identity and 'nurturing ethos' (Maggie, Barbara), is an empowering example of emphasized femininity performativity (MacGregor 2001; Moore 2008; Wibben 2016; Nagy 2017). Emphasized femininity performativity intersects within environmental activism, whereby essentialism/constructivism, strategically appropriated by women, strengthens their social and environmental change goals (Doyle 2005; Di Chiro 2008; Buechler and Hanson 2015).

One's sense of self-esteem is related to ego, or specifically, masculinist forms of egoism. I found that women's agency is less dependent on ego. In support, Maxine's criticism of 'conservative gender politics' within conservation eNGOs, suggests that egoism underpins women's experiences of inequity/injustice. Evidently, 'a boys club' frames ruling class masculinity and egoism, relative to men's hegemony. As a self-identified 'feminist', Parliamentarian Maxine 'challenged them' plus 'the male-dominated group mentality'. Being 'the only female head of an environment group', and as a social change-oriented politician, Maxine strived to achieve both sustainable and gender reforms.

Women's apparent attraction to the soft sciences, such as, 'biodiversity', 'green home team' and 'teaching' (Deborah [audio] 2010), does not delineate their agency nor capacity to competently lead on renewable technological solutions (Mackenzie and Stoljar 2000; Rees and Garnsey 2003; Gow and Leahy 2005; Canty 2017; RenewableUK 2017; Clean Energy Council 2018). My interview results show that women are actively constructing their feminist, environmentalist and activist identities, and such constructivism disrupts the masculine hegemony pervading environmental politics (Gaard 2001; Mortimer-Sandilands 2008; MacGregor 2010; Maleta 2011b; Vildåsen et al. 2017). By disrupting hegemony, patriarchy is also being disrupted (Walby 1990, 2013, 2015; Connell 1995; Plumwood 1997, 2002; Cockburn 2013). Moreover, agentic competence is not entirely specific to one's feminist identity, for it encompasses one's motivation for the environmental cause, and desire to make a difference. Participants who resist gender differences acquire a keen sense of identity through their environmental work. The 'I' in one's identity is situated in performative skill and passion (Butler 2007, 2015). I should not delineate from the fact that women-led emphasized femininity performative strategies are reinvigorating both the women's and environmentalist NSMs (Diani 1992; Glazebrook 2005; McLellan 2009; Butler 2011; Di Chiro 2011; Staggenborg 2016; BWE 2018).

Mara, an eNGO salaried Director and voluntary community activist, identifies gender distinctions in the grassroots, but contests the notion that being a woman differentiates her; rather, this opens up opportunities for resistance:

there can be gender role distinctions in circles, but there is diversity… I participated in direct action blockading in forests and the coal industry, and sometimes gender roles become marked, but I know exceptions for it to be a fair reflection of the direct action crew on coal and forests. I heard people remark the tendency for women to gravitate or be chosen for facilitating roles, and for men to be given action campaign roles… the challenges women in Australia face vary according to their socio-economic circumstances, ethnicity, sexual preference. I don't experience challenges in work–life that I associate with being a woman. In social movements, it is an advantage to be a woman, because there are tools available for us to disrupt dominant or status quo patterns that may not be available to men.

(Mara [audio] 2010)

Mara's account, in turn, is subversive to patriarchy, through an emphasis on disruption and women's empowerment in eNSMs and its eSMOs. While Mara contemplates 'gender role distinctions', she points to 'diversity' and disputes the idea that being a woman frames her 'work–life' balance (Pocock 2003; Pocock et al. 2013). The above commentary alludes to gender-specific and gender-neutral insights (Prokhovnik 1998; Foster and Meinhard 2005; Connell 2006; MacGregor 2006). Gender operates as a barrier and enabler; whereby, my interviews reveal contradictions through women's experience as insider/outsider in the paid/unpaid arm of the eNSM (Prokhovnik 1998; Culley and Angelique 2003; Jonnergård et al. 2010; Maleta 2012; Haynes et al. 2015; Edge et al. 2017). Interestingly, Mara pinpoints one's sociocultural status as a potential barrier and/enabler to inclusion (ABS 2016a; AHRC 2017b; Canty 2017). My Act's Initiatives address sociocultural forms of inequity/injustice, by focussing on minority women's (*my six groups*) performative prowesses in WW & SE technological leadership (Ahern and Hendryx 2008; DAWN 2015; BWE 2018; EREF 2018; EUREC 2018). As above, an empowering women-led framework is expressed, for there is an 'advantage to [being] a woman' so as 'to disrupt dominant or status quo patterns'. This retrospection frames emphasized femininity resistance to hegemonic masculinity. Women possess the agency to destabilise hegemony: 'there are tools available for us to disrupt dominant or status quo patterns that may not be available to men' (Mara [audio] 2010). Such disruption should challenge patriarchal institutionalisation and destabilise conservatism, chauvinism, ego and misogyny. Positively though, Mara's appraisal of 'diversity' frames the potential for women and men to collaborate more so in WW & SE solutions (Leahy 2003; Connell 2005).

5.10 Recognising/Resisting Egoism and Otherness

Positive insights to diversity does not diminish the problem of 'a boys club', framing women's otherness within contemporary executive hierarchies. Other interviews point to women's experience as the dualist insider/outsider (Yoder and Aniakudo 1997; Maddison and Scalmer 2006; Kosny and MacEachen 2010;

Fisher and Kinsey 2014). While Stephanie acknowledges 'an old boys club' in her prior financial career, she disputes its existence in the eNSM, for it is 'less ego driven'. In contrast to Australia, 'the boys club' is obvious in U.K. commerce-based corporations, defined by social class, as Stephanie ([audio] 2010) contends. Arguably, the U.K. is a more class-based society, and socioeconomic divisions were paramount with the Brexit outcome (Grusky 2014; Glencross 2016; Nunlee 2016; Mount 2017). Nonetheless, in Australia, sexism can be more problematic: 'in the U.K., if you get to the upper echelons, where it's real 'old boys club', you get it there. We don't have the extremes; we have maybe a higher level of sexism' (Stephanie [audio] 2010). Stephanie explains that eNGOs have some 'power hungry' individuals, nonetheless, the sector is comparatively less egotistical:

> the superannuation industry, they're old dudes, on multiple Boards... it's definitely an old 'boys club'... I've only been around for 18 months in the environmental world. I haven't come across it. There's networks of important people; powerful people, but not as strong as the corporate world. In the NGO world, we justify it by it being for a good cause. The corporate world is very cut throat... NGOs, there'll be some power hungry people, but the majority believe in the cause than their own agenda. If you're that driven to be powerful, you'd go into the corporate world and get remunerated. Here, it's a less ego driven environment to work in.
>
> (Stephanie [audio] 2010)

Stephanie's observation of 'the corporate [superannuation] world' as 'an "old boys club" on multiple Boards' and 'very cut throat', points to an androcentric and aggressive type of ruling class masculinist culture. This insights contrast with the appraisal of eNGOs as 'less ego driven' and 'being for a good cause'. Power and egoism are not barriers within 'the environmental world' for 'the NGO world' is 'a less ego driven environment to work in'. Rather, power is appropriated by participants to justify 'a good cause'. Whereas the 'corporate world' attracts individuals 'driven to be powerful', and to 'get remunerated'. In retrospect, 'a boys club' characterises the corporate versus eNGO world. The more hierarchical and profit-based an organisation and its employees are – that is driven by 'remuneration' and 'power' – then dominant notions of hegemonic masculinity, framed by 'an old "boys club"', are more likely to prevail. Also, corporate structures are framed by neoliberal economics, whereby individualis and capitalist-oriented competition intersect – upholding masculinist hegemony plus the rule of patriarchal industrial elites (Connell 2006; Gerulis-Darcy 2010; Erickson 2011; Grady et al. 2012; Walby 2013). Undoubtedly, such cultural structures privilege older Anglo men, framing women's perpetual struggle with otherness (Poynting and Donaldson 2005; Lobo and Morgan 2012; DAWN 2015).

Although Stephanie disputed ego, she adds that some men in her eNGO perform 'an ego element'. This shows contradictions. On one hand, ego is a problem in corporations, but not so in the eNSM. Nonetheless, 'with men, there can be an ego element', even in eNGOs. However, women's performativity is resistant to egoism:

> I'd say it's more female, we've got a meeting every week and the door's always open. It's not very masculine... it's a more conducive environment to discussing ideas and questioning, someone going off on a tangent, it doesn't work. It is a more collaborative environment. We had a breakaway women's meeting, cause on Fridays, we like wine and cheese. It was productive. It's different vibe with women. Cause we'll talk about it, there were no egos, or power, or anything to protect. Whereas with men, there can be an ego element.
>
> (Stephanie [audio] 2010)

Women recognise/reject masculinist forms of ego and power: 'we'll talk about it... no egos, or power, or anything to protect'. Women's communicative approach, as 'productive' and 'collaborative' frames emphasized femininity strategic engagement and feminist empowerment (Connell 1995, 2005; Butler 2007, 2013). Women's performativity entails an accommodation of emphasized femininity, through women-led strategies, contrasting with the more domineering leadership styles of men: 'going off on a tangent, it doesn't work', and 'with men, there can be an ego element' (MacLeod 1992; Connell 1995, 2002, 2005; Leahy 2003). Women and men often perform their roles differently, even in the same organisational context (Foster and Meinhard 2005; Maleta 2009; Butler 2011, 2013; Sundström and McCright 2014). From Stephanie's excerpt, in likeness to my Greens and academic empirical results, men's leadership is, to a significant extent, androcentric and aggressive (Plumwood 1997; MacGregor 2001, 2006). Women's emphasized femininity style of leadership, defined as 'conducive' and 'collaborative', however, has the potential to transform structural relations of power that privilege men. With more women leaders, organisational structures would be flatter, more egalitarian, and ideally, less hierarchical. Emphasized femininity leadership is, consequently, conducive to my egalitarian-social democratic Republican framework: to destabilise ruling class forms of patriarchy and bureaucracy. As such, my Bill's Initiatives, legislating on women's sustainable-technological-scientific leadership development, should realise my feminist aims of (in)equity/(in)justice. I also aim to revitalise gender dynamics and improve the work and social relations between genders. Drawing upon Stephanie's commentary, my framing of emphasized femininity as empowering, is, therefore, contextualised by women's performative agentic multiple skills-set, that is resistant to patriarchy: 'the door's always open', 'it's not very masculine', 'more conducive environment to discussing ideas', 'different vibe with women' plus 'no egos, or power, or anything to protect' ([audio] 2010).

Thus far, egoism is recognised/resisted by participants. Empirical insights to 'egos' within eNGOs and diverse sectors, frame 'a boys club' and women's struggle with ruling class masculinity, men's leadership styles and patriarchal privilege (Forbes-Mewett and Snell 2006; McGregor 2009; McDonald 2011; Donaldson and Poynting 2013). However, women's emphasized femininity performative leadership, reveals an intersection of essentialism/constructivism with hegemony. Aspirations for women's WW & SE leadership (akin to my Bill's quotas), is an opportunity to: change the way (patriarchal) organisations work, challenge the rule of the patriarch (men's hegemon), and to realise my EEO-merit-competent-based ambitions, framing *my six groups* inclusion as well as feminist empowerment at work (Cockburn 1988; Walby 1990, 2011, 2012; Disability Discrimination Act 2013; AHRC 2016b, 2017b; EEO Act [1987] 2016; STEMM 2018).

For Heidi, an eNGO advocate and PhD qualified scientist, who possesses academic and third-sector industry experience, egoism is problematic within scientific academia, or with male scientists, rather than an issue in eNGOs:

> I think research scientists are driven by ego, in some ways they are well intended. There are wonderful scientists who aren't like that, but I've had two experiences now with scientists that it's really about them, it's not about working together to achieve positive outcomes… I'm enjoying the eNGO community.
>
> (Heidi [audio] 2010)

Heidi's framing of egoism captures women's struggle with 'a boys club' and masculine hegemony within scientific academia (Pollack 2015; Cohen 2016; Merchant 2016; Farr et al. 2017; STEMM 2018). As a former PhD candidate and academic employee, Heidi attacks the way in which: 'research scientists are driven by ego' and 'it's about them, it's not about working together to achieve positive outcomes'. Although Heidi ([audio] 2010) contends that 'the NGO world can be political and competitive', her eNGO is characterised by team and independent efforts: 'we work together', 'we don't step on each other's toes' and 'we have our area to look after'. In the scientific community, her eNGO has a 'good reputation' and is 'highly regarded' (Heidi [audio] 2010). Without recognising ego in her eNGO, Heidi ([audio] 2010) assesses her organisation as 'a really nice environment to work in'. In retrospect, Heidi's dualist recognition/resistance to egoism within diverse environmentalist sectors frames my standpoint that 'a boys club' is more of a barrier in the hierarchical executive arm of environmentalism, in contrast to the more egalitarian-grassroots-based eSMOs (Blackwell and Glover 2008; Alston 2011; Maleta 2011b, 2012; Pollack 2015; Cohen 2016). Academic participant Anna had illuminated women's multi-skills-set in science, but also how their leadership is curtailed by male dominance. Men's executive dominance reinforces 'a boys club' and glass ceilings, and that gender tokenism and a masculinist culture are core gender-organisational barriers (Gupta 2007; Jonnergård et al. 2010; Gheaus 2015; Haynes et al. 2015; Cadaret et al. 2017; Irvine 2017). As a result, women's merit is not fully recognised. My insight to 'a [patriarchal] boys club' is further relayed by Heidi's critique of academic conferences:

the academic community and workplaces, they are different. With men making their way up, I don't think merit is acknowledged… it's 'a boys club'. It's a lot of conferences… We hold a bi-annual conference [omit], and that's a great networking experience. It puts everyone together in one place.

(Heidi [audio] 2010)

Heidi quotation outlines 'a boys club' in academic conferences, but not so in eNGO conferences (Merchant 1994, 2013; Gheaus 2015; Pollack 2015; Cohen 2016). Her quote intersects masculine privilege/merit, for 'men [make] their way up', disputing the viewpoint that women's 'merit is acknowledged'. While women demonstrate prowess and indeed merit, patriarchy and masculine hegemony, underpins their scientific-intellectual acknowledgement (Rentetzi 2004, 2008, 2010; Maleta 2011a). As Heidi is a trained scientist, her critique of male academic scientists' egoism, is not extended to women academics, nor the competent men and women, in her eNGO, who possess sound knowledge in environmental science – although not necessarily scientists. Heidi's interview frames performative gender differences and differing levels of professionalism and accountability within academia and third sector environmentalism (Butler 1990, 1997, 2017; Shiva 2008; Mellor 2012; Sundström and McCright 2014). In relation to Heidi, one may deduce that eNGOs have a higher professional standard, pertaining to: 'positive outcomes', 'good reputation' and 'highly regarded by the scientific community'. But, also, that the advocacy environment of eNGOs, enables women (and men) to develop scientific knowledge, without necessarily being experts in the field.

My accounts outline an active recognition/resistance of egoism in the eNSM. Former eNGO Director, Helen, an academic participant, identifies egoism in large hierarchical INGOs and in the grassroots, but refrains from viewing this as gender specific:

Women are a key part of environment and climate movements, but I would not differentiate their role from that played by men. Men can be more rational and cool-headed with less bitchy behaviour, but I have experienced large egos and dominating personalities from both genders.

(Helen [audio] 2010)

Helen's experience of 'both genders' possessing 'large egos and dominating personalities', underpins an essentialist-constructivist retrospection. Helen's appraisal of women's 'key part' in the eNSM, highlights their competent-constructivist performances, suggesting that women's assertiveness and merit is integral towards environmental change (Shiva 1993; Stein 2004; MacGregor 2010; Schlembach 2011; Staggenborg 2016; BWE 2018). Also, Helen's dispute of gender differences, relays an essentialist critique, for it is not only 'men' who are 'more rationale', 'cool-headed' and 'less bitchy'. Both genders perform such acts. This account downplays dichotomies of women/femininities within dualist frames of rationality/emotionality (Rydell et al. 2009; Fleming and Sturdy 2011;

Ussher 2011; Ainsworth 2012). Moreover, her framing of ego, as a performance of 'both genders', enables me to dispute essentialist views of women/femininity as highly emotive and even irrational (Cockburn 1988; Plumwood 1997; Buckingham-Hatfield 2000; Culley and Angelique 2003; Meynell 2009; Kosny and MacEachen 2010; Maleta 2012, 2015).

Whilst Helen disputed ego as gender-specific, other participants comment on women-led resistance to egoism. Catherine ([audio] 2010), a grassroots activist and public sector employee, adds that being a grassroots leader means: 'not letting ego get in the way and being self-reflective, which is easier for women'. The notion that it 'is easier for women' to resist ego intersects essentialism/constructivism with agentic self-reflexion. Women-led direction is an empowering premise from which to subvert ego from pervading the eNSM.

Moreover, Catherine has worked well with fellow men climate activists, indicating how a common ground approach, unifies gender and social relations within the grassroots (Leahy 2003; Connell 2005; Gow and Leahy 2005; Di Chiro 2008, 2011). On the other hand, executive men's hegemony of the resource industries, in terms of 'ego' and 'control', curtails women's sustainability-social change agendas:

> It's interesting about men in industries like coal. There's something very masculine about centralising sources of energy, something very alien to think that we could have bits of energy coming from solar panels, wind and somewhere else, because there's no control. Being able to centralise the source of energy is very appealing, to make lots of money, it's very masculine.
> (Catherine [audio] 2010)

Consequently, 'a boys club', is evidenced by the masculinisation and centralisation of the coal industry: 'very masculine about centralising sources of energy'. Catherine's interview also reveals grassroots men and women's keen advocacy of sustainability and climate action initiatives, whilst the resource sector is dependent upon the extrapolation of the natural environment, relative to industrial and economic rationales (Doyle 2000, 2005; Horton 2006; Faber 2008; Doyle et al. 2015). Sustainability is about change, progress and diversity, accentuated through Catherine's appraisal of solar and wind energy. But the resource sector is old-fashioned, dated and reluctant to change. Nonetheless, sustainable-social change is akin to my sociopolitical ambition: to subvert conservatism within Australian politics – through Republicanism. Through the legislation of my Act/Initiatives, I aim to have a greater representation of *my six groups* in the renewables technology sector. Women-led 'solar panels, wind' methods align with my conceptualisation of emphasized femininity as rooted in environmental technical competence (Culley and Angelique 2010; Maleta 2012; McFarland 2014; Ajani 2015; Clean Energy Council 2018; WIE 2018). Women's greater renewables leadership should subvert industrial hegemony, framed by: 'control', 'centralise the source of energy', 'make lots of money, it's very masculine'. Such insights to the masculinisation and centralisation of the coal industry, situate 'a [patriarchal] boys club' and ruling class masculinity as core barriers, affecting WW & SE outcomes (Di Chiro 2011; Hosey 2011; Love and Garwood 2011; Mix 2011; Davis 2015; Gaard 2017).

Third-sector environmentalism is characterised by grassroots organisations, constituted of volunteer activists, and eNGOs, composed of salaried advocates and voluntary activists (Horton 2006; Unger 2008; Shepard and Corbin-Mark 2009; Mix 2011; Maleta 2012, 2015). Most grassroots women, as Catherine (2010) and Gillian (2009), esteem the cohesive work environment of the grassroots. Whilst Mara admires the performativity of 'special peoples' in 'grassroots activism', she contrasts aspects of 'nastiness' with the 'professional' arm of the eNGO climate movement:

> In the grassroots, you can be more free and independent, work according to your priorities and so everything is a gift freely given. Which is not to say that people don't work hard in the grassroots, I worked hard, but you are working according to the terms you set yourself and are more in control… When I started working in the NGO climate movement, I was struck by how much more freely people gave support, encouragement and warmth. There is a lot of nastiness, mean-spiritedness and bickering in the grassroots, and my experience has been that it is less prevalent among the paid campaigners. This is partly a consequence of having financial and reputational standing. That said, in the grassroots, the constraints people work under bring out the best in those who rise to the challenge. I know special people in grassroots activism whom I have profound admiration.
>
> (Mara [audio] 2010)

While Mara esteems the 'free and independent' flexibility enabled within the grassroots, she critiques petty performances: 'nastiness, mean-spiritedness and bickering', directly contrasting with eNGO 'paid campaigners' social engagement: 'freely' gave 'support, encouragement and warmth'. Mara's account points to different professional standards within third-sector grassroots and eNGO organisations, relative to 'having financial and reputational standing'. She acknowledges the financial constraints impacting the grassroots, but suggests that the more financially independent an organisation is, then it less likely to be characterised by 'nastiness, mean-spiritedness and bickering'. In similarity to Mara's prior reflection, this is not gender-specific but organisation-specific (Foster and Meinhard 2005; Faber 2008; Alston 2013; Organo et al. 2013). Yet, as the grassroots is female-dominated, one can assume such performativity is enacted by women activists.

Although women do not always identify with notions of otherness in their roles, as relative to their gender status within patriarchy, empirical data highlights chauvinism as a constraint experienced by participants. Insights to chauvinism reinforce 'the boys club' and ruling class masculinity as barriers (Arendt 1945; Connell 2009; Donaldson 2009; Donaldson and Poynting 2013; Pollack 2015;

Cohen 2016). In the next passage, Stephanie's boss is assessed as chauvinistic; yet, not all men managers are like this:

> In my business area, there's myself and my boss, who's a male. He's a special male. I tend to be the doer and do stuff, and he is the alpha to my beta. He will direct what is being done, and I will do it. I've worked with very good men; he's probably my first of meeting a slightly chauvinistic, old-fashioned male, which is a bit odd. He's from consulting; it is a very male-dominated background.
>
> (Stephanie [audio] 2010)

Stephanie's retrospection of 'a slightly chauvinistic, old-fashioned male' as 'a bit odd' in the eNSM, is justified by her boss's former consulting career, relative to 'a very male-dominated background'. The seeming recognition/resistance to chauvinism, even within the eNSM, suggests that a patriarchal culture of work, continues to frame women's dualist experience as insider/outsider within their eSMOs (Warren 1997; Greer 1999; Maddison 2004; Doyle 2005; MacGregor 2006, 2009; Wibben 2016; Gaard 2017). This gender differentiation can be stark or subtle. Although chauvinism was somewhat of a constraint, Stephanie's identification as 'the doer', relative to her boss, is an empowering self-reflexion of agency, supporting Butler's (1990, 2007, 2013) insight to women's performative agency, enacted by the active doing of 'I', framing their identity and feminist empowerment. Although 'he will direct what is being done', Stephanie boldly states: 'I will do it'. Whilst chauvinism exemplifies signifies hegemonic masculinity at play, this is not stopping Stephanie from performing her role. The 'doer' in Stephanie's identity also conveys an empowering emphasized femininity performance, situated in women-led agentic competence, equally resistant to men's hegemony (Connell 1995; Plumwood 1997; Leahy 2003; Moore 2008; Marshall 2011; Haynes et al. 2015; Maleta 2018b).

Other eNGO participants working in the executive arm of the SM, recognise/ resist elements of chauvinism. As the dualist insider/outsider, Barbara's explains how both misogyny and chauvinism ostracised her in within the executive arm of 'the Green Games':

> I worked with a committee... they wanted an assessment about the remediation, and was it going to be good for the Green Games? Because I didn't toe the party line, it was led by a man and a male lawyer; they wouldn't let me back on the committee and sacked me, and didn't pay me... I was sacked because I didn't deliver the report that this environmental group wanted for the games. I knew the subject, that's why I was asked to do the job... there was this cabal of blokes and a woman; the cabal of blokes just bundled me out and it was terrible. That was absolute male chauvinism... I experienced misogyny in the 1990s, I was never provided the opportunity to play an executive role in the mainstream movement.
>
> (Barbara [audio] 2010)

5.11 Discussion

In relation to Barbara's critique of the Green Games' executive hierarchy, along with that of Stephanie, Heidi and other participants – I can deduce that chauvinism, misogyny and sexism, as examples of 'a boys club', encapsulate women's struggle with middle class masculinity plus patriarchy in the eNSM and its eSMOs. A 'boys club' was critiqued in terms of: power, ego, dress, conservativeness, criticism and support of eNGOs/grassroots, gender differences and stereotypes. However, insights to emphasized femininity leadership challenges men's hegemony and patriarchal cultural-structural privilege (MacLeod 1992; Connell 1995; Leahy 2003; Meynell 2009; Walby 2013; Sundström and McCright 2014). Contentiously, there is a lack of global research on 'a boys cub', framed by chauvinism and misogyny, within the eNSM (Pollack 2015; Cohen 2016). Hence, my insights contribute cutting-edge knowledge to the interdisciplinary field (McNay 2003; Talbot and Quayle 2010; Butler 2013; Summers 2013; Britton 2017).

With a greater representation of *my six groups* (CALD, Indigenous, Anglo, disabled, socioeconomically disadvantaged and older women) in renewables technological-scientific leadership, arguably, my social (Republican) and environmental (sustainable) objectives, would be met. Such a sociopolitical change is also required in order to redress conservatism, glass ceilings and patriarchal elitism, indicative of middle class men's ruling power plus privileged statuses at work (Donaldson and Poynting 2007, 2013; Donaldson 2009; McGregor 2009; Bombora Wave Power 2018; Carnegie Clean Energy 2018). Although women are increasingly acquiring status through performative prowess, EEO laws have not adequately addressed their leadership under-representation (Connell 2009; Public Service Commission 2015; EEO Act [1987] 2016). This is where my Republican Bill of Rights Act and its' Initiatives fill a gap: legislating/advocating on the scientific leadership of my six core groups in renewables organisational governance. My feminist model should create more jobs for women in renewables science (McFarland 2014; Ajani 2015; RenewableUK 2017; BWE 2018; Clean Energy Council 2018; WIE 2018).

Conclusion

This chapter has shown that eNGO women struggle with men's resistance to their leadership in 'the executive arm of the eNSM' and in conservative, conservation-based eNGOs, led by 'old White men' (Cockburn 1991; Doyle 2005; MacGregor 2006, 2014). Analyses of 'old White men', enable me to frame Anglo male middle class privilege as a barrier, underpinning middle and working class women's leadership (Donaldson 1993; Kaufmann 2004; McGregor 2009; Grusky 2014; DAWN 2015). The more hierarchical, and indeed patriarchal an organisation is, the more problematic is gender differentiation. Nonetheless, the grassroots can be petty and engage in 'bickering' and 'nastiness', as outlined by Mara. Commentary on the 'older bearded men brigade', 'a male-dominated group mentality', 'dominated by strong male individuals' and men's dominance in 'the executive arm of the eNSM', highlights the pervasive power of hegemonic masculinity. My constructivist intersection of gender, sociocultural status and ageism with 'the boys club', reveals the conservative rule of industrial and political elites, representing core barriers for both a Republican change plus renewables future (Wantland 2005; McDonald 2011; Pollack 2015; Cohen 2016; Veri 2016; ARM 2018). Women though are committed to a sustainable change (Gaard 2001; Maleta 2011a, 2012, 2018b). Catherine ([audio] 2010) critiqued the masculinisation and centralisation of the coal industry, whereas her ambition was for solar and wind energy (Love and Garwood 2011; Tatchley et al. 2016; WIE 2018). Catherine's insight to renewable technologies frames women-led scientific competence as a social change strategy (Culley and Angelique 2003, 2010). Also, power relations are mobile and fluid; whereby masculine hegemony is subject to feminist resistance (MacLeod 1992; Connell 1995, 2005, 2009; Plumwood 1997; Buckingham-Hatfield 2000). Although Mara ([audio] 2010) resisted gender distinctions, she framed women-led subversion in the eNSM as 'disrupting the masculinist status quo'. Arguably, an integration of feminism plus egalitarianism with sustainable science is realised in my Bill's Initiatives – focussing on women-led WW & SE skills. This is a framework for feminist empowerment whilst challenging 'the masculinist status quo' or indeed middle class masculinity, framing executive hierarchies. Whilst women struggle with 'the boys club', they 'do gender' by exercising agentic power and performing multiple skills (Butler 2007, 2013). My Republican-Act's goal is to illuminate emphasized femininity performativity, as agentic and competent whilst resistant to patriarchy in order to realise the 'I' in women's identity as well as renewables and gender justice outcomes (Plumwood 1997; Butler 2007, 2013).

6   Gender Tokenism on Climate Panels

Introduction

This chapter is organised under the thematic header 'Tokenism', the second core theme associated with 'the boys club', in which I frame women's struggle with ruling-middle class hegemonic masculinity. A token woman occurs when a woman is put into a position to give the appearance of gender equity, which does not necessarily exist (Yoder and Aniakudo 1997; Terjesen et al. 2009; Gheaus 2015; Irvine 2017). Sourcing my interviews, I articulate women's experience as token members on environmental panels along with their resistance to such labelling (Fisher and Kinsey 2014; Gheaus 2015; Pollack 2015; Britton 2017). My participants comment on tokenism in terms of: 'token woman', 'the masculine cultural domination of nature', and 'where are the women speakers?' It is challenging to construct women's agency, when their panel placement 'may largely be to fill a gender gap', rather than based on merit. My empirical results pinpoint the gender barriers faced by women in science, whilst critiquing men scientists' for taking credit of women's work on climate panels – work initially performed in a grassroots or salaried capacity (Culley and Angelique 2003, 2010; Maleta 2012; Cadaret et al. 2017; Farr et al. 2017). While I question gender tokenism, I draw upon women's *agentic performative multiple skills-set*, and subversion to men's leadership privilege as well as prejudices in environmental science (Duncan 2010; Elsesser and Lever 2011; Yoder et al. 2011; Butler 2013; Cohen 2016; STEMM 2018). Arguably, women led-emphasized femininity, represents the ultimate resistance to patriarchal elitism and gender tokenism.

6.1   Women as Token Members on Climate Panels

Gendered tokenism alludes to women's equity and competence (Yoder and Aniakudo 1997; Terjesen et al. 2009; Gheaus 2015; Irvine 2017). A woman is a token woman if she has no effective power amongst the men (Connell 2009; Terjesen et al. 2009). If women are deliberately placed on male-dominated conferences in order to fill a gender gap, this implies that the woman does not necessarily deserve the position (Gupta 2007; Yoder et al. 2011; Gheaus 2015; Pollack 2015). An appearance of gender equality is affected; arguably, due to glass ceilings and masculinist hegemony, equity does not exist in the first instance (Bendl and Schmidt 2010; Butler 2011; Maleta 2011a; Cook and Glass 2014; Britton 2017; Cadaret et al. 2017). However, my Bill of Rights Act, plus its Initiatives, centred on women's *agentic performative multiple skills-set*, entails an empowering form of emphasized femininity resistance to tokenism and patriarchy (STEMM 2018). In the global scholarship, there is a lack of current research on women's tokenism in the eNSM/eSMOs. This suggests the interdisciplinary relevance of my study and its contribution to knowledge as well as meaning-making within feminism.

Regarding my conceptualisation of ruling-middle class masculinity, the commentary from my interviews provides insights to how tokenism frames women's struggle with 'the boys club' and hegemony on scientific panels: 'token woman', 'the masculine cultural domination of nature', and 'where are the women speakers?' Such commentary demonstrates women's active, engaged performative recognition/resistance to 'the boys club' and tokenism (Ussher 2011; Butler 2013, 2015; Gheaus 2015). Tokenism relays barriers and enablers. An overarching barrier is that placement is less based on merit or prowess (as mentioned), than it is on presenting an illusion to gender equity. An enabler though is that women receive the opportunity to perform as leaders, in roles that may have traditionally been awarded to a man. Hence, women are enabled with the opportunity to demonstrate their skills and exercise agency. Yet, women's deliberate placement on panels, in order to fill a gap, frames the patriarchal control of participants organisations and that men hold more power. Through tokenism, women, subsequently, experience their roles as dualist insider/outsider (Yoder and Aniakudo 1997; Fenster 2007; Nagy 2017).

While eNGO advocate, Linda ([audio] 2010), self-identifies as 'the project leader', the climate panel's topic was not her area of expertise: 'I had a colleague who was more involved, it was only a portion of my work'. The committee's reply accentuates her token status: 'that would make the panel all male, so would I stay on it?' (Linda [audio] 2010). Linda's insight to tokenism, captures her dualist experience as insider/outsider:

> I was there as the token woman because they didn't want the panel to be all male… I suggested he'd be better placed as the panellist… it's often the case I've taken on the role of creating gender balance on panels or representative bodies… we're still male-dominated in the environment field.
>
> (Linda [audio] 2010)

Academic Yvonne adds that she is often asked to make up a gender balance on committees, panels and boards, as there are not many senior women in climate science:

> I've been fortunate in the field I chose, climate change, which has become more topical and opened up a lot of opportunities that I wouldn't have had in another area… often I'm the only woman on a panel or a committee.

I've been asked to do things because they were looking for a senior woman; there are not many senior women in the area. In some ways being a woman's opened up opportunities rather than hindered me, because of the field that I'm in.

(Yvonne [audio] 2010)

While climate change has 'opened up a lot more opportunities for women'; Yvonne asserts that 'senior' women are under-represented in 'panels' and 'committees', as academic Anna ([audio] 2010) previously articulated (Valles 2015; Farr et al. 2017; Vildåsen et al. 2017). Through panel placement, academics, like Yvonne and Anna, are enabled with the opportunity to perform expert knowledge, but the fact that 'there are not many senior women in the area', underpins mature/older women's minority status, dualist experience of insider/outsider and that glass ceilings privilege men within academic science (Blackwell and Glover 2008; Bendl and Schmidt 2010; Cook and Glass 2014; Watts et al. 2015). As older women are one of my core six groupings, their extensive wisdom and expert skills-set, frames my Bill's mission to have more senior women in executive roles in environmental science (Cooper 2013; AHRC 2016b, 2017b; Edge et al. 2017; STEMM 2018).

In support to academics Yvonne and Anna's ageist commentary, medical doctor Maggie's excerpt showcases her experience as the insider/outsider in corporate meetings:

if I'm asked to address corporate meetings the men don't talk to me afterwards. I freak them out. I'm not sure what it is. If I was still pre-menopausal and attractive I could get away with it, but now I'm not, I'm part of the wallpaper.

(Maggie [audio] 2010)

On one hand, Maggie is the 'insider', for her expert skills are sought 'to address corporate meetings'. On the other hand, she is the 'outsider', regarding men's somewhat childish response to her presence: 'don't talk to me afterwards'. Being invited to attend meetings and listened to suggests inclusion, rather than gendered tokenism. But a deliberate lack of engagement with the guest speaker, by these men, reveals the intricacies of 'a boys club', relative to Maggies' otherness and exclusion. Evidently, men are threatened by competent, mature, wise women, speaking about topics in which they themselves profess expertise: 'I freak them out'. Such a chauvinistic response to a woman expert, in the comparative field, indicates that men cannot reconcile their sense of self or self-esteem (Pease 2002; Segal 2007). When women work in the same jobs, then men feel threatened (Cockburn 1988; Probert and Wilson 1993; Probert 2005; Maleta 2009). When an expert like Maggie appears to profess more knowledge than the men, or challenge them, then men may respond by challenging Maggie (or the woman in question), or by ignoring her, as was the case here. Additionally, this accounts for the existence of 'a boys club' – in how middle class men form bonds and networks, supporting each other at work and events – thereby not engaging women and others (Forbes-Mewett and Snell 2006; McDonald 2011; Fisher and Kinsey 2014; Cohen 2016). Women may be invited to address men on panels, but this presence does not mean that they are part of the club.

In retrospect, Maggie is not 100% certain why men ignore her: 'I'm not sure what it is'. Nonetheless, maturity is relayed as a defining factor for exclusion: 'if I was still pre-menopausal and attractive' but now she is 'part of the wallpaper'. Besides, would corporate men talk to a young woman in the same situation? Perhaps they would similarly ignore her, for a woman's expertise is difficult for corporate and political men to reconcile with (Shiva 2008, 2014; Terjesen et al. 2009; Maleta 2011a; Vildåsen et al. 2017). One's age, connected to the gendering of competence therefore frames women's otherness.

However, in the Greens party and grassroots-egalitarian based eSMOs, women do not experience this degree of otherness and tokenism (Mellor 1997; Carter 2007, 2013; Maleta 2011b; Gauja and Jackson 2016; Australian Greens, Gender Equality and Empowerment of Women, 2018). The notion of women being just as competent as the men is not second-guessed in such contexts and discourses. In my interviews, I have ample evidence that women out-perform men in the same roles, thereby disputing gender stereotypes of women's technical and scientific incompetence (Culley and Angelique 2003; Ahern and Hendryx 2008; RenewableUK 2017; STEMM 2018; WIE 2018). Rather than accommodating to middle class masculinity, women's performativity of emphasized femininity, defined by skills and the exercise of agency, foreground an active, engaged subversiveness, equally resistant to the patriarchal control of their eSMOs and the eNSM.

Women experience tokenism in urban and rural sociopolitical contexts. Previously, Greens politician Margaret assessed 'a boys club' within regional LGAs, and labelled women Councillors as 'token managers'. Drawing upon Margaret's judgement, I can deduce that 'a boys club' and gender tokenism, as examples of ruling-middle class masculinity, are pronounced in rural governance: 'There are some token managers. Out of 12 Councillors there's two women' ([audio] 2010). Again, this is not experienced within the Greens, but in Local Government Authorities (LGAs), constituted of diverse Councillors, representing the left to right spectrum of political persuasion. My evidence of Australian women's struggle with tokenism in regional politics, supports the work of Alston (2003, 2011, 2013) and Poiner (1990), who critiqued the lack of a gender-specific lens framing rural polities.

Another Greens politician, Maxine, questions why there were no 'women speakers' on a bushfire conference. This starkly contrasts with her party's 'pre-selection process':

> there was a conference… where are the women speakers? Like, where are female speakers on this whole thing? It was on bushfire, it's hard to get women speakers. Even when they had no women speakers in the scientists, they didn't think to get a woman speaker for a MC [Master of Ceremonies],

it wasn't on their radar... There was no rule around making sure we had to select women on to the executive. Some members of the executive said, it would be good if we had another woman or two. But it wasn't anything set? In the Greens, even our pre-selection process, when we select candidates, if the party votes three men in a row and a woman is number four, she'll get bumped up to two for gender equity in the top two.

(Maxine [audio] 2010)

In relation to this bushfire conference excerpt, Maxine censures women's absence from both scientific and sociopolitical (MC) performative roles. Also, Maxine's questioning of 'where are the women speakers?' suggests that women's deliberate placement, or even tokenism, is necessary for an equitable gender balance. Not having women at all, as Maxine struggled to contemplate, appears to be the worst gender effect. Although the conference organisers 'didn't think to get a woman speaker' for 'it wasn't on their radar', the Greens 'pre-selection process' ensures 'gender equity'. The Greens model is compatible to my quota-based modelling of minority women's (*my six groups*) WW & SE leadership equity. I strive to achieve 75% female representation in renewable scientific-technical development (McFarland 2014; Ajani 2015; Baruah 2016; RenewableUK 2017; Clean Energy Council 2018; WIE 2018). Both models are resistant to tokenism and gender labelling; in particular, I emphasise women's agentic performative skills-set, thereby envisioning a robust meritocracy as well as social egalitarian participatory democracy.

My interview-based research with women volunteers of the New South Wales Rural Fire Service (NSW RFS) considered firefighting to be a male-dominated culture framed by conceptual insights to hegemonic masculinity (Maleta 2009). Nonetheless, the voluntary nature of the work, and technological automation of equipment, enabled women to appropriate a role, traditionally accrued to a man – as often is the case in the urban fire services (Yoder and Aniakudo 1997; Maleta 2009). Also, I found that women demonstrated agentic competence in their firefighting performances, demystifying assumptions of women's technical and indeed physical incompetence (Cockburn 1988; Maleta 2009).

Still in the field of firefighting, women's dualist struggle with tokenism may be framed by one's sociocultural demographic status. In the context of U.S. urban firefighting, Yoder and Aniakudo addressed African-American women's experience of 'token difference' and 'subordination', foregrounding their status as dichotomous insider/outsider (1997: 336). On one level, they were included; but this was clouded by gender and racial bias, as the urban fire services attempted to diversify its workforce, from being dominated by White working class men (Yoder and Aniakudo 1997). As with my NSW RFS research (Maleta 2009), African-American women were competent fire fighters; however, a cultural environment conducive to one hegemon situated women's otherness and tokenism (Yoder and Aniakudo 1997; Maleta 2009). Moreover, my Bill, addresses racial/ethnic frames of (in)equity/(in)justice, by legislating on CALD and Indigenous women-led Initiatives. My conceptual application of egalitarianism, is an empowering feminist premise to redress patriarchal structures that position women as the other, even in the same organisation.

Concerning *my six groups*, I aim to legislate/advocate Initiatives, enabling socioeconomically disadvantaged (low SES) women's leadership in male-dominated sectors, such as science and politics (Maddison 2004; Maleta 2011b; STEMM 2018). Although Australia is not perceived to be a classist-society, postcolonial visions of egalitarianism, have yet to be realised (McGregor 2009; Donaldson and Poynting 2013; DAWN 2015; Veri 2016; ARM 2018). As my Act is centred on egalitarianism, supporting Initiatives should redress tokenism plus the sociocultural barriers and stigmas, hindering low SES women's leadership potential. In regard to token-exclusion, Maddison's study of young, working class women activists, in South-West Sydney, considered that: 'the political struggles of working class women have often been overlooked due to the sometimes hidden nature of their resistance to oppression and marginalisation' (2004: 38). Maddison located these young women as dualist 'insiders and outsiders' (2004: 38). Women's membership to the local feminist organisation, Young Women Who Are Parents Programme, moreover enabled their exercise of political agency and empowered collective identity (Maddison 2004: 38). My egalitarian model, draws inspiration from such grassroots women-led actions, for community leaders are integral for Republicanism. Social disadvantage does not diminish women's performativity, thus, reinforcing Maddison's insight to 'the sometimes hidden nature of their resistance' (2004: 38). Nonetheless, my Bill/Act illuminates women's visibility in sectors where they are still invisible (Kosny and MacEachen 2010; Ainsworth 2012; Hickman 2018; Patel 2018).

6.2 Discussion

As well as gendered tokenism, participants endure activist and ageist stigmas on panels (Duncan and Loretto 2004; Maleta 2012; Petherbridge 2014). Catherine's anti-mining protest, as part of a grassroots collective, was met with harsh judgment, accrued the label 'loony'. This except reveals how perceptions of activism intersect with gender:

> we protested and put in submissions against them (coal mines), I confronted [omit] to say, basically that this was going to affect our greenhouse gas emissions, I was looked at like a total loony, of course. But it was an all-male panel. It's very, very male, absolutely.
>
> (Catherine [audio] 2010)

Catherine connects tags of activism with 'an all-male panel', thus reinforcing how the experience was 'very, very male, absolutely'. Catherine's struggle with activist labels, underpins grassroots women's struggle to be taken seriously within the professional arm of the mining industry (Ahern and Hendryx 2008; Barry 2008; Irwin 2010; Gaard 2011; Maleta 2012). Women's grassroots competence is not receiving due recognition (Cockburn 1988;

Culley and Angelique 2003; Rees and Garnsey 2003; Ahern and Hendryx 2008). Tokenism encompasses both volunteer and professional women's dichotomous otherness as insider/outsider. Hence, the patriarchal control of panels frames women's inequity.

One's age, in terms of maturity and youth, evokes enablers/barriers, framed by competence, of which participants recognise/resist. Mature academics, such as Yvonne, Anna and Maggie, state that they are often the minority in senior scientific positions and on climate panels. Nonetheless, such placement points to their expertise, whilst challenging tokenism. Older Greens women, likewise, possess expert knowledge, but also struggle with 'the boys club' of Parliament. Young women, in my study, such as eNGO advocate Juliet, grassroots activist Wendy, and Greens politician Kate, add that age can act a barrier. But one's skill and passion for the cause challenges ageism. Juliet contemplates age and competence:

> I find my age, when I'm in meetings with senior government officials, I'm not taken as seriously as if someone who was 20 years older than me sitting, but it's not necessarily about my age per se, it's about my experience and knowledge and part of that is that I've been on this planet a lesser time than someone who's 20 years older who's had more exposure to issues or who has invested more time in becoming an expert in an area. But definitely at times, I feel that's a challenging factor… as soon as they meet you, they can guess roughly how old I might be.
>
> (Juliet [audio] 2010)

While Juliet contends she is 'not taken as seriously as if someone who was 20 years older', she disputes youth as the barrier: 'it's not necessarily about my age'. Rather the key factors are 'experience', 'knowledge' and being an 'expert in an area'. Undoubtedly, younger women possess less experience; but participants, like Juliet, do not permit age nor inexperience from preventing their competent performances: 'in meetings with senior government officials'. Juliet's interview suggests a thirst for acquiring more knowledge, thereby framing her leadership potential. My Act ensures women's equity at work is realised. As I address quotas on older women's leadership, I draw inspiration from young women's passion for the eNSM, especially in contexts susceptible to patriarchal privilege.

Still in the third sector, grassroots activist, Wendy, as a young woman on a media panel of experts, similarly doubted that she would be taken as seriously:

> I was more conscious about my age, potentially my cultural background, not so much my gender… It was more the age. I felt much younger, I feel at times our voice is less legitimate because we are less informed or have spent less time being experts. But, it doesn't mean that we are less legitimate. The youth voice is a very legitimate voice, especially on this issue.
>
> (Wendy [audio] 2010)

Wendy's retrospection is resistant to gender as a barrier: 'not so much my gender' or that being a woman is a form of othering or gender differentiation: 'I never thought about the women would have made much of a difference'. From Wendy's interview, one could deduce that competence, in terms of 'experts' and 'knowledge', prevails over gender tokenism: 'they have women on the panel'. Wendy's ([audio] 2010) subjective insight to 'age' and feeling 'younger' along with 'potentially' her 'cultural background', contextualise youth and ethnicity as dichotomous frames of identity/differentiation (Plumwood 1997, 2002; Butler 2004, 2007, 2015; Donaldson 2009; Wilson et al. 2010). My interviews reveal an intersection of essentialism and constructivism; on one hand, women are agentically performing/constructing their roles; on the other hand, they engage in critical self-reflections, framed by essentialised differences and notions of otherness (Glazebrook 2005; Plumwood 2006; Moore 2008; Mortimer-Sandilands 2008; Merchant 2013). Starkly, one's gender identity is not always a differentiator (Butler 1999, 2011). Despite young activists' having 'less time being experts' in comparison to the 'older leaders' and their knowledge-based '20 years of work', the voice of the youth is an empowering premise for social change: 'The youth voice is a very legitimate voice, especially on this issue' (Wendy [audio] 2010). While Wendy resists notions that the youth are 'less legitimate in terms of communication', knowledge does place youth in a complex position: 'definitely makes it harder to legitimise ourselves' ([audio] 2010). Whilst ageism entails barriers and enablers, participants' competent performances empower their agentic identities (Duncan and Loretto 2004; Maleta 2012; Butler 2013; Evans 2016; Edge et al. 2017). Older and young women's skilled panel performances downplay tokenism as a gender-specific barrier (Gupta 2007; Terjesen et al. 2009; Gheaus 2015; Pollack 2015; Cohen 2016).

Greens politicians recognise how age can act as a barrier, but their leadership performativity and resistance to men's dominance challenges tokenism. Kate is often the sole young woman in regional LGA meetings, but insists on being included:

> I am the only woman around the table of 40 men, they're at least 30 years older than me, and I have insisted on a seat at the table and being there. They found that challenging and confronting. Within the Greens, there's a very different vibe to it, we had a nearly all female campaign team in the Federal election.
>
> (Kate [audio] 2010)

Kate's reflection of the Local Government Councillors meeting frames chauvinism, age and male hegemony as dualist barriers: '40 men' who are 'at least 30 years older' than her. Older men recognise her presence as 'challenging and confronting', whereby their resistance signifies chauvinism towards young women leaders along with intersections of gendered-ageism (Cockburn 1991; Duncan and Loretto 2004; Doyle 2005; Duncan 2010; Edge et al. 2017). The fact that Australian politics is dominated by Anglo men, as Maxine ([audio]

2010) stated, 'old White men', I reiterate that ruling-middle class masculinity is a barrier to women's inclusion (Poynting and Donaldson 2005; Donaldson and Poynting 2007; McGregor 2009; Grusky 2014; DAWN 2015). Moreover, Kate's performative leadership prowess, as with other participants, challenges male hegemony and tokenism as a barrier: 'I have insisted on a seat at the table and being there'. Hence, Kate's active negotiation of agency, challenges the structural relations that privilege men's ruling power (MacLeod 1992; Connell 1995; Plumwood 1997; Butler 2004, 2007, 2011, 2013; Meynell 2009). The male dominance of the LGA meeting, sharply contrasts with Greens women's campaign leadership: 'Within the Greens, there's a very different vibe to it, we had a nearly all female campaign team in the Federal election' (Kate [audio] 2010).

Evidently, women demonstrate agentic performative expertise in panels, meeting and conferences; however, chauvinism and ageism underpin both younger and older participants' struggle with gender-organisational barriers and tokenism (Eriksson-Zetterquis and Styhre 2008; Terjesen et al. 2009; Yoder et al. 2011; Cook and Glass 2014; Gheaus 2015; Edge et al. 2017). As 'the other' to masculine hegemony, women continue to negotiate their roles as the dualist insider/outsider (Yoder and Aniakudo 1997; Maddison 2004; Maddison and Scalmer 2006; Wibben 2016; Gaard 2017; Nagy 2017). This othering is not entirely specific to the eNSM, but to the governing institutions they partake in – that is LGAs, Parliament and scientific academic panels – often assessed as 'boys clubs' (Forbes-Mewett and Snell 2006; Maleta 2011b; Fisher and Kinsey 2014; Cohen 2016). Women's experience of 'the boys club' encompasses their struggle with tokenism, along with the structural relations of power, privileging ruling-middle class industrial and governing elites (Gow and Leahy 2005; Faber 2008; Gerulis-Darcy 2010). In my conceptual framing of (in)equity/(in)justice, middle class men's power, as an extension of monarchist polities and ruling class elitism, hinders *my six groups'* greater leadership potential. Nevertheless, women's competent resistance to 'the boys club' and tokenism encompasses emphasized femininity constructivism, as an empowered subversion towards patriarchies and the ruling class.

6.3 Gender Barrier: Men Taking Credit for the Work of Women

In this section, the notion of token women is relayed by men taking credit for the work of salaried and grassroots women, whereby 'a boys club' underlies women's dualist experiences as insider/outsider in the executive arm of environmentalism. Although women demonstrate merit and prowess, they are continually differentiated because of their gender (Burn 2011; Sundström and McCright 2014; AHRC 2017b). Women's technical leadership competence and social change agendas, though, challenge tokenism and prejudices of female scientific incompetency (Cockburn 1988, 2012; Gheaus 2015; Farr et al. 2017; Irvine 2017). This section illustrates men and women's different leadership styles, with women assessed as 'conciliatory' and men more 'critical' and 'negative'. Men's behaviour underscores a type of middle-ruling class masculinity, contrasting with emphasized femininity performativity (Maleta 2015, 2018b). Patriarchy is, thus, a barrier to *my six groups* inclusion. Such barriers and tokenism are rationales for my Act's Initiatives, addressing women's (in)equity in science and other male-dominated sectors.

Regarding middle class masculinity, Catherine explains how women are doing the bulk of the grassroots work, but men scientists take credit for this on climate panels:

> Because what pisses me off, I went to the town hall a couple of weeks ago, there was this fantastic talk about beyond zero emissions, and there are these middle-aged balding men up there, every one of them, talking. I am thinking, where are the women? The women might be out on the ground doing all the work, but there's a lot of men out there taking all the kudos and writing the papers and writing the books.
>
> (Catherine [audio] 2010)

Catherine's censuring of 'middle-aged balding men' doing all the 'talking', is sharply contrasted with women's absence 'where are the women?' Maggie had remarked that she was invited to address corporate panels, relative to her expertise, but that the men ignored her afterwards. Whereas not having women speak on panels at all is contentious, particularly as it was their grassroots performativity that informed the talk: 'out on the ground doing all the work'. It is wrong and indeed unethical for men scientists to take credit for women's work, or even profess to be experts when their knowledge base encompasses a wider pool: 'a lot of men out there taking all the kudos and writing the papers and writing the books' (Catherine [audio] 2010). Activist women's articulation of climate science, without necessarily being experts, markedly downplays assumptions of grassroots women's technical and intellectual competence (Cockburn 1988; Probert and Wilson 1993; Culley and Angelique 2003, 2010; STEMM 2018). Hence, both grassroots and professional women possess the capacity to interpret science, but do not receive due recognition for their acquired and learned knowledge (Ahern and Hendryx 2008; Rentetzi 2008, 2010; Maleta 2012; Pollack 2015). While not a direct example of tokenism, women's invisibility on executive panels, in person and through writing, exemplifies how 'a boys club', reinforces gender barriers, ruling-middle class hegemonic masculinity as well as women's otherness.

Other participants detail the lack of recognition and merit accrued to grassroots women. As women and activists, women face dichotomous stigmas centred on perceptions of competence (Plumwood 1997, 2006; Barry 2008; Culley and Angelique 2010; Hosey 2011; Irvine 2017). The gendering of competence is pronounced within activism (Gaard 2001; Ahern and Hendryx 2008; Unger 2008; Maleta 2012). Whilst women are agentic performers, in paid and unpaid capacities, androcentrism is a barrier (Buckingham-Hatfield 2000; MacGregor 2006). In support, Dion outlines how scientific climate panels are dominated by men, whom take credit for grassroots women's work:

I went to a scientific panel, ten people, all men. You look at the stall, selling the reports and doing all the work behind the scenes, it's all women, there's definitely an element of that in the climate movement. There's some great women that do fantastic things in the climate movement, men are more likely to be the person who gets up in a room and says, 'We should be doing this. This is the wrong way forward', and be quite argumentative for no reason.

(Dion [audio] 2010)

Hegemonic ruling-middle class masculinity is pronounced within 'scientific panels' and 'the climate movement', as the 'ten people' speakers were 'all men'. I deduce from this climate panel excerpt, that 'a boys club' privileges men scientists and their hegemony, whilst excluding grassroots and professional women (Cohen 2016; Marfo 2017). However, women's emphasized femininity leadership and vibrant campaign competence is integral to the eNSM: 'You look at the stall, selling the reports and doing all the work behind the scenes, it's all women'. Whilst women are performing climate action initiatives, men's resistance to their expertise reveals a patriarchal culture conducive to chauvinism, misogyny and sexism (Arendt 1945; Gillard 2012; Hall 2013; Summers 2013; Manne 2017). Men's adversarial social engagement 'quite argumentative for no reason', frames hegemonic masculinity at play: 'We should be doing this. This is the wrong way forward'. Alternatively, women's emphasized femininity-constructivist performativity, is positively action-based: 'some great women that do fantastic things in the climate movement' (Dion [audio] 2010).

Regarding gender differentiated leadership, framed by intersections of hegemonic masculinity/emphasized femininity, women's more positive approach enables cohesive social and work relations within the eNSM and climate outcomes. For instance, Dion illustrated women's 'better' approach, in contrast to men's adversarial leadership styles:

Women are better at having more of a conciliatory approach. They're more happy to work together to come to a point, whereas a man is more likely to get up and say, 'I think this,' and 'What are you doing?' and definitely be more critical. The experiences I've had in the climate movement where people are directly critical and negative of what I'm doing, they're generally always men.

(Dion [audio] 2010)

Women's 'conciliatory' and 'happy to work together' social performances contrast with men's directly 'critical' and 'negative' androcentrism of women's leadership: 'What are you doing?' Dion's excerpt links masculinity to chauvinism and egoism: 'a man is more likely to get up and say, "I think this"'. But women's sense of self, or indeed self-esteem, as suggested above, is not defined by egoism or being the most obnoxious person on the panel. Women resist adversarial and aggressive 'masculinist' performances, and rather prefer to work harmoniously 'to come to a point'. I deduce that emphasized femininity performativity, akin to women-led 'conciliatory', 'happy' and 'work together' strategies, represents a positive framework for social change in climate-sustainability eNSMs, whilst challenging ruling-middle class masculinity and 'the boys club'.

The powerful status of men, relative to masculinist hegemony, pervading environmental executive hierarchies, places women in a complex position to perform their roles and to be respected as equals. Yet again, this struggle is feasible due to 'the boys club' privileging men and their hegemonic status (Connell 2005, 2009; MacGregor 2010, 2014; Marfo 2017; Nascimento and Connell 2017). Concerning uneven structural relations of power in IeNGOs, Linda blasted the 'powerful men in the movement' who 'disempower women' and 'give less regard to their viewpoint' (Linda [audio] 2010). Regarding structural power relations, Maggie elaborates on men's resistance to her leadership:

> I was deposed in my organisation by hierarchical males who were jealous of me. I hate hierarchy… we need a revolution. I don't mean blood and guts, but I mean a revolution. We had a revolution against the French tests and uranium mining… I believe in educating people and then they get out in the streets and take over… it's usually the women who induce changes and revolutions. Women started the Russian Revolution… they've usually induced most changes and then when we start to become successful the men stop putting us down, but they take over and take credit and that's happened to me time and again and it really pisses me off.
>
> (Maggie [audio] 2010)

When women work in the same jobs or organisations to men, their potential inclusion is hindered by men's active resistance to their leadership: 'I was deposed in my organisation by hierarchical males who were jealous of me'. Also, this statement underpins a highly emotive, androcentric response by men: 'jealous of me' (Maggie [audio] 2010). Such jealously locates the egoism of men, whom, in turn, cannot reconcile women's equity, nor women-led subversion: 'I don't mean blood and guts, but I mean a revolution'. Maggie is emotive in her response to men's deposition of her, using strong words like: 'I hate hierarchy… we need a revolution'. Maggie's retrospection condemns hierarchy, as a structural power relation, and patriarchy, as an interaction of ruling class masculinity, thereby arguing for a reactionary, sociopolitical change. Arguing for a 'revolution' is the ultimate expression of subversion, revealing overall dissatisfaction and one's incompatability with exiting cultural-structures of organisational governance (Arendt 1945, 1973; Doyle 2005; Merchant 2016).

Maggie's revolutionary frame is rooted in environmental change, whereby she draws inspiration from successful eNSMs led by women: 'We had a revolution against the French tests and uranium mining' ([audio] 2010). Also, Maggie's standpoint for change encompasses educative tools and grassroots democratic participatory action: 'I believe in educating people and then they get out in the streets and take over'. Education is a powerful tool for social change. Maggie's contention for greater grassroots participation signifies the validity of egalitarian-based social democratic action, dually informing my Initiatives. Social change is enabled through citizenry-based global action, whereby the power balance should shift to the grassroots, in particular, women leaders (Di Chiro 2008, 2011; Unger 2008; Mix 2011; Schlembach 2011). Women's greater participation in renewables technical-scientific development (akin to my Bill's Initiatives), should subvert the masculinist hegemony of hierarchical governing (political) and industrial (social) elites.

Maggie's interview frames the power of women-led strategies, validating my conceptual focus on emphasized femininity performativity through women's social change acts: 'it's usually the women who induce changes and revolutions. Women started the Russian Revolution' ([audio] 2010). While Maggie reasserts that women are competent, successful leaders: 'they've usually induced most changes', she attacks men's aggressive control over women-initiated campaigns/movements: 'when we start to become successful the men stop putting us down, but they take over and take credit and… it really pisses me off'. As with other participants in this section, the core gender barrier is men taking credit for women's grassroots and professional prowess, which is highly unethical and contentious. Yet, the gender enabler, for women, is their *agentic performative multiple skills-set*, framing 'change'. Comparatively, men's domineering adversarial and aggressive approach highlights hegemonic masculinity in action, whereas women-led strategies often out-perform that of men, whilst being resistant to their dominance (MacLeod 1992; Connell 1995; Plumwood 1997). Emphasized femininity constructivist performativity, akin to women's greater WW & SE leadership, frames my Bill of Rights Act's Initiatives, whilst challenging the patriarchal control of the eNSM and the hegemony of 'the boys club'.

6.4 Discussion

In summary, 'hierarchical males', assessed as 'negative' and 'critical', underscore women's struggle with androcentrism, framed by ruling-middle class masculinity and dominant social relations of power, reinforcing patriarchy as a gender-organisational barrier. Within executive hierarchies of the eNSM, women endure tokenism and prejudices, relative to false perceptions and harsh judgements, pertaining to their equal competence (to men) (Plumwood 1997; Ahern and Hendryx 2008; Connell 2009; Maleta 2012). This frames women's struggle to negotiate their agency and environmental change agendas (MacLeod 1992; Buckingham 2004; Butler 2004, 2007; Meynell 2009; Buckingham and Kulcur 2010; Buechler and Hanson 2015). Men's adversarial approach, that is resistant to women's leadership, underpins the dualist insider/outsider status of my diverse professional (salaried) and grassroots (voluntary) activists (Mellor 1997; Plumwood 1997; Buckingham-Hatfield 2000; Cadaret et al. 2017; Edge et al. 2017).

A core gender barrier is men taking credit for women's (professional and grassroots) performative prowess on climate panels and other executive meetings. This is starkly unethical but, on the other hand, reveals that women are successfully performing their scientific roles, thus disputing assumptions of women's technical-scientific incompetence (Cockburn 1988; Culley and Angelique 2003; Farr et al. 2017; STEMM 2018). Nevertheless, participants' gendered tokenism, provides evidence to 'the boys club' effect, in which ruling-middle class hegemonic masculinity, operating within the hierarchical, executive structures of the eNSM, hinders women's equity/justice (Connell 2005; Donaldson 2009; Maleta 2011b; Pollack 2015; Marfo 2017). Hence, middle class men's hegemonic dominance of the executive arm of the eNSM and its eSMOs, is a core barrier to women's greater leadership aspirations (Connell 2005; Bombora Wave Power 2018; Carnegie Clean Energy 2018; EREF 2018; EUREC 2018; SolarPower Europe 2018).

However, women-led agentic-social change strategies, akin to emphasized femininity performativity, entail successful resistance to men's hegemony, evaluated as 'aggressive' and 'adversarial', as Maggie ([audio] 2010) contemplated: 'they've [women] usually induced most changes'. Drawing upon Dion's ([audio] 2010) retrospection, I can deduce that emphasized femininity encompasses a 'more conciliatory approach', for women are 'more happy to work together to come to a point'. Women's engaged, collaborative performativity contributes to productive social and work relations, and greater social change. My aspiration for a Republican-Constitutional change depends upon grassroots and professional women's engaged, egalitarian leadership performances that are unified, but similarly resistant to hierarchical elites' supreme command status (MacLeod 1992; Connell 1995; Plumwood 1997; Butler 2007, 2013). My Bill's Initiatives, legislating/advocating on women-led scientific-technological renewable development, should achieve gender and environmental equity/justice outcomes. Further, women's emphasized femininity-constructivist performativity, strives to subvert patriarchy as a barrier across the eNSM.

Conclusion

This chapter has investigated tokenism and gender barriers, evidenced by the way Greens, academic, eNGO and grassroots women recognise/resist ruling-middle class masculinity and recognise/accommodate emphasized femininity performativity. Within the eNSM/eSMOs, my participants critiqued elite males, in control of industry and politics. The patriarchal control of environmental politics reinforces women's otherness and dualist insider/outsider status in climate panels and meetings, even in their own organisations (Plumwood 1997; Yoder and Aniakudo 1997; Maddison 2004; Maleta 2011b, 2018a). Differentiation is replicated through uneven structural relations of power, in which men/masculinities are privileged (Connell 1995; Mellor 1997; Buckingham-Hatfield 2000; Segal 2007; Gaard 2017; Nascimento and Connell 2017). Men's cultural hegemony is evident in Parliament, scientific panels, corporate boards, Professorship posts and 'the executive arm of the [eNGO] movement', to name a few. Patriarchy is a core gender barrier, whilst hierarchy is a core organisational barrier; both underpin women's dichotomous struggle to be recognised as competent experts (Plumwood 1997; Culley and Angelique 2003; Cockburn 2012, 2013; Maleta 2012; Walby 2012, 2013). Whilst Greens women members enjoy progressive internal gender equity, they struggled with 'the boys club' of Parliament and men's adversity towards them on male-dominated LGA meetings. Gendered tokenism, sex-segregation and glass ceilings, framed by ruling-middle class masculinity, therefore, underscore women's (in)equity/(in)justice, even in the 21st century (Cockburn 1991; Connell 2005, 2009; Pocock 2005; Walby 2011; Pocock et al. 2013).

Arguably, women work better in organisations informed by egalitarian principles and flatter structures, such as less-hierarchical, grassroots-based eNGOs (Doyle 2005; MacGregor 2006; Yoder et al. 2011; Maleta 2015). In support, Catherine ([audio] 2010) criticised the masculinised centralisation of the coal industry, whilst Maggie ([audio] 2010) challenged 'hierarchical males', opposing her expertise on corporate panels. My emphasized femininity focus on women-led agentic constructivist performativity, is also evidenced by radical strategic activism (Plumwood 1997; Barry 2008; Schlembach 2011; Cockburn 2012; Cockburn and Enloe 2012). Maggie ([audio] 2010) states that what is needed is 'change' and 'revolution', as a form of subversion to 'hierarchical males', but also legislation on gender equity reforms plus greater focus on renewables outcomes. Women's WW & SE social change leadership is crucial. Maggie's earlier commentary (academic section) criticised women who act like men in politics: 'the Thatchers...', whereas women need to exercise their agency and 'use their power' ([audio] 2010). In relation to emphasized femininity, Maggie's retrospection intersects essentialism/constructivism, framed through women's leadership qualities: 'We're voting for milk for children. That's got nothing to do with political lines. It's across the board, because we're nurturing and understand the intrinsic value of life. We're not into power and that terribly nasty stuff that men tend to play act' ([audio] 2010). Also, Dion commented that men were 'critical' and 'negative', whereas 'women have more of a conciliatory approach' ([audio] 2010). Such women-led strategies enable me to highlight emphasized femininity as a poignant yet compelling resistance strategy to hegemonic masculinity (Connell 2002; Leahy 2003; Donaldson and Poynting 2007, 2013).

Although emphasized femininity alludes to essentialised femininity, as *a traditional or subordinate type of femininity*, this is somewhat misleading, for women-led-emphasized strategies *are the stage for change*. My Bill of Rights is centred on women-led change, in which Initiatives should subvert androcentrism and patriarchy. In my conceptual scope, women's emphasized femininity leadership is defined by their constructive, active engagement and self-reflexive approach to work and their identity (Connell 1995; Plumwood 1997; Butler 1999, 2007, 2015). Drawing upon the Butlerian premise of gender as a 'process of doing', women's performative multiple skills-set, along with merit and social change goals, challenges the tag of 'token women' and 'the boys club' (MacLeod 1992; Butler 2004, 2007, 2013; Cohen 2016). It is wrong to assume that women are not as scientifically or technically competent as men (Culley and Angelique 2003,

2010; Maleta 2012, 2018b). After all, women often out-perform men. Yet, this does not hinder men from taking credit for women's grassroots or professional work on climate panels. My research thus questions the normative association of men/masculinities with superior competence, agency, rationality, intellect and strength (Cockburn 1988; Buckingham-Hatfield 2000; McNay 2000, 2003; Donaldson 2009; Meynell 2009; Butler 2013; Wibben 2016).

Women's emphasized femininity-aligned renewables leadership, demonstrated through robust social movement engagement, is making a positive difference in the world. Women-led prowess destabilises gender differentiation, the sexual division of labour, glass ceilings plus the patriarchal control of organisations (Mies 1986; Walby 1990; Probert 2005; Cook and Glass 2014; AHRC 2017a, 2017b; STEMM 2018). Patriarchal hierarchies should be resisted, in order to achieve: (feminist) women's equitable leadership, social (Republican) change outcomes, (egalitarian) less bureaucracy and more collaboration, and technical-scientific development (renewables/environmentalist) outcomes. Such resistance should revitalise the women's, environmental and Indigenous NSMs (Maddison 2004; McLellan 2009; Brennan 2015; Prokhovnik 2015; Kermoal et al. 2016; Gaard 2017).

The collective activism of participants is sustaining and renewing the women's and environmental NSMs, whilst subverting gendered prejudices. Women's movements are evolving and changing; they are not static or fixed in time (Taylor 1989; Cockburn 2000; Grey and Sawer 2008; McLellan 2009). Participants' engaged agentic performativity underpins the mobile hegemony of power relations within structural hierarchies, and is subject to feminist resistance and change (MacLeod 1992; Plumwood 1997; Connell 2002, 2005; Butler 2011, 2015). Maddison (2004) contends that although young Australian women's activism is less visible to prior generations, their social change activism is sustaining the ideologies and networks necessary for a strong wave of feminist activism to re-emerge.

Emphasized femininity, via empowering, progressive women-led WW & SE strategies, is a compelling resistance strategy to hegemonic middle-ruling class masculinity (McFarland 2014; Ajani 2015; Marfo 2017; RenewableUK 2017; Clean Energy Council 2018; WIE 2018). Participants' resistant femininities enable me to situate gender as an active performance, situated in competence and subversion to patriarchy (MacLeod 1992; Connell 1995, 2005; Plumwood 1997; Leahy 2003). Arguably, hegemonic masculinity is weakening, whilst emphasized femininity performativity is being revitalised; reiterating Connell's (1995) point that hegemony is not fixed nor stationary, but mobile and fluid. Indeed, women are articulate gender performers and political negotiators, whom achieve results and work well with women – and men – who share similar ideologies and goals (Connell 2005; Maleta 2012, 2018b). An overarching goal of feminism is to empower women as individuals and a collective, and to improve their work and social relations with men.

My EEO Social Democratic model, centred on Republicanism and Egalitarianism, aspires to have more women of CALD, Indigenous, low SES, older, Anglo and disabled statuses (*my six groups*) in technological-scientific leadership, in order to realise my feminist and renewables ambitions (STEMM 2018; WIE 2018). The marginalisation of such groups is dire (Cooper 2013; AHRC 2016b; Canty 2017; Edge et al. 2017). Women possess the agentic power, to succeed where men have failed, reiterating Maggie's ([audio] 2010) point. In my argument, overtly bureaucratic organisations appear to be run like machines, rather than enabling women's creative flair and intellectual scope. My Bill of Rights Act's legislation of Initiatives (plus quotas) ensure that women's skills-sets and merits are endorsed in renewables governance. My groups' inclusion, contrasting to their otherness, is achievable through the advent of Australian Republicanism (Arendt 1945; Veri 2016; ARM 2018; Patel 2018). Without a Republic, nothing will change concerning *my six groups* status. Hence, my book *Feminism, Republicanism, Egalitarianism Environmentalism*, framed by emphasized femininity-constructivist performativity, challenges ruling-middle class masculinity. My methodological ambition is to also highlight governing and industrial elites' conservativism and resistant approach to sustainable reforms. The next chapter also considers gender barriers/enablers, relative to my Republican-Bill's modelling of women-led WW & SE performativity. I consider women's struggles and efforts, in light of their performative multiple skills-set, and women-led subversion to patriarchy within environmental organisational governance.

Part III
Emphasized Femininity as an Agentic Performance

7   An Agentic Performative Multi-Skills-Set Within Environmentalism

Introduction

This chapter illuminates the diverse skills-set of my women participants, pertaining to multiple forms of leadership competence: scientific, technological/ technical, intellectual, social, egalitarian, empathetic and physical. Within eSMOs/eNSMs, I address gendered performances, intersections of constructivism and essentialism, and emphasized femininity agentic resistance towards ruling-middle class masculinity and patriarchy (Berg and Lie 1995; Crary 2001; Leahy 2003; Connell 2005; Butler 2007, 2013; Donaldson and Poynting 2013; Wibben 2016; Nagy 2017). Women's performative technical and social competencies are assessed as constructivist, for skill-based merit challenges essentialist assumptions that women are less suited to scientific leadership (MacGregor 2010; Keller 2012; Cadaret et al. 2017; Vildåsen et al. 2017). Women's 'doing of gender' thereby challenges stigmas associated with female intellectual incompetence (Cockburn 1988; Butler 1990, 1999; Culley and Angelique 2003, 2010). Rather women play a crucial role in the future of renewables technological development (Gaard 2001; McFarland 2014; Ajani 2015; RenewableUK 2017; BWE 2018; WIE 2018). However, global renewable executive boards are male-dominated, framing men's privileged leadership status (Bombora Wave Power 2018; Carnegie Clean Energy 2018; EREF 2018; EUREC 2018). Moreover, my quota-centred EEO model (akin to my Bill's Initiatives) legislates on women's leadership, ensuring women are equitably/justly represented in scientific research and management.

Environmental ethics, relative to empathy-based ethical-simplicity, underpins my scope for greater sustainable living, encompassing work, political and everyday life (Eder 1996; Warren 1997, 1999; Glazebrook 2005; Plumwood 2006; Maleta 2011b; Valles 2015; Wibben 2016). Arguably, renewable energy represents an opportunity for individual citizens to exercise their agency over their own consumption. My Republican vision is not based on a replication of corporate or government power; rather it is centred on women's greater agency over their energy output and greater leadership of renewables development. My egalitarian-socioecological democratic feminist participatory model looks to the reactionary yet progressive era of Red Vienna, and its art nouveau creative-technological flair, for inspiration (Blau 1999; Rentetzi 2004, 2010; Kershaw 2013; Mattl

2013, 2016). I add that my vision of sustainable technological development, akin to environmental ethics and sustainable-simplicity, is 'revolutionary' in its scope, thereby, supporting the 'revolutionary' vison of Maggie and other women constituting my study.

7.1 Communicational Skills: Written and Oral Prowess

The environmental competency of salaried and voluntary participants is relayed by their aural and written communication skills, along with prowess in negotiation and lobbying strategies. These excerpts highlight professional and grassroots women's multiple skills-set, and how diverse sector engagement is contributing knowledge and scope for social change:

> To be effective, you need to communicate well in written and oral form. You need to be a good teacher because the most important group that we influence are our students. I think people need to work hard; it comes back to deciding how best you can use your time to influence things. It would be better if I could do less things but do them better.
>
> (Yvonne [audio] 2010)

> Communication is important, not only the spoken but also written. One thing that is beneficial is good people skills. My people skills aren't as good as they could be. I'm more into going out by myself and do some weeding. In my activist role, you are talking to the public, politicians; communication is important.
>
> (Gillian [audio] 2009)

> The commonalities are basic skills, being able to communicate verbally and relate to people, interpersonal skills are important. You need to be in a relationship with your boss and colleagues, and doing that in a climate sense, on a stall talking to people. Written skills, we've written grants for our climate group. Those communication skills are critical. Our group has different skills sets, but I have inside information on how the government works, and that can be useful in looking at what's realistic in our achievements and what we plan to achieve as a group.
>
> (Dion [audio] 2010)

> Understand the Internet, Web skills and design skills, understand management, handle funds, to deal with people... I would like to learn more about movements, how I can bring my strengths. I have unique strengths that not a lot of people have in [omit country]... Internet skills, writing skills, online campaigning. I would like to take the skills from Australia, and see how things could be changed.
>
> (Wendy [audio] 2010)

7.2 Discussion

The agentic competence of professional and grassroots women participants (Yvonne, Gillian, Dion, Wendy) is demonstrated through a robust performative skills set: written and oral, time allocation and prioritising, campaign strategy, technical and web literacy, academic and professional competency plus political literacy (Yoder et al. 2011; Keller 2012; Sasser 2014; Wibben 2016). Skills are acquired through formal training or practical experiences on field sites, whereby academic competency is performed by employees and volunteers (Maddison and Scalmer 2006; Keller 2012). Women's performativity encompasses flexibility and meaning-making; academic activists perform well in grassroots campaigns while grassroots women perform competently in their political lobbying efforts.

In the supporting literature, Culley and Angelique (2003, 2010) outlined the professional competency of grassroots anti-nuclear campaigners, in how women's self-acquired knowledge of nuclear technology and jargon (without being experts) challenged the patriarchal control of the nuclear industry. Applied practical knowledge informs grassroots volunteers expertise, even without formal qualifications (Maddison 2004; Maddison and Scalmer 2006). The academic competence of grassroots (and professional) women, symbolises a vibrant intersection of constructivism/essentialism, challenging tags of female incompetence in scientific endeavours and stereotypes of appropriate female roles (Berg and Lie 1995; Gaard 2011; Pollack 2015; Valles 2015; Farr et al. 2017). Although patriarchal hierarchies and gendered dualisms, informed by dominant notions of hegemonic masculinity and 'subordinate' notions of essentialised femininity, are barriers to participatory inclusion (Plumwood 1997; Buckingham-Hatfield 2000; Leahy 2003), the merit shown by women in formal and informal advocacy further illustrates their agentic (negotiation of power) sustainable competence (technological-scientific leadership).

Historically, empathy has been associated with emphasized or even 'subordinate' forms of femininity (Plumwood 1997; Buckingham-Hatfield 2000). However, I argue that empathy entails an empowering constructivist social change approach. Empathy informs participants' leadership competence, whereby empathy and egalitarianism frame the conceptual focus of my Initiatives, aspiring to have more women in male-dominated fields. An empathetic-egalitarian approach enhances the technical-scientific work of women partaking in the eNSM/eSMOs (Gaard 2001, 2011, 2015; Alston 2013; Shiva 2014).

7.3 Scientific Competence: A Technical-Intellectual Framing of Change

My participants perform outstanding degrees of scientific, technical, intellectual, social, empathy, physical and leadership competence in their work. ENGO advocate Barbara has a PhD in Humanities, but no formal training in science;

yet, through acquired knowledge, works in a scientific capacity in her eNSMO. She has an intellectual flair for science, and interest in technical aspects of environmentalism and anti-toxic campaigns:

> understands the technical side like I do, as well as the campaign side... I went to a really good high school, and even though I didn't do a science degree, I did five years up to the senior level of chemistry, physics and maths. I got very high marks. When I started at [omit] I slipped into the environmental chemistry really easily. I associated with older guys who were environmental sort of people who knew about chemistry, who worked in the environment movement.
>
> (Barbara [audio] 2010)

Barbara's literacy in chemistry, physics and maths represents expert knowledge and informs her environmental campaign advocacy. Also, the above account underscores masculine performativity, pertaining to the chemistry competence of the 'older guys' in the eNSM. It was men's competence that Barbara initially identified with. Men were perceived as role models, whom Barbara had a rapport with. Through positive work relations, Barbara was an insider; but she was also an outsider, as the sole female, in a male-dominated field (Maddison 2004). Whilst I esteem Barbara's technical competence in 'environmental chemistry', I stress the problem of women's absence in environmental science (Maleta 2015, 2018b; STEMM 2018). This suggests the necessity of my EEO-framed, Bill of Rights Act's Initiatives, centring on women-led technological-scientific development.

Technological-intellectual competence underpins the work identity of Barbara in her eNSMO, as she describes herself as: 'an Australian Greenie', 'an independent thinker', 'interdisciplinary thinker' and 'intergenerational activist' ([audio] 2010). Additionally, Barbara aims to 'pass the baton' onto 'the next generation', enabling young people with 'better tools'. Hence, technology is an empowering tool, that can and should be appropriated for environmental change: 'I don't mean computers. Computers are tools, not masters. Now technology is the master' (Barbara [audio] 2010). Regarding the mastery of technology, Barbara engaged with the media, on visual and print productions, including television appearances and writing feminist publications 'on green issues', for whcih she was paid. Advocacy/activism, involves professional and grassroots responsibilities, for which women receive payment and, at other times, perform their roles voluntarily. Hence, environmentalism is not simply a nine to five job. It entails public and professional responsibilities; conceptually framed by a social democratic egalitarian model, which Maggie likewise endorses. One's intellectual engagement with technology, and appropriation of this to one's activism, contributes cutting-edge knowledge to the eNSM.

Barbara's mastery of technology was appropriated in her leadership of feminist and environmental justice campaigns. Although 'the master' is traditionally construed as masculine, in terms of the dualist 'skilled man/Master of Technology', participants' appropriation of technology in their environmental agendas signifies

constructivist empowerment, whilst challenging essentialist views of masculinity/
femininity (Plumwood 1997, 2002; Mortimer-Sandilands 2008; Gaard 2011).
Women's technical competence, in turn, challenges the masculine mastery of
technology, and enables me to emphasise constructivism over essentialism, whilst
subverting tags of female technical incompetence (Cockburn 1988; Maleta 2012).
Women are construing their identities by engaging with technology, thereby
constructivist-performative action similarly challenges biological assumptions of
women's 'natural aptitude' and capacity to comprehend 'the masculine world'.
Women's prowess encompasses empowering acts of emphasized femininity
performativity, thus challenging the androcentrism of scientific technology
(Buckingham-Hatfield 2000; Connell 2005; MacGregor 2006; Merchant 2013,
2016; Cadaret et al. 2017).

Technical scientific competencies within environmentalism and feminism
are evident through Barbara's core two campaign initiatives: anti-toxic waste
actions against pesticides, and advocacy for young mothers' rights to healthy
reproduction. Barbara's resistance to the corporate control of baby food is
juxtaposed to an emphasis on 'maternal' breast feeding. Following anti-Vietnam
war actions, Barbara's role of mother inspired her anti-toxic campaigns, aiming to
achieve healthy reproduction for mothers and their babies:

> one of my main drivers on my work on pollution was the chemicals... work
> on birth defects. So, yeah, and on breast feeding protection against bottles,
> you know, sticking bottles in newborn babies mothers'... my early justice
> work was about women's, the diet, the mother and the child, their right to
> healthy reproduction.
>
> (Barbara [audio] 2010)

Barbara's emphasized femininity nurturing identity, as a concerned-activist
mother, involves challenging corporations control of baby bottles, as a toxic
chemical pollutant, and advocating on 'women's justice' relative to the rights
of 'mother and child' to 'healthy reproduction' ([audio] 2010). This account
highlights interplays of constructivism (resistance to corporates) and essentialism
(advocating mother's independence in child rearing). Breast feeding, as a natural
physical function, along with resistance to corporatised plastic bottles, represent
emphasized femininity performativity, undermining the patriarchal control of
health and baby products (Maleta 2015). Also, Barbara's advocacy/activism
transcends core NSMs, with campaign initiatives centred on: environmental
justice, anti-toxic waste, women's liberation (historic and contemporary), human
rights, anti-war and peace (Warren 1999; Stein 2004; Keller 2012; Cockburn
2013). Barbara's interview points to 'political elements' within activism,
highlighting the complex power relations framing social change. Moreover,
mothers have the power to challenge the monopoly of corporates.

Concerning agentic competence, Maggie adds that women have superior
intellect and sharp skills; nonetheless, they are not exercising their agency: 'women
are very intelligent... and they're very good at conflict resolution too. Men
aren't... on the whole they're not and yet somehow we've given up our power...'

Maggie's esteem of women's competence, contrasting with men's weaknesses in 'conflict resolution', underpins a dualist critique of their lack of engagement with power relations: 'we've given up our power'. This reveals an intersection of constructivism (women's intellect and conflict resolution skills) and essentialism (denial of agentic power). An emphasis on women's skilled conflict resolution informs emphasized femininity resistance to patriarchy, and the power of women-led agentic performative strategies towards achieving environmental change outcomes. More women leaders of WW & SE technologies, as legislated in my Initiatives, is framed by equity/justice, and through prowess, women should succeed, where men have comparatively failed (MacGregor 2010, 2014; Maleta 2018a, 2018b).

Markedly, Maggie's argument for a gender equity law is an aspirational EEO platform, to ensure that women are equally represented in organisational governance. Although there is no universal gender equity law; rather there are anti-discriminatory measures (EEO 2016); my Act is centred on women's scientific and political leadership (*my six groups*), supported by quotas. Such legislative action, framed by women's performative prowess and merit, should inspire global feminists. Quotas ensure equity and merit as a basis from which women can elevate their careers and statuses whilst contributing to renewables development. Such civil legislation challenges glass ceilings and gender barriers as well as 'the boys club' and ruling-middle class men's hegemony (Connell 1995, 2002; Maleta 2012; Pollack 2015; Cohen 2016; Edge et al. 2017).

My methodological ambition is to address women's inequity through women-led Initiatives in male-dominated sectors, such as environmental science and politics. As mentioned, women are just as competent as men – and often out-perform men – in management positions. Participant Rachel outlines the 'equal abilities' of both genders, but also adds that men play a role in women's advocacy:

> I believe both women and men have equal abilities, particularly intellectually. I've seen some fine advocates for women's rights and fine advocates who are men. I think merit is equal between men and women. I think people should be recognised for their abilities, on their merits, irrespective of their gender.
>
> (Rachel [audio] 2010)

This retrospection does not give ground for a gender equity law (as advocated by Maggie and Maxine), for is situated in a merit-based system, rather than quota-based model. Likewise, my model is merit-based, but contends that *my six groups'* marginalisation is grounds for quotas, in order to elevate disabled, low SES and CALD (amongst others) women's workplace participation. Drawing upon STEMM (2018), my civil-rights-framed Bill of Rights Act sets out achievable, realistic female-led quotas (McFarland 2014; Ajani 2015; Baruah 2016; RenewableUK 2017). Regarding Rachel's ([audio] 2010) stand on gender neutrality: 'equal abilities' and 'equal merit', in other sections of her interview, she adds that men tend to be promoted above women. Her comments underpin the existence of glass ceilings and gender barriers (Connell 2009; Maleta

2011a; Walby 2011; Cook and Glass 2014). Rachel's commentary also points to essentialism and constructivism. On one level, participants dispute skilled differences, but, on another level, contend that women experience gender differences. This is accentuated by men's resistance to women's leadership, particularly, in the executive arm of the eNSM, as Barbara and others remarked (Cockburn 1991; Wright and Holland 2014; Marfo 2017). For this reason, male-dominated structures reinforce patriarchy as pervasive (Walby 2013; Cadaret et al. 2017; Edge et al. 2017). Nonetheless, women's performative multi-skills-set confronts this.

Academic participant Yvonne also esteems intellectual competence as a measure informing scientific prowess. The following excerpts showcase the power of scientific and social competence as measures for environmental change. Further, the role of education is crucial within academia.

> To be effective well you have to have a certain level of intelligence, I suppose. Ah, you need to be able to communicate well in both written and oral form. I mean some people are better at one than the other. I think you need to be a good teacher because... the most important group that we influence are our students you know, from an academic perspective... people need to work hard because there's a lot to do... it comes back to prioritising, deciding what you're good at, deciding how best to, how best you can use your time to influence things.
>
> (Yvonne [audio] 2010)

Yvonne points to biological aptitude and that one's effective performance is dependent upon internal strengths, such as 'intelligence', along with diligence: 'work hard' and organisational skills: 'prioritising' and 'deciding what you're good at' in order 'to influence things'. It is mandatory to be an excellent communicator of knowledge: 'both written and oral form', whereby academic expertise is crucial, and being able to communicate this to students: 'you need to be a good teacher'. Oral and written skills showcase well-rounded intellectual and practical competencies. Also, academic competency depends upon specialisation, as Yvonne ([audio] 2010) explains: 'I have this tendency to spread myself too thinly, and it would be better if I could... do less things but do them better'. While Yvonne has turned down work opportunities as a scientist, it is preferable to 'focus on fewer things, but do them better'. Hence, one's expert intellectualism and social engagement (with students) highlights the *agentic performative multiple skills-set* of participants within environmental science (Cudworth 2002, 2012; Merchant 2013, 2016).

Yvonne's intellectual scientific competence is demonstrated by publications, representing measures of knowledge, in which one's: 'effectiveness and productivity is judged' ([audio] 2010). Publications are sought within the scientific community, whilst being a frame for promotions and career mobility. One's academic recognition depends upon publications:

> Well publications are the mechanism by which science is communicated. If we don't publish we may as well not do it. I mean if you do something

and you don't publish it, it's a waste of time... you don't get promoted in a university without publications.

(Yvonne [audio] 2010)

7.4 Academic Scientific Expertise

Scientific competence is measurable by women's senior leadership or executive positions within academic institutions. Academic Anna's interview revealed that women are indeed acquiring senior roles at universities; however, men (since the 1950s) still hold a monopoly on higher-status, scientific decision-making positions (Gaard 2015; Pollack 2015; Valles 2015; Cadaret et al. 2017; Farr et al. 2017). In a historical context, Anna contemplated men's over-representation as scientists and women's over-representation as technicians. Anna's recollection contrasts with Rentetzi's (2004, 2008, 2010) research on Red Vienna, whereby women represented one third of science researcher staff at the Institute for Radium Research, rather than as support or administrative staff. Women, in my study, nonetheless, perform responsible decision-making roles, such as, departmental heads:

> Ultimately the responsibility is mine within the department. There are some decisions... that say involve, you know, large amounts of money or whatever that I would need to consult with my boss who's the dean of science, umm, but so sometimes I have to kind of pass the buck up the, up the ladder, but ultimately most decisions in the department are my responsibility.
>
> (Anna [audio] 2010)

As Head of Department, Yvonne is the key decision-maker: 'the responsibility is mine'. This decision-making process is somewhat curtailed by an executive hierarchy, or chain of command: 'consult with my boss who's the dean of science', concerning 'large amounts of money'. Although Yvonne asserts that 'most decisions in the department' are her responsibility and that women are increasingly acquiring Professorship posts, her overall interview (prior discussion on gender barriers/tokenism), revealed that the senior echelons of academia are male-dominated. This reflects that patriarchy is a barrier. Whilst the STEMM (2018) programme's focus on more women in science is realised by women scientists' achievement as heads of departments; this is framed by a historic male privilege and cultural structures conducive to men's hegemon. The Head of Department position may be critiqued as an administrative rather than scientific role. Such a role has limitations in terms of scientific innovativeness and being able to contribute to the field. Yvonne perceive this as largely an administrative role, entailing barriers to her climate objectives:

> I'm a Professor at [omit]. I'm currently Head of Department [omit], which is a three year temporary position. So yeah, my main challenge on a day to day basis is juggling my time between my administrative responsibilities... and the things I really want to do which is more research on climate change.
>
> (Yvonne [audio] 2010)

The Head of Department is a significant management position within academia; nonetheless, a feminist critique can be applied here, to being more administrative (female-oriented), rather than scientific (Cockburn 1988; Probert 2005; Alston 2011, 2013). After all, Yvonne claims that 'administrative responsibilities' were a barrier to her career and personal goals: 'I really want to do... more research on climate change'.

Participants' environmental leadership is strengthened through their professional qualifications and personal goals for social change. The bridging of physical (environmental) and social (human) sciences guides Helen's advocacy, further evident by an interdisciplinary PhD qualification. As a former eNGO Director, Helen developed a strong affinity with third-sector networks as well as collaborative leadership and management skills. As a scientific employee in a research consultancy, Helen draws inspiration from her eSMO role and from her PhD, as a foundation to develop her qualitative expertise whilst bridging the physical and social sciences:

> I mean, having a PhD is really important, [omit organisation] really values them. Umm, my networks that I've built up over the years, my leadership and management skills, most particularly from running [omit] as an organisation, my bridging of both physical sciences and social sciences, umm, they are probably the main things. Plus, you know, practical skills in social research and application of different methodologies... my PhD was all qualitative.
>
> (Helen [audio] 2010)

7.5 To Make a Difference

Across my salaried and volunteer interviews, women, like Helen (as above), Yvonne, Maggie, Catherine, Dion (to name a few), share ambitions for environmental change, performed across a spectrum of professional and grassroots contexts (Leahy 2003, 2008; Schlembach 2011; Buechler and Hanson 2015). Helen emphasised the power of 'social research', 'practical skills' and 'the application of different methodologies', in particular, a qualitative approach, as informing her eSMO engagement and climate action objectives. Around the world, women's professional and grassroots leadership is enacted in diverse, cutting-edge campaigns: sustainability, climate action, anti-nuclear and anti-toxic-waste (Di Chiro 2008; Irwin 2010; Marshall 2011; Davis 2015; WIE 2018).

Academics elaborate on the importance of public advocacy as a strategic way to make a difference. As a climate scientist, who performs public talks (without payment), Yvonne stresses that publications are not the only tools, but that her goal is to make 'a difference'. Providing up-to-date expert knowledge to the community, through talks, is part of Yvonne's social engagement and educative framework. In relation to Yvonne, being a scientist, without advocacy or activism is somewhat redundant; the social interaction – that is engagement with the community – is vital for social change to occur. Such engagement is egalitarian: for an anticipated renewable change to occur there needs to be strong network between scientists and community activists and campaign leaders. Yvonne's community talks thereby inform grassroots participatory democratic action. Hence, academic activism performativity entails intellectual, social and egalitarian competencies. Intellectual competence entails scientific knowledge through publications while the dissemination of expert information through public talks entails social competence, along with collaborative scientist-grassroots networks, as platforms for climate action: 'only publishing in the scientific literature is not enough… you have to get out and sell a message more widely than that, which is why I do the public stuff' (Yvonne [audio] 2010).

ENGO women also consider the transformative power of education, as a strategic social change tool, highlighting integrated academic and social scientific competencies. For some participants, 'change' is only achievable by leaving one's vocation:

> I used to be a science teacher… I don't want to go back to teaching, so I thought I have got to change things… We need to change the environment to make it more sustainable, so you have to have the knowledge side, you can't do this job without understanding the fundamentals.
>
> (Deborah [audio] 2010)

Deborah's decision to leave teaching and pursue postgraduate qualifications in environmental management was motivated by mutual professional-personal objectives: to achieve environmental change through sustainable management initiatives. Her goal to 'change things', is informed by 'knowledge' and 'understanding the fundamentals' (Deborah [audio] 2010). This highlights Deborah's intellectual-scientific competence and managerial skills. Knowledge surrounding the management, responsibility and accountability of the environment, relative to qualifications and performative eSMO campaign leadership, is strengthened through a specialist focus. Deborah elaborates how eNGO advocacy enabled her to engage with leaders:

> The reason I gave up teaching in the first place cause I thought, well I teach a hundred students and I can only influence a hundred students. If I am doing the job I am doing now, the outreach work… I am contacting hundreds of people, you're not influencing the way Australia does its business.
>
> (Deborah [audio] 2010)

The last statement: 'influencing the way Australia does its business', shows that sustainable change is dependent upon professional diverse sector collaboration, networking strategies and negotiations with sustainable business and governmental leaders. The above commentary also suggests that current organisational structures are not conducive to greater sustainable reform. This reflects a critique of social (industrial) and governing (political) elites, along with ruling class masculinity, replicated by the patriarchal control of renewables organisational governance (Giddens 1991; Gow and Leahy 2005; Donaldson and Poynting 2013; Bombora Wave Power 2018; Carnegie Clean Energy 2018; EUREC 2018; SolarPower Europe 2018). However, Deborah's eSMO advocacy, namely 'outreach work', is a type of emphasized femininity resistance to ruling elites (Leahy 2003; Connell 2005; Maleta 2015). Her account similarly indicates, that those in power – that is, leaders of government and business – are not proactively enabling sustainable reforms. Yet such sectors play an instrumental role in the future of renewable energy (Marshall 2011; Ajani 2015; RenewableUK 2017; Vildåsen et al. 2017). Further, Deborah's sustainable management leadership represents women-led strategic competence that is resistant to the rule of executive hierarchies (MacLeod 1992; Plumwood 1997; Gaard 2001; Cudworth and Hobden 2010, 2013). Women's multiple performative skills-set, and greater role in WW & SE management, is mandatory for renewables outcomes. My Act's Initiatives realise this, by legislating/advocating on women's scientific, technological and managerial leadership.

In support, eNGO advocate Heidi, who has a PhD in conservation, and previously worked in higher education, evaluates how eSMOs target environmental solutions, whereas academia is postured towards publications and resource allocation. As a trained scientist, Heidi esteems knowledge and other positive aspects within her eNGO:

> I'm hoping to bring more of the science into my role, actually. And that is one the lovely things about [omit organisation]… there's a lot of flexibility. I mean I am not micro managed in any way, because there is so much work to do, and so few people to do it, so I just get on with the job.
>
> (Heidi [audio] 2010)

The 'flexibility' of the eSMO role and 'not' being 'micro managed', enables Heidi's independence and work productivity plus ambitions for scientific integration: 'hoping to bring more of the science'. Also, getting 'on with the job', shows a strong work ethic, along with diligence, thereby strengthening her overall work performance. One limitation, from Heidi's retrospection, is her lack of extensive campaign experiences. In an advocacy campaign, focussing on a developing nation, Heidi ([audio] 2010) admitted that, as a trained scientist, she 'didn't have the skills'. Hence, the lack of advocate or activist experience can be a barrier for employees entering the eNGO world from other sectors. Nonetheless, academic activists, like Yvonne and Maggie, outline their robust advocacy activity through public community talks and engaging the grassroots to social change. Similarly, Heidi, is committed to integrating her scientific expertise within campaign advocacy.

My methodological ambition to have more women in WW & SE technological development is supported by academic Helen's, emphasis on: 'new technologies' plus 'wind farm installations'. Sustainable development is framed by women-led technical, scientific, leadership and social competencies. In her scientific advisory role, Helen strives to assess the social impact of climate change, particularly in regional areas:

I'll be undertaking research projects, umm, that look into sustainable agriculture and the behaviour of farmers, and decision-making around that. My other project is looking at the community acceptance of low emission technologies… my motivation comes from the concern about climate change… considering new technologies and how they cut greenhouse gasses, but how you actually successfully implement them into the communities is for me very closely related.

(Helen [audio] 2010)

This account reveals that 'community acceptance' informs the development of 'low emission technologies', and that Helen's social and technical competency is integral to her professional objectives and worldview (Shiva 1993; Culley and Angelique 2010; Irwin 2010; McFarland 2014; Ajani 2015). Helen's goal to 'cut greenhouse gases', is framed by cutting-edge 'research projects', informed by 'new technologies', devoted to 'sustainable agriculture'. Such projects assess individual behaviours and community impacts. Helen's account reveals how sustainable technological innovation, exemplifying technical-intellectual-scientific competence, and the role of farmers within rural communities, akin to interrelated social-technical competence, informs Helen's research project development.

Practicality informs effective eSMO performances and outcomes. In relation to eNGO employee Penny, who has a BA in environmental science, having scientific qualifications is not mandatory be an effective campaigner. As most employees have scientific credentials, highlighting technical knowledge, one's passion for the work is key:

a lot of campaigners have learnt their roles on the job, just because they're so keen and involved that they want to learn everything about it and there's probably quite a few that do have science backgrounds or relevant backgrounds, in tertiary education.

(Penny [audio] 2010)

This account suggests that social competence, acquired learning (without an expert background) and motivation define one's eSMO/eNSM participatory engagement. This supports the anti-nuclear research of Culley and Angelique (2003, 2010) on grassroots women's acquired mastery of technical competence through self-training knowledge and motivation, rather than initial expertise. They learned about nuclear technology and jargon in order to challenge the industry (Culley and Angelique 2003, 2010; Maleta 2018b). Nevertheless, I esteem the expert and social competencies of salaried and volunteer women, framing my constructivist approach to agency, for women working across environmentalist sectors, share a common ground social change approach in sustainability reform. Passion for environmentalism is a rationale for why participants may change their careers, moving from, say, financial investment to an eNGO, where financial agendas and the environment correlate, as Stephanie explains. A personal interest in the environment plus individual career choice informs women's lifepaths (Diani 1992; Khatibi and Indira 2011; Staggenborg 2016; Canty 2017).

Regarding exercising agency, Stephanie, who has a background in financial investment, decided to apply her skills to an eNGO:

> I get really bored with finance and investment, and I should actually spend some time figuring out what I want to do… I went to some career coaching, and it just resurfaced that I've always been really passionate about the environment, so I wanted to work in the environment… I didn't really want to throw away, all my education experience, and was thinking it could be applied in environment… that's a really good intersection of business and environmental courses.

(Stephanie [audio] 2010)

Regarding an *agentic performative multiple skills-set*, Stephanie ([audio] 2010) also identifies as 'a Jack of all trades', who is scientifically, technically and financially literate (Culley and Angelique 2003, 2010). Passion for the environment, versus the boredom of 'finance and investment', was a key motivator for changing to the eNGO sector; nonetheless, financial skills are transferable 'to work in the environment'. Positively, Stephanie applied her professional training and wisdom to this role: 'I didn't really want to throw away, all my education experience, and was thinking it could be applied in environment'. Another point is that campaign advocacy is demanding and exhausting work, relative to a heavy schedule. Hence, one's concerned environmental ethic and consciousness is paramount. If Stephine was concerned with her pay packet, she would have remained in finance and investment:

> everyone is personally on the same, sort of, wavelength. I think people are working here specifically for the cause rather than just any old job. Because there's that much, well, advocacy's just a really bloody hard job, especially if you care about it personally. So, you'd want to, yeah, why else would you be here [chuckle]? You know, there's a lot [laughing] easier stuff to do than this. And you'll get paid more.

(Stephanie [audio] 2010)

7.6 Social Competence and Affinity for the Human/Nonhuman

Participants' agentic performativity is measurable by a multiple skills-set: social, intellectual, technical, scientific and leadership competencies (Cohen 2016; Merchant 2016; Farr et al. 2017). Social interaction is a core dimension of eNSM networking and enhances an understanding of the social and natural world plus human and nonhuman dimensions (Plumwood 1997; Buckingham-Hatfield 2000; Mellor 2002; Doyle 2005; MacGregor 2006; Maleta 2011b). Participants identify with sociological dimensions in their diverse sector negotiations with industry executives and politicians, and when engaging with the various members of the public. Social competence informs the rationale and work agendas of NSM actors, whilst strengthening social and environmental change agendas (Butler 1999, 2004, 2007; Di Chiro 2008, 2011; Snow 2013; Staggenborg 2016).

Regarding a robust skills-set, Deborah's excerpt points to scientific credentials and social competence as empowering frames for interdisciplinary sector negotiation:

> I only picked up transport in the last two years, but because I have got a strong science background... having an Environmental Management degree, it means that I know how to talk to the kinds of people... In the skills area, you have got to be a good organiser because obviously you know you are running events as well and it can cross over into areas.
>
> (Deborah [audio] 2010)

Previously, Deborah identified men's hegemony in climate change, but her transport project leadership here challenges the notion of transport as a male-dominated vocation (Greer 1999; Connell 2005; Organo et al. 2013). In Deborah's interview, she disputes the idea of being treated differently as a woman or even ostracised: 'No, I think in the environmental movement, there's a lot of women involved in it, so that doesn't seem to come up so much. Well, certainly not in my experience' ([audio] 2010). This shows contradictions; on one level, Deborah identifies gender differentiated campaigns but, on another level, downplays gender as a barrier, or that women are othered. Greens participant Kate stressed how transport was male-dominated, suggesting a barrier; nonetheless, her leadership prevented men from taking over the campaign or taking credit for it (Connell 2002, 2005; Poynting and Donaldson 2005; Donaldson and Poynting 2007, 2013). The interview with Stephanie is underpinned by contradictions; women are included, but also excluded, relative to their dualist insider/outsider status. The more hierarchical eNGOs are informed by a male-dominated culture (Maddison and Scalmer 2006, Faber 2008; Kantola 2008; Maleta 2009, 2012, 2018a). The wording of 'guys' pervades scientific projects, plus patriarchal representations: 'the guys that work in policy and research... need to be a lot more over, broad issues of science, and climate stuff' (Stephanie [audio] 2010).

When women work in science, or male-dominated vocations, the complexity of gendered power relations are revealed (Connell 2009; Gilardi 2015; Pollack 2015; Farr et al. 2017; STEMM 2018). However, women's technical, scientific and social skills, emphasises their excellent performativity, and out-performance to men. Women are performing gender by negotiating their agentic power and demonstrating skill. Women-led competence should not be under-estimated; it is a platform for greater WW & SE outcomes (McFarland 2014; Ajani 2015; Gheaus 2015; BWE 2018; WIE 2018). The rule of men is susceptible to resistance; for their 'superior' scientific competence, intellectualism and rationalism is indeed a myth (Merchant 1994, 2016; Mellor 1997; Buckingham-Hatfield 2000; Ussher 2011). Constructivism, in my qualitative analysis, is contextualised by how women construct their sociopolitical subjectivities and resist ruling class masculine privilege. Social activist interaction, relayed through agentic competence, downplays essentialist views, privileging men in science (Shiva 1993; Berg and

Lie 1995; Eder 1996; Crary 2001; Culley and Angelique 2003, 2010; Gaard 2011; Nagy 2017).

Social skills, along with organisational, managerial and writing performances, are relayed in supporting excerpts. For instance, eNGO participant, Juliet, like Stephanie, identifies as a 'Jack of all trades':

> Jack of all trades, you need to go and do absolutely everything. So, we do everything from meeting with politicians, to organising events... to writing media releases, doing radio interviews, umm, writing content for our website or for newsletters, running workshops, ah, with volunteers to build up their skills and knowledge. You know, the list goes on, a bit of everything, yeah.
>
> (Juliet [audio] 2010)

The social competence of being a 'Jack of all trades', is evident by Juliet's rigorous eSMO engagement, including meeting within politicians, organising events, media skills, plus writing and aural competencies. The social aspect of the role adds a special dimension:

> I love meeting with, with people... I'm sitting behind my desk all day writing emails or, I don't know, writing stuff I get a bit antsy... that's one great thing about my job, I just get to meet so many new different, interesting people from all walks of life. Umm, so that's one aspect I really love.
>
> (Juliet [audio] 2010)

Evidently, eNGO advocacy is not strictly an office-based role, highlighting the significance of social competence and necessity to engage with 'new different, interesting people from all walks of life'. The first and final clauses above: 'I love meeting with people' plus 'that's one aspect I really love', reveal the powerful emotive connection of social engagement to campaign work. As well as possessing a passion for the environment, it is necessary to be a people person to be an effective eNGO performer. Concerning the social aspect, Stephanie also aims to 'encourage people to manage their own environmental impact' ([audio] 2010). Sustainable leadership is multi-faceted, relative to advisory, consultative and educative facets. People skills, scientific knowledge and an understanding of policy frameworks, represent eNGO women's multiple performative competencies:

> people skills, and the ability to communicate with all levels of knowledge and capability, and across different sectors as well. Umm, that's the main thing, I think. You need to be able to put together a pretty good argument, and understand, sort of, basic science concepts, 'cause you have to keep going back to that... how capital markets work, and how we tie into the rest of the world. I guess, knowledge of how government policy works, and international policy.
>
> (Stephanie [audio] 2010)

Interrelated social, scientific and technical multiple skills-sets are cornerstones to a successful eSMO work performance, contributing to women's inclusion. Other eNGO participants esteem scientific and social components in their roles. Having a natural affinity for people is perhaps not a skill immediately associated with climate change science. The technical components of science contrast with more people-focussed vocations, like healthcare and hospitality. Although trained in science, Penny enjoys getting out of the lab:

> I love the science part of it but I've always been quite a people person myself. Like I naturally enjoy chatting to people and talking to people and just networking and that kind of thing. So, I think it's probably, more of my skill set was to be out there rather than in a lab or in a sort of more closed environment.
> (Penny [audio] 2010)

Women's emphasized femininity leadership is shown by their people skills: 'enjoy chatting to people' and scientific skills: 'I love the science'. Hence, the 'science part' along with 'networking' and being 'a people person' are not mutually exclusive. The eNGO sector enables Penny's scientific performativity and social interaction: 'more of my skill set was to be out there rather than in a lab or in a sort of more closed environment' ([audio] 2010). I deduce that academia is more so a 'closed environment' (Maleta 2011b, 2012). In contrast, the third sector is defined by rigorous internal sector negotiations plus 'environmental outcomes' rather than 'publications' and 'egoism', as Heidi argued.

Social competence encompasses emphasized femininity women-led strategies, such as feminist role modelling. ENGO Director Barbara identifies as a feminist and a mature role model for younger women in her local community. Her role encompasses a grassroots and professional component, as a community leader and expert consulted by diverse peoples:

> my contribution as a feminist is a role model, I've been told. I'm a role model to many women. I'm a role model to children who would be old enough to be my grandchildren now in my local community, which is lovely. I'm consulted by a lot of people on all sorts of things, and I've achieved, you know, status in a male-dominated world. So yeah, I'm very much a feminist, but I think it's like with the eucalyptus trees, I mean, there's 300 varieties.
> (Barbara [audio] 2010)

Barbara's recognition of success is clouded by 'a male-dominated world'. This indicates that ruling class masculinity obstructs women's dichotomous insider/outsider status, relative to patriarchal frames of androcentrism (Buckingham-Hatfield 2000; MacGregor 2006; Smith and Pangsapa 2008). Nonetheless, Barbara ([audio] 2010) is 'consulted by a lot of people on all sorts of things', and has 'achieved... status' – even in 'a male-dominated world'.

Academics additionally identify consultancy, as a form of knowledge, meaning-making and social competence. Yvonne's consultation with 'some key people', informs her decision-making as Departmental Head:

I try to consult fairly widely and there are some key people in the department whose – whose judgement I trust a great deal and ah, including my deputy Head of Department, my senior lab managers, I trust them… I'm very lucky in that I've got very good people and I would always take their views into account.

(Yvonne [audio] 2010)

From Yvonne and Barbara's commentary, plus others, trustworthy work rapports with colleagues and community networks enlightens social competence as a measure of success. Barbara's egalitarian-feminist approach is situated in her grassroots advocacy: 'I'm a role model to children who would be old enough to be my grandchildren… in my local community' ([audio] 2010). Emphasized femininity activism involves women-led role modelling and egalitarian grassroots-centric resistance to androcentrism (Mellor 1997; MacGregor 2006; Smith and Pangsapa 2008; Maleta 2018b). Institutions and governments play a decisive role in sustainable reform (Banerjee 2011); nonetheless grassroots community leaders, inclusive of older and younger women, should be central to future renewable technological development. This is where my Bill of Rights Incentives fill an EEO gap (STEMM 2018).

In relation to Barbara's narrative, the articulation of feminism as encompassing '300 varieties' suggests that one's feminist identity is individualised, for each woman relays her sense of self through discursive reckonings of gender, work and social relations (Greer 1999; Pocock et al. 2013; Maleta 2015). Social competence and social change guide Barbara's environmental leadership – akin to greater grassroots community action: 'people in our valley, land owners, pick up the environmental message about, don't wait for the government, get down there and get rid of those willows' ([audio] 2010). Barbara status, as an expert, in the specialist field of 'brown ecology', evolved from the field of 'industrial pollution'. This field is innovative for 'hardly anyone does it', yet Barbara contends that 'it's very, very hard. Because it's in your face'. Her ambition to tackle 'hazardous chemicals', is shown through scientific and social advocacy within grassroots and professional contexts. Through years of experience, Barbara sums up that it is challenging to achieve a desired sociocultural change: 'You can't have that… So it's in our culture. So it's very hard to shift people's views' ([audio] 2010). Barbara's struggle to 'shift people's views' shows that society, institutions and governance are hesitant about renewable energy as a key source. Such reluctance accounts for why this sector is still considered an emerging sector (Alston 2011, 2013; Ajani 2015; Baruah 2016). However, an egalitarian social democratic model, as proposed in my Republican Constitutional-Bill of Rights, is the solution to gender-environmentalist inequities/injustices.

7.7 Egalitarian Resistance to Egoism and Ruling Elites

In this section, empirical insights highlight the way ego is reflective of ruling class masculinity, whereas women's resistance to egoism, relayed through an emphasized femininity endorsement of egalitarianism, challenges the patriarchal control of the eNSM. According to Heidi, eNGOs are more egalitarian than other sectors, such as academia, for men scientists are 'driven by ego' ([audio] 2010). This insight replicates organisational-gender barriers. The more grassroots-based eNGOs enable women's work performance and equity, whereas more hierarchical eNGOs are less egalitarian in their approach. My methodological egalitarian democratic model is supported by participatory insights to eSMOs as fertile grounds for 'collaboration' and 'consensus-building'. Women's egalitarian ethos and resistance to ego are positive frames, informing my socioecological change model. ENGO women inspire the development of my Bill of Rights Act, and their greater leadership of WW & SE solutions accompanies my Republican vision (Stein 2004; Mattl 2013; STEMM 2018; WIE 2018). Third-sector women play a vital role in a Republican Constitutional change, and my Initiatives ensure that their equity/justice is enacted through legislated Acts.

The first excerpt represents a positive framing of eNGOs, in how scientific and social competencies intersect within third sector environmentalism (Culley and Angelique 2010; Maleta 2012; RenewableUK 2017; Clean Energy Council 2018). Collaborative work efforts, aspiring 'to achieve positive outcomes', guides the advocacy of eNGO scientist Heidi:

> I think quite often research scientists are driven by ego, more than, I think in some ways they are well intended… I've had two experiences now with scientists that's really about them, umm, it's not about the common good, it's not about working together with people to achieve positive outcomes… we are all so busy, everyone has their own defined roles…. So we have each our area to look after, but we do work together when it's required.
>
> (Heidi [audio] 2010)

Whilst eNGOs aspire towards 'the common good', mirroring an egalitarian-grassroots worldview, Heidi critiques academic scientists, for being 'driven by ego'. She adds that 'research scientists' are self-centred: 'really about them', and not totally focussed on collaborative, positive environmental goals: 'it's not about working together with people to achieve positive outcomes' ([audio] 2010). Whilst Heidi contemplates that 'the NGO world, I know it can be quite political, and quite competitive as well, she concludes that 'it's not evident at all' in her NGO, due to a respectful integrated work culture that values team and individual efforts. Hence, a cohesive eNGO work context evokes collaborative efforts and independent organisational skills. The above account signifies that competence entails socialised and individualised reckonings. A successful work performance encompasses one's leadership in 'areas to look after' and being a bearer of scientific knowledge, communicated to 'the NGO world' along with diverse sectors and the community. Hence, an *agentic performative multiple skills-set* enacted by eNGO women, through teamwork and individual performances, as above, highlights valued, contemporary social and scientific knowledge. Heidi's reflection of a 'positive' versus 'negative' work environment suggests that she, and other eSMO women, possess the agentic power to prevent patriarchal elements from subverting their eNGOs. Its leaders and advocates, are strong allies for a futuristic Republican-Act. Heidi's resistance to 'ego', and emphasis on 'working together' and respecting fellow advocates' 'defined roles', stresses an egalitarian-emphasized femininity-women-led constructivist framework. Women's empowering leadership contrasts with aggression and androcentrism, thereby challenging patriarchal hierarchies and ruling elites (MacGregor 2006; Segal 2007; Donaldson 2009; Hosey 2011).

Regarding emphasized femininity resistance to hegemonic masculinity within scientific academia, Heidi, criticises the egoism of her former PhD supervisor:

> I think it's egotistical and insecure, umm, I think it's very much a male scientist trait. I don't know about males everywhere. I certainly know from friends who work in corporate sector, there is no way what went on with me would have been able to have gone on where they worked… again, it depends, some supervisors really aren't interested in it at all, but mine was more interested about getting his name was on the paper… I'm not good at conflict at all, unfortunately.
>
> (Heidi [audio] 2010)

This extract highlights elitist masculinist performances within scientific academia: 'a male scientist trait', assessed by Heidi as: 'egotistical and insecure'. Nonetheless, Heidi refrains from labelling all men as egoistical: 'I don't know about males everywhere'. On this note, she adds that corporate men are less likely to behave like men in science, for they would not be permitted to get away with it in their workplace: 'there is no way what went on with me would have been able to have gone on where they worked' ([audio] 2010). Men scientists' publication drive exemplifies their egoism, rather than being a positive frame to contribute knowledge and meaning-making: 'mine was more interested about getting his name was on the paper' ([audio] 2010). Undoubtedly, Heidi's critique of male scientists underpins emphasized femininity resistance to patriarchy (Leahy 2003; Connell 2009; Gaard 2011, 2015, 2017). Additionally, Heidi's resistance to egoism, as an example of emphasized femininity subversion to hegemonic ruling class masculinity, showcases a powerful interplay of constructivism versus essentialism (Shiva 1993; Berg and Lie 1995; Plumwood 1997; Crary 2001; Moore 2008; Mortimer-Sandilands 2008; MacGregor 2010; Gaard 2011; Vildåsen et al. 2017).

Masculinity is not static and fixed, for hegemony is discursive to mobile power relations, representing scope for plural masculinities (plus femininities) and unique gendered performances (Connell 1995, 2002, 2005; Butler 2007, 2011, 2013; Doherty and Doyle 2013). Heidi rejects the idea that all men are 'egotistical', for men in the corporate sector do not behave this way. Yet other women, including Maggie and Maxine, critique the egoism of corporate and political men. Maxine particularly scorned the conservative gender politics of conservation-based eNGOs, led by 'old White men'. Heidi elaborates that corporations have more accountability; if a complaint is made against an individual: 'it would be on his file', but 'in science [academia], they don't care' ([audio] 2010). The lack of effective complaints resolutions was a reason why Heidi did not submit a formal complaint:

Oh, just because someone would make a formal complaint, it would be on his file, and they would have been concerned about it. In science, they don't care. Even if you think about it, you are supposed to get two publications out a year, well, how many of them do? And if they don't, nothing ever happens. It's very much, I think it's partly because they run their own show all the time, and they are not managed, they are not told what to do in any way, shape or form.

(Heidi [audio] 2010)

Emphasized femininity challenges 'the assumed' certainty of patriarchy and essentialism (Connell 2002; Leahy 2003; Walby 2013; MacGregor 2014). Heidi's connection of ego to insecurity, challenges the notion of strength associated with men in science. Insecurity is traditionally linked to women/femininities, as an essentialist viewpoint, but if men are insecure then this challenges their agentic power and 'superior' competence (Plumwood 1997; Cockburn 1988; Buckingham-Hatfield 2000; McNay 2000; Culley and Angelique 2003; Mallory 2006; Ahern and Hendryx 2008; Meynell 2009). Contentiously, egoism is not uniform to men/masculinity, but to men in particular work sectors; be it here scientific academia (Alston 2013; Haynes et al. 2015; Gheaus 2015; Pollack 2015). Another point is that gender is subjective, framed by one's reckoning with self along with relative local and broader environs (MacGregor 2001; Butler 2004, 2007, 2013, 2015; Sullivan 2011; Maleta 2015). Egoism, overall, is more problematic in executive-based hierarchies, that is in elitist organisations, such as politics and academia.

My ruling class critique of egoism extends to misogyny and chauvinism – as examples of hegemonic masculinity and the patriarchal control of environmental politics (Leahy 2003; MacGregor 2009, 2010; Maleta 2011b; Carter 2013; Sundström and McCright 2014). ENGO participants Barbara and Stephanie, in support, reviewed men's leadership style as misogynist and chauvinistic in the executive arm of the eNSM. Barbara argued: 'I experienced misogyny in the 1990s, I was never provided the opportunity to play an executive role in the mainstream movement' ([audio] 2010). This critique of misogyny frames executive women's struggle with patriarchy and ruling elites within environmentalism. Executive men's leadership styles generally are not egalitarian, whereas women's engaged leadership foregrounds my aspirations for a unified institutional-grassroots social change. I aspire to unify environmental sectors (including grassroots and governance) so as to realise a Republican social democratic change, centred on an egalitarian Act. This vision is framed by *my six groups'* equity in male-dominated sectors.

Concerning my methodological review of ruling class masculinity, supporting accounts expose intersections of essentialism/constructivism, in how women recognise/resist gender differences and dualist experiences of otherness (Cockburn 1988; Walby 1990; Plumwood 1997, 2002, 2006; Buckingham-Hatfield 2000; Gaard 2017). ENGO advocate Mara considers the rationality of men, but contends that one's behaviour or egoism, is not entirely gender-specific: 'Men can be more rational and cool-headed, with less bitchy behaviour (all of which I have experienced), but I have experienced some large egos and dominating personalities from both genders' ([audio] 2010). Concurrently, women recognise plural types of masculinities and femininities (Connell 1995, 2005; Segal 2007). Moreover, women's 'apparent' egoism, as suggested by Mara, may be interpreted as emphasized femininity accommodation to patriarchy, rather than active resistance – of which I advocate (MacLeod 1992; Mellor 1997, 2013; Plumwood 1997; Leahy 2003). Most participants identify egoism, chauvinism and misogyny, as masculine performances, pronounced with executive organisational and political hierarchies. So, this signifies that ruling-middle class masculinity is a structural-cultural barrier for women.

ENGO advocate Penny adds that egoism is more so a masculine performance, whereby women tend to resist ego and embrace compassion in their advocacy/ activism:

> I think a lot of the problems that I see, this is a very personal point of view, but in positions of power is an egotistical, umm, how do you state that, but an egotistical, yeah, that presence of power means that you lose a lot of the compassionate values that we need to change in terms of a lot of our campaigns. And I think the only way you're going to get that is not to necessarily shift the, shift it the other way, but just to have that equal sort of footing between men and women, and spread the power role so that there is that gender equity there.
>
> (Penny [audio] 2010)

A more equitable gender representation, pertaining to an 'equal footing between men and women', strategically challenges ruling class masculinity along with egoism. Penny's case for women's 'gender equity', informs my EEO-framed Bill, in its subversion of the structural relations of power that replicate patriarchal hierarchies and men's privileged statuses. Comparatively, the ruling class elitism and performative egoism associated with men's leadership is juxtaposed to women's ambitions for gender unity and 'compassionate values', as Penny remarked. Penny's ([audio] 2010) interview emphasises 'compassion' and 'change', which suggests that women-led campaigning is compatible with empathetic objectives.

With more women in power, compassion, change and empathy are achievable in work, society and governance. In order to fully realise this worldview and structural change, it is necessary to reject a Monarchist type of governance – that replicates ruling-middle class power, and rather endorse a Republican sociopolitical change, framed by *my six groups'* agentic performative plural skills-set. Republicanism would be realised by greater women-led networks within the eNSM and its institutions (grassroots, eNGOs, political, academia).

The media plays a role in sociopolitical change. Participants' interpretation of the media illuminates their social and technical competence, and leadership advocacy. Academic Maggie has achieved status internationally as a public anti-nuclear orator, whereby the media plays a defining educative role in social change: 'People follow me… but I need more media attention, so I can educate all the people and the only way to do that is through the media' ([audio] 2010). For Maggie, social change is achievable by citizens' grassroots democratic action, supported by the media, as an influential tool of knowledge.

Maggie's interview highlights a compelling critique of ruling class masculinity, in how powerful figures in the media are culpable leaders of social change, yet fail to do so:

> They should be aspiring to enormous power to save the planet… the way you do that is fundamentally to organise a grassroots but you can't organise a grassroots without educating them and how do you educate them? Only through the media. [omit] is one of the most wicked men on the planet. He controls… broadcasts… He could help to save the Earth.
>
> (Maggie [audio] 2010)

This excerpt indicates that ruling class men, situated in supreme positions of power, be it as representatives of the media, politics or corporations, are disjointed from the mainstream grassroots population. Ruling class male figures, who do not support renewables-social change, are motivated by power and economic gain. This is linked to capitalism and neoliberal economic structures, replicated through an emphasis on the individual (Martin 2011; Walby 2011, 2012; Butler 2013; Cornish 2017; Jones 2017). Arguably, Anglo middle class men are the most privileged individuals (also as a collective) in Australia and English-speaking countries (Kaufmann 2004; Poynting and Donaldson 2013; DAWN 2015; ABS 2016a; Sheppard 2017). Ruling class Anglo men's accommodation of neoliberal individualisation counters with my egalitarian-social democratic model. My Bill, focussing on *my six groups'* collective agency, acts on EEO equity/justice, in which self-centred approaches are rejected/resisted, in favour of a greater emphasis on the integration of the social and natural world (Thampapillai 2005; Campbell et al. 2006; Sioufi and Bourhis 2017; STEMM 2018). Elite male figures may be critiqued for lacking compassion for the planet and, all the more so, their children's future:

> Psychic numbing and blocking out the real evil of what they're doing, ah chopping down our forests… when their children are dying or on their deathbed themselves that's often when they recant… they change at that point. They know underneath but… join societal norms to achieve and become rich and powerful.
>
> (Maggie [audio] 2010)

In relation to Maggie, a compassionate and empathetic approach is lacking in the leadership styles of ruling class men: 'real evil of what they're doing', 'children are dying', 'recant', 'change at that point', 'rich' and 'powerful'. My professional and grassroots participants, however, readily perform empathetic and technical leadership qualities (Cockburn 1988; Mellor 1997; Plumwood 1997; RenewableUK 2017; WIE 2018). More women in sustainable leadership is necessary, so as to protect humans and nonhumans, inclusive of the social and natural world (Shiva 1993, 2005, 2008; Ajani 2015; Buechler and Hanson 2015; Canty 2017). Rather than focussing on the continuing extrapolation of the natural environment/nature for economics and profit, more focus should be on safer sustainable development, framed by women-led technological-scientific strategic performativity (Shiva 2008, 2014; Baruah 2016; WIE 2018). The technology is there and ready to go; the agentic leadership of women, in greater numbers, is vital to realise this ambition.

7.8 Constructing Performativity: 'We [Women] Need to Change'

Regarding Maggie's grassroots leadership standpoint, women play an important role in a renewable future, but need to use their own power, rather than let men run the world:

> So we put ourselves down and I think that's conditioning and that pisses me off too… women need to change. Men won't. We need to change…. Women? Well, I think we're brought up to please people… it's usually the women who induce changes and revolutions.
>
> (Maggie [audio] 2010)

Maggie's passage underscores emphasized femininity resistance to both hegemonic masculinity and essentialised femininity, relative to the statement: 'men need us to change'. Women do 'induce changes and revolutions', thereby accentuating their strength and competence. Rather contradictorily, the latter comment, from Maggie, counters essentialised representations of women as passive, docile or submissive to men (Mellor 1997; Plumwood 1997; Barry 2008; Meynell 2009; Cooper 2013). Maggie's criticism is framed by women not exercising the agency at their disposal, thus highlighting a lack of agency (MacLeod 1992; McNay 2000, 2003; Butler 2007, 2013, 2015). Women's apparent unwillingness to negotiate their power and status replicates the hegemony of ruling class men (MacLeod 1992; Connell 1995, 2002; Poynting and Donaldson 2013; DAWN 2015). Women's inactive negotiation of power, plus lack of agency, is a contentious feminist issue. Contentiously, this underpins renewables development. Without more women in organisational governance, akin to their performative agentic competence, then materialist structures and ideologies conducive to patriarchy are likely to prevail. Comparatively, a culture of meritocracy, framed within a neoliberal democracy, falls short in addressing women's equity (Connell 2006; Walby 2012; Gheaus 2015; Cornish 2017; Jones 2017). An EEO-focussed Bill of Rights, akin to women's greater leadership within renewables technological development, is legitimised by their skilled prowess in multi-faceted areas. Hence, nothing will change; but change is mandatory to my interrelated feminist, environmentalist and republican ambitions.

Other academics similarly suggest that women need to change. A view by some women, including Barbara and Rachel, is that compliance to feminism is not necessarily the solution. In her rejection of the Women's Liberation Movement, assessed by academic Rachel as led by 'whinging, self-centred, self-obsessed neurotics'; Rachel defined her strategy: 'I just flipped and left them, and as Voltaire said, cultivated my own garden, and, yeah, just worked, worked my own way through' ([audio] 2010). This points to women's individualism as offering an innovative way forward. It does not though evoke individualism as a form of neoliberal-capitalist-aligned economics, which ruling class men tend to ascribe to. But it does show that women's self-centredness, as Rachel critiqued, portrays some feminists as non-egalitarian in their approach. The common ground cause for change though involves women, as individuals and collectives, working together, in a positive unified effort for change.

Following on from Maggie's point, women's seeming compliance to men entails that men will always dominate, and continue to run the world. Critically, this frames a subordinate femininity, that is essentialist in its sociocultural representation, of which feminists have historically rejected (Walby 1990; MacLeod 1992; Buckingham-Hatfield 2000; Butler 2004, 2007; Merchant 2013). Also, men's ruling power prevails in the mining of uranium and fossil fuels, and fracking (Rankin and Gale 2003; Shiva 2008; Cuomo 2011; Maleta 2011b; Alston 2013; Heuer and Yan 2017). Fracking, like these sources, involves an aggressive extrapolation of the natural environment, and there is much criticism of its contamination of the water supply of farmers and residents in rural communities (Heuer and Yan 2017). More women WW & SE leaders, positively, should strengthen the 'emerging' renewables sector, whilst challenging men's hegemon of the resource sector, in order to achieve a greater diversity of technological development; thus reinvigorating the global energy sector (Alston 2011, 2013; Banerjee 2011; Maleta 2011a; Ajani 2015; REA 2018; SolarPower Europe 2018; WIE 2018). A Republican-Bill makes this vision a reality, akin to its Initiatives, that challenge the hegemony of resource-based industrial governance.

7.9 Discussion

Although patriarchy constrains women's leadership equity; hegemony, as Connell (1995: 77) stated: 'is a historically mobile relation', in that gendered power relations are susceptible to women-led resistance and elevated feminist identities (MacLeod 1992; Plumwood 1997; Gaard 2001; Connell 2002, 2005; Maleta 2015, 2018a, 2018b). Feminist empowerment, in my methodological scope, is relayed through women's agentic negotiation of power and assertion of a dynamic skills-set. Regarding performativity, my interviews highlight women's social, scientific and intellectual qualities. Gendered power relations, depend upon women's active, self-reflective acts of social change within discursive contexts (Butler 1990, 2007, 2013). Hegemony is not fixed in time nor stationary, but susceptible to women-led subjective subversion, envisioning altered horizons and amended visions for the future (Connell 1995;

Plumwood 1997; Butler 1999; Leahy 2003; Maleta 2011a). My Republican-egalitarian modelling of emphasized femininity resistance to ruling-middle class masculinity, further, challenges the power relations that privilege men's hegemony.

The masculinist control of global renewables governance frames women's (in)visibility along with their dualist experience as the insider/outsider within environmental politics (Yoder and Aniakudo 1997; Maddison 2004; Maddison and Scalmer 2006; Kosny and MacEachen 2010; Maleta 2011b; Carnegie Clean Energy 2018; EREF 2018; EUREC 2018). Also, this (in)visibility is accentuated by men scientists taking credit for women's grassroots and professional work on climate panels. Furthermore, middle class masculinity must be challenged through legislative reform, whereby my Republican constitutional change aims for social democratic governance, in which *my six groups* play a special leadership role. Their leadership though depends upon performative skill and merit.

Maggie's ([audio] 2010) point that 'men need us to change', may be compared to the performance of women in global governance. Maggie draws upon former British Prime Minister, the late Dame Margaret Thatcher, whose 'strong' leadership style was, in turn, admired by male colleagues:

> Men actually like strong women. That's why Thatcher was popular… a lot of the men came from public schools, that means private schools in Britain, where they were beaten and hit, you know, corporal punishment and stuff and she was a bit like that and they, sort of, like that. They like strong women. They like women to know their own mind, to be assertive and it's time we bloody did it.
>
> (Maggie [audio] 2010)

Thatcher's seeming 'strong' gender performativity in British politics; moreover, may be critiqued in terms of compliance to ruling class masculinity, therefore, contrasting with emphasized femininity resistance to patriarchy (Greer 1999; Connell 2009; Petherbridge 2014). When women politicians, or others in senior executive positions, act like ruling-middle class men, such performativity reaffirms masculine power (MacLeod 1992; MacGregor 2006; Greer 2010b; Alston 2013; Butler 2013). Critically, I cannot deduce empathy in Thatcher's political performance. Maggie's narrative, as with others, though, signifies that empathising with the human and nonhuman, and the exercise of agency and performative prowess, should be accompanied by a grassroots-women-led social democratic change, whereby women citizens are the egalitarian leaders of a sustainable technologically-informed future. To reiterate, women's leadership is the key to this goal.

7.10 Empathy as Agentic: Constructivist/Essentialist Dichotomies

Emotive discourses have been critiqued by feminists for their over-representation with essentialised 'subordinate' femininities (Connell 1995, 2009; Plumwood

1997; Buckingham-Hatfield 2000). Globally, there is no research that links empathy to agentic technical-scientific competence, in terms of interrelated intellectual and sociocultural competencies, whereby my research fills a gap in the global field (Cockburn 1988, 2012; Culley and Angelique 2003). Regarding my interviews, women demonstrate empathy in their sustainable change leadership by identifying with the betterment of the human and nonhuman (Mellor 2002; MacGregor 2006; Irwin 2010; Maleta 2011a, 2011b). ENGO advocate Penny, and academic activist Maggie, pointed to the empathy of women leaders, whilst contemplating their greater equity in the future of renewables development (Di Chiro 2008; Banerjee 2011; McFarland 2014; Ajani 2015; Baruah 2016; Clean Energy Council 2018). Women's emphasized femininity performance of empathy challenges patriarchal hegemonic privilege (Connell 2002, 2005; Leahy 2003; Maleta 2015, 2018a, 2018b; Bombora Wave Power 2018; Carnegie Clean Energy 2018).

My interview analysis shows that empathy is an empowering women-led strategy and has the potential to redress structural gender inequality whilst improving gender relations. For Helen, her leadership goal is to reduce conflict whilst improving work relationships:

> my staff at [omit organisation], and I, we worked hard to move beyond, umm, a lot of territoriality and conflict that existed within the NGO movement on climate change to a much more cohesive working relationships.
>
> (Helen [audio] 2010)

The above narrative relays intersection of constructivism/essentialism. In relation to Helen, cohesion, as an example of empathetic competence, diminished conflict from potentially subverting the NGO climate movement. Women's constructivist leadership, through empathetic 'cohesion', in turn, improved workplace relations. Regarding constructivism/essentialism, not all women are empathetic, for empathy, and degrees of this, depends on one's subjectivity and motivation as an environmentalist (Plumwood 1997; Maleta 2015). It is also discursive to one's background and status in the eNSM.

Mothers in the grassroots arm of the eNSM are often motivated out of concern for their children, and apply a personalised nurturing ethos in their activism (Maleta 2012, 2015). Professional salaried advocates, like Maggie, Stephanie, Barbara, etc., leading renewables technological development, are motivated by concerns for their children and communities, along with healthier, safer sustainable futures. Hence, motherhood, framed by empathy and personalised identity, underpins women's strategic rationales, informing their grassroots and professional social change agendas (Maleta 2011a, 2011b, 2015).

Men's leadership styles are critiqued by participants as lacking empathy, particularly in the executive arm of organisational governance. Greens politicians, academics and eNGO advocates, characterise men-led strategies as 'aggressive' and 'androcentric', which supports global ecofeminist analyses (Buckingham-Hatfield

2000; MacGregor 2006, 2010, 2014; Hosey 2011). However, women-led approaches, are more so 'conciliatory' and 'consensus-based', framed by a common ground team-approach that is empathetic and socially egalitarian, in reckonings with fellow humans and the nonhuman world. Although 'the boys club' of Parliament lacks empathy; it is in such male-dominated environs that women advocate for more empathy. Women's emphasized femininity leadership of empathy represents scope for more egalitarian organisational structures, whilst equally resistant towards patriarchal hierarchies (Plumwood 1997).

Empathy symbolises an empowering form of emphasized femininity agentic leadership resistance to the patriarchal control of environmental politics (Maleta 2011b, 2015). In likeness to Maggie, Deborah ([audio] 2010) esteems the media as an educative tool for social change. She recognises the importance of empathy, relative to a public reach: 'being able to empathize with the community' (Deborah [audio] 2010). Deborah elaborates on the power of media skills, contemplating empathy and women-led approaches in politics:

> I did a radio interview and you have to empathise with what they're asking... not all women have empathy... women politicians I have come across are very emphatic, and happy to talk to you, not at you. They're nicer to deal with... there wasn't that patriarchal concept coming from the women... Some of the male politicians have been wonderful and very helpful... I haven't seen gender as the issue so much as politicians wanting to tell you how good they are.
>
> (Deborah [audio] 2010)

Empathy is a skill that women endorse – in practice and as part of their identity. According to Deborah, empathy contrasts with 'that patriarchal concept', whereby women politicians, for the most part, are: 'very emphatic, and happy to talk to you, not at you' and 'nicer to deal with'. On the other hand, Deborah ([audio] 2010) adds that 'some men are inclined to blow their trumpet and say this is how it is'. Nonetheless, Deborah contends that 'not all women have empathy', which supports ecofeminist critiques (Merchant 1994; Mellor 1997; Plumwood 1997, 2006; MacGregor 2010). Deborah's ([audio] 2010) additional retrospection indicates gender-neutral insights, disputing the notion that behaviour is entirely gender-specific: 'Some of the male politicians have been wonderful' whilst 'some are typical politicians, they're trying to sell a vote, so they're politicians first' (Connell 2006; Lewis 2006; Gupta 2007; Jonnergård et al. 2010; Cockburn 2013). Considering green political theory, Plumwood (1997: 9–10) had argued that not all women have empathy nor treat the earth with a nurturing or maternal ethos of care (Merchant 1994, 2013; Mellor 1997; Maleta 2015). Plumwood adds that: 'The simple fact of being female does not guarantee an affinity with an ecological consciousness' (1997: 10). However, Plumwood contends that women have played a significant role in resisting the patriarchal control of the eNSM, which underscores my emphasized femininity resistant approach: 'Women have played a major role, largely unacknowledged, in the male-dominated environment movement, in resisting the assault on nature' (1997: 9–10). Comparatively, my framing of women's scientific-technical competence, parallel to empathetic-egalitarian performances, entails individual-collective performative resistance to ruling-middle class masculinist social and industrial elites (Mellor 1997; Gaard 2001; Leahy 2003; Gow and Leahy 2005; Merchant 2016).

While Deborah's interview esteems women's performative empathy, she claimed that the role of politician distorts its authenticity: 'politicians wanting to tell you how good they are' ([audio] 2010). Hegemonic masculinity, located in 'that patriarchal concept', curtails women's capacity to validate elevated empathy, and to negotiate their agentic sociopolitical change agendas (Connell 1995, 2002, 2009; Maleta 2011a, 2011b; Butler 2013, 2017). Patriarchy, as a gender-organisational barrier, situated in work and social environs assessed as less empathetic, underscores women's lower agency and marginalisation (McNay 2000, 2003; Butler 2004, 2007, 2011; Edge et al. 2017). Within a materialist and cultural sense, empathy and agency are susceptible to the patriarchal control of eSMOs, entailing lower agentic representations. However, women demonstrate empathy and agency in their roles – despite a masculinist cultural environment resistant to emphasized femininity leadership (Mellor 1997; Plumwood 1997; Kosny and MacEachen 2010; Maleta 2018a, 2018b).

Empathy, akin to the agentic performative multiple: technical, scientific, intellectual, social leadership prowess of *my six groups*, informs my Act's goals. For instance, CALD and disabled women (part of my grouping), ideally, would identify with empathy in their strategic engagement with other CALD and disabled women. Through my Bill's Initiatives, I envision robust, informed networks between women (and fellow men), strengthened through constructivist-women-led collaborative teamwork efforts, centred on progressive renewables technological development. Emphasized femininity entails women-led skills and resistance to androcentrism. In the next passage, constructivism/essentialism intersect with empathy, for women's performative empathetic leadership in their eSMOs/eNSMs, accentuates agency, all the while, testing patriarchal power:

> My strong belief is we would be more effective if we had more women involved in senior leadership roles in the environment movement... we have a culture as a movement, and certainly within the established part of that movement as in the paid funded organisations; we have a culture of combatativeness and competitiveness and underminingness, which my experience of working with the women in the movement, I believe we would be less likely to behave in that way and more likely to build more consensus and more, collaboration.
>
> (Linda [audio] 2010)

Linda's analysis of men's 'senior leadership roles in the environmental movement', in terms of 'combatativeness', 'competitiveness' and 'underminingness', supports Barbara's censure of patriarchal hierarchies, omnipresent within the executive-arm of the eNSM. Such recollections frame ruling-middle class masculinity as both a cultural and structural obstacle, hindering women's equity and otherness, even in the same position to men (Maleta 2012; Donaldson and Poynting 2013; DAWN 2015; Cadaret et al. 2017; Edge et al. 2017). However, emphasized femininity agentic resistance to patriarchal leadership is relayed by women's focus on 'more consensus' and 'more collaboration', as Linda stated. Also, more women in senior leadership should challenge hegemonic male privilege and structural inequity, replicated through executive hierarchies of power: 'the established part of that movement' plus 'the paid funded organisations' (Linda [audio] 2010). Women's leadership competence is situated in an empathetic strategy centred on teamwork and unity. Empathy/empathetic leadership represents an assertion of emphasized femininity agency, whilst representing a rejection/resistance to androcentrism and ruling masculinist elites. On this point, grassroots participants, in similarity to others, elaborate on empathy as a defining women-led skill:

> Women probably have better skills at communicating and understanding, having more empathy than some men… sometimes men are more confident and sure they are right. Maybe it's not really good in public; you've got to be more sympathetic and understanding of other peoples' views.
>
> (Linda [audio] 2009)

One's empathetic skill and exercise of power frames one's constructivist-performative agency – evoking an active, subjective process 'of doing', thus, elevating the 'I' in one's identity (Butler 1990, 2007, 2013). Other grassroots accounts connect empathy to women-led competence. In a critique of the masculinisation of politics, Wendy outlines her feminist goal of embracing 'empathy', as a leadership strategy in the climate eNSM:

> I'd like to bring the feminine into my leadership through my style of campaigning, of bringing emotions into what I do. I feel that politics is very male-dominated, a very male style of thinking. Emotions often aren't as legitimate as facts or logic, that's a male concept, that's something men do more naturally. I feel that women more naturally communicate in emotions in terms of empathy, I think logic and rationality isn't always about outcomes, it's about the relationships. I can't say it's men versus women, it's more the masculine and the feminine, which I think are different. My leadership is helping people understand their emotional side, and the concepts of forgiveness among activists.
>
> (Wendy [audio] 2010)

7.11 Discussion

The notion of empathy, as an empowering activist strategy, challenges essentialist views of empathy as a 'subordinate' type of femininity, viewed as docile, weak and passive to men/masculinities (Cockburn 1988; Mellor 1993, 1997; Plumwood

1997; Buckingham-Hatfield 2000; Connell 2009; Maleta 2015). Empathy, as a women-led strategy, transforms and strengthens campaigns. For example, 'empathy', 'emotions', 'forgiveness' and 'relationships' frames Wendy's social change leadership, contrasting with a 'male style of thinking' ([audio] 2010). Although Wendy's emotivity, may be perceived as somewhat essentialist, her appropriation of empathy illuminates a constructivist-emphasized femininity performance, situated in environmental change and subversion to patriarchy (Berg and Lie 1995; Connell 1995, 2002; Leahy 2003; Maleta 2018b). Empathy informs Wendy's social change agenda, as a campaign strategy, and, thus, is constructivist in its representation. The essentialist element of emotivity is being appropriated and reworked by women within their robust activism. Simultaneously, Wendy identifies the differences in masculine/feminine leadership, for emotions are not perceived as legitimate within the masculinisation of politics. The masculinisation of politics and industry are framed by logic and rationality, whereby emotionality, is 'othered' as a feminine performance (Mellor 1997; Butler 2004, 2007, 2015; Meynell 2009; Wright and Holland 2014). For Wendy, it is not about 'men versus women'; however, women's strength in understanding 'their emotional side' enables them to be more effective leaders in the eNSM. Hence, empathy, appropriated by women campaigners, accentuates their agentic performative plural skills-set. It highlights a dynamic interplay of essentialism and constructivism, resulting in feminist empowerment.

This section has shown that empathy, relative to women's performative agentic multiple competencies, intersects with essentialism/constructivism (Berg and Lie 1995; Crary 2001, 2011; Gaard 2001; Moore 2008; Mortimer-Sandilands 2008; Wibben 2016). Also, empathising with the environmental cause enables professional and grassroots women to effectively perform their roles, negotiate their power, status and social change goals, whilst achieving the 'I' in their identity (Butler 1990, 1999, 2004; Maleta 2012, 2015). My interviews highlight the way women are indeed empowered agents of environmental change (Butler 2007, 2011, 2013, 2015; Snow 2013; Maleta 2018b). Empathy, as an egalitarian performance, is conducive to my feminist framing of a Bill of Rights, that is equally resistant to 'adversarial' and 'aggressive' patriarchal hierarches (MacLeod 1992; Plumwood 1997; Gaard 2001). In my resistance to ruling-middle class men, and their hegemony of structural-cultural relations of power, my emphasized femininity approach validates empirical insights of: 'communicating' 'understanding' 'sympathetic' 'outcomes'. As Linda contends, more women in senior leadership, strengthened by their 'consensus' and 'collaboration', should strengthen unity in eSMOs.

Conclusion

Women's *agentic performative multiple skills-sets* (scientific, social, intellectual, technical, physical, empathy) demonstrate how women's leadership is positively contributing to renewables technological development, whilst transforming the eNSM and its eSMOs (Ahern and Hendryx 2008; McFarland 2014; Ajani

2015; RenewableUK 2017; BWE 2018). Emphasized femininity performative leadership is reinvigorating the women's and environmentalist NSMs, whilst demonstrating how women-led constructivism is challenging ruling-middle class men's hegemony (Berg and Lie 1995; Connell 1995, 2005; Crary 2001; Gaard 2001, 2017; Poynting and Donaldson 2005; Maleta 2011a). Empathy is conducive to my conceptual: constructivist, egalitarian, feminist and republican ambitions, aspiring for an enlightened progressive sociocultural democracy, and methodological vision for a sustainable-simplicity-technologically defined future. Also, my vision of sustainable-simplicity, markedly, is framed by a self-reflective performative ethical existence: living a life that is clean-cut, sincere and authentic, framed by one's empathy and warmth of character, along with concern for other humans and all species inhabiting the planet. In relation to my appropriation of empathy, I aim to construct a simpler yet smarter way of living, in which consumerism, personal greed and androcentrism is resisted (Buckingham-Hatfield 2000; MacGregor 2006; Maleta 2018b). My Bill of Rights model, plus its Initiatives, focussing on women's greater renewables technological development, undoubtedly strives for women's greater leadership in this sector. My Republican vision addresses citizens' greater agency and control of their personal energy consumption, whilst resisting the monopoly of corporations and governments, whereby I aim to subvert their hegemony of the resource-based and renewables sectors (Faber 2008; Gerulis-Darcy 2010; McFarland 2014; Ajani 2015; RenewableUK 2017; BWE 2018). My Act's emphasis on women-led WW & SE solutions represents an obstacle to the extrapolation of the natural environment/nature. Women's empowered agentic scientific-technical performativity of this technology underscores my egalitarian-feminist-constructivist approach.

Environmental ethics, relative to empathy-based ethical-simplicity, underpins my scope for greater sustainable living, encompassing work, political and everyday life contexts (Eder 1996; Warren 1997, 1999; Glazebrook 2005; Plumwood 2006; Maleta 2011b; Valles 2015; Wibben 2016). Arguably, sustainably-simplicity, exemplifying environmental ethics, entails resistance to designer clothes and labels, and undoubtedly, the corporate control of global energy sources (Warren and Cady 1996; Banerjee 2011; Gaard 2011, 2014; Shiva 2014). The grassroots, everyday citizen, should have more control of their personal energy use plus consumption (Shiva 2005, 2008, 2016). I resist the profit-centred agenda of corporates in the energy sector, including renewables, as an emerging sector (Mellor 1993; Shiva 1993; Sullivan 2013; Ajani 2015; Baruah 2016). Simultaneously, stricter government regulation is essential to curtail corporate control.

Regarding environmental ethics, renewable energy represents an opportunity for individual citizens to exercise their agency over their own consumption. My emphasized femininity insight to environmental ethics is contextualised by women's scientific-technical leadership (Bill of Rights Act/Initiatives) of renewables technologies, and goal for women to exercise agentic power over their personal energy use. My feminist ambition is to accentuate the empowerment of women-led grassroots communities and that of individualised women citizens. Hence, my feminist framing of empathy is egalitarian in its social democratic modelling. Simultaneously, my Act is subversive to the corporate-capitalist-economic control and profit-individualised-incentive-drives, underpinning the way in which global companies control the environment (Mellor 1997; Faber 2008; Shiva 2008, 2014; Gerulis-Darcy 2010). Currently, the environment and its resources are being extrapolated by multinational companies (MNCs) and transnational companies (TNCs) for profit, conducive to a global ruling neoliberal, capitalist, economic order (Gaard 2001; Cudworth 2002; Rankin and Gale 2003; Leahy 2008; Gerulis-Darcy 2010; Sullivan 2013; Shiva 2014; Maleta 2018a). In my legislative focus on renewables solutions, I aim for women to have more power over the future of energy development, and for women everyday citizens to have more individualised control of their own economic consumption. This emphasized femininity approach is, consequently, resistant to ruling class masculinity and the hegemony of social (industrial) and political (governing) elites.

My Republican vision is not based on a replication of corporate or government power; rather it is centred on women's greater agency over their energy output and greater leadership of renewable development. My model is *empathetic*, egalitarian and democratic in its social, cultural, economic and political outlook. My egalitarian-socioecological democratic feminist participatory model, furthermore, looks to the reactionary yet progressive era of Red Vienna, and its art nouveau creative-technological flair, for inspiration (Blau 1999; Rentetzi 2004, 2010; Kershaw 2013; Mattl 2013, 2016). I add that my vision of sustainable technological development, akin to environmental ethics and sustainable-simplicity, is 'revolutionary' in its scope, thereby supporting the 'revolutionary' vison of Maggie as well as other women participants constituting my study.

8   Physical Competence and Civil Disobedience

Introduction

The notion of physical competence is a tag largely associated with men/masculinities (Cockburn 1988, 1991; Barnes 2000; Ahern and Hendryx 2008; Maleta 2009; Cooper 2013). Historically, men are perceived to be physically stronger than women, and this is a justification to exclude women from certain jobs, such as firefighting and forestry (Yoder and Aniakudo 1997; Childs 2006; Mallory 2006; Maleta 2009). Moreover, women are marginalised in scientific and intellectual jobs, along with engineering and information technology (IT), which do not necessarily involve a corporeal component (Pollack 2015; Cohen 2016; Cadaret et al. 2017; Farr et al. 2017). Arguably, this chapter shows that women's physical performativity, in scientific and grassroots capacities, demystifies the hegemonic representation of strength with men. My emphasized femininity method is strengthened by linking physical competence to women's *agentic performative multiple skills-set*, relative to their empathetic, intellectual, scientific and social leadership prowess.

Also, in this chapter, I highlight radical and conservative performative femininities. Radicalism, as a constructivist approach, is shown by civil disobedience, such as Greens women protesting at Parliament and grassroots women's collective actions at Climate Camp. Whereas conservatism, as an essentialist approach, is shown by women using talk to engage in social change. Comparatively, grassroots, eNGO and political participants, adopt radical (direct) and/or passive (indirect) strategies in their quest for improved sustainability polices. Also, women's technological-scientific leadership is assessed as assertive, confident and principled. Emphasized femininity performativity, strategically, should contribute to a less androcentric, militant world (Warren 1999; Cockburn 2010, 2012, 2013; MacGregor 2014; Wibben 2016; WIE 2018). Such women-led action defies hegemonic masculinity. Women's 'toughness' evokes constructivism, and challenges subordinate, traditional notions of essentialised femininity (MacGregor 2006, 2010). This enables my Republican aims, framed by agentic resistant femininities, pursing greater WW & SE change goals.

In relation to Butler, gender performativity entails bodily gestures and actions; it is a corporeal and intellectual reckoning, framed by how women are actively doing gender, exercising the 'I' in their identity, whilst pursing social change goals (Butler 1999, 2006, 2007, 2011, 2013; Loizidou 2007; Chambers and Carver 2008; Jagger 2008). My interviews reveal how professional and grassroots women's physical prowess exemplifies emphasized femininity resistance to ruling-middle class men's hegemony (DAWN 2015). My empirical material accentuates constructivism, for women's corporeal performativity, is testing essentialist views of women's 'subordinate' strength (Butler 1990, 2006; Maleta 2015). My emphasized femininity argument, consequently, is that women are not compliant to men nor patriarchy (Connell 1995; Plumwood 1997; Leahy 2003; Maleta 2018b).

In my prior interview-based research with women volunteer members of the New South Wales Rural Fire Service (NSW RFS), I found that women fire fighters performed well, agentically and competently, as individuals and collectively, within a traditional masculinist cultural environment (Maleta 2009). Women's performativity was enhanced through their appropriation of the technological automation of equipment, and collaborative teamwork efforts between women and men members (Maleta 2009). The heavy lifting and physical demanding aspect of the job, was enabled by technology; but also by the fact, that women can lift heavy equipment. While men generally are 'physically stronger', with larger muscles and commanding physiques, this biological composition does not hinder women's corporeal competence in male-dominated jobs (Cockburn 1988, 1991; Culley and Angelique 2003; Maleta 2009). Nonetheless, women continue to encounter barriers in work contexts, relative to stigmas associated with their technical-corporeal competence, and that physical work is more suitable to men (Cockburn 1988; Maleta 2012; STEMM 2018).

8.1 'You Can't Be Afraid of Getting Your Hands Dirty or Have Good Nails'

Participants' gender performativity entails their negotiation of 'normative' masculinity/femininity, whereby femininity 'as subordinate', is undergoing defiance (Cockburn 1988; Culley and Angelique 2010; Butler 2011; Maleta 2012). Women-led subversion evokes an empowering work-based performance, extending to social movement goals, striving for sustainable-social change (Butler 1999, 2006; Banerjee 2011; Di Chiro 2011; Schlembach 2011; Buechler and Hanson 2015; WIE 2018). My results emphasise that women are not afraid of getting their hands dirty and performing hard fieldwork:

> You can't be afraid of getting your hands dirty or have good nails or anything like that. It can be physically hard. Recently, we did an experiment with 800 pots, and all of them were 10 kilograms each. We had to move them all the time. Some people don't like doing that sort of thing. But that's the sort of science I do. You find more women in biochemistry, that is purely lab based stuff, rather than, so there are less women in field based sort of work that I do.
> (Anna [audio] 2010)

Anna's performative statement 'it can be physically hard', and her lifting of '800 pots' weighing '10 kilograms', in turn, encapsulates emphasized femininity-aligned corporeal strength in biological science. While Anna contends that women tend to be more represented in 'biochemistry' and 'lab based stuff', her field-based biological work reveals women-led multiple performative prowess in traditional male-dominated stratas of science (Culley and Angelique 2003; Blackwell and Glover 2008; MacGregor 2010; Rentetzi 2010; Farr et al. 2017). Additionally, the opening statement 'you can't be afraid of getting your hands dirty or have good nails' challenges essentialist connotations of women's grooming, along with dainty images of femininity, relative to an assumed obsession with appearance (Kwan and Trautner 2009). Evidently, women recognise/resist that performing 'dirty' field work is not something typical of women. As an activist, Gillian perceives herself to be 'not a typical woman'. As a former teacher, she was similarly labelled, as 'different', but adds that activists who worry about getting their 'fingernails dirty' are pretending to be activists:

> As far as being an activist, there are advantages to being a woman, but I'm not a typical feminine woman, so maybe it makes a difference… what people perceive women as like, painting their fingernails and not liking to get their hands dirty. I'm not like that. I've been told I'm different by some of the male teachers in my last school, they made comments about the other girls didn't want to get their hands dirty, like work in the garden, and I said, 'I don't care about that'. They said, 'Oh yes, but you're not typical, you're different.' I think that's true… the ones that worry about getting their fingers or hands dirty, maybe pretend to be activists.
>
> (Gillian [audio] 2009)

Grassroots activist Gillian's rejection of feminine perceptions: 'painting their fingernails and not liking to get their hands dirty', suggests that environmental activism performativity is not conducive to docile, dainty nor passive femininity: 'I'm not like that'. On that note, Gillian's subjectivity displays emphasized femininity resistance to traditional notions of femininity, rooted in dainty grooming and beauty care (Kwan and Trautner 2009). Constructivism is relayed by Gillian's corporeal and physical reckoning as 'not a typical woman', whereby essentialised views of women/femininities are dually confronted: 'I don't care about that' ([audio] 2009). Another point is that men are equally resistant to subversive, non-normative forms of femininity; labelling Gillian as 'not typical' and 'different', stating: 'the other girls didn't want to get their hands dirty, work in the garden'. While Gillian ([audio] 2009) recognises her performance as not characteristic of women in general: 'I think that's true', authentic activists ought not to 'worry about getting their fingers or hands dirty'. Following on from Gillian's testing of pretentious imagery: 'maybe pretend to be activists', activism encompasses emphasized femininity-constructivism resistance to essentialised notions of femininity and men's assessment of their physical appearance (Maleta 2012, 2015).

Constructivism is shown by women's agentic self-reflective negotiation of their gendered roles and work-based identities. I do not deter from accommodating essentialism as a form of feminist empowerment within environmental activism (Maleta 2015). Thus, I have demonstrated that women-led skills frame agentic empowerment whilst challenging men's hegemony (Connell 1995; Butler 1999, 2006, 2011; Maleta 2011b, 2018b). In my constructivist framing of feminist agentic competence, I consider participants view of 'the common ground' approach relative to genders in terms of a 'rationalist' framework. In the next excerpt, Barbara recognises essentialist differences whilst identifying as a 'humanist technocrat', framing a competence placed within scientific prowess plus human empathy:

> I think the absolutely essential element of feminism is to recognise the essential differences between men and women, and the common ground we must share. So I am more of a sort of humanist, really, probably, a humanist technocrat or something, a rationalist humanist… than a feminist, because it's bad language. Yes. But I'm, I've led lots of things, I've led the charge a lot. I've been acknowledged as being very brave, as well as physically brave, too.
>
> (Barbara [audio] 2010)

Barbara's recognition of feminism through 'the essential differences between men and women' enables me to assess women-led skills as different but also empowering. A 'common ground' approach, 'between men and women' enables unity rather than dissent. While Barbara's interview underscores gender differences, her narrative simultaneously frames the greater potential for collaborative efforts between men and women, as an 'element of feminism'. Hence, the goal of feminism is not for men and women to work apart, nor in opposition, but through shared, mutual acts, especially acts of social-environmental change. Barbara's narrative evokes dichotomous appraisals/critiques of 'feminism', relative to 'its bad language', contrasting with a potential greater gender unity between the sexes. Rather Barbara self-identifies as a 'humanist technocrat' or 'a rationalist humanist', which has scope for a greater common ground approach, as advocated here. As this subjective reckoning encompasses intellectual 'humanist' plus 'rationalist' and technical 'technocrat' performative competencies, Barbara's corporeal-intellectual qualities underpin women-led multiple performative prowess: 'I've led lots of things, I've led the charge a lot… very brave, as well as physically brave' ([audio] 2010). In similarity to my other accounts, Barbara's 'physical bravery' and assertive leadership skills challenge essentialist views of women/femininities as passive and less physically able (Cockburn 1988; Plumwood 1997; Buckingham-Hatfield 2000; Pease 2002; McNay 2003; Cooper 2013). Women's bodily strength 'physically brave', and empathy 'the common ground we must share' along with assertiveness 'led the charge', highlights their plural corporeal-intellectual-empathetic-agentic performative skills-set. My empirical insights reiterate Butler's (1999, 2006, 2007) point that agency depends upon a self-reflective reckoning, entailing exercising the 'I' in one's identity and active doing of gender. Women-led performative acts, striving for social change, enable feminist agency and empowerment (Butler 1990, 2004, 2011, 2013; Maleta 2018b). In similarity to Gillian and Anna, Barbara elaborates on the bodily and intellectual aspects, framing her identity:

> I've always been physically confident. Because I've done so much… because of the life I led as a child, I was physically, I was confident, you know? A lot of women aren't so physically confident now because they don't, they haven't played, you know, they haven't played tennis, and they haven't done all that stuff, fallen over a million times and gone camping and, women don't do that.
> (Barbara [audio] 2010)

Like the other participants, Barbara assesses that physically strength is not typical of most women: 'A lot of women aren't so physically confident'. Comparatively, Barbara's recollection evokes emphasized femininity resistance to 'subordinate' or delicate femininity (Cockburn 1988; Plumwood 1997; Leahy 2003; Connell 2005, 2009; Maleta 2015, 2018b). Although physical assertion is not characteristic of women/femininities, women's physicality underscores their identity whilst challenging gender stereotypes: 'as a child, I was physically confident, you know?' Barbara's questioning here underscores her femininity as non-normative, or an unusual feminine performance. However, Barbara's connection between body and mind highlights a compelling intersection of constructivism/essentialism. Certainly, women's constructed physicality defies the perception of strength as hegemonic to men/masculinities (Donaldson 1993; Connell 1995; Pease 2002; Poynting and Donaldson 2005; Maleta 2009; Donaldson and Poynting 2013).

8.2 Competitive, Tough Performative Femininities

Women's gender performativity is not conducive to one type of femininity. Competitive femininities and toughness supports my conceptual insight to women's physical competence. Emphasized femininity performativity entails women's 'tough behaviour', in terms of '[getting] their hands dirty', 'being very brave… physically brave too' and 'bossy, pushy'. Competitive performative forms of femininity, such as bossy and pushy, point to women's assertion rather than passivity. My participants have extensively censured the adversarial, aggressive leadership styles of men in the executive arm of the eNSM and patriarchal-Parliamentary contexts. Barbara critiqued the misogyny and chauvinism of executive men leaders of the Green Games. However, here, she adds that women, aspiring to be CEOs of an eNGO, can act just the same way as men:

> in the environment movement, there are a lot of women who are well placed… they are bossy, pushy. They've been told they were a princess, and they make their way to the top, they don't care whose head they tread on, they're just the same as men. They operate in a dynamics where if they want

to be the CEO of an eNGO, they will operate just as ruthlessly as men. Maybe they have to do it even more because there's still those inherent glass ceilings... But these things take time.

(Barbara [audio] 2010)

Executive eNGO women's apparent 'bossy, pushy' and 'ruthless' approach, on one hand challenges the notion of aggression as characteristic to men/hegemonic masculinity (Connell 1995, 2005; Buckingham-Hatfield 2000; MacGregor 2006; Segal 2007). On the other hand, Barbara's insight to 'inherent glass ceilings' shows that women's 'ruthlessness', is underpinned by their historic position of marginalisation and gender-organisational barriers, endemic to patriarchy (Walby 1990, 2013; Connell 2009; Cook and Glass 2014; Edge et al. 2017). The patriarchal control of the executive arm of the eNSM encourages women to act 'ruthlessly', aspiring to achieve career pinnacles, whilst 'hopefully' breaking glass ceilings. The commentary on women as 'princess' and 'well placed' points to executive women's privileged statuses and relative agency, in which they actively negotiate their social statuses and career aspirations. Women's agentic power, and goal for better jobs in their eSMOs challenges men's hegemonic privilege. The above interview also suggests that the more hierarchical-based eNGOs are sites for more competitive performances of femininity, contrasting with the more grassroots-based eNGOs.

8.3 Discussion

I would deduce from the above excerpt that being ambitious for one's career and acting 'pushy' or 'bossy' parallels to emphasized femininity resistance. 'Ruthlessness' is not an egalitarian approach; but then acting 'tough' and competitive accompanies one's career objective for a prestigious position: 'they make their way to the top, they don't care whose head they tread on, they're just the same as men... if they want to be the CEO of an eNGO...' (Barbara [audio] 2010). Moreover, I refrain from attacking women's tough performances and assertiveness; rather toughness highlights intellectual-physical strength. Moreover, potentially quashing other women, who may be aspiring for similar jobs, is not an ethical performance, nor grounds for a harmonious work environment. Besides, Barbara's account reveals that women operate in a masculinist culture, which underscores their aggressive performances: 'they don't care whose head they tread on, they're just the same as men. They operate in dynamics... just as ruthlessly as men'. Hegemonic masculinity underlines women's inequity/injustice; however, emphasized femininity leadership, accentuated through agentic performances, entails feminist empowerment, whilst destabilising male privilege. Women are skilled agents of change, but are equally resistant to men's power (Plumwood 1997; Gaard 2001, 2017; Meynell 2009; Butler 2011, 2013; Clean Energy Council 2018).

Women-led physical-intellectual assertiveness should challenge Anglo middle class men's exclusivity of environmental governance (Donaldson 1993, 2009; DAWN 2015; Bombora Wave Power 2018; Carnegie Clean Energy 2018). In summary, women's emphasized femininity performativity, as tough and confidently assertive, reveals a dynamic interplay of constructivism/essentialism that is justly defiant to ruling governing and industrial elites. Women's bodily and intellectual strength frames their emphasized femininity leadership, and are vibrant qualities for Republicanism. *My six groups'* agency is located in their skills-sets and potential to subvert middle class men's control of executive governance.

8.4 Radical Performative Femininities: Civil Disobedience

Regarding my theme of physical competence, women's civil disobedience, in terms of 'getting arrested' is viewed by several of my grassroots and political participants, as a valid activist strategy. In this section, my participants performative civil disobedience underlines women's dissatisfaction with political structures and governance. Also, I consider participants' conservative, performative femininities, in which peaceful, less confrontational approaches likewise validate social change goals. These insights inform my rather 'revolutionary' framework. Women-led subversion, that is, on the one hand, politically radical, and, on the other hand, centred on communicative, 'quiet' reactionary methods, informs my anti-war ethos. In my peacemaking democratic model, I aim to realise my groups equity/justice, in which a Republican constitution should replace Monarchist governance and the Westminster Constitution. This egalitarian model is inclusive of my groups, aspiring for their greater representation in male-dominated sectors. It is equally resistant to middle class men's hegemony (Plumwood 1997; Donaldson and Poynting 2013; Ajani 2015; WIE 2018).

Concerning physical competence, grassroots and professional women's prowess is shown by an appropriation of radical methods that challenge the authorities. They engage in bravery, camaraderie and dedication. Climate Camp, an annual Australian third-sector protest event organised by eNGOs and the grassroots, has a strong women-led contingent, in opposition to industrial and governing elites. At Climate Camp, Greens politician Margaret indicates no fear of arrest or legal repercussion in pursuit of the cause:

> There's a few of us prepared to be arrested at Climate Camp, and there's one coming up, so we will be quite happy to be arrested. We feel as though we're helping. There's a lot of young activists that are brave, that put their careers on the line and we feel that we can help them. We advocate for other people.
> (Margaret [audio] 2010)

Margaret's civil disobedience at Climate Camp shows the radical determinism, framing women's social change acts. Margaret's evaluation of being part of a group that was 'quite happy to be arrested' and 'we feel we're helping', frames an intersection of positive/negative connotations. Although getting arrested is stereotypically a negative incident, women's emotiveness, articulated by feelings of happiness on 'helping the cause' and putting 'their careers on the line', reveals that social change parallel to emphasized femininity-led non-compliance, is necessary to spur on civil reform and political urgency on climate action (Mellor 1997; Doyle 2005; Barry 2008; Wilson et al. 2010; Schlembach 2011). Such radical climate action is situated in the fact that Australia does not have an Emissions Trading Scheme or Federal legislative policies centred on capping carbon emissions, unlike many other post-industrial, advanced democracies (Shepard and Corbin-Mark 2009; EU ETS 2018; McIlroy 2018; NZ ETS 2018). My Act's four Initiatives, affiliated with women's scientific-technical leadership, informs positive frames of sustainable technological development (Gaard 2001; McFarland 2014; Clean Energy Council 2018).

Margaret's ([audio] 2010) positively framed emotive adjectives/verbs: 'happy', 'feel', 'helping' and 'advocate', accentuated through 'we', evoke the power of emphasized femininity collective – environmental change acts, whereby the group dynamic, that is compassionate, dedicated women activists, denote tough defiance towards ruling authorities. Also, the bravery of 'young activists', signifies their corporeal-intellectual capabilities. The 'climate advocacy' of mature (Margaret) and younger women, signifies demographical unity within activism. A dynamic group force, of young and older women's performative acts, is necessary for social change. According to Barbara ([audio] 2010), older women are inspirational role models for young activists. Each age demographic inspires the other. Mature women's wisdom, inspires my Initiatives; I contest older, CALD and disabled women's marginalisation in the workforce (Ainsworth 2002; Cooper 2013; DAWN 2015; AHRC 2016b; Evans 2016; Edge et al. 2017).

In relation to Margaret's commentary: 'happy to be arrested', fellow Greens politician, Stacey was part of a group, where over 100 people were arrested outside Federal Parliament. There is an interesting power dynamic here, when politicians – people with political authority – are exercising the laws of the land, but also challenging this:

> I went to Canberra and was part of a protest where 130 people got arrested outside Parliament House and I was one of them. It was about highlighting to the government before they went to Copenhagen, they needed to be serious about reducing emissions, having a proper mandatory target and expanding the coal industry and logging forests was not going to address the issues... You can be activated and very engaged... They don't see themselves as environmental activists. I hope that somebody like me can say to Mums and Dads, you are already an activist. You are fighting for the environment because you think about your kids.
>
> (Stacey [audio] 2010)

Such a radical protest event, for Stacey, was critical for climate reform: 'where 130 people got arrested outside Parliament House', in order to spur politicians' serious policy reforms on reducing carbon emissions and having 'a proper mandatory target' rather than continued extrapolation/destruction of the natural environment: 'expanding the coal industry and logging forests'. In relation to Stacey, everyday citizens, in particular concerned parents, are already 'activated and very engaged', which supports my research on mothers' nurturing identity as central to their sustainable-climate campaigning (Maleta 2011b, 2015, 2018a). While Stacey's excerpt frames her 'radical' subversiveness and civil disobedience towards ruling political leaders, her narrative puts emphasis on the role of a politician, as a concerned advocate of citizenry: 'I hope that somebody like me can say to Mums and Dads, you are already an activist', whereby parents also play a crucial, informative role in advocating for the environment, although, 'they don't see themselves as environmental activists' ([audio] 2010). In my egalitarian scope for sustainable technical-scientific development, social change is contingent upon 'very engaged', 'activated' individual-collective acts by politicians and the grassroots. The mutual efforts of citizens 'Mums and Dads' and advocacy of politicians with legislative power are powerful forces for a more sustainable, healthier, ethical world (Prokhovnik 1998; MacGregor 2006, 2014; Smith and Pangsapa 2008; Sundström and McCright 2014; Maleta 2018a)

Professional and grassroots women undoubtedly place 'their careers on the line' (Margaret) and put themselves in confronting, danger-ridden scenarios, susceptible to law and prosecution: 'arrested outside Parliament House' (Stacey), in order to achieve their environmental goals. Climate activist Dion pinpoints the abuse activists endure:

> People came in the middle of the night and jumped on tents, and came drunk and started abusing people and people threw eggs at us the next day. It's scary when you're in that situation… they see us as a direct threat to their livelihoods, 'cause they work on the mine and we were saying it shouldn't continue.
>
> (Dion [audio] 2010)

Whilst radical-grassroots initiatives places climate activists in a 'scary' situation, the local miners respond radically and partake in their own type of subversive civil 'drunken' disobedience, by jumping on tents, 'abusing people' and throwing eggs. The miner's incivility is due to their view of climate activists as 'a direct threat to their livelihoods'. Nonetheless, women continue with sustainability-informed climate resistance, highlighting their corporeal-intellectual capabilities plus bravery, tenacity and strength of character.

The above excerpt, furthermore, underscores gender and class dimensions. As miners are mainly working class men (Gow and Leahy 2005; Barry 2008; Unger 2008; Gaard 2011); I deduce that their 'abusiveness' evokes a type of tough, aggressive, working class masculinist resistance to 'middle class' anti-mining campaigners. There is a class differentiation here between working class miners and middle class women (and men) climate activists. Hegemony is discursive to one's status and position in social hierarchies (Connell 1995, 2005; Donaldson 2009; Maleta 2011a; Nascimento and Connell 2017), whereby one's class may define how men/women respond to their environs, particularly when they feel challenged. In addition, men's 'abuse' of women activists signifies a type of aggressive, adversarial hegemonic masculinity that is resistant to emphasized femininity leadership (Connell 1995,

2005; Leahy 2003; Maleta 2015, 2018b). Across my interviews, women critique men's aggressive, adversarial performances. I contend that middle class and working class men perform adversarial masculinities, framed by androcentrism; however, working class men's performance here tends to be more physical. Men of different classes resist women's leadership; however, executive men's resistance is a core barrier, underpinning glass ceilings in organisational governance (Giddens 1991; Donaldson and Poynting 2007, 2013; Connell 2009; McGregor 2009; Grusky 2014). In relation to *my six groups'* inequity/injustice, arguably, it is middle class Anglo men that are the core barrier, rather than working class men, for they control environmental hierarchies, which underscores the lack of progressive sustainable technological development. My Initiatives meet this gap; for women empower such change.

The direct, radical action of women in the firing line details women's assertive performances in acts not deemed conventionally feminine (Buckingham-Hatfield 2000; Pease 2002; Unger 2008; Kwan and Trautner 2009). Such action emphasises constructivism as agentic, whilst downplaying essentialist assumptions of female incompetence (Cockburn 1988; Berg and Lie 1995; Crary 2001; MacGregor 2010; Vildåsen et al. 2017). Similarly, Greens participant Tanya elaborated on radical strategies at Climate Camp, such as, stopping the coal trains:

> I attend rallies, I've been to the last two climate camps. The last one; we marched to the entrance of the coal facility. The year before we marched to the rail yards and stopped the coal trains from taking their coal.
>
> (Tanya [audio] 2010)

The women in my study, especially older women, convey a bold, proud history in climate change-sustainably initiatives along with anti-war-nuclear peace-oriented activism. My Bill of Rights is framed by an anti-war ethos and peacemaking agenda, in which military approaches involving warfare and atomic energy are sharply resisted (Warren and Cady 1996; Butler 2009; Cockburn 2010; Cockburn and Enloe 2012; Wibben 2016). Warfare is an extension of patriarchy and hegemonic masculinity, replicated through the androcentric ruling power of governing elites (Warren 1999; Gaard 2001; Cockburn 2012, 2013). However, emphasized femininity-sustainable leadership, corresponding to women-led anti-war and anti-atomic-anti-nuclear initiatives, underlie my peacemaking methodological quest, to have more strategic investment of renewable technologies (Cockburn 2012, 2013; McFarland 2014; Ajani 2015; Clean Energy Council 2018). Such technologies are not supported by atomic energy or dangerous toxins, and, thus, accompany my peacemaking agenda for a safer, more sustainable, less militant, androcentric world (Rankin and Gale 2003; MacGregor 2006; Culley and Angelique 2010; Cockburn 2012).

In a landmark Australian peace collective action, women's anti-war resistance, outside the U.S. army base, Pine Gap, in the Northern Territory, highlighted empowering emphasized femininity leadership:

one of the most exciting actions was in 1983 when 700 women camped outside Pine Gap, a U.S. military installation outside Alice Springs, that was a very powerful action by these hundreds of women to say no to war.

(Jennifer [audio] 2010)

The peace-oriented nature of this protest event shrouded the potential of these '700 women' to be arrested in large numbers. This example highlights their collective, courageous bravery, and how their peaceful ethos, driven by a mutual declaration of 'no to war', was an educative, encouraging experience, accentuating their knowledge plus skills base. In relation to this Pine Gap action, Jennifer adds that she: 'learnt a great deal at the time' and: 'had real pleasure working with those women' ([audio] 2010). Likewise, this historic event, mirrors the 'radical-peace activism' of global women anti-nuclear campaigners, during the 1980s, as with British women's anti-military, anti-atomic energy initiatives at the Greenham Common Peace Camp (Rankin and Gale 2003; Cockburn 2012; Cockburn and Enloe 2012; Maleta 2018b).

In current sociopolitical climes, anti-nuclear campaigning is accompanied by vigorous sustainably actions; my Act legislates on renewable development, whilst viewing nuclear energy as the most dangerous technology on the planet (Rankin and Gale 2003; Culley and Angelique 2010; Caldicott 2014). Every ten years or so there is a nuclear-oriented disaster: the partial-nuclear melt-down at Three Mile Island (TMI), Pennsylvania, U.S.A., in 1979; the nuclear power plant explosion at Chernobyl, USSR, 1986; and the Fukushima nuclear power plant meltdown, caused by an earthquake and tsunami, in Japan, 2011 (Culley and Angelique 2003; Unger 2008; Caldicott 2014; Maleta 2018b; World Nuclear Organisation 2018). Moreover, renewable technology is unquestionably safer, yet requires more investment and women-led direction, for its true potential to be realised.

8.5 Conservative Performative Femininities: Aspirations for Social Change

In support to 'radical' and 'competitive' femininities, in this section I consider women-led 'conservative' approaches. Conservative femininities are seemingly representative of less agentic or less activated femininities; however, I argue that women appropriate this in their leadership, as compelling acts of social change. Women engage in radical (direct, confrontational) and/or conservative (indirect, less confrontational) performative femininities, responding differently to ruling class masculinity along with patriarchal-framed environments (MacLeod 1992; Sandilands 1995; Mellor 1997, 2013; Plumwood 1997; Mortimer-Sandilands 2008; Buechler and Hanson 2015). Conservativeness does not delineate from women's agentic competence, or goals for policy reform and political changes. Concerning conservative femininity, Abigail rejected Climate Camp, due to the fear of potential arrest:

It takes courage to do it… I find it intimidating to interact with the police in that way. I went to Climate Camp, and I couldn't participate in sitting on the road because I didn't want that interaction with the police. I don't think the police are violent or unreasonable. I don't have the courage. I'm not real convinced how effective it is, but my temperament doesn't fit very well; but I admire people who do it… but I don't think social change is more likely to come about because of those actions. It's more about talking to people, standing for something. I understand why people do it, I'm just not sure how well it advances what we're on about.

(Abigail [audio] 2010)

Although Abigail did not want a direct confrontation with the police at Climate Camp: 'I couldn't participate in sitting on the road', and contemplated her lack of 'courage'; her social change agenda was defined by communicative, less confrontational engagement: 'talking to people'. Abigail's rejection of civil disobedience: 'I don't think social change is more likely to come about because of those actions', does not delineate her passion for the cause nor her admiration for climate activists. Abigail's emphasized femininity leadership is 'more about talking to people, standing for something' whereby social interaction is viewed as the solution to climate reform. While Abigail's performativity draws attention to a conservative feminine performance, in her resistance to radicalised Climate Camp, I deduce, from my excerpts, that 'conservative' (talking, communicating, negotiating, lobbying) and 'radical' (protest events, challenging the authorities) techniques are necessary for legislative reform and community consensus, thereby informing sustainable development goals. Radical and conservative performative women-led strategies contribute to environmental change outcomes (Prokhovnik 1998; Gaard 2001; Connell 2005; Butler 2006, 2013).

My Republican approach is radical in arguing for the end of Monarchism (Snow 2016; Veri 2016; ARM 2018; Australian Monarchist League 2018; Australians for Constitutional Monarchy 2018). It hinges upon dissatisfaction with conservative, redundant political structures along with governing and industrial leaders' reluctance to embrace sustainable technological development. Patriarchy underscores my subversion (Walby 1990, 2013; Plumwood 1997; Cockburn 2010, 2012, 2013). In my egalitarian resistance to ruling-middle class masculinity, a Republican-constitutional-framed Bill of Rights Act, supported by robust Initiatives, is an opportunity to challenge the patriarchal control of politics and achieve a more inclusive, democratic model, relative to *my six groups*' equity/justice.

CALD women constitute one of my six groupings, and, in the following interview, Wendy, of Asian heritage, elaborates on sociocultural-gender framed enablers/barriers within activism. Concerning insights to radicalism/conservativism, Wendy explains that by choosing to be an activist, she is subverting from family expectations:

It hasn't been a huge a barrier for me, but to get involved in activism as a young [Asian] person is culturally difficult, it's not the normal way to pursue your life path. With women, it's a big pressure on getting married and finding the right family. I think any woman who wanted, at my age, to devote her life to social change, would be very challenging within her family. They are afraid what the community would think, afraid for the future of their daughter, how will she get married? It's not an Australian phenomenon so much… But I am born and brought up here, so there is a difference if I had been brought up there. I'm not sure if I would have been empowered in the same way as I have been empowered here.

(Wendy [audio] 2010)

8.6 Discussion

In retrospect, Wendy's decision to engage in 'social change' acts manifests itself as 'a huge a [cultural] barrier', for 'a young [Asian] person', deviating from family norms and sociocultural expectations: 'it's not the normal way to pursue your lifepath'. Despite cultural barriers and family expectations, 'afraid for the future of their daughter, how will she get married?', Wendy's choice to pursue activism, 'But I am born and brought up here, so there is a difference', indicates her radicalism and empowerment as a young first-generation Australian woman, pursuing community social change: 'I have been empowered here'. The above narrative reveals a compelling intersection of conservatism/radicalism with constructivism/ essentialism. Wendy's constructivism is located in her agentic identity as an empowered activist, exercising gendered power relations and negotiating the 'I' in her identity through robust performative acts (Butler 1990, 2006, 2007, 2015; Connell 1995, 2005). Simultaneously, essentialist views of young Asian women's 'conservative' appropriate role in society is being reworked. Wendy's evident success as a young woman community campaigner demonstrates that such performativity is not necessarily shameful or dishonourable; but an inspirational act, inspiring others in the community, ideally.

This section has shown that Greens politicians and grassroots participants, adopt radical (direct) and less confrontational (indirect) strategies in their quest for a more sustainably peaceful, less patriarchal, militant world (Warren and Cady 1996; Warren 1999; Butler 2009; Cockburn 2010; Maleta 2011b; Australian Greens, Participatory Democracy, 2018). In support to my method, MacLeod's (1992) resistance theory enables me to consider conservatism/radicalism by how women may choose to accept/accommodate to hierarchy, and/or reject/ resist patriarchy. Similarly, Plumwood (1997) contends that women have the choice to adopt a resistant femininity, which supports Connell's (1995, 2002) foregrounding of emphasized femininity as compliant or resistant to patriarchy.

Differentiated women-led 'radical' and 'conservative' approaches do not delineate women's *agentic performative multiple skills-set*. Women's radicalism highlights their physical competence, whilst their conservative-social change initiatives highlight their intellectual competence. Corporeal and intellectual performative qualities intersect across my interviews, framing women's emphasized femininity empowerment, relative to diverse radical/conservative performative femininities. Evidently, 'conservative' (talking, communicating, negotiating, lobbying) and 'radical' (protest events, challenging the authorities) techniques are necessary for legislative reform and community consensus, informing sustainable development goals. Radical and conservative performative women-led strategies, contribute to environmental change outcomes (Prokhovnik 1998; Gaard 2001; Connell 2005; Butler 2006, 2013). Such action is not complaint to men nor patriarchy (Warren 1999; Cockburn 2010, 2012, 2013; MacGregor 2014; Wibben 2016; WIE 2018). Women's 'toughness' evokes constructivism, and challenges 'subordinate' notions of essentialised femininity (Cockburn 1988, 2012; Culley and Angelique 2003; MacGregor 2006, 2010; Farr et al. 2017; Maleta 2018b). My integration of constructivism with emphasized femininity enhances my Republican-Initiatives, framed by agentic resistant femininities, pursing greater WW & SE change goals (WIE 2018).

Conclusion

My vision for a Republican-Bill of Rights Constitutional change is reinforced by emphasized femininity performative plural competencies: corporeal (physical strength, bravery, confidence, assertion, radicalism) and intellectual (technical, scientific, talking, communicating, negotiating). Women's civil disobedience and communicative negotiation strategies foreground my rationale for a Republican change and Initiatives, legislating on *my six groups'* leadership of male-dominated sectors, such as politics and science (Maleta 2011b; Pollack 2015; Cohen 2016; STEMM 2018). My Act draws upon women's physical-bodily and intellectual-scientific-technical strengths. Toughness, exemplified through career drives within eSMOs, and as an act of civil disobedience, has emerged as a core theme from this chapter, supporting my insight to women's performative physical competence. Emphasized femininity performativity entails women's 'tough behaviour', in terms of '[getting] their hands dirty', 'being very brave... physically brave too' and 'bossy, pushy'.

Competitive performative forms of femininity, such as, 'bossy' and 'pushy', signpost several points. One, executive women are particularly ambitious for career advancement and elevated statuses; similarly, they aspire to be, justly and fairly, economically rewarded for their performative expertise. Two, the more hierarchical-structured eNGOs are characteristic of competitive femininities (contrasting with grassroots-based eNGOs), whereby performative-based merit is a decisive factor in career elevation. Three, *my six groups* would struggle more to achieve leadership equity in the executive arm of the eNSM, due to its 'less inclusive' work culture. As such, hierarchical-based eNGOs, led by executive men (and some executive women) are sites that are less likely to entice elevated input from minority women, including, disabled, CALD and Indigenous groups (my six categories). Four, women being ambitious for their careers, and acting tough to achieve this, should not be overtly criticised. Such toughness frames an emphasized femininity performative leadership, situated through women's physical-intellectual assertion. Similarly, ambitious women, are not content to be wallflowers. They strive for more important, influential positions in their organisations; this is vital, in order for women's eminent leadership to be realised. Five, more women in positions of power is the solution to a more sustainable world, whereby women play a vital role in renewable technological development (Baruah 2016; RenewableUK 2017; BWE 2018; Clean Energy Council 2018; WIE 2018). This frames my Act's legislative scope, along with its equity/justice-based Initiatives. Six, women's apparent 'ruthlessness', is underpinned by the patriarchal control of their eSMOs, for men hold superior statuses in the upper echelons of the eNSM (Connell 2009; Edge et al. 2017; EREF 2018; EUREC 2018; SolarPower Europe 2018). Seven, Anglo middle class men's privileged hegemony, continues to hinder women's career elevation (DAWN 2015; Bombora Wave Power 2018; Carnegie Clean Energy 2018). Women's toughness and exercise of agency, however, defies glass ceilings and ruling class masculinity, as Barbara and Maggie argued. Women's performative, subversive 'doing of gender', thus contributes to environmental change (Plumwood 1997, 2002, 2006; Gaard 2001; Butler 2006, 2013).

My excerpts indicate that there is no singular feminine way of behaving (Cockburn 1988; Connell 1995, 2002, 2005; Pease 2002; Segal 2007; Wibben 2016). Women partake in competitive, radical and conservative femininities, and each of these represents a valid social change leadership strategy. Also, women's agentically competent leadership performativity, reveals that they are not submissive or compliant to men (MacLeod 1992; Connell 1995; Mellor 1997; Plumwood 1997; Butler 2011, 2015; Gaard 2011). Rather they are performing resistant femininities, shown to be physically and intellectually assertive thereby representative of constructivism, whilst challenging essentialism. Further, corporeal and mind-based prowess, accentuates women's bodily and intellectual empowerment (Butler 1999, 2004, 2007). Women's 'tough' approach, hence, challenges subordinate notions of femininity, and such tough-based leadership informs my Republican model. Although I reject adversarial strategies, women-led assertion evokes emphasized femininity resistance to patriarchy, and is necessary for a reactionary, revolutionary change. Women's intellectual confidence and physical strength along with bravery, compassion and warmth, underlines my Initiatives, centred on women's performative plural skills-set. This section has integrated the bodily and mind-based qualities of participants, and such empowered performances inspire my methodological vision for women's defined leadership of sustainable technological development and a Republican sociopolitical change.

9 Age as a Barrier/Enabler
Older and Younger Women's Agentic Resistance

Introduction

I have, so far, demonstrated how participants (Juliet, Wendy, Maggie and Kate) identify age/ageism (being too young or too old) as a barrier, pertaining to labelling, positioning women as the dualist outsider/insider within climate conferences, panels and at work (Yoder and Aniakudo 1997; Maddison 2004; Nagy 2017). In this chapter, academics and eNGO women comment on age as a barrier/ enabler, framed through stigmas and perceptions of female scientific-technical incompetence (Cockburn 1988; Culley and Angelique 2010; Yoder et al. 2011; Maleta 2012). Anna, Rachel and Stephanie pinpoint the chauvinism of older men, reflecting how ruling-middle class men's hegemony 'others' women, even in their own academic institutions and eNGOs (Donaldson 1993; Donaldson and Poynting 2013; Grusky 2014). Older and younger women advocates' otherness is discursive to constructivist-essentialist framed perceptions of knowledge, and, comparably, relayed though intersections of age, gender, competence and hegemony (Cockburn 1988; Culley and Angelique 2003, 2010; Maleta 2011a, 2015). As young (and older) women struggle with tags of technical incompetence, their 'knowledge sharing' (Juliet) and performativity of 'social and environmental importance' (Helen), represents an interactive, constructivist performance. Women-led constructivist empowerment accompanies an emphasized performative resistant femininity, framed by social-intellectual-scientific-physical competencies akin to agentic sustainable-social change ambitions (Leahy 2003; Connell 2005; Butler 2006, 2007; Jagger 2008; Maleta 2012, 2018b).

9.1 Framing Women's Liberation: Women as Technicians, Men as Scientists

Scientific academic Anna considers age as a barrier for older women re-entering the workforce. She explains that older women scientists, re-entering academia after extended maternity leave, are deemed 'too old', especially for 'physical' field work:

> women have time out to have children and by time they perhaps reach
> the stage where they'd be ready for a senior research position, then they're

too old. I think it's harder for research, because it's more physical than social science. You know, you have to do the experiment; you have to get out in the field and collect the data... so time consuming doing interviews and things like that. And you have a lot more failures, like the glasshouse will break down and the temperature will go up and all the plants will die, and you have to start again.

(Anna [audio] 2010)

Physical-intellectual-scientific prowess is demonstrated by Anna's biological research, performed out on the: 'field', 'glasshouse', 'experiments', boldly stating that: 'you have to get out in the field and collect the data' and possess skills in tenacity and perseverance: 'the temperature will go up and all the plants will die, you have to start again'. However, she admits that the physicality of this is a barrier for mature women re-entering the workforce: 'they perhaps reach the stage where they'd be ready for a senior research position, then they're too old' (Anna [audio] 2010). The notion of age and performing hard field work is difficult to reconcile, when women struggle to perform the corporeal, bodily aspects of the task at hand. To a certain extent, this excerpt reflects stigmas associated with age, gender and incompetence (Cockburn 1988; Culley and Angelique 2003; Duncan and Loretto 2004; Keller 2012; Maleta 2012; AHRC 2016b). Nonetheless, women, like men, have certain limitations, bounded by their physique and maturity. As a feminist, there is no shame in stating that age can be a limitation in one's performative scope. In retrospect, I infer that older women can still engage in performative scientific field work, but they may require some help in the physical demanding aspects of the role. While I (and Anna), evidently empathise with women's 'physical' limitations, I refrain from conceding that older women cannot perform field work. As suggested, seeking assistance from other staff, or even appropriating the technological automation of equipment, could enhance mature women's agentic performance within biological, physical-field science, whilst diminishing the toughness of it (Cockburn 1988; Maleta 2009; Meynell 2009; Merchant 2013, 2016).

Within an historic reflective context, Anna's interview points to women's physical sex-segregation in professional science (Alston 2011, 2013; Pollack 2015; Cohen 2016; STEMM 2018). In the framework of the 1950s–60s (shortly before the Women's Liberation Movement), Anna contemplates the physical segregation of women in academia: 'All the technicians were females. All the scientists were males... only one female scientist where I worked... in microscopy, which is... a more feminine thing' ([audio] 2010). Women's scientific over-representation as 'technicians' and in 'feminine' 'microscopy', suggests segregation is discursive to degree of (in)competence (Cockburn 1988; Ahern and Hendryx 2008; Kermoal et al. 2016). To this day, women still struggle with labels of scientific-intellectual incompetence (Culley and Angelique 2003; Payne 2009; Maleta 2018a; STEMM 2018). Despite men's dominance in the higher-status position of scientist, women competently performed their roles in a technical capacity (Cockburn 1988; Probert and Wilson 1993; Lindsay 2008; Maleta 2009; Pollack 2015; Farr et al. 2017).

Physical segregation extends to separate dining facilities. During the 1960s, Anna ([audio] 2010) explains how men scientists and women technicians were socially differentiated: 'they had tea rooms that were separate for technicians and the women sat in one and all the male scientists sat in the other'. Moreover, women's scientific competence should not be under-estimated, for their technical work enabled men to simulate research results: 'The men sat in their office writing, doing whatever they did [laugh]… the technicians did all the work…' (Anna [audio] 2010). Hence, it was women's technical-scientific performances, that enabled men to write 'their' findings (Culley and Angelique 2003; Maleta 2018b). This harks to my prior point, on scientific men taking credit for the professional and grassroots work of women on climate panels. It also highlights constructivism/essentialism, for women are 'doing all the work', whilst men partake in the more passive role: 'in their office writing'. Women's constructivism is, consequently, relayed through technical-scientific performative prowess (Shiva and Moser 1995; Crary 2001; Butler 2004, 2006; MacGregor 2010, 2014).

Preceding the women's liberation NSM, women in science, were subject to aggressive physical contact, which would be considered sexual harassment or assault nowadays (Freeman 1973; Greer 1999, 2010b; Burn 2011; AHRC 2017a). Anna ([audio] 2010) states that men 'used to pinch our bums and everything. We never dared say anything'. Such behaviour should be defined as sexual assault; although this still occurs, EEO civil laws have made it clear that men's, touching of women, is highly inappropriate and dually susceptible to criminal legislation (Ainsworth 2012; AHRC 2017a, 2017b). Anna's excerpt underpins women's invisibility within a culture of silence: 'We never dared say anything' (Prokhovnik 1998; Crary 2001; Ainsworth 2002; Lewis 2006; Segal 2007). This underscores men's ruling status and authoritative power, and that a complaint initiated by a woman would be ignored (Yoder and Aniakudo 1997; Poynting and Donaldson 2005; AHRC 2017b). Or if a women dared to challenge a man/men, she would be susceptible to workplace dismissal, further reiterating their unfair treatment (Sullivan 2011; Ussher 2011; AHRC 2017a). Before the women's NSM of the 1970s, sexism, misogyny and chauvinism were rampant; exemplified through adversarial and androcentric performances of middle class masculinity, underscoring women's historic to contemporary struggle with gender-organisational barriers as well as patriarchy (Taylor 1989; Donaldson 1993; Connell 1995, 2002; Butler 2007, 2011; Maleta 2012; Summers 2013; Walby 2013; Manne 2017).

Anna's above commentary, 'we never dared say anything', perhaps links to Maggie's critique of women not using their power and letting men run the world. As women's liberation was a collective global action against sexism and discrimination, centred on reversing women's (in)equity in the workplace, perhaps women's silence, before this NSM, enabled chauvinism and the patriarchal control of organisational governance (Walby 1990; Crary 2001; MacGregor 2006, 2009; Ainsworth 2012). Women's seeming accommodation or compliance to patriarchy, critically, frames their 'subordination' (MacLeod 1992; Connell 1995; Plumwood 1997; Buckingham-Hatfield 2000; Butler 2004). Nonetheless, women's liberation, symbolised women's successful collective mobilisation against endemic gender harassment and improved workplace entitlements, including higher pay (Freeman 1973; Taylor 1989; Pocock 2003, 2005; McLellan 2009). Contentiously, women still receive less pay (than men), as Jennifer and other participants illustrated (Greer 1999; Walby 2011, 2013; Pocock et al. 2013; Plibersek 2016).

9.2 Chauvinism, Misogyny and Sexism Within Academia

Following on from my discussion of women's liberation, framed by its struggles and successes, my empirical themes reveal that chauvinism, misogyny and sexism, are still problematic within environmentalist executive hierarchies. This section considers women's contemporary struggle with ruling-middle class masculinity in academia and hierarchical eNGOs (Eder 1996; Probert 2005; Connell 2009; McGregor 2009; Grusky 2014; AHRC 2017b). Turning to 2010 or thereabouts, Anna contemplates how women's work and social relations have changed: 'there's been a big change, that was sort of in the late 50s. I think things have improved' ([audio] 2010). While 'things have improved', glass ceilings hinder academics:

> There are a lot of women in administration in universities, and our university had one of the first female vice chancellors, but there are still not a lot of women in research itself, you know, that reach the top. So we're trying to recruit a Director for this institute, and, I can't think of a woman who's at the stage of their career that I can ask to apply, yet I can think of a hundred men. So that sort of reflects the pros, where the women are in their careers.
>
> (Anna [audio] 2010)

In relation to Anna, women are achieving status as 'vice chancellors', one of the most important executive roles in universities; however, they remain under-represented in 'top' research positions (Probert 2005; AHRC 2016b, 2017b; Marfo 2017; STEMM 2018). This is evident through Anna's struggle to recruit women as institute Directors. Also, the fact that men hold more research experience: 'I can think of a hundred men' is contrasted with women's lack of proportionate leadership expertise: 'I can't think of a woman who's at the stage of their career that I can ask to apply' (Anna [audio] 2010). I infer that women's contentious position in scientific research is not reflective of their competence, but due to men's privileged status, whereby a patriarchal culture enables their career elevation: 'reflects the pros, where the women are in their careers'. Additionally, this relates to Anna's assessment, that after women's re-entry to scientific academia, upon maternity leave, they are situated at a significant gap in career development – unable to compete with men, for high-status positions (Rentetzi 2010; Gilardi 2015; Pollack 2015; Cohen 2016). However, after maternity leave, women, should be supported and encouraged in their own organisations, through knowledge-based, career-development initiatives (Ainsworth and Cutcher 2008; Baxter and Chesters 2011; Maleta

2015; STEMM 2018). My Act's Initiatives, centred on mature women's career development in scientific leadership, aims to counter the barriers working mothers (akin to *my six groups*) experience, whilst improving their work–life balance (Ainsworth 2002; Pocock 2003; Ainsworth and Cutcher 2008; Baxter and Chesters 2011; Pocock et al. 2013; Britton 2017).

Chauvinism is related to my key theme of 'a boys club', and evokes the structural-cultural ruling power of middle class men plus their hegemony of executive hierarchies. In the international gender studies field, there is a lack of current research on chauvinism, as an example of ruling class masculinity, relative to the global eNSM and its eSMOs, whereby my research fills a cutting-edge gap (Forbes-Mewett and Snell 2006; Maleta 2011b, 2018b; Fisher and Kinsey 2014; Wibben 2016; EREF 2018; EUREC 2018). My empirical insights to chauvinism, misogyny and sexism are supported by a number of mature academic critiques. Rachel considers the chauvinism of 'men of a certain age'. While chauvinism and harassment occur in the workplace, this is not uniform to all men:

> up again at the bar, you'll get comments about, once upon a time, in the 90s, the early 90s, men of a certain age, who would now be in their 60s, would still have that chauvinistic attitude… Umm, harassment, there was one barrister, he was on the same floor as I was, who used to come on to every woman. I just found that giving him as good as he got… his middle name was William, so I'd refer to him as 'Little Willie'.
>
> (Rachel [audio] 2010)

In the context of 'the early 90s, older men 'of a certain age', are more likely to possess chauvinistic, misogynist attitude towards women. I infer, from Rachel and Anna's excerpts (plus other participants) that Anglo middle class men, represent a cultural-structural barrier to women's workplace equity and career aspirations (Kaufmann 2004; Donaldson and Poynting 2007, 2013; McGregor 2009; DAWN 2015). As Maxine contended, 'old White men' are not enlightened, in terms of progressive gender politics and realising women's leadership within conservation-based eNGOs. Although these men would have come through the women's liberation NSM, chauvinism curtails their social attitudes and work relations towards women. Rachel's ([audio] 2010) account underscores male harassment, as a type of sexualised, middle class masculinity: 'harassment, there was one barrister, he was on the same floor as I was, who used to come on to every woman'. His conduct though was not perceived to be a direct threat to Rachel or other women: 'I just found that giving him as good as he got' (Rachel [audio] 2010).

9.3 Mocking the Sexualised Performativity of Male Bosses

Professional academics, like Rachel, mock the sexualised performativity of men. The example of a pet name, naming the barrister 'Little Willie', denotes a humorous caricature to experiences of sexism: 'coming on to every woman'.

Although women, like Rachel, identify this as 'harassment' and exemplifying a 'chauvinistic attitude', they do not personalise this behaviour or become personally offended. Rather women respond by mocking and mimicking their male harasser, thereby placing him in a comical light, rather than as a potential dangerous perpetrator. This reveals a fine line between the actual violation of women's civil rights and women's rejection of male chauvinism, sexism and misogyny (Gaard 2011; Summers 2013; Manne 2017). Besides, Rachel's interview shows that chauvinism is particularly characteristic of the older, maturing male group and their old-fashioned attitude to women, thereby revealing an intersection of age, gender and perceptions of competence (Greer 1999, 2010a; Maleta 2012). Chauvinism and sexism are framed by men's expectations of women's conformity to 'subordinate' roles plus their resistance to women's leadership; thus replicating patriarchy (Arendt 1945; Cockburn 1991; Mellor 1993; Segal 1999, 2007; Wright and Holland 2014; Cadaret et al. 2017).

Scientist, Helen, a former eNGO Director, likewise draws attention to stigmatised labelling from older men. Her observation foregrounds women's struggle with ruling class masculinity and middle class management, underscoring the contentious, 'subordinate' status of women in mining corporations (Buckingham-Hatfield 2000; Irwin 2010; Gaard 2011; Donaldson and Poynting 2013; Haynes et al. 2015). In my line of questioning: 'As a female, do you ever feel that you are treated differently for what you can do or how you perform? Please give me an example of when gender may have been an issue?'

> Being young and female has sometimes set me apart. The main realisation of this was when I worked in mining advocacy in my early 20s. I was young, female, in AGMs of mining companies full of old men in suits, and raising questions of social and environmental importance in a financial profits-focused setting. That made me feel different and aware of my gender and age. But it also made me stand out, which was good for task!
>
> (Helen [audio] 2010)

Helen's critique of 'mining companies full of old men in suits' highlights the hegemonic privilege of older middle class Anglo men in resource-based industries (Rankin and Gale 2003; Donaldson and Poynting 2007; Donaldson 2009; McGregor 2009; Nunlee 2016). Such privilege is replicated in global sustainability management, whereby executive men dominate the leadership hierarchy of renewable boards (Doyle 2000; Gaard 2011; Bombora Wave Power 2018; Carnegie Clean Energy 2018; EREF 2018; EUREC 2018; SolarPower Europe 2018). Although Helen's age and gender: 'in my early 20s... young female', initially sets her apart, this is an enabling framework from which to question the 'financial profits-focused setting' of the mining sector, and incorporate values centred on 'social and environmental importance'. While Helen felt 'different and aware [of her] gender and age', ultimately, this 'was good for the task!' Her youth underscored a fresh, innovative approach to social change. Helen's career move, from mining AGMs 'in [her] early 20s' to eNGOs and thereafter, sustainability-scientific research, represents a stark rejection of 'mining advocacy' and extrapolation of the natural environment 'in a financial profits-focused setting' ([audio] 2010). Distinctly, Helen's sustainable change involves advocating for human and nonhuman betterment (Mellor 1997, 2002; Irwin 2010; Maleta 2011b, 2018a). This supports my methodological conceptual focus on the powerful premise of emphasized femininity resistance to industrial and governing resource-based elites (Leahy 2003; Gow and Leahy 2005; Gerulis-Darcy 2010; Alston 2011; Doherty and Doyle 2013; Doyle et al. 2015). As a dualist insider (employee)/outsider (young woman), Helen's emphasized femininity focus on 'social and environmental importance' challenged hierarchical-chauvinism. Being an insider/outsider, entails an empowering women-led egalitarian framework for social change (Doyle 2000, 2005, 2008; Maddison and Scalmer 2006; Fenster 2007; Faber 2008; Leahy 2008; Maleta 2018a, 2018b).

Concerning my sub-theme of male chauvinism, relative to the core theme of 'a boys club', eNGO advocate Stephanie perceives this as a behaviour of older men in the eNSM, framing how women are treated differently, even in comparative positions to men:

> I think there's a general disrespect for female colleagues. He can be quite antagonistic. But he's never really as antagonistic to male colleagues as he is to female colleagues... his behaviour, I go, if I was his age, and a male, would he be doing that to me then? And it's nothing really outrageous, it's just, sort of, his, mannerisms and ways of doing stuff... It would just be silly things... it's, sort of, the steamrolling of ideas through, and not really being open to discussion, umm, sort of, delegating indirectly.... just a general lack of, equality, and, no discursive sort of nature, it's more benevolent dictatorship [laughs].
>
> (Stephanie [audio] 2010)

Stephanie's observation demonstrates an androcentric performance of masculinity, and negative connotations, framing the workplace as sexist for 'female colleagues', in terms of: 'disrespect', 'antagonistic', 'his age', 'male', 'lack of equality' and 'benevolent dictatorship'. Clearly, older men treat women differently: 'his, mannerisms and ways of doing stuff' and in a patronising way: 'a male, would he be doing that to me then?' whereby women's voice is not included: 'not really being open to discussion... delegating indirectly'. Stephanie's recollection, reinforces Cockburn's (1988, 1991, 2010, 2012, 2013) patriarchal condemnation of men's resistance to women's leadership in organisations and NSMs. Sex-based discrimination remains problematic in the 21st century, although recruitment programmes, like STEMM (2018) and other Initiatives, including renewable employment drives, attempt to minimise women's workplace marginalisation (McFarland 2014; Ajani 2015; AHRC 2016b, 2017a, 2017b; RenewableUK 2017). My Bill of Rights Act, focussing on women's agentic performative plural skills-set, supported by WW & SE leadership quotas, challenges such shortfalls, endemic to a patriarchal-capitalist framed neoliberal meritocracy (Levine and Strube 2012; Walby 2012, 2013; Gheaus 2015; Watts et al. 2015; Cornish 2017; Jones 2017; Hickman 2018).

In similarity to Rachel, Stephanie's chuckling and laughing demonstrates women's capacity to mock their male colleagues, rather than to be insulted by their chauvinism, sexism and downright misogyny. Her analysis of 'his mannerisms' and 'silly things', shows how women ridicule their male bosses. I infer women's performance as a type of emphasized femininity resistance to men's patronising attitude and seeming otherness. Stephanie's assessment of his behaviour as not 'outrageous' and linked to 'mannerisms', downplays chauvinism as a threat (Coronel et al. 2010; Jonnergård et al. 2010; Cadaret et al. 2017; Edge et al. 2017). Participants' humorous framing of their male bosses evokes dichotomous resistant labelling – women towards men – indicative of reverse discrimination. Women-led caricatures and comical responses do not, however, diminish men's adversity: 'He can be quite antagonistic.' Gender as a barrier prevails (Culley and Angelique 2003, 2010). Stephanie's ([audio] 2010) final articulation on the 'lack of equality' and 'it's more benevolent dictatorship', frames the issue more directly as gender differentiation (Poiner 1990; Levine and Strube 2012; Maleta 2012; Sundström and McCright 2014). Participants emphasized femininity strategies, parallel to agentic performances, challenge men's performative ostracisation, and subvert the patriarchal control of their eSMOs (Connell 2002; Leahy 2003; Butler 2006, 2013). Women do not permit gender differences to cloud their competence nor capacity to contribute positively within an eNGO context.

Maturity is a source of wisdom. My accounts reveal how women's maturity enables their work performances. In my line of interview questioning to Deborah: 'In the workplace, have you had any experiences of sexism, discrimination?', she replied:

> Not that I have noticed… I haven't noticed it but then I grew up with three brothers and I had to learn to tough it out when I was a child, to be tough and I'm a tough person… I don't notice it personally, but then I'm very vocal. So I don't know… if being older is helpful… I find that sometimes that is helpful because, and also you know you have got to when you are going to meet politicians, you have to look like you're part of their part of their scene.
> (Deborah [audio] 2010)

Deborah's contemplation of how 'being older is helpful', frames her assertive-subjective resistance to gender and ageism as potential barriers, for age was actually an enabler (Maleta 2012; AHRC 2016b; Evans 2016; Edge et al. 2017). Maturity also frames one's potential to be taken seriously, especially 'when you are going to meet politicians' for it is mandatory 'to look… part of their scene'. Deborah's self-assessment, as 'tough' and 'vocal', reveals adjectives that thwart men or her 'brothers' from treating her differently. Deborah's gender performativity highlights her physical prowess, supporting my thematic insight to toughness as a forceful form of emphasized femininity leadership. In likeness to fellow eNGO advocate Stephanie and academic Rachel, Deborah does not personalise gendered experiences: 'I don't notice it personally'. Overall, Deborah rejects sexism and discrimination as an issue of marginalisation: 'Not that I have noticed… I haven't noticed it' ([audio] 2010). However, in other parts of her interview, she identified gendered differentiated campaigns, with men's dominance of the 'hard' sciences and women's dominance of 'soft' sciences, such as, 'biodiversity' and the 'green home', educative, teaching team. She even remarked that she was more interested in the softer sciences. Thus far, my interviews reveal contradictions. I deduce that women continually negotiate gender. Gender performances inform the overall work-based roles and gendered identities of participants (Butler 1999, 2004; Maleta 2009, 2011b, 2015).

9.4   Grassroots Collectives: Older and Younger Women's Lead

Mature participants recollection of age as an enabler suggests that young women, with less experience or possibly wisdom, may struggle more with recognition, status and career development. Being young was initially a barrier for Juliet, which I will discuss, shortly. Nevertheless, Helen, an advisory scientist and former eNGO Director, alludes to both older and younger women's aptitudes within grassroots climate action collectives:

> Community based groups… each group is a totally different profile, but there are some very dedicated older women who have devoted themselves significantly to their climate action group… they are a different generation, and their husbands might still be working, and this has become their passion. So, the volunteer level, there are some groups who represent that. There's others that are all young people, and all totally diverse gender. So yeah, there's not one model.
>
> (Helen [audio] 2010)

Helen's overview of 'diverse gender' representation and 'there's not one model' within 'community based' climate action groups, underpins mature and youthful women-led performative competencies: 'very dedicated older women' and 'others that are all young people'. Such performativity is framed by passion for the cause, for they are 'dedicated' and have 'devoted themselves significantly'. Egalitarianism underscores this account. Participatory inclusion, along gender and age lines, is strengthened through grassroots organisational structures that are egalitarian, along with women's performance of egalitarianism; thus, strengthening women's empowerment (Di Chiro 2008, 2011; Yoder et al. 2011; Butler 2013, 2015; Maleta 2015; Veri 2016). The grassroots are not conducive to rigid hierarchies, nor patriarchal privilege, but enable a diverse intersectionality; consequently, framing the greater equity/justice of *my six groups* (Buckingham and Kulcur 2010; Walby 2011; Summers 2013; MacGregor 2014; DAWN 2015). My empirical themes enable me to accentuate the grassroots arm of the eNSM as inclusive of mature and youthful women; nonetheless, older men are also central actors (Maddison 2004; Maleta 2012). In relation to women's narratives, I also found that older men play an active role in grassroots climate initiatives, which challenges assumptions that grassroots voluntary activism is dominated by women, or indeed young women (Maddison 2004; Unger 2008; Maleta 2011a, 2011b, 2012). Whilst the grassroots models egalitarianism, enabling young and older women's performances, it is, likewise, an agentic, empowering model for improved work relations and gender unity. Egalitarianism is, thus, central to my Republican social model.

Positive appraisals of the grassroots do not delineate ageism as a matter of differentiation for women partaking across diverse sectors. Although Deborah disputed sexism within her eNGO, she pointed to ageism as a barrier within Local Government:

Umm, not sexist, no I've had ageist. Yeah, ageist definitely because you're applying for a job and I was actually told by one particular local government, when I applied for this job and I didn't even get the interview and I rung up to find out why not, he said oh well, you know we looked at when your degree was, you know when you got your degree and we basically, he admitted on the phone to me that umm I was too old. So ageist I've had definitely, ageist is more an issue than sexist… He let it slip… No, I just thought I don't want to work there anyway, if they're that moronic I don't want to work there.

(Deborah [audio] 2010)

Deborah's last statement 'they're that moronic', as a rationale for why she does not 'want to work there', reinforces Stephanie's comical assessment of her 'old-fashioned' boss, plus Rachel's caricature of her 'chauvinistic' supervisor, 'Little Willie'. While women experience differentiation or indeed otherness, because of their age or simply as women, they do not necessarily personalise this, but respond by mocking the men that attempt to other and ostracise them. Men, therefore, have failed in their attempt to exclude women. Participants' social-scientific-technical performative prowess, further, thwarts men's otherness. Nonetheless, Deborah's rejection for a job interview, because of her age, shows that mature women experience barriers in employment (Ainsworth 2002; AHRC 2016b; Evans 2016; Edge et al. 2017). My Initiatives should redress older women's marginalisation, focussing on their wisdom, extensive skills-set, and capacity to positively transform the eNSM. Likewise, I view mature and young women as leaders of scientific-technological renewable development (McFarland 2014; Pollack 2015; BWE 2018; Clean Energy Council 2018; WIE 2018). My republican intersection of feminism/egalitarianism/environmentalism, challenges barriers and stigmas surrounding age, gender and technical (in)competence, whilst conferring power to older and young women across the eNSM (Ainsworth 2002; Maleta 2012; Evans 2016; Edge et al. 2017).

Questionably, the othering of older women is to the detriment of workplaces and productivity, for older women possess a wealth of experience and knowledge, such as strategic negotiation and communication expertise (AHRC

2016b; Evans 2016; Maleta 2018b). Although Deborah disputed sexism as an overarching barrier, it is intriguing that it was a male that denied her the job interview. I infer that 'othering' evokes degrees of Anglo male middle class privilege that, in turn, is not supportive to Anglo middle class women, let alone all the sociocultural demographics, constituting *my six groups* (Giddens 1991; Donaldson and Poynting 2007, 2013; Donaldson 2009; McGregor 2009). If the scenario was reversed, and it was a male of the same age – would he be treated differently, and secure an interview?

9.5 Cultural-Ageist Dimensions Framing Emphasized Feminine Constructivism

If the applicant was a woman of a Non-English Speaking Background (NESB) or CALD status, in her fifties, and resident of a low-income suburb; undoubtedly, she would encounter multiple forms of exclusion (Lobo and Morgan 2012; DAWN 2015; Haynes et al. 2015; Cole 2016; Canty 2017). This would be convert; but perhaps overt, as Deborah suggested. Othering, relative to one's cultural/race minority status, is not so visibly in your face. This frames women's (in)visibility in global governance (Lewis 2006; Kosny and MacEachen 2010; Gheaus 2015). In my critique of ruling-middle class masculinity, Anglo men's dominance of the business and political world, covertly or overtly, positions women as 'the other' to the hegemon (Kaufmann 2004; Connell 2009; ABS 2016a; AHRC 2016b).

Regarding dichotomous insights to race/ethnicity/culture, in relation to age, gender and competence, eNGO advocate, Juliet, considers her prior international eSMO role in a developing nation. While Juliet contemplates her potential exclusion, her experience was contextualised by complex gendered power relations and 'knowledge sharing':

> I was maybe 20 or 21, you know, a White Western female. Umm, so there was a lot, going on there in terms of, umm, power relations... Being young, being White, umm, being female... not being a migrant worker, like there was more differences, than there were similarities. However, I developed really amazing positive working relationships with everyone I worked with and felt incredibly welcomed and incredibly humbled by what was given to me, yeah, in terms of, I guess, knowledge sharing and the thanks that people gave me.
>
> (Juliet [audio] 2010)

Therefore, Juliet's skilled 'knowledge sharing', as 'a White Western female', performing in a traditional patriarchal culture, undermined the notion of age, gender and competence as potential barriers. Nonetheless, Juliet experienced her role as a dualist insider/outsider (Yoder and Aniakudo 1997; Cockburn 2000, 2010, 2012; Maddison 2004; Maddison and Scalmer 2006; Fenster 2007). In the first instance, Juliet perceived herself, as an outsider, parallel to 'more differences, than similarities'. Simultaneously, she was an insider – for her 'knowledge' and 'being young, being White, female… not being a migrant worker' was a premise for respect and status, in a seemingly patriarchal context: 'I developed really amazing positive working relationships with everyone… felt incredibly welcomed' (Greer 1999; Doyle 2005; Nagy 2017).

Women's agentic performative plural skills-set strengthens my constructivist-interactionist approach, thereby subverting gender hegemony, middle class masculinist industrial and political elitism, and essentialist viewpoints of women's 'appropriate role' in global organisational governance (Moore 2008; Mortimer-Sandilands 2008; Gaard 2011; Maleta 2011a, 2011b, 2015, 2018b). Juliet's emphasized femininity leadership is bounded by knowledge, thus disrupting the 'power relations' omnipresent with ruling class masculinity (Donaldson 1993; Connell 1995, 2009; Greer 2010b; Butler 2011, 2013; Grusky 2014; Wasson 2017). Women-led emphasized femininity performative skill challenges tags of age, gender, ethnicity and competence (Maleta 2012, 2015). Young and older women possess the power to challenge male privilege. Yet, some women, framed by mature wisdom, endeavour to relive their actions. Maggie reflects on her youth, when she lacked the esteem to challenge Ivy League Professors; however, now strives for more social change leadership:

> I was depleted; I was still a little girl. These guys were Professors at [omit]; I didn't have the emotional security, the self-esteem to take them on. Now, it would never happen but I'm [omit age] and it's too bloody late. I'd like to relive my life… We are sitting here ready to go and it would increase the GDP and employ hundreds of thousands of workers. Why don't we do it? Because the politicians are scientifically illiterate. They listen to corporations and their propaganda.
>
> (Maggie [audio] 2010)

9.6 Discussion

In relation to Maggie, women should 'use their power' and 'act like women' rather than 'a little girl' or 'the Thatchers…'. Maggie's passage additionally highlights how maturity is related to confidence and assertion: 'these guys were Professors…'. The above extract shows how younger women struggle with 'self-esteem' and 'emotional security', whereas, older men, 'Professors', protected by 'the boys club' within Ivy League academia, perhaps bully or ostracise younger women: 'I was depleted' (Probert 2005; Maleta 2012; Fisher and Kinsey 2014; Gheaus 2015). This extract exposes the way in which ageism and gender intersect, framing ruling-middle class masculinity as a barrier to women's participation (Duncan and Loretto 2004; Cooper 2013; Donaldson and Poynting 2013).

In summary, older and younger women environmental activists/advocates endure stigmas associated with their age, be it that they are too old or too young. This stigmatisation is framed through perceptions of knowledge, whereby scientific-technical competence-defined barriers/enablers, encompass intersections of age, gender and hegemony (Cockburn 1988; Culley and Angelique 2003, 2010;

Maleta 2011a, 2018a, 2018b). Although young women struggle with labels of technical incompetence, their demonstration of 'knowledge sharing' (Juliet) and advocacy of 'social and environmental importance' (Helen) represents an interactive constructivist performance – parallel to an emphasized resistant femininity, striving for sustainable change goals, whilst subversive to the rule of privileged patriarchal elites (Connell 1995; Leahy 2003; Butler 2007, 2013).

According to Anna ([audio] 2010), older women scientists, re-entering academia, after extended maternity leave, are deemed 'too old', especially for the 'more physical' field work. To a certain extent, this comment is judgemental of older women's (in)competence (Cockburn 1988, 1991; Cooper 2013; Evans 2016; Edge et al. 2017). Even if a job is physically demanding, and women may protest; it is the responsibility of the employer to support the agentic prowess of women, rather than labelling them as too old or unemployable (Ainsworth 2002; Maddison 2004; AHRC 2016b, 2017b). Women perform well in diverse capacities, and should have the opportunity to work accordingly to their physical preference. Although Deborah was deemed 'too old' for a job interview by a male recruiter; she adds that being older is 'helpful'. Older and younger women, demonstrate significant physical and intellectual prowess, and denying women a position because of age is detrimental to the workplace. Older women possess a wealth of knowledge and immeasurable experience: a framework for sustainable technological development (BWE 2018; SolarPower Europe 2018; WIE 2018). Young women possess innovative skills, energy and vibrancy, along with a degree of naïveté – which should not be under-estimated either; they are as passionate, committed environmentalists as their 'older sisters' in the eNSM. Such youthful energy and mature wisdom intersect, challenging the dinosaurs that control 'mining AGMs' and executive ruling resource-based hierarchies (Maleta 2011b).

Conclusion

In her resistance to patriarchal-framed glass ceilings, Maggie ([audio] 2010), as discussed in Chapter 5, had advocated a universal gender law: 'there should be a law that 53% of every corporation, academic, Parliamentary body is women'. Relative to this framework, my Act's Initiatives, supported by a Republican feminist-egalitarian change, should redress EEO gaps and achieve equity/justice for *my six groups* (Marshall 1995, 2011; AHRC 2016b, 2017b; Veri 2016; ARM 2018; Hickman 2018; STEMM 2018). It ensures that women's competence and merit is dually recognised. Women-led strategies, often defined by 'consensus-building' and 'collaboration' across my interviews, are discursive to emphasized femininity resistance to 'the boys club' and middle class masculinised institutionalised power. Emphasized femininity leadership is defined by plural performative skills: social, empathetic, scientific, technical, intellectual and an egalitarian ethos. Women's WW & SE leadership parallels my sociocultural democratic model, advocating/legislating for egalitarian-feminist methods of organisational governance. My participatory model, evokes the progressive Republican era of Red Vienna, whereby ruling class masculinity was challenged

(Rentetzi 2010; Lagi 2012; Rodriguez-Ruiz and Rubio-Marin 2012; Mattl 2013). In the sociopolitical context of Red Vienna, women secured suffrage, whilst the working and middles classes flourished through technical and intellectual ingenuity (Gruber 1991; Jeffery 1995; Bader-Zaar 1996; Kershaw 2013). As such, my Bill accentuates women-led grassroots and professional agentic competencies.

My Bill of Rights' Initiatives, methodologically aligned to frames of (in) justice/(in)equity, centre on the agentic (technological-intellectual-scientific-social-egalitarian ethos) competence of young and mature women, framing their greater WW & SE leadership in sustainable renewable development (Ajani 2015; Baruah 2016; Clean Energy Council 2018). Constructivism is relayed through women's emphasized femininity performative leadership, involving an exercise of agentic power and aspirations for greater career statuses, whilst challenging patriarchy, as Maggie stated (Shiva and Moser 1995; Leahy 2003; MacGregor 2006, 2010; Cockburn 2012, 2013; Maleta 2015). Constructivism entails an active negotiation of self to one's sociocultural environs, enabling subjective empowerment, whereby women actualise the 'I' in their identities (Butler 1999, 2007, 2015). On this point, I aim for women to dominate green energy, and to reinvigorate this sector – from an emerging to dominant sector of energy (Shepard and Corbin-Mark 2009; McFarland 2014; Ajani 2015; RenewableUK 2018). Women-led authority here should challenge traditional resource-based approaches, along with the worldwide hegemony of nuclear technology as a reliant energy source (Rankin and Gale 2003; Culley and Angelique 2010; Caldicott 2014; Maleta 2018b; World Nuclear Organisation 2018).

My Bill contends that a meritocracy has failed women, in particular, *my six groups*. As I address competence plus merit, I reject the notion that sociopolitical structures are inclusive. Within executive hierarchies, men/masculinities remain privileged, which is dually replicated in the ruling class power of industrial and political elites; framing patriarchy as a barrier – discursive to the global politics of the environment (McGregor 2009; Buckingham and Kulcur 2010; Maleta 2011b; MacGregor 2014; Doyle et al. 2015). However, my legislation of a Republican-constitutional sustainable-technological sociopolitical change, focussed on women's 75% leadership in renewables development, should reverse the historic privilege of men and the supremacy of middle class masculinity (Donaldson 1993, 2009; McFarland 2014; Bombora Wave Power 2018; Carnegie Clean Energy 2018; WIE 2018). Accordingly, my model aspires to inform nations' leaders – for women's renewables leadership is a cutting-edge EEO-egalitarian model, framing change.

10 Activism as Egalitarian and Anti-hierarchical

Introduction

Following on from my discussion of older and younger women's agentic performative skills-set, this chapter develops my egalitarian-emphasized femininity insight to activism as anti-hierarchical, relative to participatory-framed patriarchal resistance (Connell 1995, 2005; Lowry 2009; Maleta 2011a; Walby 2011, 2013; MacGregor 2014). My contention is that egalitarianism unifies women campaigners in their advocacy, whilst hierarchy represents a barrier for feminism and environmental change. Arguably, bureaucracies, dually informed by rigid hierarchy and patriarchal privilege, operate like machines, and, for the most part, are not flexible, fluid, nor inclusive work environments. Hence, unyielding bureaucracy makes the voice of women (in)visible, clouding their sustainable-climate reformative goals (Shiva and Moser 1995; Prokhovnik 1998; Crary 2001; Lewis 2006; Kosny and MacEachen 2010). As participants struggle with bureaucracy, emphasized femininity performative leadership, subverts the hegemony of patriarchal hierarchies (Plumwood 1997; Segal 1999; Connell 2002; Leahy 2003; Wasserman 2012). My methodological esteem of egalitarianism, akin to a Republican-Bill of Rights, challenges men's global control of executive environmental governance (Maleta 2012; Mattl 2013, 2016; ARM 2018; Hickman 2018; Patel 2018). In my framing of emphasized femininity resistance to patriarchy, women are active subjects, challenging dualist experiences of domination/subordination (MacLeod 1992; Plumwood 1997; Buckingham-Hatfield 2000; Butler 2004, 2007; Cockburn 2010, 2012). Thus, feminist empowerment is indeed possible.

10.1 Egalitarianism as an Enabler

In the first excerpt, Abigail explains how egalitarian structures enable women's advocacy, in terms of 'creativity' and 'vision':

> It requires creativity, imagination, vision; it's about people skills, relationships. If you want to turn it into a bureaucracy, go somewhere else. We try and be egalitarian, but I'm very happy not to have to worry about running this, we're

always running things by each other. But as president, you've got influence of how bureaucratic it's going to be… I want it to be somewhere where people feel inspired and it's about co-operative relationships, and enjoying meetings. We have to comply with certain requirements, but that doesn't mean we have to be a bureaucracy.

(Abigail [audio] 2010)

Although bureaucracy and 'certain [hierarchical] requirements' are counterpoint to egalitarianism, Abigail's contention is that compliance 'with certain requirements' does not evoke an overall endorsement of bureaucracy ([audio] 2010). Instead, Abigail argues: 'If you want to turn it into a bureaucracy, go somewhere else'. In a positive egalitarian framework, Abigail's ([audio] 2010) emphasized femininity leadership is shown through: 'creativity', 'vision', 'people skills, relationships', 'egalitarian', 'feel inspired', 'co-operative relationships' and 'enjoying meetings'. Her hierarchical resistance is discursive to a rejection of bureaucracy, whereby as a woman leader: 'president', she has certain control of 'how bureaucratic it's going to be'.

Across my findings, women tend to adopt egalitarianism in their work engagement and social relations, but the capacity to perform this relates to the extent to which organisations enable gender equity, or are more rigidly hierarchical and patriarchal. Hence, hierarchy and patriarchy are not mutually exclusive – pertaining to framing the otherness of women. Bureaucracy, similarly, hinders egalitarianism, along with women's capacity to exercise their emphasized femininity-social change leadership (Leahy 2003, 2008; Maleta 2015). Whereas an egalitarian work structure, in a materialist and ideological premise, enables women and men to cooperate, despite some men wanting to dominate: 'there is a more egalitarian feeling about men in the progressive movements… they can be dominant or have difficulties in their personalities, that they don't know how to manage in a group situation' (Abigail [audio] 2010). Masculine middle class hegemony is replicated through patriarchal-hierarchical-framed bureaucracies (Maleta 2018b). Although some men share a progressive ideology, evident through social change acts – masculinist-bureaucratic performativity, nevertheless positions women on the outer: as 'in a group situation', Abigail adds.

Competitiveness, as an example of hegemonic masculinity, subverts a potential gender unity plus aspirational environmental change goals (Mellor 1997; Plumwood 1997; Buckingham-Hatfield 2000; Connell 2002, 2005; Poynting and Donaldson 2005). In support, Connell's (2005) research on Australian men environmental activists highlighted their rejection of hegemonic masculinity and appraisal of egalitarian-ecofeminist principles, consequently unifying the collaborative efforts of men and women within green political contexts. Similarly, the grassroots-based eNSM and its eSMOs are defined by progressive egalitarian viewpoints, whereby many grassroots men respect the role and equity of women (Maleta 2012). It is too simplistic to state that all women are oppressed; for a shared environmental ethos, egalitarian ethics and empathetic compassion are performed by both genders. While women often adopt a maternal/caring position in their activism, a number of men, likewise, care about gender rights and environmental protection. Gillian conveys the value of gender diversity and that men activists are challenging the same power relations:

> There are plenty of men that are very active… but women tend to be more caring. Look at these men who are challenging that same power. My husband would feel just as strongly about the role of women in society.
>
> (Gillian [audio] 2009)

This grassroots account sets the framework for an empowering feminist-egalitarian performative ethos: to strengthen the work and social relations of men and women, whilst challenging the dominant power relations that run counterpoint to a common ground social change agenda. Egalitarianism, exemplified by fluid, less hierarchical structures, enables women and men to cooperate. Such engaged performative leadership tests gender stereotypes and destabilises labels of female technical-scientific incompetence (Cockburn 1988; Ahern and Hendryx 2008; Duncan 2010; Ussher 2011; Yoder et al. 2011; Maleta 2018a). Nonetheless, a maternal 'caring' ethos motivates women's activism and rationale for change, as Gillian adds: 'I did this after my mother more than after my father' ([audio] 2009). Similarly, Amanda, a grassroots campaigner, articulated how a feminist-egalitarian ideology was central to her group, and how a maternal identity guides her ethic. In a female-dominated apolitical organisation, the goal is to prevent hierarchical structures and power dynamics from subverting the structure: 'we worked hard to create a structure that was open, inclusive and protect it from other organisations that have more hierarchy, and probably a little bit predatory agendas politically' (Amanda [audio] 2010). Being apolitical, strategically, ensures that multiple viewpoints are heard:

> we [our group] decided that if climate change was to be fixed, then you have to include everybody… We have to get Liberal people standing next to Greens people, and you need bi-partisan support to get the whole system to change. It's central that we're apolitical, non-aligned. We're clean politically; it means that people can work with you, because they know you're not pushing a political agenda. So to set up a structure that we can all communicate and work collectively.
>
> (Amanda [audio] 2010)

A grassroots focus on 'bi-partisan support', 'non-aligned', 'clean politically', embodies the integrity of social democratically egalitarian eSMO collectives. My empirical examples symbolise emphasized femininity resistance to middle class cultural structures: bureaucracy, hierarchy and patriarchy. My thematic insights frame the egalitarian focus of my Bill, targeting women's 75% WW & SE technical-scientific leadership. Nonetheless, my goal is to improve gender relations within renewables organisational governance (Maleta 2018a, 2018b). Women and men's collaborative efforts are required for a Republican constitutional change

(Veri 2016; ARM 2018). Whilst women lead this charge, a unified gender effort is a platform for social and environmental change goals to be realised in praxis.

10.2 A Grassroots-Egalitarian Approach to eNSMs/eSMOs

Women's grassroots leadership of eNSMs/eSMOs strengthens my sociocultural democratic-egalitarian participatory Republican model, reinforced through EEO-Initiatives, envisioning *my six groups'* equity/justice. In supporting grassroots analyses, Gillian ([audio] 2009) elaborates how her organisation avoids hierarchical people and hierarchical structures. Again, gender diversity, plus unity, is strengthened through apolitical practices, consensus-building and a greens justice ethic. At the annual Climate Summit, Gillian ([audio] 2009) condemned some large International NGOs, regarding how they: 'wanted control of the communication of the group, whereas it was a grassroots summit'. Comparatively, eNGO participants confront the patriarchal control of executive-hierarchies within their eSMOs. In my emphasis on ruling-middle class barriers, I draw upon Barbara, Maxine and Linda's censuring of 'combativeness' and 'competitiveness' within male-dominated executive hierarchies. Gender as a barrier is additionally replicated through cultural-structural barriers. ENGO women evaluated the lack of merit, inadequate maternity provisions plus heavy workload.

Greens women, aligned with grassroots socioecological democratic principles, reinforced through party policies, protest about hierarchy, as a core barrier within Parliamentary governance (Mellor 1993, 1997; Maleta 2011b; Australian Greens, Our Policies, 2018, Participatory Democracy, 2018). Although I am not a party member, I esteem their inclusive modelling of a Bill of Rights, framing a potential Republican political change (Australian Greens, Constitutional Reform and Democracy, 2018). In support to my egalitarian mode, Tanya, an LGA Councillor, rejects hierarchy and 'absolute power structures' in governance and everyday life, rather advocating: 'communalism and less consumption' ([audio] 2010). Jacquie, another LGA Councillor, perceives hierarchy to be more of an issue than gender. As her party is grassroots; this contrasts with mainstream politics:

> I haven't found that to be the difficult thing to deal with because of my gender. It is more the hierarchy. It is having to know who to speak to; I find that difficult, the Greens do not operate that way. Everything is grassroots and locally done. So to go from that headspace of coming to decisions by consensus as a local group, and then having to deal with the different parties and levels of government and administration and knowing who is the boss, that's hard to negotiate the two.

> (Jacquie [audio] 2010)

In contrast to the Greens, mainstream parties tend to be structurally and culturally defined by hierarchy, which is a challenge for the Greens – defined by 'consensus as a local group'. While Greens women mostly view hierarchy as a point of differentiation to Greens policies and practices, Ruth adds that hierarchy is, at times, adopted for media consultations:

> well, there's definitely a hierarchy at the [omit], it's quite clear and established... the same thing goes with the Greens. I mean, in terms of policy and media, if you were interviewed by journalists, you would want to ensure that your interpretation of Greens policy was accurate. There's people in the Greens who advise. So there's definitely a bureaucracy and a hierarchy of people to refer to. However, any organisation has to have that to an extent, but there's opportunities to question that. For example, there's a State Delegates Committee, a meeting of all the [omit] groups where they discuss policy issues. It's allowing everyone to have a say about how things work, the process, the policy. There's opportunities for people to be involved, even though there is a certain hierarchy there.
>
> (Ruth [audio] 2010)

Whilst a key Greens policy is grassroots participatory democracy, evidently, women cannot entirely avoid hierarchy in their negotiations (Maleta 2011b; Australian Greens, Our Policies, 2018, Participatory Democracy, 2018). As grassroots-eNSMs are defined by egalitarian resistance to patriarchal hierarchies, SMOs and SM political parties are characterised first and foremost by their political allegiances and policies (Diani 1992; Hawkins 2014; Staggenborg 2016). The use of bureaucracy, relative to media diplomacy, shows that SM political parties and SMOs cannot entirely avoid hierarchy (Diani 1992; Staggenborg 2016). Although the Greens adopt hierarchy in media negotiations; they mostly endorse a grassroots framework: 'allowing everyone to have a say', as Ruth ([audio] 2010) remarked. Such empirical data accentuates Greens women's emphasized femininity-egalitarian performativity. Additionally, Greens women's emphasized femininity resistance to bureaucratical-informed patriarchal hierarchies is shown during state and LGA meetings. Women's performativity pinpoints a multi-faceted diplomatic approach, rather than a one-dimensional strategy. Principally, the party remains loyal to its grassroots principles. The Greens have an egalitarian Bill of Rights policy, and sympathise with an Australian Republic Constitutional change (Australian Greens, Constitutional Reform and Democracy, 2018).

10.3 Intersections of Bureaucracy, Hierarchy and Patriarchy

Greens women's subversion to three core interrelated gender barriers: bureaucracy, hierarchy and patriarchy, is a framework for me (without being a party member) to develop an empowering egalitarian-feminist Bill of Rights model, in which *my six groups* are included, rather than ignored, in leadership positions. Additionally, focussing on the grassroots, as a powerful political force, enables/ empowers the electorate to vote for an Australian Head of State, rather than an assumed hereditary (foreign) monarch (Kumarasingham and Power 2014; Glencross et al. 2016; Veri 2016; ARM 2018). As I aim for my women groups'

(CALD, Indigenous, mature, disability statuses, low SES, Anglo) greater (75%) representation in renewables technological-scientific energy development, this defies the globalised patriarchal control of institutionalised environmentalist politics (Maleta 2011b; Carter 2013; Doherty and Doyle 2013; Doyle et al. 2015; SBS 2016; Canty 2017). More women in environmental science, aligns with STEMM (2018) goals; moreover, my Bill ensures that such leadership quotas are met – relative to performative competence and merit. Hence, a human-rights ethos frames my Act, supported by sub-frames of (in)equity/(in)justice. Concerning women-led Republican-sustainable advocacy, EEO outcomes are achievable through legislated quotas – affirmed by women's skills-sets. Agentic environmental technical competence is, thus, a premise for women's career mobility.

Within the framework of a university setting, academic activists recognise/resist hierarchy. Anna highlights her personal resistance to rigid hierarchies: 'I'm not very good with hierarchies. I trample it!' ([audio] 2010). She adds that hierarchy frames university accountability, but formal and informal structures reflect degrees of flexibility:

> It depends on the relationships and trust between members within that hierarchy. I wouldn't do what somebody told me to do, if I didn't respect their view. I can't do something that I never believe is right or practical. You've got formal hierarchies and informal hierarchies. I see them both working together.
>
> (Anna [audio] 2010)

Academic and IeNGO women esteem hierarchy as an enabling structure, whilst others emphasise the value of grassroots techniques. Helen ([audio] 2010) contends that hierarchy is 'there for a reason' , but is measured by power relations, suggesting degrees of (in)equity. Gendered power relations, informing executive hierarchies, underpin the organisational complexity farming women's capacity to construct empowered identities. Linda ([audio] 2010) explains how her IeNGO is hierarchical rather than consensus-based, which contrasts with perceptions. Nonetheless, the work culture enables independent decision-making:

> The culture isn't so hierarchical in that people have a lot of autonomy in decision-making provided they do well. There's a misunderstanding in this organisation and other NGOs about whether they are hierarchical or practice consensus decision-making because we're not a consensus-based organisation… in practice we might spend a lot of time trying to build consensus, but at the end of the day it's a hierarchical top-down decision-making organisation.
>
> (Linda [audio] 2010)

While IeNGOs and grassroots collectives constitute the third sector, bureaucratic hierarchal structures, are more evident within large IeNGOs

(Maleta 2012). I confer that middle class masculinity is more problematic in the executive arm of the eNSM, as Barbara, Maxine, Maggie, etc. contemplated. Volunteer activist Wendy adds that IeNGOs are hierarchical, but that grassroots organisations are decentralised and have a flatter, more inclusive structure. Pointing to third-sector partnerships, Wendy ([audio] 2010) explains that youth grassroots organisations operate in a 'decentralised structure, in comparison to the civil society INGOs, that are fairly hierarchical'. Wendy adds that uniform decision-making is difficult when the grassroots work with INGOs, in light of 'overarching bureaucracy and tiers of management', and that men are usually in 'decision-making leadership roles within civil sector NGOs, whereas the super grassroots tends to be female dominated'. In my critique of ruling class masculinity, the patriarchal control of the eNSM and its eSMOs, in terms of 'overarching bureaucracy', shows that elitism contrasts with egalitarianism (Kaufmann 2004; Donaldson and Poynting 2013; Grusky 2014; AHRC 2017b). While I contend that Anglo male middle class privilege is a key barrier, I hope for improved gender relations, seeking inspiration from Wendy's advocacy of unified gender balances, integrating male and female competencies, within decision-making leadership.

10.4 Discussion

This chapter has demonstrated the extent to which hierarchy and bureaucracy, represent the patriarchal control of environmental organisational governance, whereby ruling-middle class masculinity underpins women's leadership inequity/injustice (Giddens 1991; Kaufmann 2004; Donaldson 2009; McGregor 2009; Grusky 2014; Bombora Wave Power 2018). Hegemonic masculinity, relative to Anglo middle class men's control of the global eNSM and its eSMOs, contrasts with egalitarian-emphasized femininity leadership. Besides, eSMOs that are egalitarian, grassroots, flexible and non-hierarchical enable women's performative advocacy (Gaard 2001; Di Chiro 2011; Butler 2013; Davis 2015). While egalitarianism enables women's performance – it is also an ethic that women practice in their activism and everyday life contexts. As an approach, it contrasts with ruling class masculinity and dominant power relations that are elitist. To reiterate, egalitarian ideals, supported by women's WW & SE leadership, provide an empowering frame for change.

My interviews suggest that hierarchy is not always an obstacle. Some IeNGO and academic women view hierarchy as enabling internal work operations. Concerning enablers, Helen ([audio] 2010) argued that hierarchy 'makes things flow better', while Anna ([audio] 2010) added that 'formal and informal hierarchies' provide relevant structure to universities. Ruth ([audio] 2010) remarked that the Greens was hierarchical in its media strategy, revealing that, even in parties of a strong grassroots ecological democratic persuasion, it is not possible to eradicate hierarchy. Hierarchy, thus, uncomfortably informs the global politics of the environment (Carter 2007, 2013; Maleta 2011b; Doherty and Doyle 2013; Doyle et al. 2015).

Leading IeNGOs, like Greenpeace International, are hierarchically organised; nevertheless, they are well-represented by female International Executive Directors (Greenpeace International, Annual Report 2016, International Executive Directors 2018, Management Structure 2018). This points to women's competence and merit, but also shows that an egalitarian ethos, even within a hierarchically organised eNGO, does not hinder women's leadership equality. Women can work well, then, in hierarchical organisations. Nonetheless, the interviews with women (across chapters) shows the way hierarchical bureaucracies replicate gender-organisational barriers. In relation to masculinist hegemony, my theme of 'a boys club' is supported by insights to glass ceilings, misogyny, sexism and chauvinism (Maleta 2011b, 2012; Pollack 2015; Cohen 2016; Marfo 2017).

However, women's emphasized femininity leadership, situated in their agentic competence and resistance to patriarchy, is an empowering frame for renewable technological development (McFarland 2014; Ajani 2015; BWE 2018; Clean Energy Council 2018; WIE 2018). Organisations led by women, discursive to a feminist-egalitarian ethos, are proactive sites to resist masculine hegemony (Maddison 2004; Schlembach 2011; Maleta 2012). Supporting studies esteem egalitarianism in women-led SMOs, thereby contributing to feminist empowerment (Diani 1992; Butler 1999, 2006, 2011; Yoder et al. 2011; Staggenborg 2016). Despite gender barriers, my participants engage in protest femininities, exemplifying emphasized femininity resistance in action (MacLeod 1992; Connell 1995; Mellor 1997, 2012, 2013; Plumwood 1997, 2002; Leahy 2003; Maleta 2015).

Similarly, Greens and grassroots women protest against patriarchal hierarchies, in favour of egalitarian-feminist methods (Maleta 2011b; Australian Greens, Gender Equality, 2018). Women-led egalitarian resistance to bureaucracy, is central to grassroots ethics, as Abigail ([audio] 2010) explains: 'If you want to turn it into a bureaucracy, go somewhere else. We try and be egalitarian...' An egalitarian ethos enables women and men to collaborate, despite gender differences in leadership styles. Abigail adds that egalitarian approaches enabled women and men to cooperate despite some men wanting to dominate: 'there is a more egalitarian feeling about men in the progressive movements. But not always, they can be dominant or have difficulties in their personalities...' Hence, the incorporation of egalitarian ideals, framed by women's leadership, undermines the patriarchal control of the eNSM.

Conclusion

Women's agentic performative skills-set (scientific-technical-intellectual-social-egalitarian-empathetic) and leadership of a renewable energy future, underpins my Republican-Bill of Rights Act. My *six groups'* emphasized femininity-performative constructivism of a renewables future – that is less reliant on resource-based industries and the rule of industrial and political elites – shapes my Initiatives. In my legislative scope, I aim for professional and grassroots women leaders to have more control of renewable scientific-technical development, thereby moving the power from corporates (Leahy 2003; Faber 2008; Gerulis-Darcy 2010; Maleta 2018a, 2018b; WIE 2018). My egalitarian-grassroots model, enables everyday citizens to exercise their agency and have individual control over their energy consumption – thereby challenging corporatised industrial and economic control (Shiva and Moser 2005; Shiva 2008, 2014; Sullivan 2013).

Although not all women, across my research study, identify hierarchy as a pressing obstacle, most participants advocate a non-hierarchical stance, which constitutes my legislative scope for a feminist-egalitarian Act and its Initiatives. Women are the leaders of a renewables-technological future. In support to this claim, Linda ([audio] 2010) argued: 'we would be more effective if we had more women involved in senior leadership roles in the environment movement'. Cultural structures and men's leadership styles are conductive to hegemonic masculinist performativity: 'We have a culture as a movement and in the paid funded organisations of combatativeness and competitiveness and underminingness… we [women] would be less likely to behave that way and more likely to build more consensus and more collaboration' (Linda [audio] 2010). Women's emphasized femininity leadership of 'consensus' and 'collaboration', contrasts with men's 'combatativeness', 'competitiveness' and 'underminingness'; thus framing my egalitarian-feminist-republican goal for change.

11 Indigenous Women's Leadership
Envisioning an Indigenous Treaty

Introduction

Indigenous and non-Indigenous women participants in my research study outline their Indigenous advocacy in relation to social, environmental and feminist campaigning. The quest for Indigenous rights, in particular, Indigenous women's justice, informs participants' activism. Greens politician, Tanya, a Climate Camp activist, outlines her interest in environmental and social justice: 'I'm involved with a lot of issues. I speak about Indigenous problems, rallies against the Northern Territory Intervention. I also do work with homelessness. I speak at a lot of anti-war rallies' (Tanya [audio] 2010). Women participants' sustainable change ethos is, thus, linked to goals for social and gender justice, showing how they care about other women and diverse issues (Merchant 1994, 2013; Maddison 2004; Mellor 2013; SBS 2016; Canty 2017). Indigenous women's leadership, and that of other women who support Indigenous women's rights/equity, informs my Act's conceptual development of an Indigenous Treaty (Brennan 2015; Prokhovnik 2015; Gaard 2017; Nagy 2017). Additionally, the active voice of Indigenous and non-Indigenous women, as collectives and individuals, frames a republican-sustainable technical sociocultural change.

11.1 Barbara's Retrospection: 'A Very Feminine Caring, Nurturing, Mother Earth Angle'

ENGO advocate Barbara self-identifies as an Indigenous Tasmanian, along with mixed European descent, whose activism is framed by a maternal ethic and anti-toxic-chemical-industrial-pollutant environmentalist position. Barbara's Indigenous identity entails a spiritual connection and feminine subjectivity, framed by a 'nurturing' and 'mother earth angle'. The idea of an Indigenous identity as core to one's activism adds a compelling dimension to my empirical thematic analysis, as explained in the below two extracts:

> in the 1820s in my Tasmanian history, there may have been an Indigenous person... I have, six generations back some Indigenous roots, it was a tiny part... I think these things have come my way, people often say I'm just very

honest, and it's about my kids, and a fairer world. Often the angle I'm coming from is a very feminine sort of caring, nurturing, mother earth angle.

(Barbara [audio] 2010)

It's activism; you learn by doing, you lead by example. If you want something done, do it yourself. I'm very individualistic, but I believe in the collective. You must have strong individuals to lead... The satisfaction is having people in our valley, land owners, pick up the environmental message, don't wait for the government, get down there. Then the bush appreciation, my Indigenous part.

(Barbara [audio] 2010)

These narratives show how Barbara's Indigenous cultural identity is a rationale for her social movement participation: 'the bush appreciation, my Indigenous part' ([audio] 2010). Barbara's affinity for a 'mother earth' angle, reveals an intersection of maternalism with essentialism/constructivism, in how 'the role of mother' – a traditional female role, is appropriated by women, as a motivation for social change within environmental activism (Maleta 2015). Participators' empathy for the environment and active performativity of constructivism counters essentialist critiques of women/femininities as subordinate or compliant/submissive to patriarchy (Shiva 1993; Eder 1996; Mellor 1997; Plumwood 1997; Buckingham-Hatfield 2000; MacGregor 2010; Merchant 2013; Nagy 2017). Evidently, Barbara ([audio] 2010), has a strong ecological-justice ethos that is subjective (self-reflective) and performative (activist-based) (Butler 1990, 2004, 2007, 2015). Her 'nurturing' ethos and message for change is egalitarian and political: 'it's about my kids, and a fairer world' (Barbara [audio] 2010). The maternal role captures her environmental activism: 'It was my kids... it was my love for the environment' (Barbara [audio] 2010). Although Barbara debates the feminist label, she pinpoints women's leadership inequity in executive hierarchies: 'I'd love there to be higher representation by women' ([audio] 2010). Barbara's vibrant vision underpins my goal for an egalitarian, women-led participatory democracy.

Indigenous women, around the world, possess a proud history in grassroots leadership initiatives, such as, anti-nuclear-anti-toxic waste campaigns (Havemann 1999; Gaard 2001, 2017; Culley and Angelique 2003; Prokhovnik 2015; Kermoal et al. 2016). Indigenous women-led collectives validate their resistance against traditional tribal, rural lands being used as dumping grounds for industrial pollution and chemical waste, or any other type of waste (Maddison 2004; Doyle 2005; Maddison and Scalmer 2006; Brennan 2015; Canty 2017). Barbara's retrospection is grassroots centric: 'our valley', emphasising egalitarian-rural leadership: 'environmental message(s)', enticing all members of her community, 'the collective', in social change acts. Simultaneously, it is the role of community leaders to 'lead by example', inspiring local grassroots action: 'don't wait for the government' ([audio] 2010). The performative role of 'activism; you learn by doing' (Barbara [audio] 2010), adds substance to Butler's (1990, 2004, 2006) message that agency is realised through engaged, repetitive, subversive acts. Through performative social change, women experience a corporeal-intellectual reckoning, accentuating the 'I' in their identity (Butler 1999, 2007, 2013). What I further deduce from Barbara's above recollection is that grassroots-egalitarian-framed activism underscores the vitality of an integrated urban-rural based movement. Concurrently, it is vital that everyday citizens, along with the leaders of eNSMs/eSMOs, are not submissive in their action. In order for real change to be achieved, everyday citizens need to be involved (MacGregor 2006; Barry 2008; Faber 2008; Butler 2013; Maleta 2018b).

Non-Indigenous participants outline the agentic skill of Indigenous women leaders. In an NGO event in Canberra, Indigenous women advocates and women politicians from diverse parties discussed family challenges. The forum addressed the health of Mums and babies, young people's access to safe sex education, and access issues for elderly patients:

> I felt often working with Aboriginal women here in [omit city] that there's a lot of really strong, great, wonderful, powerful women who will really fire up, umm, and make sure stuff gets, gets done and I saw some of the interactions, kind of, happening between, umm, some of the State MPs, ah, who came along, especially the female one, and these female, kind of, umm, Aboriginal leaders that… who were there at the event, umm, and there's kind of a, kind of some nice automatic affinity that happens, I think, really based on that same gender.
>
> (Juliet [audio] 2010)

Juliet summed up the event as a uniting experience for Indigenous and non-Indigenous women, coming together from diverse sectors. Juliet elaborates on the 'safety and inclusion-ness of it being women in that space' and was 'amazed by the number of powerful Indigenous women as leaders' ([audio] 2010), and how an automatic affinity developed: 'based on that same gender'. In my argument, the future direction of the eNSM and Republican-Bill of Rights Act, relative to an Indigenous Treaty, depends upon the leadership of Indigenous women campaigners (Brennan 2015; Prokhovnik 2015; Gaard 2017; Nagy 2017). Indigenous women's leadership, along with other women, constituting *my six groups*, informs the development of my proposed Indigenous Treaty (Gaard 2001, 2017; Nagy 2017). In a Republican Constitution, Indigenous and CALD women's equity/justice is formalised through legislated leadership in workplace equity, such as WW & SE solutions. This is accentuated through agentic competence plus merit. The above accounts reveal how Indigenous women's leadership is highly skilled, as well as subversive and passionate for change, representing a framework to transform the eNSM and governance. As non-Indigenous women support Indigenous women-rights, I confer a united 'sisterhood' inclusive of diverse women groups as well as a force for feminist equity.

Penny's ([audio] 2010) advocacy is focussed on 'justice for nature' and protecting the rights of 'traditional owners of the land'. This except shows how Indigenous rights underpins the environmentalist, social and gender justice ethos of women in the eNSM and its eSMOs:

But I think there's also the justice element of the communities that we work with, the tradition, the traditional owners of our land, and all the rural settings out there. Like people that don't necessarily have the power to create, like protection and change for the environment that they want to. I think that's the sort of vision that I see for what we do here and how justice plays a part in it. I suppose, if you look at climate change, obviously justice, you know, becomes a major part of what, of what the campaign should look like. If you speak, we do a lot of nature and conservation based campaigns here but personally, like justice is going to become, well, justice issues are going to become a major part of the climate change debate.

(Penny [audio] 2010)

11.2 Discussion

The framing of (in)justice/(in)equity compels Indigenous and non-Indigenous women's advocacy, evidenced through rigorous environmentalist, social and gender justice campaign initiatives. I conclude that an Indigenous voice is crucial to the future development of the eNSM, and foreseeable Republican change, plus proposed Indigenous Treaty. Indigenous women and that of *my six groups*, are key leaders for such a sociopolitical-sustainable change (Brennan 2015; Prokhovnik 2015; Gaard 2017; Nagy 2017; Kawharu 2018). From my interview results, Indigenous women are passionate about a renewables future, rather than the continued extrapolation of the natural environment/nature (Doyle 2005; Shepard and Corbin-Mark 2009; Banerjee 2011; Prokhovnik 2015; Maleta 2018a). Barbara elaborated on her 'mother earth angle' (Merchant 1994; Warren and Cady 1996; Sandilands 1997; Maleta 2015). She highlighted her spiritual 'Indigenous' connection to the land, and that as a mother. Barbara's ethics encompass care for the environment and future sustainability of the planet. Henceforth, motherhood and Indigenous identity intertwine with an environmental justice ethos (Maleta 2015). Women's ethical performances connect constructivism/essentialism as discursive to environmental activism (Shiva and Moser 1995; Plumwood 1997, 2002; Crary 2001; Glazebrook 2005; Moore 2008; Maleta 2012). Women's activism is situated in social change, envisioning a safer, sustainable world for future generations. Indigenous women are inspiring leaders, whose affinity and identity with land and communities, is a premise for change (Maddison 2004; Di Chiro 2011; SBS 2016; Gaard 2017). My proposed Republican change, akin to a Bill of Rights Act, supports this vision.

Conclusion

Anglo male middle class privilege is a barrier for Indigenous women's social change leadership and participation in organisational governance, as with my other five groups of women (Poynting and Donaldson 2005; Donaldson 2009; DAWN 2015; ABS 2016a; Canty 2017). Sociopolitical structures privilege the dominant hegemon, whereby Indigenous cultural frames, or empathy for

Indigenous legislative reform are disjointed. Moreover, Anglo privilege does not delineate Indigenous women's justice ethos nor robust grassroots performativity. Whilst Barbara experienced misogyny and chauvinism in the executive arm of the eNSM, she perceived herself to be equally, if not more skilled, than the men. Barbara's experience of ostracisation was not relayed to racial discrimination, but to sexist discrimination; for as a woman in a male-dominated hierarchy, she did not receive due credit for her performative expertise and merit (Rentetzi 2004; Maleta 2012).

My proposition of an Indigenous Treaty runs counterpoint to the ruling government's rejection of Aboriginal and Torres Strait Islander Recognition (or formal amendment, recognising this, to the Westminster Constitution). Former Prime Minister Turnbull's assessment of the voting electorates' conservativism, contrasts with the public's decision, via a national referendum, in 2017, to recognise same-sex marriage (ABS 2017; Jacks 2017). Of January 2018, it became legal for LGBTQI individuals to marry in Australia (Philpot et al. 2016; Tomazin and Koziol 2017). Although same-sex marriage represents a progressive act of social change within Australian politics and rigorous challenge to conservatism, Indigenous sovereignty remains fraught and unreconciled (Brennan 2015; ABS 2017; Nagy 2017; Pemberton 2017; Kawharu 2018; Patel 2018).

My vision of a Bill of Rights Act, is one in which the Westminster Constitution is discarded – as a remnant of the Monarchy, whereby Republicanism represents an opportunity for Indigenous sovereignty (Smith et al. 2012; Veri 2016; ARM 2018; Hickman 2018). In support to this Act, a Treaty would, be driven by the agentic voice and passionate leadership of Australian Indigenous women. The future achievement of a Treaty, in anticipation, is a polity for reconciliation between Indigenous and non-Indigenous citizenry. It is an egalitarian legislative measure, supported by Indigenous and non-Indigenous women's advocacy (*my six groups*), reinforced through conceptual frames of (in)justice/(in)equity. Thus, a Treaty is a platform for Indigenous sovereignty and nation-wide reconciliation (Prokhovnik 2015; Gaard 2017; Nagy 2017; Patel 2018). This is mandatory to account for the Stolen Generation and 'genocidal acts' towards the Indigenous population, particularly, in the early colonial era. While one participant, in my research, was identified as an Indigenous Tasmanian, this demographic is an extreme rarity, for it is impossible to find a full-blooded Tasmanian Aboriginal (Morris 2017).

Emphasized femininity performative leadership, evidenced as: 'nurturing' 'caring', 'love for the environment', 'my kids', connects constructivism (politically reformative) and/essentialism (motherhood as an agentic model for social change) (Maleta 2012, 2015). Barbara's egalitarian approach and environmental ethics inspires my sociocultural participatory model, striving for *my six groups'* justice/ equity. My Republican change involves drawing inspiration from contemporary and historic modes of governance. Turning to Red Vienna, with the advent of Austrian Republicanism, working and middle class women, benefited considerably from this remarkable social egalitarian model (Gruber 1991; Jeffery 1995; Kelsen 1996, 2004; Blau 1999; Rentetzi 2004, 2008). While Viennese women were politicians and scientists, they did not receive due recognition for their social-scientific-intellectual competence, replicated through the structural remnants of patriarchal monarchism, of which my research contended (Arendt 1945; Rentetzi 2005, 2010; Mattl 2013, 2016). Furthermore, my Republican-Bill of Rights Act plus Treaty, legislates (and advocates) sustainable technological leadership Initiatives in organisational governance, drawing inspiration from Indigenous women's passionate drive for environmental change.

Part IV
Conclusion

12 Conclusion

Emphasized Femininity/Hegemonic Masculinity and Constructivism/ Essentialism

Introduction

This book has addressed a gap on the interplay of emphasized femininity/ hegemonic masculinity and constructivism/essentialism within the eNSM and its eSMOs. Utilising my interviews with Australian women members of renewables organisational governance (IeNGOs, grassroots organisations, academic institutions and the Greens party), I applied a constructivist approach to emphasized femininity, arguing that women-led sustainable-social change strategies, strengthened through participants' agentic technical-scientific performative competencies (and multiple skills-set: intellectual, social, empathetic and physical), challenges the patriarchal control of global politics and rigid structures of hierarchy and bureaucracy. More women in sustainable technological leadership should contribute to global peace as well as desired gender justice outcomes.

My Republican Constitutional vision for sociopolitical change, supported by an egalitarian Bill of Rights Act and its Initiatives, strives to challenge Anglo middle class men's dominance of organisational governance (Kaufmann 2004; Donaldson and Poynting 2007, 2013; DAWN 2015; ABS 2016a; AHRC 2017b). My thematic insights to 'a boys club' and glass ceilings, nonetheless, underscore women's ongoing struggle with ruling class masculinity, plus women's perpetual otherness within patriarchal bureaucratic hierarchies (Connell 2009; Cook and Glass 2014; Pollack 2015; Cohen 2016). My feminist peacemaking model, focussed on innovative human-rights-equity-justice Initiatives, is conceptually framed by an emphasis on *my six groups'* scientific-technical leadership in technological renewable development (Butler 2007; Cockburn 2010, 2013; AHRC 2016b, 2017b). My model emphasises women's constructivist performance of emphasized femininity, situated in their agentic competence, and resistance to patriarchy (Walby 1990; Plumwood 1997; Gaard 2001; Maleta 2015, 2018b). Regarding my thematic insights, constructivism is relayed by the way women defy male-dominated cultural-structures, critiqued as 'aggressive' and 'androcentric', and accommodate emphasized femininity, in terms of 'less aggression', 'collaboration' and 'consensus-building' (Warren 1999; Connell 2005; Gaard 2014, 2017; MacGregor 2014). Hence, emphasized femininity performativity, parallels to empowering women-led WW & SE social change-driven Initiatives (Butler 2013; Wibben 2016; BWE 2018; Clean Energy Council 2018; WIE 2018).

Whilst women work in the same professions to men, they are not equally represented, especially in senior executive positions (Connell 2009; Cook and Glass 2014; STEMM 2018). My Initiatives fill this gender-organisational leadership gap (Ajani 2015; Marfo 2017; Clean Energy Council 2018). Also, women still earn less than men, and struggle with an equitable work–life balance (Pocock 2005; Pocock et al. 2013; Maleta 2015). Greens' Parliamentary interview material, along with that of women partaking in 'the executive arm of International eNGOs' and upper echelons of academia, reveals dissatisfaction with 'a boys club', gendered tokenism and conservative neoliberal practices (Connell 2006; Arthur 2012; Cornish 2017; Jones 2017). Some women are deliberately placed as 'token women' on climate panels – to fill a gap – which presents an illusion of gender equality (Terjesen et al. 2009; Gheaus 2015; Cohen 2016). Yvonne elaborated on how women are increasingly acquiring Professorships; however, men's hegemony is a barrier (Connell 2009; Maleta 2012). Globally, climate science is male-dominated, suggesting that workplaces replicate male privilege, underscoring the gendering of competence and patriarchal structural hierarchies (Cockburn 1988, 1991; Walby 2011, 2013; Cadaret et al. 2017). Women, in my study, however, are assertive, agentic leaders, relative to their multiple-skills-set, framed by confidence, diligence and passion for the cause. Their technical, scientific, empathetic, physical and intellectual performances should not be under-estimated, as a real challenge to the 'boys club' of science and politics (Maleta 2011b; RenewableUK 2017; Vildåsen et al. 2017; EREF 2018; EUREC 2018; REA 2018). Henceforth, labels of 'female technical incompetence' are being destabilised through women's scientific prowess (Cockburn 1988; Maleta 2009; Keller 2012; Farr et al. 2017).

12.1 My Bill of Rights Act in Action: An Evolutionary Framework

The STEMM (2018) programme, defined as Science, Technology, Engineering, Mathematics and Medicine, aims to recruit more women leaders in male-dominated fields. My Bill of Rights Act, accentuated through my conceptual modelling of *Republicanism, Environmentalism, Egalitarianism and Feminism*, foregrounds a compelling legislative challenge to female inequity/injustice, setting a policy benchmark for women's scientific-technological leadership in renewables organisational governance, especially that of my six categories. As such, a Republican-Bill counters women's marginalisation through targeted quotas on women's leadership in environmental science and other male-dominated fields. My constitutional model is supported by the key frame of human rights, and sub-frames of (in)equity/(in)justice. A Bill of Rights serves as a human-rights template, focussing on four key Sections: Section 1. *Women's Renewables Technological Leadership Initiative*; Section 2. *Minority Women's Leadership in Renewables Organisational Governance Initiative*; Section 3. *Women's Leadership Equality in Male-dominated Work Sectors Initiative*; and, Section 4. An *Indigenous*

Treaty. My articulation of minority women includes: CALD, Indigenous, older, socioeconomically disadvantaged, disabled and Anglo-Celtic. My Sections envision a more inclusive social egalitarian democracy. My Bill of Rights, as such, has several goals: 1. to replace the Westminster Constitution with a Republican Constitution; 2. to legislate an Australian Head of State; 3. to reinvigorate governance – revise dated policies with new, improved policies; 4. to articulate an innovative framework for an inclusive egalitarian social participatory democracy; 5. to target women's (75% representation) WW & SE renewables leadership; 6. to provide scope for a national renewables policy framework; plus, 7. to initiate the framing for an Indigenous Treaty.

From a materialist and ideological standpoint, my Bill aims to subvert structural relations of power and cultural representations of gender, privileging men's leadership within patriarchal bureaucratic hierarchies. My Act is centred on women's leadership development of Wind, Wave and Solar Energy Solutions – ideally supported by diverse sector investment (Alston 2011; McFarland 2014; BWE 2018; Carnegie Clean Energy 2018; WIE 2018). The integration of *my six groups* in under-represented sectors, such as politics and science, strategically, should subvert glass ceilings and structural barriers (Ainsworth 2002; Maleta 2011b; DAWN 2015; AHRC 2016b; Canty 2017; STEMM 2018). Further, Indigenous sovereignty is best supported through Republican Constitutional recognition, formalised through a Treaty – dually driven by Indigenous women's voice for political change (Brennan 2015; Kermoal et al. 2016; Nagy 2017).

My Bill aspires for 75% women in WW & SE leadership, akin to their constructivist, engaged performances. Such performativity, reinforced by feminist-egalitarian-republicanism, is a framework to challenge the patriarchal control of the eNSM. Additionally, I dispute assumptions that women are less competent, in the same roles, to men (Cockburn 1988; Culley and Angelique 2003; Maleta 2009, 2012). Women often out-perform men, and, my interviews show, that they tend to be 'less driven by [androcentric] emotivity', 'aggression', 'ego' and 'power'. This viewpoint challenges essentialist frames of women/ femininities, especially as technically or scientifically incompetent (Cockburn 1988; Mellor 1997; Plumwood 1997; Buckingham-Hatfield 2000; Culley and Angelique 2003; Mortimer-Sandilands 2008; Alston 2011, 2013; Pollack 2015; Maleta 2018b).

My findings on women-led emphasized femininity performativity reveals that masculine hegemony is not fixed or static (Connell 1995, 2005; Leahy 2003; Maleta 2011a, 2018b). Drawing upon Connell (1995, 2002, 2005), I contend that patriarchal hierarchies are hegemonic – for hegemony entails a mobile, changing social relation of power, susceptible to women-led subversion (MacLeod 1992; Plumwood 1997; Leahy 2003). Constructivism, as a performative act, encompassing women's negotiation of self and place, defies essentialist assumptions of women's 'appropriate place' in society, their organisations, and indeed, the world (Butler 2007, 2011, 2013). Constructivism is situated through women's negotiation of power (agency); resistance to masculine hegemony; performative multiple skills-set (competence); and subjective empowerment (assertive work and social relations)

(Plumwood 1997; Buckingham-Hatfield 2000; Connell 2009; MacGregor 2009, 2014). Women's constructivist-emphasized femininity performative leadership foregrounds my Republican-sustainable technological model.

Many EEO programmes allude to gender equity, whereas I actualise this through my Bill's Initiatives. While STEMM (2018) is a proactive recruitment programme; my Act is a legislative measure that ensures gender equity and robust sustainable action; it directly addresses women's skill in the technological-scientific development of sustainable science, rather than alluding to it. Hence, my Bill is unique, on a global scale, for its capacity to address women's (in)equity/(in)justice. My model, ideally, inspires leaders of global nations to legislate on such feminist-egalitarian-sustainable Initiatives. Nations that are Republican or have a Bill of Rights in place advisably, could amend their Sections, whereby improved legislation, supported by targeted quotas, should elevate women's status in science, politics and male-dominated sectors (Maleta 2011b, 2018b; WIE 2018).

Women's greater leadership is, therefore, central to my a. Republican-social change manifesto and b. Sustainable technological development polity. My resistance to hereditary monarchism, is necessary to subvert the ruling power of Anglo middle class elites as well as chauvinism and misogyny (Arendt 1945; Donaldson 2009; Donaldson and Poynting 2013; Summers 2013; DAWN 2015). Henceforth, women play a strong part as leaders in a Republican future, and the integration of *my six groups* informs such a revolution. Regarding such a prospective change, Maggie presented a compelling critique of patriarchal hierarchies, in her advocacy of a sustainable world:

> I was deposed in my organisation by hierarchical males who were jealous of me. I hate hierarchy... we need a revolution. I don't mean blood and guts but I mean a revolution. We had a revolution against the French tests and uranium mining... I believe in educating people and then they get out in the streets... Women started the Russian Revolution... they've usually induced most changes and then when we start to become successful the men stop putting us down but they take over and take credit and that's happened to me time and again and it really pisses me off.
>
> (Maggie [audio] 2010)

12.2 Women-Led Renewable Technological Development Initiatives

In relation to Maggie's above 'revolutionary' standpoint akin to 'changes' led by women, the *Women's Renewables Technological Leadership Initiative* enables this vision. It is a cornerstone of my Bill of Rights Act and Republican Constitutional change agenda. In support, I draw upon global women-led recruitment models and professional renewables associations (BWE 2018; WIE 2018), whilst critiquing the middle class control of renewables organisational governance (Bombora Wave Power 2018; Carnegie Clean Energy 2018). Men's dominance of renewables executive boards, underpins women' inequity/injustice. However, participants' agentic performative skills-sets frame the need for more women to lead global renewables development (Ajani 2015; Baruah 2016).

Women In Energy (WIE 2018), formed in 2013, aimed to address Australian women's gap in the energy industry. The association aims: 'to enable women to advance their careers in the energy sector by delivering education, training, advocacy and networking' (WIE 2018). Although women represent approximately 20% of the energy sector, they account for 6.3% of managerial positions (WIE 2018). As a result, WIE's (2018) recruitment programme aspires for more women leaders in renewables, whilst providing a valuable networking pool for women. Still in the Australian context, the Clean Energy Council (2018), similarly aims to recruit more women to sustainable leadership. The *Women in Renewables Initiative* has five core goals, centred on empowering women:

- To showcase the contribution of women in renewables;
- To provide professional development opportunities and advice for women in renewables;
- To foster a sense of valued community, and wider industry pride in Women in Renewables;
- To provide opportunities for informal self-guided development and support for women in renewables;
- To foster positive change in the renewables industry so it can be more inclusive and supportive of women (Clean Energy Council 2018).

The Clean Energy Council's (2018) *Women in Renewables Initiative* is a positive recruitment-leadership model, providing scope for my Act's Initiatives. In addition, the Women in Renewables Scholarship enables a talented woman to work with some key leaders in the industry: 'The CEC's annual scholarship supports a female employee within a CEC member company to undertake the Australian Institute of Company Directors (AICD) Foundations of Directorship course' (Clean Energy Council 2018). Like WIE (2018), the Council has a mailing list of events for women and offers e-mentoring, thereby enabling women's leadership plus networking opportunities. Its annual luncheon recognises competent women in the industry (Clean Energy Council 2018). Comparatively, these examples are compatible with STEMM's (2018) goals: to have more women working in scientific and other male-dominated areas. Energy sector recruitment programmes show that women are being encouraged to be leaders in environmental science, akin to their merit and agentic technical competence. Nonetheless, this is framed through inequity/injustice, relative to gender-organisational gaps, accounting for the necessity for such programmes. Whilst these recruitment programmes are inspirational, my Act goes further in its legislation/advocacy of targeted quotas, ensuring that *my six groups* are indeed, *equitably* and *justly* represented in renewables leadership. Like WIE (2018) and the Clean Energy Council (2018), women's performance is based upon merit and competence. My quota-base drive though ensures their leadership equality in diverse sectors – without alluding to this – as is characteristic of meritocracy. My *Women's Leadership Equality in Male-dominated Work Sectors Initiative* ensures women's leadership in other fields.

Overall, my four Initiatives envision STEMM's (2018) ambitions and that of professional associations.

Turning to a global context, RenewableUK is regarded as Britain's leading renewable energy trade association, specialising in onshore wind, offshore wind, and wave and tidal energy (RenewableUK, How we work 2018). It has a large corporate membership, ranging from small independent companies to large international corporations (RenewableUK, How we work 2018). Women partake in middle management; however, men dominate executive hierarchies. Such findings point to gendered tokenism and executive men's supremacy on boards (Gupta 2007; Terjesen et al. 2009; Gheaus 2015). Regarding its senior management structure, two Chief Directors are male, while the third executive Director, is a woman (RenewableUK, Organisational Structure 2018). In its gender makeup, the executive hierarchy is constituted of five women on the Board of Directors; but men still dominate – with a total of 11 male board members (RenewableUK, Organisational Structure 2018). Despite women's 'good representation', indicating that their competence is recognised; men's dominance of the executive hierarchy, frames the patriarchal control of European renewable boards (EREF 2018; EUREC 2018; SolarPower Europe 2018). In two Australian wave energy boards, there were no females at board level, which is even more contentious! (Bombora Wave Power 2018; Carnegie Clean Energy 2018). Having no women on boards reveals that 'the boys club' of renewables governance, is juxtaposed to women's prowess and merit as well as sustainable technological-scientific development.

Professional renewable associations, like WIE (2018), the Clean Energy Council (2018) and RenewableUK (2018), proactively recruit women through progressive Initiatives. RenewableUK (2017), launched the *Women Into Wind Initiative*, targeting women's greater representation in male-dominated roles, such as mariners, engineers and CEOs. Considering overarching gaps, RenewableUK's Executive Director, Emma Pinchbeck outlined the rising role of women in wind energy development:

> It's great to see this new power list highlighting the important role women are now playing in the wind industry… British women in some of the world's most powerful firms are playing a significant role in taking the wind industry forward. It's an encouraging sign that our sector is becoming more inclusive, but the number of women in senior management roles still needs to increase. We should ensure that women across the country see wind energy as an open and attractive industry to work in. This means promoting renewable skills and opportunities to a new generation of women entering the workforce.
> (*Women Into Wind Initiative*, cited in RenewableUK 2017)

In relation to Pinchbeck's assessment of the *Women Into Wind Initiative*, women's merit-competence performativity is: 'taking the wind industry forward' (RenewableUK 2017). Although RenewableUK has women board members in the executive hierarchy, the senior management team and Board of Directors, are mostly men (RenewableUK, Organisational Structure 2018). However, these Initiatives redress men's control of the emerging renewables sector (Ajani 2015; RenewableUK 2017; Clean Energy Council 2018; WIE 2018). Concurrently, my legislative stand on women-led quotas in environmental scientific polity is essential to challenge endemic male privilege. It should subvert 'the boys club', underscoring the global eNSM and political terrains (Maleta 2011b).

12.3 A Pervasive 'Boys Club' Within Environmentalist Executive Hierarchies

The 'boys club' is replicated in a number of European renewable energy associations, but women are not entirely excluded from leadership (EREF 2018; REA 2018). Comparatively, women experience their work role as the dualist insider/outsider within organisations/movements (Yoder and Aniakudo 1997; Maddison 2004; Maleta 2009, 2011a; Yoder et al. 2011; Nagy 2017). The European Renewable Energies Federation (EREF), has a male President, supported by an array of male Vice-Presidents and Advisory members, on its executive board (EREF 2018). Most of these men represent West European nations, with the exception of one from the Czech Republic. This sociocultural demographical representation suggests that East European nations are not visible in renewables development nor its management, and thereby lag behind the West. Regarding demographical under-representation, at EREF, there are two women board members: one who represents the UK's Renewables Energy Association and another, who is additionally a member of Germany's Bundesverband WindEnergie eV (The German Federal Wind Energy Association [BWE]) (BWE 2018; EREF 2018). Concerning the U.K. example, it is questionable whether Britain will be included in European Energy Boards following Brexit, which is supposed to occur in 2019. The German woman member of BWE, moreover, points to scientific-technical expertise in wind energy development (BWE 2018). A common finding, nonetheless, is replicated in BWE's hierarchy: the CEO is male, the Federal Executive has two male presidents, along with one female deputy president plus one female in the position of Treasurer, while the remaining five executives are all males (BWE 2018). As the organisational structure is male-dominated, women's deputy President and Treasurer posts, still accentuates their merit and contribution to renewables technologies. But, pessimistically, women's placement on executive boards, indicates gender tokenism or that women are deliberately placed to fill a gender gap on male-dominated panels (Gupta 2007; Terjesen et al. 2009; Gheaus 2015). If tokenism applies, then gender performativity – arguably, is less indicative of merit or even competence.

SolarPower Europe (professional renewable association) has males as CEO, Deputy CEO, CFO and Head of Marketing. Simultaneously, the Policy Director is female – to reiterate, the lone female in a pool or, indeed, sea of men (SolarPower Europe 2018). Whilst women are visible, the visibility of men is more obvious, further, highlighting women's insider/outsider status, in their organisations and across the eNSM.

In addition, the European Renewable Energy Research Centres Agency (EUREC), an association representing research centres and university departments – contentiously, has only one female executive amongst a pool of eight men Board Directors! (EUREC 2018) Whilst the President and Vice-President and other Directors are men, the (sole) female board member is involved in its Energy Innovation Centre. As the gender gap at EUREC is striking, the woman's technical performative role in energy development, within an expert research setting, highlights a woman's/women-led scientific and intellectual competence.

The rule of middle class men is replicated in their control of global environmental governance. The UK's Renewable Energy Association has five male executives, including Chairman (REA 2018). It also has two female executives: Chief Executive and Independent Non-Exec Director (REA 2018). One woman accounts for a top internal executive position, while the other, is an external 'Non-Exec Director'. Perhaps the external directorship role is not as influential as the internal executive post. These examples reveal further contradictions. Men dominate the executive, whilst women tend to be represented in middle management (Mellor 1997, 2013). My Act's clause on 'Minority' categories, ensures that CALD, low SES, disabled, mature and Indigenous women, who are currently under-represented in workplace hierarchies, partake at a board level, rather than as token women, in a pool of men, clouded by ruling class masculinist cultural-structural elitism.

But would Indigenous or CALD women, as with my other groups, enjoy working with privileged middle class Anglo males? In response, I pose that through increased representation of my groups in environmentalist sectors, this diversity should make workplaces more harmonious and cohesive for my 'under-represented' categories. A point to reiterate is that organisational structures and workplace cultures need to change in order to become more inclusive of women. Arguably, more women in renewables leadership would create an environment of inclusion, representing multiple, diverse voices and not solely a privileged group. I found that Indigenous women, like Barbara, are passionate about protecting the environment along with children and communities, framed by a nurturing ethos, and cultural or indeed spiritual affinity for their land (Maleta 2015). From my assessment of Barbara's recollection, Indigenous women are empathetic towards renewable energy, for it does not involve a violent extrapolation of the land or natural environment, and represents a viable healthier, sustainable option, for communities and children. Such a cultural standpoint, rather moralistic and ethical in its vision, is, therefore an empowering frame of enablement, aligned with emphasized femininity-sustainable leadership. Indigenous women, in supporting global studies, have long resisted their traditional lands being used as dumping grounds for toxic waste pollutants by corporates and governing authorities (Gaard 2001, 2017; Brown 2011). Concurrently, women's greater role in wind, wave and solar energy technological development contests the hegemony of resource-based industries, and contributes to a safer, healthier, more sustainable world (Gaard 2001; Stein 2004; Schlembach 2011; Ajani 2015; Baruah 2016).

12.4 My Act's Initiatives' Modelling of Merit and Competence

The quotas in my Bill of Rights Act model, plus Initiatives, are performative, accentuated through merit and competence. Legislating on women-led quotas does not delineate from women's multiple skills-set (technical, scientific, social, intellectual, physical and empathetic), and their quality performances across the eNSM and its eSMOs. Certainly, emphasized femininity-constructivist leadership strategically contests 'the boys club' and strengthens the renewables energy sector, transforming it from an emerging to growth sector (Maleta 2011b; McFarland 2014; Ajani 2015; RenewableUK 2017; Clean Energy Council 2018; WIE 2018). Women-led WW & SE direction is based on the premise that women's agency in the development of this technology defies the corporate-government control of environmental technologies, whilst defying over-reliance on resource-based approaches, including uranium mining, oil extrapolation, and fracking (Ajani 2015; Heuer and Yan 2017; Maleta 2018b). As well as empowering women's agency in sustainable technology, my egalitarian model engages grassroots citizen's solar power usage – enabling everyday citizens to exercise their agency over their personal, individualised energy consumption (Horton 2006; Smith and Pangsapa 2008; Arthur 2012; MacGregor 2014). More power to women and the grassroots (including individuals and grassroots eSMOs) challenges the corporate-governmental control of renewables (Di Chiro 2008; Shiva 2008, 2014; Sundström and McCright 2014; Maleta 2018a). In my feminist-egalitarian-republican model, agency is discursive to women and global citizenry.

Although men dominate senior management, women are competently performing their scientific research roles, thus reinforcing the findings of Rentetzi (2004, 2005, 2008, 2010), relative to women's radium research prowess in the Red Vienna period. Critically, my focus is not on radium technology, and, undoubtedly, is on the sophisticated development of renewable technology. Women, additionally, should be encouraged, through rigorous recruitment drives (as legislated in my Bill of Rights Act and Republican Constitutional framework) to contribute more so and visibly, as leaders, in the future of sustainable technology. After all, in my qualitative analysis and supportive studies, women partake in professional (advocacy, salaried) and grassroots (activist, volunteer) capacities, motivated by mutual passionate drives for a renewables versus resource-based future (Gaard 2001; Di Chiro 2011; Maleta 2015, 2018a, 2018b).

One retrospection is that a gender mix entails a healthy mix; representing a productive work environment, whereby, female and male voices are heard, elevated by mutual goals for environmental change. Shared gender efforts, is an inspiring framework for renewables development. Moreover, I previously shared office space with nurses. There were a couple of men nurses in the department – whom were nicer and less clannish than the women nurses. Hence, having a robust gender mix enables diversity, for women and men can work well together. Gender can act as an enabler rather than a barrier (Maleta 2012).

12.5 An Agentic Performative Multi-Skills-Set: Emphasized Resistance to Tokenism

Having one or two women on executive boards does not demonstrate an equitable gender mix, nor does this point to women's workplace inclusion. Rather this shows that women are marginalised in patriarchal contexts, thereby revealing that feminist concerns for equity and justice are still valid in the 21st century. Women often out-perform men when placed in the same or similar positions (as evident from my qualitative analysis). As a feminist-environmentalist, aiming to incorporate an egalitarian-human-rights framed Republican Constitutional Bill of Rights Act, I strive to reverse the gender-based discrimination, sexism and misogyny that has been characteristic of so many scientific and technological work sectors (Connell 2009; Culley and Angelique 2010; STEMM 2018). As renewables are still regarded to be an emerging sector, at this 'so-called early' stage, it is essential that women are included in its leadership structure and scientific development. Such inclusion should reverse historical to contemporary gender injustices/inequities, whereby men have been – and still are, privileged in executive scientific leadership (Pollack 2015; Cadaret et al. 2017; Farr et al. 2017). I demonstrated how women perform an expert skills-set: egalitarian, social, scientific, technical, intellectual and physical competencies. Thus, it is to the detriment of the industry to have women placed as token women, for their talent and passion should reinvigorate and revitalise this sector. Undoubtedly, women-led performative acts, akin to agentic technical-scientific competence, contest the patriarchal control of global environmentalist organisational governance. Women's constructivist-emphasized femininity performativity is instrumental in downplaying the middle class masculine hegemony of resource-based industries and ruling governing (political) and industrial (social) elites. Greater women-led emphasis in renewables, frames a safer, more sustainable human and nonhuman world (Gaard 2001, 2017; Shiva 2014).

In support to my Act's legislative scope for women's greater managerial and technical leadership, Baruah (2016) positioned renewables energy as a growth sector, with significant scope for women to contribute substantially to its development. Within a global context, Baruah (2016) identified a gender gap in the renewables sector, particularly in technical and managerial positions: 'Worldwide women constitute fewer than six per cent of technical staff and below one per cent of top managers in the renewable energy sector'. Women's under-representation here is further comparable to their under-representation in science, technology, engineering and math (STEMM) fields (STEMM 2018). Baruah (2016) adds that the renewables sector should benefit women and men, but that proactive action policies should be in place, to realise women's greater leadership potential:

> we must be proactive about enabling women to establish a stronger equity stake to compensate for historical and contemporary economic injustices and

unequal outcomes. This will require more concrete and proactive actions and policies. Simply creating opportunities for training and employment in new fields and suggesting that women are not unwelcome in them is obviously not enough.

Baruah's (2016) emphasis on 'concrete and proactive actions and policies' framed through 'historical and contemporary economic injustices and unequal outcomes' adds context to my conceptual framing of inequity/injustice. In order to address women's under-representation in renewables scientific development, it is necessary to go beyond STEMM as the benchmark, but to implement proactive recruitment-driven legislative Acts, like my Bill of Rights Act's Initiatives. My four Initiatives legislate on women's greater leadership in this technology, thereby meeting my conceptual-methodological equity/justice ambitions along with gaps in the global renewables literature. In support, Baruah (2016) contemplated: 'training and employment' is 'not enough'; I also realise this and, therefore, aim to advocate a Bill of Rights Act in order to inform national policy direction, whilst strengthening citizens' agency of energy consumption. My Bill's particular Sections/Articles, ensure that minority women, that is those with disabilities, mature, Indigenous, socioeconomically disadvantaged and CALD, are equally represented in this emerging growth sector, whilst strengthening its scientific-technical development.

McFarland's (2014) research, parallel to Baruah (2016), highlighted the gender gaps framing women's marginalisation in green energy. Focussing on Canadian empirical data, McFarland adds that stricter equity programmes need to be developed, which dually informs my robust recruitment model, that envisions change, rather than alluding to this:

> The evidence that I have gathered – from New Brunswick as well as some from Nova Scotia and Canada as a whole – shows that given women's current patterns of participation in jobs and training in the trades, almost none of the green jobs created would go to women, 13 either now or in the future. We need equity programs both on the job and in training and those equity programs need to be strictly monitored, tracked, reported and enforced. Only with such equity programs will there be any chance for women to get a reasonable share of the green jobs created.
>
> (2014: 12–13)

12.6 Sustainable Energy Programmes and Empowering Quotas

McFarland's (2014) emphasis on gender equity programmes, relative to clean energy, efficiency and environmental protection, envisions women's greater leadership in the intellectual-scientific-technical development of wind power and solar energy (BWE 2018; Clean Energy Council 2018; WIE 2018). In my standpoint, women's (in)equity/(in)justice underpinning 'green jobs' can only be 'enforced' through a policy framework that is legislative and reformative.

Nonetheless, this is also framed by women's agentic competence and merit, thereby entailing a performative act. Performativity entails an intellectual to corporeal reckoning, situated in agentic negotiations, resulting in an empowered identity (Butler 1999, 2006, 2013). My proposed Republican Constitutional model, emphasises gender performativity, in a rigorous review of dated environmental policies. Through women's WW & SE Initiatives, I aim to contribute policy recommendations for a sustainable technological development programme. In order to expand and develop the industry, my ambition is for a 75% representation of women in this sector. Arguably, women's technical contribution and merit should subvert gender imbalances.

I envision that nations that have a Bill of Rights in place, such as New Zealand, Canada and Britain, should revise their legislative Acts in order to be more inclusive of a women-led renewables framework (Hiebert and Kelly 2015; Hickman 2018). As well as no Bill of Rights nor Indigenous Treaty, Australia lacks a Federal renewable technological policy framework (Brennan 2015; Prokhovnik 2015; Kermoal et al. 2016; EU ETS 2018; Yaxley 2018). Our political establishment, currently led by the Liberal National Party (LNP) Coalition, is characterised by extreme conservative neoliberalism, but also volatility and instability; evident by the ousting of several Prime Ministers within the last decade (Greer 2010b; Sweeney and Belot 2018; Yaxley 2018). Following an internal LNP Leadership spill (rather than enacted by the voting electorate), on the 24 August 2018, Scott Morrison became the sixth Australian Prime Minister within a decade (Sweeney and Belot 2018; Yaxley 2018). Comparatively, Malcolm Turnbull was ousted as Prime Minister, having served less than three years (Sweeney and Belot 2018; Yaxley 2018). This is endemic to Australian politics. It also reveals the androcentrism of ruling-middle class masculinity.

12.7 Envisioning Greater Agency for Women and Grassroots Citizenry

My sociopolitical model, moreover, is egalitarian and empathetic in its vision; it is supportive to women and the grassroots – encompassing everyday citizens (Maleta 2018a). A greater investment in renewables technology frames agentic economic choice, enabling grassroots populaces to exercise control of their own energy consumption. With a greater diversity of renewables solutions, individuals can choose particular options rather than relying on energy companies (Gaard 2001; McNay 2003; Meynell 2009; Cuomo 2011; Khatibi and Indira 2011; AGL 2018). Such choice defies the supremacy of ruling and industrial elites, along with their 'centralised' control of energy output and consumption.

Certainly, the renewables sector is a progressive example of technological development, with less catastrophic impact upon the social and natural world, encompassing human and nonhuman dimensions (Maleta 2011a, 2011b; Ajani 2015; RenewableUK 2017; BWE 2018; SolarPower Europe 2018). Renewables energy is compatible with women-led direction, and my theoretical-methodological framing of emphasized femininity leadership acts as a defining counterpoint to ruling class masculinity and the patriarchal control of the eNSM.

It challenges the supremacy of resource-based industrial elites as with, mining, oil extrapolation and fracking (Ajani 2015; Heuer and Yan 2017; Maleta 2018a). Women more so reject unsustainable technologies, like nuclear energy and uranium, due to the danger these technologies pose to children and communities (Maleta 2015, 2018b). Hence women, as mothers and 'non-mothers', recognise the human and nonhuman connection, framing 'dangerous' resource-based energy, versus 'safer' sustainable technological methods. Such a premise is an empowering scope to realise my emphasized femininity vision, framed by women's empathetic performative leadership. Consequently, mothers and non-mothers engage with sustainability in everyday life. This underscores women's strength in social (Republican) and sustainable developments.

12.8 Discussion

My Republican social egalitarian model is juxtaposed to the conservatism framing Australian governance and polities. Australia's Federal environmental policies are dated, and require revised changes in order to redress *my six groups'* greater WW & SE technological leadership development. The Environment Protection and Biodiversity Conservation Act 1999: 'provides a legal framework to protect and manage nationally and internationally important flora, fauna, ecological communities and heritage places' (EPBC Act [1999] 2018). The EPBC Act is centred on matters of a national significance, whereby the sociocultural participation element, relative to inclusive human and nonhuman aspects, requires greater focus and integration. In my proposed Republican Constitutional sociopolitical change, my Bill of Rights Act integrates an ethical-human-rights framework, framed by (in)equity/(in)justice, thereby integrating the social and natural world (Wibben 2016; Hickman 2018). My feminist-egalitarian-human-rights-technological framework also challenges the centralisation of the energy industry, whereby the community, led by women working in this field, are enabled to choose their energy consumption and have greater agency on how much they spend. With greater economic agency and choice, the grassroots, inclusive of its individuals and collectives, are not reliant upon the ruling governing and industrial elite for energy output. Women's leadership in this development, such as through solar panels at home, or development of wind turbines in regional and rural areas, and wave energy – centred on tidal energy sources, either on the Pacific or Indian coastlines – are enabled by the multiple skills-sets of women. Also, Australians, as other nationalities around the world, can appropriate their natural environment in a sustainable rather than extrapolative, or indeed destructive way. The technology and environment should support this social and environmental change.

Conclusion

To sum up, managerial and technical leadership roles should be opened up, more so, for my six categories of women. Hence, my Republican reformative

Constitutional framework aims to make this vision a reality, rather than a fantastical dream. Why should the scientific and technical side, or even managerial side of renewables be a preserve of men, as with other scientific and technical industries? After all, it is an emerging sector, and women should be enabled rather than disabled from its participatory inclusion (McFarland 2014; Ajani 2015; Baruah 2016; RenewableUK 2017; BWE 2018; WIE 2018). Women are passionate about sustainable energy, and their dynamic skills-set, in technical development and management, should reinvigorate and transform the renewable energy sector. It is to the detriment of the industry, on a global scale, if women are not included, particularly in a managerial and scientific-technical capacity, within this industry (Ajani 2015). Concurrently, nations that are Republican or have a Bill of Rights in their Constitution, can take advice from my model by incorporating Sections that address women's sustainability leadership. It is mandatory that this technology is supported by greater investment, across sectors, encouraging women around the world to partake in higher numbers, whilst drawing upon their agentic technical prowess. Regarding my Acts' conceptual modelling of egalitarianism, feminism and republicanism, I further refer to Red Vienna, as a landmark example of social democratic mode of governance, enabling women's agentic-academic competence, whereby, middle and working class women experienced greater civil and civic liberties as well as empowerment (Rentetzi 2004).

13 Conclusion

Republican Red Vienna: An Inspirational Feminist Model of Egalitarian Governance

Introduction

My Republican Constitution-Bill of Rights Act, is inspired by *Red Vienna* (1919–34), a landmark social egalitarian democracy. In this era, robust social policies were enacted, conducive to 'republican', 'egalitarian', 'feminist' and 'inclusive' ideals. An impressive equilibrium was reached across social groups along with improved civil and civic liberties for working and middle class women (and men) (Gruber 1991; Jeffery 1995; Rentetzi 2004; Mattl 2009, 2013). Women worked as research scientists and politicians, highlighting their prowess (Rentetzi 2008, 2010; Mattl 2013, 2016). This dispels assumptions that women were not scientifically or politically literate in the early 20th century. Although women's intellectualism was a reality, they did not receive due credit, which my 21st-century research, likewise, reaffirms (Bader-Zaar 1996; Rentetzi 2004; Mattl 2009; Kershaw 2013; Zarkov 2017).

Women still struggled with barriers, framed by patriarchy, a structural-cultural remnant of the Imperial age (Rentetzi 2010; Mattl 2016). Today, a lack of credit persistently positions women/femininities as 'the other' to men/masculinities (Plumwood 1997; Buckingham-Hatfield 2000). Yet, women perform well in roles 'deemed best suitable for men'. Concurrently, I would not delineate their prowess, but reiterate that ruling class masculinity frames women's ongoing struggle (Donaldson and Poynting 2013; DAWN 2015). Red Vienna, however, exemplifies an enlightened social democracy, aiding women's multiple skills-set. But the limitations of patriarchy were not eroded. Although Austria remains a Republic, Austrian women, like others in Western democracies, are under-represented in leadership within organisational governance (Bader-Zaar 1996; Zarkov 2017). This suggests a need to point back to the enlightened age of Red Vienna.

Despite gender barriers, I adhere to the contemporary Austrian Republic model. Vienna is one of the most liveable cities in the world (*Economist* 2018). Notably, Viennese working mothers receive free day care for their children (City of Vienna, Childcare Centres 2018). Arguably, Vienna remains a mode of social egalitarian governance, enabling middle and working class women. Its robust social and workplace polices, enabled women to either work as scientists or in factories, supported by an improved eight-hour day (Hautmann 2012). Industrial strength was an integral model of Red Vienna.

As such, Red Vienna and contemporary Austria are viable participatory democratic models of republicanism, egalitarianism and feminism. My conceptual modelling of sustainable technological development further draws inspiration from the art nouveau architecture and intellectual creativity of Red Vienna (Blau 1999). In summary, Red Vienna was a reformative Social Democratic model, whereby its Republican Constitution is an inspirational point, to improve women's leadership in renewables organisational governance. My book has integrated nature within the arts, science and technology, relative to my six women groups' performative skills-set in WW & SE leadership. Henceforth, my emphasized-feminist-constructivist plus environmentalist-egalitarian-republican sociopolitical-change model is situated in a. women-led agentic competence and b. resistance to oppressive patriarchal bureaucratic hierarchies that privilege men.

13.1 Women's Performativity as Research Scientists, Not Technicians

Rentetzi's (2004) study illustrated Austrian women's expertise as scientists at the Viennese Institute for Radium Research (famous for Nobel Prize winners and distinguished alumni). The Institute was founded in 1921, and now is part of the Austrian Academy of Sciences (Rentetzi 2004, 2005; OEAW 2018). Although most of the Nobel Prize winners were men, this somewhat 'patriarchal institution' was not oblivious to women's intellectual and scientific performative prowess. Comparatively, Rentetzi's (2004) analysis of women scientific academics and Mattl's (2016) case study of Charlotte Glas, a founding member of the Austrian Social Democratic Party (politically active during the Habsburgs age and Red Vienna), provides evidence that it is a myth or naïve to assume that Viennese women were absent from professional and political life (or that of other women in the world) in the early 20th century. The radical socialism of this time further empowered women's agency.

Rentetzi's (2004) investigation of gender-politics at the Institute for Radium Research highlighted women's significant contribution to scientific academic knowledge. In the sociopolitical context of Red Vienna, Rentetzi emphasises women's empowerment: 'the politics of Red Vienna and the culture of radioactivity research specific to the Viennese setting encouraged exceptional gender politics within the Institute for Radium Research in the interwar years' (2004: 359). Supporting my conceptual-methodological appraisal of women's agentic plural performative proficiencies, her assessment also speaks against: 'stereotypical images of women in science to explain the disproportionately large number of women in radioactivity research' (Rentetzi 2004: 359). Her confrontation of gender stereotypes and labels of female scientific incompetence are conceptually-methodologically developed in the articulation of my participants' multi-skills-set (intellectual, scientific, technical, social, empathetic, egalitarian, physical etc.).

The social democracies of Austria and Australia, to a certain extent, enable women; yet, men's privileged status – conducive to the patriarchal control of organisational governance, hinders women's competence in conjunction with merit from being fully actualised. As men remain privileged in science, and other male-dominated vocations, women – when enabled with the opportunity – perform well in such roles (Pollack 2015; Cohen 2016; Farr et al. 2017). At the Viennese Institute, men were the project leaders, but several women physicists were part of the research team. As experts, women worked in radiophysics and radiochemistry, and formed their own groups; but also worked with men physicists (Rentetzi 2004: 360). Rentetzi esteems women's, individual and collective, excellence in scientific research

> between 1919 and 1934 more than one third of the institute's personnel were women. They were not technicians or members of the laboratory support staff but experienced researchers or practicum students who published at the same rate as their male counterparts.
>
> (Rentetzi 2004: 360)

On the other hand, academic activist Anna's retrospection of the 1960s, pointed to women's over-representation in technical support roles rather than scientific positions. However, in Red Vienna, one third of Institute women were radium researchers. They were better represented in the scientific research side, rather than as technicians or lab support staff (Rentetzi 2004: 360). This frames women's expert knowledge, parallel to a progressive, enlightened 'Red Viennese' social democracy. Simultaneously, following Austrian suffrage, Viennese women were further empowered (Bader-Zaar 1996; Rodriguez-Ruiz and Rubio-Marin 2012; Mattl 2016). Women's emphasized femininity leadership, evidenced through performative scientific proficiencies, challenged Austrian middle class men's privileged status.

13.2 Patriarchy, Still a Barrier

The ruling power of the patriarch or patriarchy (as a cultural-structural representation), framed by men's leadership dominance of organisational governance, still prevailed in Red Vienna, as in many other male-dominated contexts, of that time (Bader-Zaar 1996; Rentetzi 2008, 2010; Mattl 2016). To reiterate, the patriarchal figure – within patriarchy – entails an omnipresent historical to contemporary structural-cultural barrier. Even in Red Vienna, arguably the most progressive municipal governance in Europe of the early 20th century, women dominated private, domesticated roles. It is rather optimistic or naïve to assume that all women were empowered; some were, but most were curtailed by patriarchy and male hegemony. One's class or sociocultural connections represented certain enablement. Although women were radium scientists, this grouping was predominantly middle class women, which indicates degrees of privilege. Moreover, women's job placement depends upon their expertise and merit, even within a patriarchal profession. Mattl's (2016) historic-based Austrian research highlighted women's political activism in the suffrage Movement; simultaneously, harking to the Habsburg (the late 19th century) age. Markedly, women were not sitting at home, letting men do all the scientific and political work.

The Austrian Republican Constitution was written by Hans Kelsen, who, in later years was forced to flee, due to the rise of Nazi fascism (and demise of Viennese republican-socialism) (Kelsen 1996, 2004; Lagi 2012). Red Vienna was an enlightened, egalitarian democracy, empowering women and their dynamic skills; but it did not erode the structural relations of power, in which patriarchy was replicated. Austria remains a Republic; however, Austrian women, like others in Western democracies, are under-represented in organisational governance (Bader-Zaar 1996; Zarkov 2017). This suggests a need to draw inspiration from Red Vienna in how republicanism and egalitarianism elevated women's participatory engagement, along with a vibrant social class equilibrium.

With the demise of the Monarchy or Habsburgs, the Bourgeoisie and Proletariat gained more power and status, whilst the power of the ruling class somewhat lessened (Barker 2012; Rauchensteiner 2014; Mattl 2016). In contrast to the Russian Revolution (for the Austrian royal family were not assassinated), a parallel 'peaceful' transition to republicanism occurred (Mack 1993; Rauchensteiner 2014). Working class families, benefited from many municipal housing projects and socialist polices enacted by the local government – the most famous being Karl Marx Hof (which is a current tourist attraction) (Kitchen 1988; Gruber 1991; Jeffery 1995) This transfer of power, from Monarchism to Republicanism, enabled the working and middle classes (in contrast to the privilege of the royalist elite) to have more power at their disposal. This was reflected in polity and polices.

Republicanism, consequently, challenged patriarchal practices and ruling class masculinity. Red Vienna, therefore, remains a successful Social Democratic model. Its egalitarian mode of governance challenged the ruling power of privileged elites, and enabled diverse individuals and communities to ascertain a more defined 'agentic' position at work and society. Critically, many nations have not achieved such an equitable equilibrium between social classes (Gardner and Stevens 1992; Rentetzi 2004, 2008; Mattl 2016). Feminist sociopolitical empowerment evolved through Viennese women's greater participation in academic (middle class) and industrial (working class) employment; nonetheless, these classes were empowered by Austrian suffrage (Bader-Zaar 1996; Rentetzi 2004, 2010). Such social equilibrium frames an empowering feminist-egalitarian model of republicanism, which I aim to endorse with a Republican-Bill of Rights Act.

13.3 The Federal Republic of Austria: A Viable Contemporary Model?

In my Republican Constitutional framing of social egalitarian women-led participatory democratic governance, I draw inspiration from the contemporary Austrian Federal Parliamentary model (Republic of Austria, Parliament 2018).

The Austrian Parliament's structural leadership is composed of a President and Chancellor, and supported by a Federal Council and National Council. Elected members serve on the National Council via proportional representation (Republic of Austria, Parliamentary Dimension 2018). Similarly, the Australian Parliament has proportional representation, while its two houses of Parliamentary governance are called the Lower House (House of Representatives) and Upper House (the Senate) (Bolton 2005; Smith et al. 2012; Parliament of Australia 2018). The Lower House has 150 elected MPs or political representatives, and represents Federal governance and the running of the nation (Parliament of Australia, House of Representatives, 2018). The Senate is composed of 76 Senators, and is where most of the nation's laws are negotiated and voted upon – that is, either legislated or rejected (Smith et al. 2012; Parliament of Australia, Senate 2018). Australia, like Austria, is a Federal Parliamentary democracy, yet differs in its Constitutional monarchy/Westminster constitution and Republican Constitutional framework (Kumarasingham and Power 2014; Republic of Austria, Parliament 2018, Parliamentary Dimension 2018).

Austria is a successful model for Australian Republicanism, particularly in how policies and polity are enacted in social, everyday life. The city of Vienna is consistently esteemed for its high standard of living, and recently overtook Melbourne as the most liveable global city (*Economist* 2018). Vienna undoubtedly is a leading mode of egalitarian governance, relative to middle and working class women's enablement. For instance, Viennese working mothers receive free day care for their children (City of Vienna, Child-care Centres 2018). This is a viable model for worldwide social democracies to adhere to, reflective of a productive, harmonious work–life balance (Pocock 2005; Pocock et al. 2013).

One point of contention is that Austria does not have a Bill of Rights in place. Rather Austria has Constitutional-based Acts, relative to its national Republican legislative framework, whereby civil rights are legislated on (Republic of Austria, Parliamentary Dimension 2018). Moreover, Monarchist, Commonwealth nations, like New Zealand (1990) and Canada (1960), have respective Bill of Rights Acts (Canadian Bill of Rights 1960; Hickman 2018). Australia has an Australia Act (1986); this is not a Civil Rights Act, but is indicative of a sovereign Federal legislation. Although the Australia Act (1986) terminated Britain's power to legislate on Australian law, it did maintain the Westminster Constitution, and thereby retained the Monarchy (Smith et al. 2012; Australia Act 1986). I should mention that as early as 1688, Britain established a Bill of Rights Act (Bill of Rights 1688), which still serves as a legal civil rights document by the Crown. The monarchist connection though is rather redundant, when a Bill of Rights Act can be just as well administered by Parliament. Also, a futuristic Head of State, leading New Zealand or Canada, within a prospective Republican Constitutional framework, could make revisions and amendments to their existing Bill of Rights. The signature of the Monarch, hence, serves a ceremonial capacity, and such action can be performed by elected MPs and Senators, in Australia, or indeed, Britain. I would again point to one Head of State, rather than the dualist roles of Prime Minister, Governor General and Monarch.

13.4 A New Model: One Head of State

While Austria's Federal and National Council model is plausible; Australia's Parliamentary model of Upper and Lower Houses is also a viable mode to maintain (Republic of Austria, Parliament 2018, Parliamentary Dimension 2018). This model can be structurally applied to a Republican Constitutional framework. I seek inspiration from Austria's Federal Republican Constitution; but would disband with multiple roles of President and Chancellor, in favour of one leader: a Head of State. The Head of State can perform multiple Parliamentary and ceremonial roles, including meeting with dignitaries and running the country, while upholding the Parliamentary democracy. It is economically viable to have one functionary role here. The Head, or perhaps, Leader of the Nation, would be accountable to the grassroots electorate, whom vote for their leader via proportional representation (Smith et al. 2012). This model ensures egalitarian governance.

In my Australian reformative Parliamentary model, unquestionably, I would disband with the dualist roles of Governor General/Monarch, for these are largely ceremonial roles and dichotomous representations of hereditary privilege; rather than a necessary performative function for egalitarian, robust Republicanism (Commonwealth of Australia Constitution Act [1977] 2013; ARM 2018; Commonwealth of Australia, Governor General 2018). The Australian Republican Movement (ARM 2018), led by Peter FitzSimons, critiques the Governor General role as a subsidiary to the Monarch: 'The Governor-General is only their representative to act on their behalf and has to approve every law made by our Parliament, every election and the appointment of every government' (ARM, What Is a Republic 2018). Moreover, the ARM, both advocates and legislates, for a local Head of State: 'For Australia to become a republic, we need to replace having a King or Queen and a Governor-General with having an Australian as our head of state – someone chosen by Australians to serve Australia' (ARM, What Is a Republic 2018). In my resistance to pomp and ceremony, and focus on agentic economic savviness, one Head of State is financially sustainable and doable, rather than exerting multiple leadership roles in governance, essentially performing the same or similar political function.

As other Commonwealth nations, Australia's Governor General represents the Sovereign Monarch, and this position serves to inform the Queen of significant legislative amendments and Parliamentary leadership changes affecting the Westminster Constitution (Commonwealth of Australia Constitution Act [1977] 2013; ARM 2018; Commonwealth of Australia, Governor General 2018). In a symbolic act, the Governor General signs on Prime Ministerial changes – of which there have been several over the last decade – more so than other democracies (Commonwealth of Australia Constitution Act [1977] 2013; Commonwealth of Australia, Governor General 2018; Sweeney and Belot 2018; Yaxley 2018). Such signatory authority is supported (or rejected) by the Monarch. Mostly, the Queen has supported proposed changes (WhitlamDismissal 2017).

Nonetheless, Prime Ministerial changes are initiated by the political parties themselves (most recently the Liberal-National Coalition) (Greer

2010b; Sweeney and Belot 2018). Additionally, political parties' leadership are influenced by the voting electorate and opinion polls (Newspoll 2018). The role of the media in influencing Prime Ministerial changes is contentious, in terms of presenting an image of leaders that is inauthentic (Greer 1999, 2010b; Maleta 2011b; Wright and Holland 2014). On the other hand, opinions are made real through Opinion Polls; framed by the electorate's view of Parliament, and their (dis)satisfaction with particular leaders and parties (Newspoll 2018). Public polls reflect the opinion of the grassroots electorate and voting base, thereby informing the Parliamentary democratic process and system of governance. However, having several, manoeuvring Prime Ministers over the last decade is contentious; for this reveals the way 'a boys club' operates in an adversarial rather than professional way (Greer 1999, 2010b; Maleta 2011b).

13.5 Sovereignty, Democratic Egalitarianism and Sustainable Economics

Whilst the Westminster Constitution is in place, it is undergoing degrees of subversive resistance (ARM 2018). Nevertheless, there are conservative NSMs that endorse the Monarchy, plus private individuals and influential members of the ruling political establishment, intent on maintaining the same constitutional framework (Australian Monarchist League 2018; Australians for Constitutional Monarchy 2018). One could add that individuals (most likely of a privileged, or indeed Anglo middle-ruling class background) possess degrees of socioeconomic interest in maintaining the Monarchy.

Considering progressive (Republican) and conservative (Monarchist) viewpoints, upholding the Constitutional Monarchy, in turn, evokes fraught notions of ruling class elitism, colonialism, misogyny and chauvinism (Arendt 1945; Gillard 2012; Donaldson and Poynting 2013; Petherbridge 2014; Wright and Holland 2014). Debatably, pomp and ceremony is not conducive to my egalitarian-Republican reformative model – for I continue to resist hereditary ruling class privilege plus the replicated power of privileged Anglo male middle class elites (Poynting and Donaldson 2005; DAWN 2015; ABS 2016a). In order to address structural-sociocultural inequities/injustices, my Act legislates on Minority Women's (disabled, CALD, Indigenous, low SES, mature) leadership representation in renewables technological-scientific development. My Act facilitates individuals' and communities' economic agentic choice in energy consumption, thus testing the hegemony of national energy companies and associated corporatisation (Gaard 2001; Shiva 2008, 2014; AGL 2018). Economic agency is applied to the fiscal modelling of my Bill of Rights Act. My vision for one Head of State, akin to an egalitarian Federal model, is dually informed by the voting power of the grassroots electorate.

The sovereignty and *greater egalitarianism* of Australia and other monarchist nations, like New Zealand and Canada, are clouded by the overarching status of the Monarch. As Head of State, the Monarch can technically intervene in Commonwealth governance. The Queen rarely exercises her sovereign authority;

but did so in the controversial sacking of Labor Prime Minister Gough Whitlam (PM between 1972 and 1975); supporting Governor General Kerr's request to dissolve Parliament, thus disposing Whitlam's leadership (Sheckels 2012; Bramston and Whitlam 2015). Whitlam is one of the most revered Australian Prime Ministers, due to his enactment of egalitarian democratic policies and social polity; his dismissal remains controversial (WhitlamDismissal 2017).

My Constitutional-Federal framing of a Republican-Bill of Rights Act rejects a foreign figurehead as an exertion of postcolonial power and cultural chauvinism (Arendt 1945; ARM 2018). This resistance is discursive to women's and grassroots individuals' greater economic agency, and the expense of adhering to a Constitutional Monarchy along with numerous governing representatives (*The Telegraph* 2004; Praderio 2017; ARM 2018; *Financial Review* 2018). In Britain, the Privy Purse, accrued to the Monarch and certain members of the Royals, is funded by public monies (*The Telegraph* 2004; Praderio 2017; ARM 2018; *Financial Review* 2018). As such, British taxpayers, and the voting, grassroots electorate, fund the Royal family. When the Royals visit Australia, we also pay, via public funding (from tax sources) (*The Telegraph* 2004; Praderio 2017; ARM 2018; *Financial Review* 2018). This is an economic drain upon the electorate and Parliament, whereby such public monies could be better spent on health, education and investment in renewables infrastructure. Australia is supposedly an independent nation, established as the Commonwealth of Australia in 1901; and then reaffirmed by the Australia Act in 1986 (Australia Act 1986; Selway 2003; Smith et al. 2012; Commonwealth of Australia Constitution Act [1977] 2013). However, the Westminster Constitution, akin to the rule of a hereditary Monarch, delineates our sovereignty and points to historic and contemporary contradictions, framing the extent to which we are an independent, sovereign nation?

13.6 Brexit and the Monarchy

In June 2016, in a national referendum on the European Union (E.U.), by a slight majority (51.9 to 48.1% of the electorate), Britain voted to leave or exit the E.U.: what is referred to as Brexit (Hunt and Wheeler 2018). Some key reasons for this outcome were: sovereignty concerns, Brussels having too much political power (the Capital of the European Parliament) and unrestricted migration to Britain from other E.U. nations (Glencross 2016; Black 2017; Fabbrini 2017; Mount 2017). Most of these concerns were from older Brits, whereas the younger population mostly preferred to remain in the E.U., revealing a striking contrast between the mature and youth demographic (Shuster 2016). Regarding sovereignty concerns, I argue that the E.U. Parliament does not have the final say in British politics or the internal running of its nation state (Kaplan 2018). Britain – via its Parliamentary democratic Constitutional Monarchy, constituted of the House of Commons and the House of Lords – governs the nation and decides on its legislation and laws, whilst the Monarch oversees this (Parliament UK 2018). Legislation is signed by the Monarch thereby akin to

Britain's constitution (Parliament UK 2018). Since Coronation, the Queen has not refused Parliament's proposed legislative changes (Parliament UK 2018).

Although the Monarch is perceived to not be directly involved in the running of the country (Parliament UK 2018); as an overarching figurehead, debatably the Queen has more power and influence than the E.U. The Monarch's signature to the nation's Acts represents the ultimate blueprint (Selway 2003). Contentiously, the Monarch refrains from legislative resistance. Her role seemingly supports the Parliamentary structures in place. Some controversial laws, advisably, could have been challenged by the sovereign. The deportation of thousands of British children to Australia, after World War II, up until the 1970s, is a contentious example (Buti 2002; Bannister 2011). According to Bannister (2011), some of these children were very young (three or four) and deported without the consent of their parents: 'The UK authorities often told those children that their parents were dead and that a better future awaited them on the other side of the earth; in a land of "oranges and sunshine"'. In retrospect, this is where the role of figurehead and sovereign authority intertwine rather complexly – regarding the capacity to act on behalf of the citizenry.

With the lack of challenge to legislative Acts and laws, the Monarch is largely removed from the democratic mode of governance and the grassroots voting electorate. As such, legislation that may be viewed as unfavourable or contentious is more likely than not to be approved by the Monarch (Parliament UK 2018). Concerning Brexit and that status of Britain, if the Brits are discontent with their lot, particularly with social, cultural, political and economic life, then perhaps there is scope to scrutinise the Constitutional Monarchy and its leadership impact upon the nation. To reiterate, there is the cost factor to consider. After all, the British electorate fund the Monarchy (Sturgess and Boyfield 2013; *Financial Review* 2018). What an economic drain upon society! Perhaps, the Brits would be better off as a Republic? Undoubtedly, Australia would (ARM 2018).

I am not convinced that by leaving the E.U., societal dissent or dissatisfaction with governance would be resolved. Britain has significant social inequalities and class-based divisions, more so than Commonwealth nations like Australia and New Zealand (Walby and Armstrong 2010; Walby 2011, 2015; UK Income Inequality 2017). This is remnant of the ruling class power of privileged elites, replicated through a monarchist polity. Australia and New Zealand are comparatively more egalitarian; but there is the issue of Anglo male middle class hegemonic privilege within organisational governance (Poynting and Donaldson 2005; Donaldson and Poynting 2013; DAWN 2015). Middle class Anglo masculinist power is more problematic in post-colonial nations, like Australia and New Zealand, rather than peerage-based elitism. Moreover, the Republic of Austria has a higher standard of living than Anglo neoliberal democracies, which suggests that a Republican change could improve economics and reinvigorate governance (*Economist* 2018).

Henceforth, what I am arguing for is the separation of the Royals from governance. I am not pointing to a bloody revolution, but a peaceful transition from Monarchy to Republicanism – as occurred with Red Vienna's social egalitarian-democratic model. Further, republicanism is an important opportunity to revise, rework and rewrite our constitution, along with its legislative Acts (my proposed Bill of Rights Act). Our policies are dated, old-fashioned and sharply conservative. Consequently, a robust human-rights-framed Bill of Rights Act, should redress sociocultural inequalities, along with gender gaps, conceptually framed by inequity/injustice and privilege. Such an Act legislates (and advocates) on the performative scientific-technical leadership of my six categories: CALD, Indigenous, low SES, mature, disabled and Anglo women in renewables governance. Although not strictly a minority group, Anglo women are more disadvantaged than Anglo men; hence, why they are part of my grouping. In my conceptual model, overall, I aim to integrate republican, egalitarian, environmentalist (sustainable) and feminist (emphasized femininity) methodological ambitions, whilst challenging the patriarchal control of organisational governance. As Anglo middle class men are the most privileged group in work and politics, the talent of women, relative to their agentic performative multi-skills-set, should be redressed within such a revised participatory Republican framework. Thus, I aim to realise an egalitarian-ecological-feminist mode of social democratic governance.

13.7 *My Six Groups'* Scientific-Technical Leadership of WW & SE Solutions

Regarding the Red Viennese model, and its enablement of the working and middle classes, emphasising women's elevated civic and political statuses; my egalitarian Bill of Rights Act is a model for social inclusion as well as legislative-framed gender and environmental justice outcomes. A Republican Constitutional change is an opportunity to confront conservative, dated, old-fashioned policies, whereby practitioners (like me and others) would eagerly write and develop new legislative Acts and social policies. Likewise, republicanism, is an opportunity to revise and improve EEO laws, such as, the Equal Employment Opportunity Act along with concurrent gender gaps and glass ceilings (Connell 2009; Public Service Commission 2015; EEO Act ([1987] 2016). The EEO Act would be replaced with my Bill of Rights Act, whereby my Sections/articles, ensure gender equity through leadership quotas, but also through women-led performative competence and merit. By rewriting and reframing EEO laws, I aim to address *my six groups'* marginal status, particularly within executive leadership. Republicanism, therefore, challenges hereditary privilege and privileged ruling-middle class elites as well as men's hegemony of organisational governance (Poynting and Donaldson 2005; Donaldson and Poynting 2013; DAWN 2015).

Although positions of employment are ideally based on merit, minority women, in particular women with disabilities, endure inequality and disadvantage in the workforce (Walby 2011; Butler 2013; Disability Discrimination Act [1992] 2013; AHRC 2016, 2017a, 2017b). Whilst Federal EEO laws, such as the Disability Discrimination Act ([1992] 2013) aspire to address the discrimination of disabled peoples in the workforce, this does not account for disabled women's marginalisation from leadership positions (AHRC 2016b; Evans 2016; Farr et al.

2017). Disabled women are significantly under-represented in governmental and corporate positions (Shiva 2014; Gilardi 2015; Watts et al. 2015; Wibben 2016). Debatably, this is a flaw within meritocracy, whereby the privileged remain so. It is catastrophic that women are not enabled to offer their full skills- set to the workforce. In summary, EEO laws and policies fall short in addressing intersectional diversity and women-led qualities. By targeting women's leadership, at a 75% proportionate representation, my emphasized femininity model aspires to realise CALD, Indigenous, Anglo, low SES, mature/older and disabled women's performative talent. This is an ambitious target; nonetheless, with more minority women in technical-scientific leadership, STEMM goals should be realised (Sharp et al. 2008; Gillard 2012; Summers 2013; Cook and Glass 2014; STEMM 2018). Glass ceilings should also lessen.

My Act, therefore, ensures that the Anglo male is not the dominant force in politics or science (Poynting and Donaldson 2005; Donaldson and Poynting 2013; DAWN 2015; STEMM 2018). I view CALD, disabled, mature, low SES and Indigenous women as competent leaders; however, structural power-based imbalances, curtailed by flaws in meritocracy and ruling elites' hegemony, are why my women are not equally represented in decision-making. This is not due to their lack of competence, or negligence from the women themselves, but rather reminiscent of 'a boys club', that operates either covertly or overtly (Wantland 2005; Culley and Angelique 2010; Maleta 2011b). My interview findings accentuated 'a boys club' through men's dominance as scientists and politicians (Maleta 2011b; Pollack 2015; Farr et al. 2017). Patriarchal bureaucratic hierarchies may include women in certain aspects of work, but then tend to exclude them from others – especially higher up the ladder of power (Yoder and Aniakudo 1997; Maddison 2004). That is why we have gender barriers and gaps (Maleta 2012). Such systems are structurally and culturally discursive to ruling class masculinity, and cannot be eroded overnight (Connell 2009; Donaldson and Poynting 2013; Wasson 2017). But a Republican Constitutional change would challenge this; supported by a human-rights framed Bill of Rights, and Sections/articles focussed on: Renewables Technological Development; Women's Leadership Equality in Male-dominated Work Sectors; Minority Women Groups' Equality in Renewables Organisational Governance; and an Indigenous Treaty.

While most Westernised Parliamentarian neoliberal democracies ascribe to gender equity measures, women in advanced, post-industrial nations still earn less than men (Rankin and Gale 2003; Pocock 2005; Butler 2013; Pocock et al. 2013). I have demonstrated though how women are agentic competent performers in masculine fields, and their agentic performativity is a viable model, informing the future of WW & SE technological development (McFarland 2014; Ajani 2015; Clean Energy Council 2018; Maleta 2018a, 2018b). More women in science and politics, akin to my Republican-Bill, discursive to women-led performative technical, intellectual, social, physical, egalitarian and empathetic talents, ensures that merit and competence are realised, rather than a fantastical dream.

13.8 Connecting My Bill of Rights to an Indigenous Treaty Framework

My conceptual modelling of egalitarianism, feminism, republicanism and environmentalism, ideally, would inspire futuristic social democratic republican nations. Other monarchist nations, such as Canada and New Zealand, should be inspired to follow my lead (Nagy 2017; Patel 2018). Although New Zealand and Canada have Bills of Rights and Indigenous Treaties, this does not deter from Anglo male middle class men still constituting the ruling class group in these respective nations (Havemann 1999; Kermoal et al. 2016; Bachand 2017; Nagy 2017). Despite English and French being official languages in Canada, Anglo men dominate the business sector (Colson and Field 2016; Bachand 2017; Sioufi and Bourhis 2017; Freeman-Maloy 2018). A Republican Constitutional framework, proposed in 'transitional monarchist' nations, is an opportunity to revise legislative Acts, and existing Bills of Rights, in order to represent a more inclusive, egalitarian social mode of governance. Hence, my Republican scope reinvigorates national governance, along with plural social, feminist and national identities, plus notions of sovereignty. The replacement of the Westminster Constitution with a Republican Constitution thus addresses gender (in)equity/(in)justice, and provides policy frames for cutting-edge renewables technological-scientific development. Simultaneously, my advocated Bill of Rights strives for improved Indigenous sovereignty and reconciliation.

An Indigenous Treaty, akin to my Act, is necessary to formalise Indigenous sovereignty, whilst officially dispelling myths of 'Terra Nullius' (Plumwood 1997; Havemann 1999; Doyle 2005; Brennan 2015; Prokhovnik 2015). In particular, I envision Indigenous women's leadership as integral to its development (Maddison 2004; Maddison and Scalmer 2006; Brown 2011; Kermoal et al. 2016; Gaard 2017; Nagy 2017). In 2008, former Labor Prime Minister Rudd made a formal public apology to the Indigenous Stolen Generation at Federal Parliament, which was a landmark speech towards reconciliation (Rudd 2008; AIATSIS 2018). In support to this speech, a Treaty represents a formal platform to engage with past wrongs, and to enable Indigenous communities to ascertain greater agentic political leadership, framing the national process of reconciliation. This applies to Native Title Rights and entitlements (Smith et al. 2012; Brennan 2015; Kawharu 2018). In New Zealand, the Treaty of Waitangi (1840), empowered the Maori to address their native land rights, and remains a legal document for elders to negotiate agency in 'disputed' or unresolved land entitlements (Ministry for Culture and Heritage 2017; Pemberton 2017; Godfery 2018). The Treaty of Waitangi though is a contested document, relative to particular interpretations of what it means for Pakeha (White European descent) and Maori (Indigenous) peoples (Ministry for Culture and Heritage 2017; Godfery 2018; Kawharu 2018). In my contribution to the policy development of a Treaty, I aim to ensure that the Indigenous case is clear, and that the voice of Aboriginal and Torres Strait Islander peoples are not misinterpreted; hence, avoiding its framing as a White-centric-patriarchal-postcolonial, legal document. The Treaty and Act is dually informed by Indigenous quests for equity/justice, therefore entailing an empowering legislative scope for sovereignty and reconciliation.

Conclusion

Separation from a Monarchist form of governance entails independent modes of operation that are intrinsically reworked and revitalised; for Republicanism is an opportunity to reinvigorate governance. 'Our' Westminster Constitutional is dated, old-fashioned and in need of change (Butler 2001; Commonwealth of Australia Constitution Act 2013; Snow 2016; ARM 2018). Women are the ideal leaders of a Republican (political change) and sustainable technological-scientific development (environmental change). Republicanism should challenge chauvinistic and paternalistic views of nationhood, along with cultural-privileged elitist envy, replicated through a monarchist polity (Arendt 1945; Summers 2013; Mattl 2016; Patel 2018). Reliance on the Monarchy suggests Australia is a colony of Britain. Republicanism, however, supported by a Bill of Rights Act, and women-led Initiatives, challenges the legacy of colonialism, unresolved issues between White and Indigenous communities, whilst being a framework for *my six groups'* (disabled, CALD, socioeconomically disadvantaged, Indigenous, mature/older women, Anglo) agentic performative leadership of renewable energy development. My model of egalitarian democratic-participatory republicanism, thus, confronts patriarchal privilege, conducive to one's gender, ethnic and sociocultural status (Gaard 2001; Bolton 2005; Veri 2016; Canty 2017; ARM 2018; Clean Energy Council 2018; WIE 2018).

Conclusively, a Republican Constitutional-Bill of Rights Act, is strengthened by my constructivist approach to emphasized femininity, framed by Initiatives, legislating and advocating, on women's greater leadership of WW & SE solutions. My stand for sociopolitical change, parallel to emphasized femininity performative agentic competence, defies ruling class masculinity and the patriarchal control of the global eNSM and its institutions. My Bill of Rights Act, as a dynamic, reactionary, conceptual-methodological model, integrates egalitarian, constructivist, feminist and environmentalist ambitions – thus, representing an empowering framework for nations, aspiring to Republican nationhood.

References

ABS. 2016a. *Cultural Diversity in Australia. 2016 Census Data Summary*. Available from: www. abs.gov.au/ausstats/abs@.nsf/Lookup/by%20Subject/2071.0~2016~Main%20 Features~Cultural%20Diversity%20Article~60 (Accessed 22 April 2019).

ABS. 2016b. *Australian Bureau of Statistics (ABS) Annual Report, 2015–16*. Available from: www.abs.gov.au/ausstats/abs@.nsf/Lookup/by%20Subject/1001.0~Report%20on%20 ABS%20performance%20in%202015-16~Main%20Features~ABS%20Annual%20 Report%202015-16~1 (Accessed 22 April 2019).

ABS. 2017. *Australian Marriage Law Postal Survey*. Available from: www.abs.gov.au/ ausstats/abs@.nsf/mf/1800.0 (Accessed 22 April 2019).

AGL. 2018. Homepage. Available from: www.agl.com.au/ (Accessed 21 July 2018).

Ahern, M.M., and Hendryx, M. 2008. Health disparities and environmental competence: A case study of Appalachian coal mining. *Environmental Justice*, 1 (2), 81–86.

AHRC (Australian Human Rights Commission). 2016a. *Australian Human Rights Commission (AHRC) Annual Report, 2015–16*. Available from: www.humanrights.gov. au/sites/default/files/document/publication/AHRC%20Annual%20Report%202015- 2016.pdf (Accessed 20 April 2019).

AHRC. 2016b. *Willing to Work: National Inquiry into Employment Discrimination against Older Australians and Australians with Disability*. Available from: www.humanrights. gov.au/our-work/disability-rights/projects/willing-work-national-inquiry-employment- discrimination-against (Accessed 22 June 2016).

AHRC. 2017a. *Change the Course: National Report on Sexual Assault and Sexual Harassment at Australian Universities*. August 2017. Available from: www.humanrights. gov.au/sites/default/files/document/publication/AHRC_2017_ChangeTheCourse_ UniversityReport.pdf (Accessed 2 August 2017).

AHRC. 2017b. *A Conversation in Gender Equality*. March 2017. Available from: www. humanrights.gov.au/sites/default/files/document/publication/AHRC_conversation_ gender_equality_2017_2.pdf (Accessed 13 April 2017).

AIATSIS (Australian Institute of Aboriginal and Torres Strait Islander Studies). 2018. *The National Apology to the Stolen Generations*. Available from: https://aiatsis.gov.au/ explore/articles/apology-australias-indigenous-peoples (Accessed 2 July 2018).

Ainsworth, J. 2012. The performance of gender as reflected in American evidence rules: Language, power, and the legal construction of liability. *Gender & Language*, 6 (1), 181–95.

Ainsworth, S. 2002. The 'feminine advantage': A discursive analysis of the invisibility of older women workers. *Gender, Work & Organization*, 9 (5), 579–601.

Ainsworth, S., and Cutcher, L. 2008. Expectant mothers and absent fathers: Paid maternity leave in Australia. *Gender, Work & Organization*, 15 (4), 375–93.

Ajani, A. 2015. More power to women in renewables. *Eco-Business*, 26 January. Available from: www.eco-business.com/opinion/more-power-to-women-in-renewables/ (Accessed 13 January 2017).

Albinski, H.S. 2016. *Australian Policies and Attitudes toward China*. Princeton, NJ: Princeton University Press.

Alston, M. 2003. Women's representation in an Australian rural context. *Sociologia Ruralis*, 43 (4), 474–87.

Alston, M. 2011. Gender and climate change in Australia. *Journal of Sociology*, 47 (1), 53–70.

Alston, M. 2013. Gender mainstreaming and climate change. *Women's Studies International Forum*, 47, 287–94.

Anderson, D. 2010. Does Australia need a Bill of Rights? *Sydney Morning Herald*, 21 September. Available from: www.smh.com.au/national/education/does-australia-need-a-bill-of-rights-20100920-15jk5.html (Accessed 21 November 2012).

Arendt, H. 1945. Imperialism, nationalism, chauvinism. *Review of Politics*, 7, 441–63.

Arendt, H. 1958. *The Origins of Totalitarianism*. London: George Allen & Unwin.

Arendt, H. 1959. *The Human Condition*. New York: Doubleday Anchor.

Arendt, H. 1973. *On Revolution*. Harmondsworth [England]: Penguin.

Arendt, H., and Kohn, J. 2005. *The Promise of Politics*. New York: Schocken Books.

Arthur, C.J. 2012. *Financial Literacy Education: Neoliberalism, the Consumer and the Citizen*. Rotterdam: SensePublishers.

Australia Act. 1986. C2004A03181. Federal Register of Legislation. Canberra: Office of Parliamentary Counsel, Australian Government. Available from: www.legislation.gov.au/Details/C2004A03181 (Accessed 8 March 2018).

Australian Energy Council (AEC). 2018. Homepage. Available from: www.energycouncil.com.au (Accessed 28 July 2018).

Australian Greens. 2018. Constitutional Reform and Democracy. Available from: https://greens.org.au/policies/constitutional-reform-and-democracy (Accessed 10 July 2018).

Australian Greens. 2018. Gender Equality and Empowerment of Women. Available from: https://greens.org.au/policies/gender-equality-and-empowerment-women (Accessed 12 September 2018).

Australian Greens. 2018. Our Federal MPs. Available from: https://greens.org.au/mps (Accessed 8 June 2017).

Australian Greens. 2018. Our Policies. Available from: https://greens.org.au/policy (Accessed 4 July 2018).

Australian Greens. 2018. Participatory Democracy. Available from: https://greens.org.au/policies/wa/participatory-democracy-core-policy (Accessed 1 July 2018).

Australian Monarchist League. 2018. Homepage. Available from: www.monarchist.org.au (Accessed 29 May 2018).

Australian Republican Movement (ARM). 2018. *Our Plan to Achieve a Republic by 2022*. Available from: www.republic.org.au/about#our-plan (Accessed 1 September 2018).

Australian Republican Movement (ARM). 2018. *What Is a Republic?* Available from: www.republic.org.au/faq/ (Accessed 2 September 2018).

Australian Women's Leadership Symposium. 2017. *The 2017 Australian Women's Leadership Symposium*, APSCo, 6–7 June. Sydney: International Convention Centre. Available from: https://awia.org.au/event/australian-womens-leadership-symposium/ (Accessed 20 April 2019).

Australians for Constitutional Monarchy: No Republic. 2018. Homepage. Available from: https://norepublic.com.au (Accessed 30 May 2018).

Austrian Academy of Sciences (OEAW). 2018. *History of the OEAW*. Available from: www.oeaw.ac.at/en/the-oeaw/about-us/history-of-the-oeaw/ (Accessed 24 July 2018).

Bachand, M. 2017. Disunited daughters of the confederations: Creoles and Canadians at the intersection of nations, states, and empires. *Journal of the Civil War Era*, 7 (4), 541–69.

Bader-Zaar, B. 1996. Women in Austrian politics, 1890–1934. In: D.F. Good, M. Grandner, and M.J. Maynes, eds., *Austrian Women in the Nineteenth and Twentieth Centuries: Cross-disciplinary Perspectives*. Providence, RI: Berghahn, 59–90.

Baldwin, B. 2017. *207: Among the Trumps, Ha Ha*. London: Dennis Publishing.

Banerjee, S.B. 2011. Embedding sustainability across the organization: A critical perspective. *Academy of Management Learning and Education*, 10 (4), 719–31.

Bannister, B. 2011. 'Oranges and Sunshine': A film about the other stolen generation. *ABC Radio Perth*, 25 May. Available from: www.abc.net.au/local/stories/2011/05/25/3226507.htm (Accessed 19 August 2016).

Barker, A. 2012. *Fictions from an Orphan State: Literary Reflections of Austria between Habsburg and Hitler*. Rochester, NY: Camden House.

Barnes, B. 2000. *Understanding Agency: Social Theory and Responsible Action*. London: Sage.

Barry, J.M. 2008. A small group of thoughtful, committed citizens: Women's activism, environmental justice, and the Coal River Mountain Watch. *Environmental Justice*, 1 (1), 25–33.

Baruah, B. 2016. There's a gender gap in the global renewable energy workforce. *Huffington Post*, 8 March. Available from: www.huffingtonpost.ca/development-unplugged/renewable-inequityglobal_b_9402854.html (Accessed 8 December 2016).

Baxter, J., and Chesters, J. 2011. Perceptions of work-family balance: How effective are family-friendly policies? *Australian Journal of Labour Economics*, 14 (2), 139–51.

Bell, D. 2016. *Reordering the World: Essays on Liberalism and Empire*. Princeton, NJ: Princeton University Press.

Bendl, R., and Schmidt, A. 2010. From 'glass ceilings' to 'firewalls' – Different metaphors for describing discrimination. *Gender, Work & Organization*, 17 (5), 612–34.

Berg, A.J., and Lie, M. 1995. Feminism and constructivism: Do artifacts have gender? *Science, Technology, & Human Values*, 20 (3), 332–51.

Bill of Rights. 1688. UK Legislation, The National Archives Crown. Available from: www.legislation.gov.uk/aep/WillandMarSess2/1/2 (Accessed 30 July 2018).

Bill of Rights Institute. 2018. Bill of Rights of the United States of America (1791). Bill of Rights Institute. Available from: https://billofrightsinstitute.org/founding-documents/bill-of-rights/ (Accessed 2 February 2018).

Black, J. 2017. *A History of Britain, 1945 to Brexit*. Bloomington: Indiana University Press.

Blackwell, L., and Glover, J. 2008. Women's scientific employment and family formation: A longitudinal perspective. *Gender, Work & Organization*, 15 (6), 579–99.

Blau, E. 1999. *The Architecture of Red Vienna, 1919–1934*. Cambridge, MA: MIT Press.

Bogdanor, V. 1995. *The Monarchy and the Constitution*. Oxford: Clarendon.

Bolton, G. 2005. Thoughts of an elitist republican. *Sydney Papers*, 17 (1), 105–9.

Bombora Wave Power. 2018. Board of Directors. Available from: www.bomborawave.com/about-us (Accessed 1 June 2018).

Bourdieu, P. 1985. The social space and the genesis of groups. *Theory and Society*, 14 (6), 723–44.

Bramston, T., and Whitlam, G. 2015. *The Whitlam Legacy.* Annandale, NSW: Federation Press.

Brennan, F. 2015. *No Small Change: The Road to Recognition for Indigenous Australia.* Chicago: University of Queensland Press.

Britton, D.M. 2017. Beyond the chilly climate: The salience of gender in women's academic careers. *Gender & Society*, 31 (1), 5–27.

Brown, R. 2011. Religion, political discourse, and activism among varying racial/ethnic groups in America. *Review of Religious Research*, 53 (3), 301–22.

Buckingham, S. 2004. Ecofeminism in the twenty-first century. *Geographical Journal*, 170 (2), 146–54.

Buckingham, S., and Kulcur, R. 2010. Gendered geographies of environmental injustice. In: R. Holifield, M. Porter, and G. Walker, eds., *Spaces of Environmental Justice*. Oxford: Wiley-Blackwell, 70–94.

Buckingham-Hatfield, S. 2000. *Gender and Environment*. New York: Routledge.

Buechler, S., and Hanson, A.M.S., eds. 2015. *A Political Ecology of Women, Water and Global Environmental Change*. Abingdon, Oxon: Routledge.

Bundesverband WindEnergie eV (BWE). 2018. Board. Bundesverband WindEnergie eV (The German Federal Wind Energy Association). Available from: www.wind-energie.de/english/association/board/ (Accessed 1 September 2018).

Burn, S.M. 2011. *Women Across Cultures: A Global Perspective*. New York: McGraw-Hill.

Buti, A. 2002. British child migration to Australia: History, Senate inquiry and responsibilities. *Murdoch University Electronic Journal of Law*, 9 (4). Available from: http://classic.austlii.edu.au/au/journals/MurUEJL/2002/47.html (Accessed 10 December 2015).

Butler, J. 1990. *Gender Trouble: Feminism and the Subversion of Identity*. New York: Routledge.

Butler, J. 1997. *Excitable Speech: A Politics of the Performative*. New York: Routledge.

Butler, J. 1999. *Gender Trouble: Feminism and the Subversion of Identity*. New York: Routledge.

Butler, J. 2004. *Undoing Gender*. New York: Routledge.

Butler, J. 2006. *Gender Trouble: Feminism and the Subversion of Identity*. New York: Routledge.

Butler, J. 2007. *Gender Trouble: Feminism and the Subversion of Identity*. New York: Routledge.

Butler, J. 2009. *Frames of War: When Is Life Grievable?* London: Verso Books.

Butler, J. 2011. *Bodies That Matter: On the Discursive Limits of Sex*. Abingdon: Routledge.

Butler, J. 2013. *Dispossession: The Performative in the Political*. Hoboken: Wiley.

Butler, J. 2015. *Senses of the Subject*. New York: Fordham University Press.

Butler, J. 2017. Academic freedom and the critical task of the university. *Globalizations*, 14 (6), 857–61.

Butler, P. 2001. The referendum on an Australian Republic. *Verfassung und Recht in Ubersee / Law and Politics in Africa, Asia and Latin America*, 34 (1), 6–23.

Cadaret, M.C., Hartung, P.J., Subich, L.M., and Weigold, I.K. 2017. Stereotype threat as a barrier to women entering engineering careers. *Journal of Vocational Behavior*, 99, 40–51.

Caldicott, H. 2014. *Crisis without End: The Medical and Ecological Consequences of the Fukushima Nuclear Catastrophe*. New York: The New Press.

Campbell, T., Goldsworthy, J.D., and Stone, A. 2006. *Protecting Rights without a Bill of Rights: Institutional Performance and Reform in Australia*. Aldershot: Ashgate.

Canadian Bill of Rights. 1960. Government of Canada, Consolidated Acts. Available from: http://laws-lois.justice.gc.ca/eng/acts/C-12.3/page-1.html (Accessed 11 April 2018).

Canty, J.M., ed. 2017. *Ecological and Social Healing: Multicultural Women's Voices*. Abingdon, Oxon: Routledge.

Carnegie Clean Energy. 2018. Board of Directors. Available from: www.carnegiece.com/about/board-of-directors/ (Accessed 22 July 2018).

Carp, B.L. 2010. *Defiance of the Patriots: The Boston Tea Party & the Making of America*. New Haven, CT: Yale University Press.

Carter, N. 2007. *The Politics of the Environment: Ideas, Activism, Policy*. Cambridge: Cambridge University Press.

Carter, N. 2013. Greening the mainstream: Party politics and the environment. *Environmental Politics*, 22 (1), 73–94.

Chambers, S.A., and Carver, T., eds. 2008. *Judith Butler and Political Theory: Troubling Politics*. Oxford: Routledge.

Chapman, P. 2007. Operation Corporate – The Sir Galahad bombings. Woolwich Burns Unit experience. *Journal of the Royal Army Medical Corps*, 153, 37–40.

Childs, M. 2006. Counting women in the Australian Fire Services. *Australian Journal of Emergency Management*, 21 (2), 29–34.

City of Vienna. 2018. Child-care Centres. Available from: www.wien.gv.at/english/social/childcare/ (Accessed 13 June 2018).

City of Vienna. 2018. *Municipal Politics: 'Red Vienna' – A Success Story*. Available from: www.wien.gv.at/english/history/commemoration/housing.html (Accessed 22 January 2018).

Clean Energy Council. 2018. *Women in Renewables*. Available from: www.cleanenergy council.org.au/advocacy-initiatives/women-in-renewables (Accessed 19 April 2019).

Cockburn, C. 1988. *Machinery of Dominance: Women, Men and Technical Know-how*. Boston: Northeastern University Press.

Cockburn, C. 1991. *In the Way of Women: Men's Resistance to Sex Equality in Organizations*. Ithaca, NY: ILR Press.

Cockburn, C. 2000. The women's movement: Boundary-crossing on terrains of conflict. In: R. Cohen and S. Rai, eds., *Global Social Movements*. London: Athlone Press, 46–61.

Cockburn, C. 2010. Gender relations as causal in militarization and war. *International Feminist Journal of Politics*, 12 (2), 139–57.

Cockburn, C. 2012. *Antimilitarism: Political and Gender Dynamics of Peace Movements*. Basingstoke: Palgrave Macmillan.

Cockburn, C. 2013. War and security, women and gender: An overview of the issues. *Gender and Development*, 21 (3), 433–52.

Cockburn, C., and Enloe, C. 2012. Militarism, patriarchy and peace movements. *International Feminist Journal of Politics*, 14 (4), 550–57.

Cohen, M. 2016. The only woman in the room: Why science is still a boys' club by Eileen Pollack. *Mathematical Intelligencer*, 38 (3), 91–93.

Cole, M. 2016. *Racism: A Critical Analysis*. London: Pluto Press.

Collins, P. 2017. From misery to momentum: The strange rebirth of the Labour Party. *NewStatesman*, 9 July. Available from: www.newstatesman.com/politics/uk/2017/07/misery-momentum-strange-rebirth-labour-party (Accessed 20 July 2017).

Colson, R., and Field, S. 2016. Socio-legal studies in France: Beyond the law faculty. *Journal of Law and Society*, 43 (2), 285–311.

Commonwealth of Australia Constitution Act (The Constitution). [1977] 2013. C2013Q00005. Federal Register of Legislation. Canberra: Office of Parliamentary Counsel, Australian Government. Available from: www.legislation.gov.au/Details/ C2013Q00005 (Accessed 11 July 2017).

Commonwealth of Australia, Governor General. 2018. Homepage. Available from: www. gg.gov.au/ (Accessed 30 May 2018).

Connell, R.W. 1995. *Masculinities*. St Leonards, NSW: Allen & Unwin.

Connell, R.W. 2002. *Gender*. Cambridge: Polity Press and Blackwell.

Connell, R.W. 2005. *Masculinities*. Crows Nest, NSW: Allen & Unwin.

Connell, R.W. 2006. The experience of gender change in public sector organizations. *Gender, Work & Organization*, 13 (5), 435–52.

Connell, R.W. 2007. *Southern Theory: The Global Dynamics of Knowledge in Social Science*. Crows Nest, NSW: Allen & Unwin.

Connell, R.W. 2009. *Gender: In World Perspective*. Cambridge: Polity.

Cook, A., and Glass, C. 2014. Women and top leadership positions: Towards an institutional analysis. *Gender, Work & Organization*, 21 (1), 91–103.

Cooper, H. 2013. Defamiliarising passivity with the disabled subject: Activism, academia and the lived experience of impairment. *Graduate Journal of Social Science*, 10 (3), 125–37.

Copley, G.R. 2018. Trump as Julius Cæsar; as Churchill. *Defense & Foreign Affairs Strategic Policy*, 46 (1), 2.

Cornish, A. 2017. Cornel West doesn't want to be a neoliberal darling. *New York Times Magazine*, 3 December, 66–68.

Coronel, J.M., Moreno, E., and Carrasco, M.J. 2010. Work–family Conflicts and the Organizational Work Culture as Barriers to Women Educational Managers. *Gender, Work & Organization*, 17 (2), 219–39.

Cowell, A. 2013. Prince William to leave the British military: Foreign desk. *New York Times*, 12 September. Available from: www.nytimes.com/2013/09/13/world/europe/ prince-william-to-leave-british-military.html (Accessed 1 November 2016).

Crampton, R.J. 1997. *Eastern Europe in the Twentieth Century and After*. London: Routledge.

Crary, A. 2001. A question of silence: Feminist theory and women's voices. *Philosophy*, 76 (297), 371–95.

Cretney, S.M. 2008. Royal marriages: Some legal and constitutional issues. *Law Quarterly Review*, 124, 218.

Cudworth, E. 2012. Community resilience in natural disasters. *Contemporary Sociology: A Journal of Reviews*, 41 (3), 392.

Cudworth, E. 2002. *Environment and Society*. New York: Routledge.

Cudworth, E., and Hobden, S. 2010. Anarchy and anarchism: Towards a theory of complex international systems. *Millennium – Journal of International Studies*, 39 (2), 399–416.

Cudworth, E., and Hobden, S. 2013. Of parts and wholes: International relations beyond the human. *Millennium – Journal of International Studies*, 41 (3), 430–50.

Culley, M.R., and Angelique, H.L. 2010. Nuclear power: Renaissance or relapse? Global climate change and long-term Three Mile Island activists narratives. *American Journal of Community Psychology*, 45 (3/4), 231–46.

Culley, M.R., and Angelique, H.L. 2003. Women's gendered experiences as long-term Three Mile Island activists. *Gender Society*, 17 (3), 445–61.

Cuomo, C.J. 2011. Climate change, vulnerability and responsibility. *Hypatia*, 26, 690–714.

Davey, J.D. 2012. *The Shrinking American Middle Class: The Social and Cultural Implications of Growing Inequality*. New York: Palgrave Macmillan.

Davis, B. 2015. A brief cosmogeny of the West German Green Party. *German Politics and Society*, 33 (4), 53.

DAWN. 2015. Dai le: We need more than women in leadership, we need cultural diversity. *DAWN*, 27 May. Available from: https://dawn.org.au/2015/05/27/we-need-more-than-women-in-leadership-we-need-cultural-diversity/ (Accessed 24 May 2016).

Delanty, G. 2005. *Social Science: Philosophical and Methodological Foundations*. Maidenhead, UK: Open University Press.

Diani, M. 1992. The concept of social movement. *Sociological Review*, 40 (1), 1–25.

Di Chiro, G. 2008. Living environmentalisms: Coalition politics, social reproduction, and environmental justice. *Environmental Politics*, 17 (2), 276–98.

Di Chiro, G. 2011. Acting globally: Cultivating a thousand community solutions for climate justice. *Development*, 54 (2), 232–36.

Disability Discrimination Act. [1992] 2013. C2013C00022. Federal Register of Legislation. [This compilation was prepared on 8 January 2013 taking into account amendments up to Act No. 169 of 2012]. Canberra: Office of Parliamentary Counsel, Australian Government. Available from: www.legislation.gov.au/Details/C2013C00022 (Accessed 20 August 2015).

Dixon, P. 2012. *The British Approach to Counterinsurgency: From Malaya and Northern Ireland to Iraq and Afghanistan*. New York: Palgrave Macmillan.

Doherty, B., and Doyle, T., eds. 2013. *Environmentalism, Resistance and Solidarity: The Politics of Friends of the Earth International*. Houndmills, Basingstoke: Palgrave Macmillan.

Doherty, C. 2016. Theresa May's first speech to the nation as prime minister – in full: New PM vows to look after the interests of the many rather than just 'the privileged few'. *Independent*, 13 July. Available from: www.independent.co.uk/news/uk/politics/theresa-mays-first-speech-to-the-nation-as-prime-minister-in-full-a7135301.html (Accessed 23 August 2016).

Donaghue, N. 2015. Who gets played by 'The Gender Card'? *Australian Feminist Studies*, 30 (84), 161–78.

Donaldson, M. 1993. What is hegemonic masculinity? *Theory and Society*, 22 (5), 643–57.

Donaldson, M. 2009. *Migrant Men: Critical Studies of Masculinities and the Migration Experience*. New York: Routledge.

Donaldson, M., and Poynting, S. 2007. *Ruling Class Men: Money, Sex, Power*. Bern: Peter Lang.

Donaldson, M., and Poynting, S. 2013. Peering upwards: Researching ruling-class men. In: B. Pini and B. Pease, eds., *Men, Masculinities and Methodologies*. London: Palgrave Macmillan, 157–69.

Doyle, T. 2000. *Green Power: The Environment Movement in Australia*. Sydney: UNSW Press.

Doyle, T. 2005. *Environmental Movements in Minority and Majority Worlds*. New Brunswick, NJ: Rutgers University Press.

Doyle, T. 2008. *Environment and Politics*. New York: Routledge.

Doyle, T., McEachern, D., and MacGregor, S. 2015. *Environment and Politics*. London: Routledge.

Duncan, L.E. 2010. Women's relationship to feminism: Effects of generation and feminist self-labeling. *Psychology of Women Quarterly*, 34 (4), 498–507.

Duncan, C., and Loretto, W. 2004. Never the right age? Gender and age-based discrimination in employment. *Gender, Work & Organization*, 11 (1), 95–115.

Economist. 2018. Vienna overtakes Melbourne as the world's most liveable city. *Economist*, 16 August. Available from: www.economist.com/graphic-detail/2018/08/14/vienna-overtakes-melbourne-as-the-worlds-most-liveable-city (Accessed 17 September 2018).

Eder, K. 1996. *The New Politics of Class: Social Movements and Cultural Dynamics in Advanced Societies*. London: Sage.

Edge, C.E., Cooper, A.M., and Coffey, M. 2017. Barriers and facilitators to extended working lives in Europe: A gender focus. *Public Health Reviews*, 38 (2), 1–27.

Elsesser, K.M., and Lever, J. 2011. Does gender bias against female leaders persist? Quantitative and qualitative data from a large-scale survey. *Human Relations*, 64 (12), 1555–78.

Environment Protection and Biodiversity Conservation Act 1999 (EPBC Act). 1999. Canberra: Department of the Environment and Energy, Australian Government. Available from: www.environment.gov.au/epbc (Accessed 12 August 2018).

Equal Employment Opportunity (Commonwealth Authorities) Act (EEO Act). [1987] 2016. C2016C00775. Federal Register of Legislation. [This is a compilation of the Equal Employment Opportunity (Commonwealth Authorities) Act 1987 that shows the text of the law as amended and in force on 1 July 2016 (the compilation date)]. Canberra: Office of Parliamentary Counsel, Australian Government. Available from: www.legislation.gov.au/Details/C2016C00775 (Accessed 12 December 2016).

Erickson, B. 2011. Recreational activism: Politics, nature, and the rise of neoliberalism. *Leisure Studies*, 30 (4), 477–94.

Eriksson-Zetterquist, U., and Styhre, A. 2008. Overcoming the glass barriers: Reflection and action in the 'Women to the Top' programme. *Gender, Work & Organization*, 15 (2), 133–60.

EU Emissions Trading System (EU ETS). 2018. European Commission, EU action: A 'cap and trade' system. EU Emissions Trading System (EU ETS). Available from: https://ec.europa.eu/clima/policies/ets_en (Accessed 30 June 2018).

European Renewable Energies Federation (EREF). 2018. Board & Advisory members. Available from: www.eref-europe.org/about-us/board-advisory-members/ (Accessed 30 August 2018).

European Renewable Energy Research Centres Agency (EUREC). 2018. Board of Directors. Available from: www.eurec.be/en/About/Board-of-Directors/ (Accessed 27 August 2018).

Evans, E. 2016. Diversity matters: Intersectionality and women's representation in the USA and UK. *Parliamentary Affairs*, 69 (3), 569–85.

Fabbrini, F. 2017. *The Law & Politics of Brexit*. Oxford: Oxford University Press.

Faber, D. 2008. *Capitalizing on Environmental Injustice: The Polluter-Industrial Complex in the Age of Globalization*. Lanham, MD: Rowman & Littlefield.

Farr, C.M., Bombaci, S.P., Gallo, T., Mangan, A.M., Riedl, H.L., Stinson, L.T., Wilkins, K., Bennett, D.E., Nogeire-McRae, T., and Pejchar, L. 2017. Addressing the gender gap in distinguished speakers at professional ecology conferences. *BioScience*, 67 (5), 464–68.

Fedorowich, K., and Thompson, A.S. 2013. *Empire, Migration and Identity in the British World*. Manchester: Manchester University Press.

Fenster, T. 2007. Reinforcing diversity: From the 'inside' and the 'outside'. *Gender, Place & Culture: A Journal of Feminist Geography*, 14 (1), 43–49.

Financial Review. 2018. Royal Family reveals how much it cost taxpayers this year (and it's gone up). *Financial Review*, 29 June. Available from: www.afr.com/news/world/europe/royal-family-reveals-how-much-it-cost-taxpayers-this-year-and-its-gone-up-20180629-h1211v (Accessed 19 April 2019).

Fisher, V., and Kinsey, S. 2014. Behind closed doors! Homosocial desire and the academic boys club. *Gender in Management: An International Journal*, 29 (1), 44–64.

Fleming, P., and Sturdy, A. 2011. 'Being yourself' in the electronic sweatshop: New forms of normative control. *Human Relations*, 64 (2), 177–200.

Forbes-Mewett, H., and Snell, D. 2006. Women's participation in 'a boys club': A case study of a regional Trades and Labour Council. *Labour & Industry*, 17 (2), 81–98.

Foster, M., and Meinhard, A. 2005. Women's voluntary organizations in Canada: Bridgers, bonders, or both? *Voluntas*, 16 (2), 143–59.

Fraser, A. 1989. *The Warrior Queens*. New York: Knopf.

Freeman, J. 1973. The origins of the Women's Liberation Movement. *American Journal of Sociology*, 78 (4), 792–811.

Freeman-Maloy, D. 2018. The international politics of settler self-governance: Reflections on Zionism and 'Dominion' status within the British empire. *Settler Colonial Studies*, 8 (1), 80–95.

Gaard, G. 2001. Women, water, energy: An ecofeminist approach. *Organization & Environment*, 14 (2), 157–72.

Gaard, G. 2011. Ecofeminism revisited: Rejecting essentialism and re-placing species in a material feminist environmentalism. *Feminist Formations*, 23 (2), 26–53.

Gaard, G. 2014. What's the story? Competing narratives of climate change and climate justice. *Forum for World Literature Studies*, 6 (2), 272–91.

Gaard, G. 2015. Ecofeminism and climate change. *Women's Studies International Forum*, 49, 20-33.

Gaard, G. 2017. *Critical Ecofeminism*. Lanham, MD: Lexington Books.

Gahrton, P. 2015. *Green Parties, Green Future: From Local Groups to the International Stage*. London: Pluto Press.

Gardner, S., and Stevens, G. 1992. *Red Vienna and the Golden Age of Psychology, 1918–1938*. New York: Praeger.

Garrett, P.M. 2013. *Social Work and Social Theory: Making Connections*. Bristol: Policy Press.

Garry, P.M. 2012. *Limited Government and the Bill of Rights*. Columbia, MO: University of Missouri Press.

Gauja, A., and Jackson, S. 2016. Australian Greens party members and supporters: Their profiles and activities. *Environmental Politics*, 25 (2), 359–79.

Gerulis-Darcy, M. 2010. Capitalizing on environmental injustice: The polluter-industrial complex in the age of globalization. *Environmental Justice*, 3 (1), 37–39.

Gheaus, A. 2015. Three cheers for the token woman! *Journal of Applied Philosophy*, 32 (2), 163–76.

Giddens, A. 2009. On rereading the presentation of self: Some reflections. *Social Psychology Quarterly*, 72 (4), 290–95.

Giddens, A. 1991. *Modernity and Self-identity: Self and Society in the Late Modern Age*. Cambridge: Polity Press in association with Basil Blackwell.

Gilardi, F. 2015. The temporary importance of role models for women's political representation. *American Journal of Political Science*, 59 (4), 957–70.

Gillard, J. 2012. Julia Gillard's Misogyny Speech. *Network Ten*, 10 October. Available from: www.youtube.com/watch?v=SOPsxpMzYw4/ (Accessed 16 May 2013).

Glazebrook, T. 2005. Gynocentric eco-logics. *Ethics & the Environment*, 10 (2), 75–99.

Glencross, A. 2016. *Why the UK Voted for Brexit: David Cameron's Great Miscalculation*. London: Palgrave Macmillan.

Glencross, M., Rowbotham, J., and Kandiah, M.D. 2016. *The Windsor Dynasty 1910 to the Present: 'Long to Reign Over Us'?* London: Palgrave Macmillan.

Godfery, M. 2018. The crown: Is it still 'White' and 'English-speaking'? *The Round Table*, 107 (4), 493–506.

Gow, J., and Leahy, T. 2005. Agency and environmental risk in the Hunter region. *Journal of Sociology*, 41 (2), 117–41.

Grady, J., Marquez, R., and McLaren, P. 2012. A critique of neoliberalism with fierceness: Queer youth of color creating dialogues of resistance. *Journal of Homosexuality*, 59 (7), 982–1004.

Greenpeace International. 2016. *Annual Report 2016*. Available from: https://storage. googleapis.com/planet4-international-stateless/2018/11/6188faf2-greenpeace_international_annualreport2016.pdf (Accessed 22 April 2019).

Greenpeace International. 2018. International Executive Directors. Available from: www.greenpeace.org/archive-international/en/about/how-is-greenpeace-structured/management/executive-director/ (Accessed 21 July 2018).

Greenpeace International. 2018. Management Structure. Available from: www.greenpeace. org/archive-international/en/about/how-is-greenpeace-structured/management/ (Accessed 16 May 2018).

Greer, G. 2010a. Greer takes swipe at 'clown' Abbott. *Sydney Morning Herald*, 25 August. Available from: www.smh.com.au/politics/federal/greer-takes-swipe-at-clown-abbott-20100825-13qqn.html (Accessed 18 April 2019).

Greer, G. 2010b. Pragmatism rules over principles. *Herald Sun*, 28 June. Available from: www.heraldsun.com.au/news/pragmatism-rules-over-principles-for-julia-gillard/news-story/14bff243983732825f55dba9943efd18?sv=33240dcbc4d98de9e16b2404a4e36340 (Accessed 17 April 2019).

Greer, G. 1999. *The Whole Woman*. London: Doubleday.

Gregory, M.R. 2009. Inside the locker room: Male homosociability in the advertising industry. *Gender, Work & Organization*, 16 (3), 323–47.

Grey, S., and Sawer, M. 2008. *Women's Movements: Flourishing or in Abeyance?* London: Routledge.

Gruber, H. 1991. *Red Vienna: Experiment in Working-Class Culture, 1919–1934*. New York: Oxford University Press.

Grusky, D.B., ed. 2014. *Social Stratification: Class, Race, and Gender in Sociological Perspective*, 4th edn. Emeryville, CA: Avalon Publishing.

Gupta, N. 2007. Women research scholars in IITs: Impact of social milieu and organisational environment. *Sociological Bulletin*, 56 (1), 23–45.

Haberman, M. 2016. Nikki Haley chosen as U.N. Ambassador. *New York Times*, 23 November. Available from: www.nytimes.com/2016/11/23/us/politics/nikki-haley-donald-trump-un-ambassador.html (Accessed 1 December 2017).

Hacohen, M.H. 2000. *Karl Popper, the Formative Years, 1902–1945: Politics and Philosophy in Interwar Vienna*. Cambridge: Cambridge University Press.

Hale, H.C. 2008. The development of British military masculinities through symbolic resources. *Culture & Psychology*, 14 (3), 305–32.

Hall, B. 2013. Julia Gillard surprised by impact of misogyny speech. *Sydney Morning Herald*, 26 July. Available from: www.smh.com.au/federal-politics/political-news/julia-gillard-surprised-by-impact-of-misogyny-speech-20130726-2qp4q.html/ (Accessed 2 August 2013).

Hannam, J., Auchterlonie, M., and Holden, K. 2000. *International Encyclopedia of Women's Suffrage*. Santa Barbara, CA: ABC-CLIO.

Haute, E.V. 2016. *Green Parties in Europe*. Farnham: Ashgate.

Hautmann, H. 2012. Vienna: A city in the years of radical change 1917–20. In: C. Wrigley, ed., *Challenges of Labour: Central and Western Europe 1917–1920*. London: Routledge, 87–104.

Havemann, P. 1999. *Indigenous Peoples' Rights in Australia, Canada and New Zealand.* Auckland: Oxford University Press.

Hawkins, M. 2014. *Global Structures, Local Cultures.* South Melbourne, VIC: Oxford University Press.

Haynes, N., Jacobson, S.K., and Wald, D.M. 2015. A life-cycle analysis of minority underrepresentation in natural resource fields. *Wildlife Society Bulletin*, 39 (2), 228–38.

Hazel, R. 1966. White Anglo-Saxon Protestant. *Hudson Review*, 19 (4), 551–84.

Healey, K. 1998. *A Republic: Yes or No?* Balmain, NSW: Spinney Press.

Heuer, M., and Yan, S. 2017. Marcellus Shale fracking and Susquehanna River stakeholder attitudes: A five-year update. *Sustainability*, 9 (10), 1713.

Hickman, T. 2018. The New Zealand Bill of Rights Act: Going beyond declarations. *Policy Quarterly*, 10 (4), 39–45.

Hiebert, J., and J.B., Kelly. 2015. *Parliamentary Bills of Rights: The Experiences of New Zealand and the United Kingdom Experiences.* Cambridge: Cambridge University Press.

Hochman, E.R. 2016. *Imagining a Greater Germany: Republican Nationalism and the Idea of Anschluss.* Ithaca, NY: Cornell University Press.

Horton, D. 2006. Demonstrating environmental citizenship? A study of everyday life among green activists. In: A. Dobson & D. Bell, eds., *Environmental Citizenship.* Cambridge, MA: MIT Press, 127–50.

Hosey, S. 2011. Canaries and coalmines: Toxic discourse in The Incredible Shrinking Woman and Safe. *Feminist Formations*, 23 (2), 77–97.

Howell, P. 1998. An Australian convention conceived in controversy. *The Round Table*, 87 (347), 343–355.

Hudson, W., and Kane, J. 2000. *Rethinking Australian Citizenship.* New York: Cambridge University Press.

Hunt, A., and Wheeler, B. 2018. Brexit: All you need to know about the UK leaving the EU. *BBC News*, 22 September. Available from: www.bbc.com/news/uk-politics-32810887 (Accessed 25 September 2018).

Irvine, J. 2017. Chances are, she's smarter than you: The truth about that 'token' woman you dismiss. *Sydney Morning Herald*, 27 March. Available from: www.smh.com.au/comment/chances-are-shes-smarter-than-you-the-truth-about-that-token-woman-you-dismiss-20170325-gv6jvf.html (Accessed 20 April 2017).

Irving, H., and Murray, A. 2001. *Trusting the People: An Elected President for an Australian Republic.* Cottesloe, WA: Design by Design Practitioners.

Irwin, R. 2010. *Climate Change and Philosophy: Transformational Possibilities.* London: Continuum International.

Jacks, T. 2017. Turnbull warns Australian voters 'conservative' on constitutional change. *Sydney Morning Herald*, 27 May. Available from: www.smh.com.au/national/turnbull-warns-australian-voters-conservative-on-constitutional-change-20170527-gwegxt.html (Accessed 12 June 2017).

Jagger, G. 2008. *Judith Butler: Sexual Politics, Social Change and the Power of the Performative.* London: Routledge.

Jeffery, C. 1995. *Social Democracy in the Austrian Provinces, 1918–1934: Beyond Red Vienna.* London: Leicester University Press.

Johnson, V., and Gurung, R. 2011. Defusing the objectification of women by other women: The role of competence. *Sex Roles*, 65 (3/4), 177–88.

Jones, B. 2017. *Alternatives to Neoliberalism: Towards Equality and Democracy.* Bristol: Policy Press.

Jones, B.T., and McKenna, M. 2013. *Project Republic: Plans and Arguments for a New Australia*. Collingwood, VIC.: Black.

Jonnergård, K., Stafsudd, A., and Elg, U. 2010. Performance evaluations as gender barriers in professional organizations: A study of auditing firms. *Gender, Work & Organization*, 17 (6), 721–47.

Jonsson, S. 2013. *Crowds and Democracy: The Idea and Image of the Masses from Revolution to Fascism*. New York: Columbia University Press.

Kadi, J. 2015. Recommodifying housing in formerly 'Red' Vienna? *Housing, Theory and Society*, 32 (3), 247–65.

Kantola, J. 2008. 'Why do all the women disappear?' Gendering processes in a political science department. *Gender, Work & Organization*, 15 (2), 202–25.

Kaplan, Y. 2018. (Re)considering sovereignty in the European integration process. *Asian Journal of German and European Studies*, 3 (1), 1–11.

Karp, P. 2018. Greens MP Jeremy Buckingham urged to stand aside over harassment allegations. *The Guardian*, 3 August. Available from: www.theguardian.com/australia-news/2018/aug/03/greens-lee-rhiannon-jeremy-buckingham-sexual-harassment-inquiry (Accessed 30 August 2018).

Kaufmann, E.P. 2004. *The Rise and Fall of Anglo-America*. Cambridge, MA: Harvard University Press.

Kawharu, M. 2018. The 'unsettledness' of Treaty claim settlements. *The Round Table*, 107 (4), 483–92.

Keller, J.M. 2012. Virtual feminisms. *Information, Communication & Society*, 15 (3), 429–47.

Kelsen, H. 1996. *Introduction to the Problems of Legal Theory: A Translation of the First Edition of the Reine Rechtslehre or Pure Theory of Law*. Oxford: Clarendon.

Kelsen, H. 2004. *A New Science of Politics: Hans Kelsen's Reply to Eric Voegelin's 'New Science of Politics'. A Contribution to the Critique of Ideology*. Berlin: De Gruyter.

Kemp, S.P. 2011. Recentring environment in social work practice: Necessity, opportunity, challenge. *British Journal of Social Work*, 41 (6), 1198–210.

Kershaw, A.D. 2013. *Women in Europe between the Wars: Politics, Culture and Society*. Farnham: Ashgate.

Kermoal, N.J., Altamirano-Jiménez, I., and Horn-Miller, K. 2016. *Living on the Land: Indigenous Women's Understanding of Place*. Edmonton, AB: AU Press.

Khatibi, F.S., and Indira, M. 2011. Empowerment of women through self help groups and environmental management: Experiences of NGOs in Karnataka state, India. *Journal of Human Ecology*, 34 (1), 29–40.

Kitchen, M. 1988. *Europe between the Wars: A Political History*. London: Longman.

Kopecek, L. 2009. The Slovak Greens: A complex story of a small party. *Communist and Post-Communist Studies*, 42 (1), 115–40.

Kosny, A., and MacEachen, E. 2010. Gendered, invisible work in non-profit social service organizations: Implications for worker Health and Safety. *Gender, Work & Organization*, 17 (4), 359–80.

Kmec, J.A., and Skaggs, S.L. 2014. The 'state' of equal employment opportunity law and managerial gender diversity. *Social Problems*, 61 (4), 530–58.

Knowles, L., and McClymont, A. 2018. 'I was shocked and afraid': Women say Greens botched their sexual misconduct complaints. *ABC News*, 3 August. Available from: www.abc.net.au/news/2018-08-02/women-say-greens-botched-sexual-misconduct-complaints/10060954 (Accessed 17 August 2018).

Kumarasingham, H., and Power, J. 2014. Semi-presidential regimes: Some lessons for Australian Republicans? *The Round Table*, 103 (4), 423–32.

Kwan, S., and Trautner, M.N. 2009. Teaching and learning guide for 'beauty work: individual and institutional rewards, the reproduction of gender, and questions of agency'. *Sociology Compass*, 3 (6), 1017–21.

Lagi, S. 2012. Hans Kelsen and the Austrian Constitutional court (1918–1929). *Co-herencia*, 9 (16), 273–95.

Leahy, T. 2003. Ecofeminism in theory and practice: Women's responses to environmental issues. *Journal of Interdisciplinary Gender Studies*, 7 (1/2), 106–25.

Leahy, T. 2008. Discussion of 'global warming and sociology'. *Current Sociology*, 56 (3), 475–84.

Levine, D.S., and Strube, M.J. 2012. Environmental attitudes, knowledge, intentions and behaviors among college students. *Journal of Social Psychology*, 152 (3), 308–26.

Lewis, P. 2006. The quest for invisibility: Female entrepreneurs and the masculine norm of entrepreneurship. *Gender, Work & Organization*, 13 (5), 453–69.

Lindsay, S. 2008. The Care–tech link: An examination of gender, care and technical work in healthcare labour. *Gender, Work & Organization*, 15 (4), 333–51.

Lipenga, K.J. 2018. Voicing marginality: Disability in Leila Aboulela's Lyrics Alley. *Journal of African Cultural Studies*, 30 (1), 93–104.

Lobo, M., and Morgan, L. 2012. Whiteness and the city: Australians of Anglo-Indian heritage in suburban Melbourne. *South Asian Diaspora*, 4 (2), 123–37.

Loizidou, E. 2007. *Judith Butler: Ethics, Law, Politics*. Abingdon, Oxon: Routledge.

Love, T., and Garwood, A. 2011. Wind, sun and water: Complexities of alternative energy development in rural northern Peru. *Rural Society*, 20 (3), 294–307.

Lowry, D. 2009. Age, the life course, and environmental justice. *Environmental Justice*, 2 (3), 109–16.

MacGregor, S. 2001. A matter of interpretation: On the place of 'lived experience' in ecofeminist research. *Women & Environments International Magazine*, 52/53, 34.

MacGregor, S. 2006. No sustainability without justice: A feminist critique of environmental citizenship. In: A. Dobson and D. Bell, eds., *Environmental Citizenship*. Cambridge, MA: MIT Press, 101–26.

MacGregor, S. 2009. A stranger silence still: The need for feminist social research on climate change. *Sociological Review*, 57, 124–40.

MacGregor, S. 2010. Gender and climate change: From impacts to discourses. *Journal of the Indian Ocean Region*, 6 (2), 223–38.

MacGregor, S. 2014. Only resist: Feminist ecological citizenship and the post-politics of climate change. *Hypatia*, 29 (3), 617–33.

Mack, K. 1993. Austrian research on eastern and southeastern Europe. *Kultursoziologie*, 2 (1), 126–133.

Mackenzie, C., and Stoljar, N. 2000. *Relational Autonomy: Feminist Perspectives on Automony, Agency, and the Social Self*. New York: Oxford University Press.

MacLeod, A.E. 1992. Hegemonic relations and gender resistance: The new veiling as accommodating protest in Cairo. *Signs*, 17 (3), 533–57.

MacSmith, J. 2016. Public support for a republic hits record high as Turnbull and Shorten show their support. *News Corp Australia Network*, 21 December. Available from: www.news.com.au/national/politics/public-support-for-a-republic-hits-record-high-as-turnbull-and-shorten-show-their-support/news-story/cf8c6f2c424202c2d0e8fb7d70c f0a89 (Accessed 5 January 2017).

Maddison, S. 2004. Young women in the Australian Women's Movement: Collective identity and discursive politics. *International Feminist Journal of Politics*, 6 (2), 234–56.

Maddison, S., and Scalmer, S. 2006. *Activist Wisdom: Practical Knowledge and Creative Tension in Social Movements*. Sydney: University of New South Wales Press.

Maleta, Y. 2009. Playing with fire: Gender at work and the Australian female cultural experience within rural fire fighting. *Journal of Sociology*, 45 (3), 291–306.

Maleta, Y. 2011a. Social dimensions of gender and hegemony within environmental organisations and communities. *International Journal of Diversity in Organizations, Communities and Nations*, 10 (6), 79–91.

Maleta, Y. 2011b. The politics of the environment: Australian women's activism in the Greens party. *International Journal of Interdisciplinary Social Sciences*, 5 (11), 187–200.

Maleta, Y. 2012. Activism as a barrier and gender dynamics within Australian Third Sector Environmentalism. *Third Sector Review* [Special issue: Environmental Organisations], 18 (1), 77–97.

Maleta, Y. 2015. Nurturing identity and the "role of mother" within Australian environmental advocacy. *International Journal of Interdisciplinary Environmental Studies*, 10 (4), 1–13.

Maleta, Y. 2018a. A sociocultural insight to feminist activist sustainable citizenship. *International Journal of Sustainability in Economic, Social, and Cultural Context*, 14 (2), 31–44.

Maleta, Y. 2018b. Australian women's anti-nuclear leadership: The framing of peace and social change. *Journal of International Women's Studies*, 19 (6), 70–86.

Mallory, C. 2006. Ecofeminism and forest defense in Cascadia: Gender, theory and radical activism. *Capitalism, Nature, Socialism*, 17 (1), 32–49.

Manne, K. 2017. *Down Girl: The Logic of Misogyny*. New York: Oxford University Press.

Marfo, A. 2017. Breaking through the Boys' Club at NACA. *Women in Higher Education*, 26 (4), 9.

Marshall, A. 2002. Organizing across the divide: Local feminist activism, everyday life, and the election of women to public office. *Social Science Quarterly*, 83 (3), 707–25.

Marshall, J. 1995. Working at senior management and Board levels: Some of the issues for women. *Women in Management Review*, 10 (3), 21–25.

Marshall, J. 2011. En-gendering notions of leadership for sustainability. *Gender, Work & Organization*, 18 (3), 263–81.

Martin, G. 2011. Showcasing security: The politics of policing space at the 2007 Sydney APEC meeting. *Policing and Society*, 21 (1), 27–48.

Mason, D. 2003. *Explaining Ethnic Differences: Changing Patterns of Disadvantage in Britain*. Bristol: Policy Press.

Mattl, S. 2009. The ambivalence of modernism from the Weimar Republic to National Socialism and Red Vienna. *Modern Intellectual History*, 6 (1), 223–34.

Mattl, S. 2013. The case of Red Vienna. *Lua Nova – Revista de Cultura e Politica*, 89, 191–213.

Mattl, S. 2016. Between socialism and feminism: Charlotte Glas (1873–1944). *Religions*, 7 (8), 1–10.

May, T. 2016. Speech: Statement from the new Prime Minister Theresa May. *Gov.UK*, 13 July. London: The Rt. Hon Theresa May MP, Prime Minister's Office. Available from: www.gov.uk/government/speeches/statement-from-the-new-prime-minister-theresa-may (Accessed 1 August 2016).

McDonald, S. 2011. What's in the "old boys" network? Accessing social capital in gendered and racialized networks. *Social Networks*, 33 (4), 317–30.

McFarland, J. 2014. Are there jobs for women in green job creation? *Women & Environments International Magazine*, 94/95, 22–25.

McGovern, P. 2017. *Small Voluntary Organisations in the 'Age of Austerity': Funding Challenges and Opportunities*. London: Palgrave Macmillan.

McGregor, C. 2009. *Class in Australia*. Ann Arbor, MI: Viking Penguin.

McIlroy, T. 2018. National Energy Guarantee reliability component critical to future policy: business. *Financial Review*, 9 September. Available from: www.afr.com/new/national-energy-guarantee-reliability-component-critical-to-future-policy-business-20180909-h154mk (Accessed 13 September 2018).

McIvor, D.W. 2016. *Mourning in America: Race and the Politics of Loss*. Ithaca, NY: Cornell University Press.

McLellan, B. 2009. *Unspeakable: A Feminist Ethic of Speech*. Townsville, QLD: OtherWise Publishing.

McNay, L. 2000. *Gender and Agency: Reconfiguring the Subject in Feminist and Social Theory*. Malden, MA: Polity Press.

McNay, L. 2003. Agency, anticipation and indeterminacy in feminist theory. *Feminist Theory*, 4 (2), 139–48.

Mellor, M. 1993. Building a new vision: Feminist, Green Socialism. In: R. Hofrichter, ed., *Toxic Struggles: The Theory and Practice of Environmental Justice*. Philadelphia: New Society Publishers, 36–46.

Mellor, M. 1997. *Feminism & Ecology*. Cambridge: Polity Press.

Mellor, M. 2002. Ecofeminist economics. *Women & Environments International Magazine*, 54/55, 7–10.

Mellor, M. 2010. Escaping from bondage. *Capitalism Nature Socialism*, 21 (4), 86–88.

Mellor, M. 2012. Money as a public resource for development. *Development*, 55 (1), 45–53.

Mellor, M. 2013. *Feminism and Ecology*. Oxford: Wiley.

Merchant, C. 1994. *Ecology*. Atlantic Highlands, NJ: Humanities Press.

Merchant, C. 2013. *Reinventing Eden: The Fate of Nature in Western Culture*. Abingdon, Oxon: Routledge.

Merchant, C. 2016. *Autonomous Nature: Problems of Prediction and Control from Ancient Times to the Scientific Revolution*. Abingdon, Oxon: Routledge.

Meynell, L. 2009. *Embodiment and Agency*. University Park: Pennsylvania State University Press.

Mies, M. 1986. *Patriarchy and Accumulation on a World Scale: Women in the International Division of Labour*. London: Zed Books.

Ministry for Culture and Heritage. 2017. *Treaty of Waitangi*. Wellington: Ministry for Culture and Heritage, New Zealand Government. Available from: https://mch.govt.nz/treatyofwaitangi (Accessed 26 July 2017).

Mix, T. 2011. Rally the people: Building local-environmental justice grassroots coalitions and enhancing social capital. *Sociological Inquiry*, 81 (2), 174–94.

Moore, N. 2008. Eco/feminism, non-violence and the future of feminism. *International Feminist Journal of Politics*, 10 (3), 282–98.

Morris, L. 2017. The last Indigenous Tasmanian. *National Geographic*, 8 May. Available from: www.nationalgeographic.com.au/australia/the-last-indigenous-tasmanian.aspx (Accessed 3 February 2018).

Mortimer-Sandilands, C. 2008. Eco/feminism on the edge. *International Feminist Journal of Politics*, 10 (3), 305–13.

Mount, H. 2017. *Summer Madness: How Brexit Split the Tories, Destroyed Labour and Divided the Country*. London: Biteback Publishing.

Murphy, K. 2013. Julia Gillard reveals what she thought when she gave the misogyny speech. *The Guardian*, 26 July. Available from: www.theguardian.com/world/2013/jul/26/julia-gillard-misogyny-kevin-rudd/ (Accessed 1 August 2013).

Nagy, R. 2017. Can reconciliation be compelled? Transnational advocacy and the Indigenous–Canada relationship. *Peace & Change*, 42 (3), 313–41.

Nascimento, M., and Connell, R. 2017. Reflecting on twenty years of masculinities: An interview with Raewyn Connell. *Ciencia and Saude Coletiva*, 22 (12), 3975–80.

Newspoll. 2018. Opinion polls: Federal politics. *Newspoll*. Available from: www.newspoll.com.au/opinion-polls-2/opinion-polls-2/ (Accessed 4 September 2018).

New Zealand Emissions Trading Scheme (NZ ETS). 2018. Ministry for the Environment, Climate Change. Available from: www.mfe.govt.nz/ets (Accessed 10 November 2018).

Nunlee, M. 2016. *When Did We All Become Middle Class?* New York: Routledge.

Organo, V., Head, L., and Waitt, G. 2013. Who does the work in sustainable households? A time and gender analysis in New South Wales, Australia. *Gender, Place & Culture: A Journal of Feminist Geography*, 20 (5), 559–77.

Otnes, C.C., and Maclaran, P. 2018. Royalty: Marketplace icons. *Consumption Markets & Culture*, 21 (1), 65–75.

Palmer, R.R. 2014. *The Age of the Democratic Revolution: A Political History of Europe and America, 1760–1800*. Princeton, NJ: Princeton University Press.

Parliament of Australia. 2018. Homepage. Available from: www.aph.gov.au/ (Accessed 19 June 2018).

Parliament of Australia. 2018. House of Representatives. Available from: www.aph.gov.au/About_Parliament/House_of_Representatives (Accessed 19 June 2018).

Parliament of Australia. 2018. Senate. Available from: www.aph.gov.au/About_Parliament/Senate (Accessed 19 June 2018).

Parliament UK. 2018. The Monarch and Parliament. Available from: www.parliament.uk/education/about-your-parliament/mps-lords-monarch/the-monarch-and-parliament/ (Accessed 31 July 2018).

Patel, J. 2018. Will New Zealand inevitably become a Republic, 'just as Britain will be blurred into Europe'? *The Round Table*, 107 (4), 429–12.

Payne, J. 2009. Emotional labour and skill: A reappraisal. *Gender, Work & Organization*, 16 (3), 348–67.

Pease, B. 2002. *Men and Gender Relations*. Croydon, VIC: Tertiary Press.

Perkins, A. 2016. Theresa May's speech: What she said and what she meant. *The Guardian*, 14 July. Available from: www.theguardian.com/politics/ng-interactive/2016/jul/13/theresa-mays-speech-what-she-said-and-what-she-meant (Accessed 16 September 2017).

Pemberton, G. 2017. Why New Zealand's Maori got a Treaty, and Australia's Indigenous peoples didn't. *Sydney Morning Herald*, 3 June. Available from: www.smh.com.au/federal-politics/political-news/why-new-zealands-maori-got-a-treaty-and-australias-indigenous-peoples-didnt-20170601-gwhysd.html (Accessed 30 June 2017).

Petherbridge, D. 2014. The Season of the Witch. *The Independent*, 28 September

Philpot, S.P., Ellard, J., Duncan, D., Dowsett, G.W., Bavinton, B.R., Down, I., Keen, P., Hammoud, M.A., and Prestage, G. 2016. Gay and bisexual men's interest in marriage: An Australian perspective. *Culture, Health & Sexuality*, 18 (12), 1347–62.

Plibersek, T. 2016. Tanya's Record. Tanya Plibersek, MP [Member for Sydney]. Sydney Office. Available from: www.tanyaplibersek.com/record (Accessed 30 June 2018).

Plumwood, V. 1997. *Feminism and the Mastery of Nature*. London: Routledge.

Plumwood, V. 2002. *Environmental Culture: The Ecological Crisis of Reason*. New York: Routledge.

Plumwood, V. 2006. The concept of a cultural landscape: Nature, culture and agency in the land. *Ethics and the Environment*, 11 (2), 115–50.

Pocock, B. 2003. *The Work/Life Collision: What Work Is Doing to Australians and What to Do about It*. Annandale, NSW: Federation Press.

Pocock, B. 2005. Work/care regimes: Institutions, culture and behaviour and the Australian case. *Gender, Work & Organization*, 12 (1), 32–49.

Pocock, B., Charlesworth, S., and Chapman, J. 2013. Work-family and work-life pressures in Australia: Advancing gender equality in 'good times'? *International Journal of Sociology and Social Policy*, 33 (9/10), 594–612.

Poiner, G. 1990. *The Good Old Rule: Gender and Other Power Relationships in a Rural Community*. Sydney: Sydney University Press in association with Oxford University Press.

Pollack, E. 2015. *The Only Woman in the Room: Why Science Is Still a Boys' Club*. Boston, MA: Beacon Press.

Poynting, S., and Donaldson, M. 2005. Snakes and leaders: Hegemonic masculinity in ruling-class boys' boarding schools. *Men and Masculinities*, 7 (4), 325–46.

Praderio, C. 2017. Here's where the royal family gets their money. *Insider*, 12 January. Available from: www.thisisinsider.com/where-does-the-royal-family-get-money-2017-1 (Accessed 28 January 2018).

Prazmowska, A. 2000. *Eastern Europe and the Origins of the Second World War*. Basingstoke; New York: St. Martin's Press.

Probert, B. 2005. 'I just couldn't fit it in': Gender and unequal outcomes in academic careers. *Gender, Work & Organization*, 12 (1), 50–72.

Probert, B., and Wilson, B.W. 1993. *Pink Collar Blues: Work, Gender and Technology*. Carlton, VIC: Melbourne University Press.

Prokhovnik, R. 1998. Public and private citizenship: From gender invisibility to feminist inclusiveness. *Feminist Review*, 60, 84–104.

Prokhovnik, R. 2015. From sovereignty in Australia to Australian sovereignty. *Political Studies*, 63 (2), 412–30.

Public Service Commission. 2015. *Annual Report, 2014-15*. Sydney: Public Service Commission, NSW Government. Available from: www.apsc.gov.au/annual-report-2014-15 (Accessed 1 February 2019).

Punch, K.F. 2005. *Introduction to Social Research: Quantitative and Qualitative Approaches*, 2nd edn. London: Sage.

Rankin, G., and Gale, F. 2003. Keep them in the dark: Australian government strategy to weaken activism against Australia's new nuclear reactor. *Capitalism, Nature, Socialism*, 14 (3), 137–58.

Rauchensteiner, M. 2014. *The First World War: And the End of the Habsburg Monarchy, 1914–1918*. Berlin: De Gruyter Open.

Raunio, T. 2015. The Greens and the 2015 elections in Finland: Finally ready for a breakthrough? *Environmental Politics*, 24 (5), 830–34.

Rees, B., and Garnsey, E. 2003. Analysing competence: Gender and identity at work. *Gender, Work & Organization*, 10 (5), 551–78.

Renewable Energy Association (REA). 2018. REA Board Members. Available from: www.r-e-a.net/about/board-members (Accessed 2 August 2018).

RenewableUK. 2017. UK women dominate new wind energy rankings. Women Into Wind Initiative. News & Publications, Press Releases. Available from:

www.renewableuk.com/news/news.asp?id=334349&hhSearchTerms=%22women+and +wind%22 (Accessed 24 April 2018).

RenewableUK. 2018. Homepage. Available from: www.renewableuk.com/ (Accessed 18 April 2018)

RenewableUK. 2018. How we work. Available from: www.renewableuk.com/page/Work (Accessed 26 April 2018).

RenewableUK. 2018. Organisational Structure. Available from: www.renewableuk.com/ page/structure (Accessed 27 April 2018).

Rentetzi, M. 2004. Gender, politics, and radioactivity research in interwar Vienna: The case of the Institute for Radium Research. *Isis*, 95 (3), 359–93.

Rentetzi, M. 2005. Designing (for) a new scientific discipline: The location and architecture of the Institut für Radiumforschung in early Twentieth-Century Vienna. *British Journal for the History of Science*, 38 (3), 275–306.

Rentetzi, M. 2008. *Trafficking Materials and Gendered Experimental Practices: Radium Research in Early 20th Century Vienna*. New York: Columbia University Press.

Rentetzi, M. 2010. Gender, politics, and radioactivity: The case of Red Vienna. *Travail, genre et societies*, 1, 127–46.

Republic of Austria. 2018. Parliament. Available from: www.parlament.gv.at/ENGL/ (Accessed 28 August 2018).

Republic of Austria. 2018. Parliamentary Dimension. Available from: www.parlament. gv.at/ENGL/EU2018/ (Accessed 29 August 2018).

Rodriguez-Ruiz, B., and Rubio-Marin, R. 2012. *The Struggle for Female Suffrage in Europe: Voting to Become Citizens*. Boston; Leiden: Brill.

Ross-Smith, A. and Huppatz, K. 2010. Management, women and gender capital. *Gender, Work & Organization*, 17 (5), 547–66.

Ruane, J.M. 2005. *Essentials of Research Methods: A Guide to Social Research*. Malden, MA: Blackwell.

Rudd, K. 2008. *Apology to Australia's Indigenous Peoples*. Canberra: Australian Government. Available from: www.australia.gov.au/about-australia/our-country/our-people/apology-to-australias-indigenous-peoples (Accessed 11 July 2015).

Rydell, R.J., McConnell, A.R., and Beilock, S.L. 2009. Multiple social identities and stereotype threat: Imbalance, accessibility, and working memory. *Journal of Personality & Social Psychology*, 96 (5), 949–66.

Sandilands, C. 1995. From natural identity to radical democracy. *Environmental Ethics*, 17 (1), 75–91.

Sandilands, C. 1997. Wild democracy: Ecofeminism, politics, and the desire beyond. *Frontiers: A Journal of Women Studies*, 18 (2), 135–56.

Sasser, J.S. 2014. The wave of the future? Youth advocacy at the nexus of population and climate change. *Geographical Journal*, 180 (2), 102–10.

Savage, M. 2017. Jeremy Corbyn gives more power to new Labour party members. *The Guardian*, 9 July. Available from: www.theguardian.com/politics/2017/jul/08/ jeremy-corbyn-labour-party-members-birmingham-council-vote (Accessed 17 July 2017).

SBS. 2016. Linda Burney to become first female Indigenous MP in Australia's history. *SBS News*, 2 July. Available from: www.sbs.com.au/news/article/2016/07/02/linda-burney-become-first-female-indigenous-mp-australias-history (Accessed 1 August 2016).

Schlembach, R. 2011. How do radical climate movements negotiate their environmental and their social agendas? A study of debates within the Camp for Climate Action (UK). *Critical Social Policy*, 31 (2), 194–215.

Schutte, V. 2017. *Unexpected Heirs in Early Modern Europe: Potential Kings and Queens.* Cham: Springer International.

Segal, L. 1999. *Why Feminism: Gender, Psychology, Politics.* New York: Columbia University Press.

Segal, L., ed. 2007. *Slow Motion: Changing Masculinities, Changing Men.* Basingstoke: Palgrave Macmillan.

Selway, J.B.M. 2003. The Constitutional role of the Queen of Australia. *Common Law World Review*, 32 (3), 248–74.

Seton-Watson, H. 1945. *Eastern Europe between the Wars, 1918–1941.* Cambridge: The University Press.

Sharp, E.A., SoRelle-Miner, D., Bermudez, J.M., and Walker, M. 2008. The glass ceiling is kind of a bummer: Women's reflections on a gender development course. *Family Relations*, 57 (4), 530–41.

Sheckels, T.F. 2012. *Political Communication in the Anglophone World: Case Studies.* Lanham, MD: Lexington Books.

Shepard, P.M., and Corbin-Mark, C. 2009. Climate justice. *Environmental Justice*, 2 (4), 163–66.

Sheppard, S. 2017. Obama Wasn't No FDR. *USA Today* (March 2017), 145 (2862), 22–24.

Shiva, V. ed. 1993. *Ecofeminism.* Melbourne, VIC: Spinifex.

Shiva, V. 2005. *Earth Democracy: Justice, Sustainability, and Peace.* Cambridge, MA: South End Press.

Shiva, V. 2008. *Soil, Not Oil: Climate Change, Peak Oil and Food Insecurity.* London: Zed Books.

Shiva, V. 2014. Biofortification, genetic engineering and corporate interests: False solutions to malnutrition. *Development*, 57 (2), 268–73.

Shiva, V. 2016. *Stolen Harvest: The Hijacking of the Global Food Supply.* Lexington: University Press of Kentucky.

Shiva, V., and Moser, I. 1995. *Biopolitics: A Feminist and Ecological Reader on Biotechnology.* London: Zed Books.

Shuster, S. 2016. The U.K.'s old decided for the young in the Brexit vote. *Time*, 24 June. Available from: http://time.com/4381878/brexit-generation-gap-older-younger-voters/ (Accessed 1 March 2017).

Sioufi, R., and Bourhis R.Y. 2017. Francophone intergroup attitudes and readiness for interprovincial migration in Canada. *Canadian Ethnic Studies*, 49 (1), 43–65.

Skard, T. 2014. *Women of Power: Half a Century of Female Presidents and Prime Ministers Worldwide.* Bristol: Policy Press.

Smith, M.J., and Pangsapa, P. 2008. *Environment and Citizenship: Integrating Justice, Responsibility and Civic Engagement.* London: Zed Books.

Smith, R., Vromen, A., and Cook I., eds. 2012. *Contemporary Politics in Australia: Theories, Practices and Issues.* Cambridge: Cambridge University Press.

Snow, D.A. 2013. *The Wiley-Blackwell Encyclopedia of Social and Political Movements.* Hoboken: Blackwell.

Snow, D. 2016. Malcolm Turnbull disappoints crowd at Australian Republican Movement birthday. *Sydney Morning Herald*, 18 December. Available from: www.smh.com.au/national/malcolm-turnbull-disappoints-crowd-at-australian-republican-movement-birthday-20161218-gtdk5f.html (Accessed 16 May 2018).

SolarPower Europe. 2018. Management. Available from: www.solarpowereurope.org/about/our-team/ (Accessed 29 August 2018).

Staggenborg, S. 2016. *Social Movements.* New York: Oxford University Press

Stein, R. 2004. *New Perspectives on Environmental Justice: Gender, Sexuality, and Activism.* New Brunswick, NJ: Rutgers University Press.

STEMM. 2018. *Gender Equity in STEMM.* Science in Australia Gender Equity (SAGE). Available from www.sciencegenderequity.org.au/gender-equity-in-stem/ (Accessed 21 August 2018).

Stoddart, M.C.J., and Tindall, D.B. 2011. Ecofeminism, hegemonic masculinity, and environmental movement participation in British Columbia, Canada, 1998–2007: 'Women always clean up the mess'. *Sociological Spectrum,* 31 (3), 342–68.

Sturgess, B., and Boyfield, K. 2013. How the Crown Estate could become Britain's first sovereign wealth fund. *World Economics,* 14 (4), 1.

Sullivan, S. 2011. Supposing truth is a woman? A commentary. *International Feminist Journal of Politics,* 13 (2), 231–37.

Sullivan, S. 2013. Banking nature? The spectacular financialisation of environmental conservation. *Antipode,* 45 (1), 198–217.

Summers, A. 2013. *The Misogyny Factor.* Sydney: NewSouth.

Sundström, A., and McCright A.M. 2014. Gender differences in environmental concern among Swedish citizens and politicians. *Environmental Politics,* 23 (6), 1082–95.

Sweeney, L., and Belot, H. 2018. Scott Morrison beats Peter Dutton in Liberal spill to succeed Malcolm Turnbull; Julie Bishop loses Deputy position. *ABC News,* 24 August. Available from: www.abc.net.au/news/2018-08-24/live-scott-morrison-replaces-malcolm-turnbull-as-pm-after-spill/10159462 (Accessed 28 August 2018).

Talbot, K., and Quayle, M. 2010. The perils of being a nice guy: Contextual variation in five young women's constructions of acceptable hegemonic and alternative masculinities. *Men & Masculinities,* 13 (2), 255–78.

Tatchley, C., Paton, H., Robertson, E., Minderman, J., Hanley, N., and Park, K. 2016. Drivers of public attitudes towards small wind turbines in the U.K. *PLoS One,* 1 (3), 1–16.

Taylor, A. 2004. *Lords of Misrule: Hostility to Aristocracy in Late Nineteenth and Early Twentieth Century Britain.* Basingstoke, Hampshire: Palgrave Macmillan.

Taylor, B. 2007. *Australia as an Asia Pacific Regional Power: Friendships in Flux?* New York: Routledge.

Taylor, D. 1997. *Disappearing Acts: Spectacles of Gender and Nationalism in Argentina's 'Dirty War'.* Durham, NC: Duke University Press.

Taylor, V. 1989. Social Movement continuity: The Women's Movement in Abeyance. *American Sociological Review,* 54 (5), 761–73.

The Telegraph. 2004. Demands on the privy purse. *The Telegraph,* 25 June. Available from: https://www.telegraph.co.uk/news/uknews/1465445/Demands-on-the-privy-purse.html (Accessed 12 December 2018).

The Telegraph. 2019. Prince William booed and heckled at service to mark 50 years of Royal Navy's nuclear submarines. *The Telegraph,* 3 May. Available from: www.telegraph.co.uk/news/2019/05/03/prince-william-booed-heckled-nuclear-deterrent-service/ (Accessed 5 May 2019).

Terjesen, S., Sealy, R., and Singh, V. 2009. Women Directors on corporate Boards: A review and research agenda. *Corporate Governance: An International Review,* 17 (3), 320–37.

Thampapillai, V. 2005. *A Bill of Rights for New South Wales and Australia: Discussion Paper.* Sydney: The Law Society of New South Wales. Available from: https://books.google.com.au/books/about/A_Bill_of_Rights_for_New_South_Wales_and.html?id=ZoKJnQAACAAJ&redir_esc=y (Accessed 11 April 2019).

Thoma, D. 2012. Democracy and dictatorship after Freud. A controversy on the relationship between politics and the generation game. *Psyche-Zeitschrift für Psychoanalyse und ihre Anwendungen* [Journal of Psychoanalysis and its Applications], 66 (5), 408–32.

Tomazin, F., and Koziol, M. 2017. High Court gives the green light to Turnbull government's same-sex marriage survey. *Sydney Morning Herald*, 7 September. Available from: www.smh.com.au/federal-politics/political-news/high-court-gives-the-green-light-to-turnbull-governments-samesex-marriage-survey-20170906-gybqm8.html (Accessed 14 September 2017).

UK Income Inequality. 2017. The scale of economic inequality in the UK. *The Equality Trust*. Available from: www.equalitytrust.org.uk/scale-economic-inequality-uk (Accessed 19 March 2018).

Unger, N.C. 2008. The role of gender in environmental justice. *Environmental Justice*, 1 (3), 115–20.

Ussher, J.M. 2011. *The Madness of Women: Myth and Experience*. London: Routledge.

Valles, S.A. 2015. Bioethics and the framing of climate change's health risks. *Bioethics*, 29 (5), 334–41.

Veri, F. 2016. Minimalist citizenship and national identity in the Australian Republican Movement. *Studies in Ethnicity and Nationalism*, 16 (1), 3–19.

Vildåsen, S.S., Keitsch, M., and Fet, A.M. 2017. Clarifying the epistemology of corporate sustainability. *Ecological Economics*, 138, 40–46.

Walby, S. 1990. *Theorizing Patriarchy*. Oxford: Blackwell.

Walby, S. 2011. Is the knowledge society gendered? *Gender, Work & Organization*, 18 (1), 1–29.

Walby, S. 2012. Globalization and varieties of modernity. *EurAmerica*, 42 (3), 391–417.

Walby, S. 2013. *Patriarchy at Work: Patriarchal and Capitalist Relations in Employment*. Hoboken, NJ: Wiley.

Walby, S. 2015. *Crisis*. Malden, MA; Cambridge: Polity Press.

Walby, S., and Armstrong, J. 2010. Measuring equalities: Data and indicators in Britain. *International Journal of Social Research Methodology*, 13 (3), 237–49.

Wantland, R. 2005. Feminist frat boys? Fraternity men in the (women's studies) house. *NWSA Journal*, 17 (2), 156–63.

Warren, K.J. 1997. *Ecofeminism: Women, Culture, Nature*. Bloomington: Indiana University Press.

Warren, K.J. 1999. Peacemaking and philosophy: A critique of justice for hero and now. *Journal of Social Philosophy*, 30 (3), 411–23.

Warren, K.J., and Cady, D.L., eds. 1996. *Bringing Peace Home: Feminism, Violence, and Nature*. Bloomington: Indiana University Press.

Wasserman, J. 2012. The Austro-Marxist struggle for 'intellectual workers': The lost debate on the question of intellectuals in interwar Vienna. *Modern Intellectual History*, 9 (2), 361–88.

Wasson, E.A. 2017. *The British and Irish Ruling Class, 1660–1945*. Berlin: De Gruyter Open.

Watts, S.M., George, M.D., and Levey, D.J. 2015. Achieving broader impacts in the National Science Foundation, Division of Environmental Biology. *BioScience*, 65 (4), 397–407.

WhitlamDismissal.com. 2017. Homepage. Available from: http://whitlamdismissal.com/ (Accessed 3 February 2018).

Wibben, A.T.R. 2016. *Researching War: Feminist Methods, Ethics and Politics*. Abingdon, Oxon: Routledge.

Williams, K. 2015. *Young Elizabeth: The Making of the Queen*. New York: Pegasus Books.

Wilson, S.M., Richard, R., Joseph, L., and Williams, E. 2010. Climate change, environmental justice, and vulnerability: An exploratory spatial analysis. *Environmental Justice*, 3 (1), 13–19.

Women In Energy (WIE). 2018. Women In Energy [Professional association]. Available from: www.womeninenergy.com.au/index.html (Accessed 1 August 2018).

Woodford, B. 2013. Perceptions of a Monarchy without a King: Reactions to Oliver Cromwell's Power. Montréal: McGill-Queen's University Press.

Woodward, R., and Winter, P. 2006. Gender and the limits to diversity in the contemporary British army. *Gender, Work & Organization*, 13 (1), 45–67.

World Nuclear Organisation. 2018. Fukushima Daiichi accident. World Nuclear Organisation. Available from: www.world-nuclear.org/information-library/safety-and-security/safety-of-plants/fukushima-accident.aspx (Accessed 30 June 2018).

Wright, K.A.M., and Holland, J. 2014. Leadership and the media: Gendered framings of Julia Gillard's 'sexism and misogyny' speech. *Australian Journal of Political Science*, 49 (3): 455–68.

Yancy, G. 2017. *Black Bodies, White Gazes: The Continuing Significance of Race in America*. Lanham, MD: Rowman & Littlefield.

Yaxley, L. 2018. Scott Morrison asked why he has replaced Malcolm Turnbull as Prime Minister. *ABC News*, 10 September. Available from: www.abc.net.au/news/2018-09-10/scott-morrison-asked-why-he-is-prime-minister-not-turnbull/10222804 (Accessed 13 September 2018).

Yoder, J.D., and Aniakudo, P. 1997. 'Outsider within' the firehouse. [African American women firefighters] *Gender & Society*, 11 (3), 324–41.

Yoder, J.D., Tobias, A., and Snell, A. 2011. When declaring 'I am a feminist' matters: Labeling is linked to activism. *Sex Roles*, 64 (1/2), 9–18.

Zarkov, D. 2017. Populism, polarization and social justice activism. *European Journal of Women's Studies*, 24 (3), 197–201.

Index

244   Index

Great War, the 41–43; *see also*
Red Vienna; World War I
Greenham Common: Peace Camp
36–37; Peace Chain 36–37; *see also*
Cockburn, C.
Greenpeace International 6, 21, 179
Greens party, the (Australian) 5, 8–13,
24–26, 38, 63–64, 95, 189; *see also* My
research project

Head of State 4, 35, 46, 176, 191,
207–09
hegemony 45, 49, 57, 85, 96, 118, 134,
168, 184
hegemonic: masculinity 5, 12–17,
21–23, 31, 37–39, 62–63, 68–71, 76,
82–83, 89–91, 92, 96, 101–07, 113,
129–30, 133, 138, 148, 151–52, 173,
178, 189
hegemony: masculine 15–19, 24, 29, 31,
68, 81, 85–86, 91, 100, 179, 191, 198;
masculinist 23, 77, 83, 93, 103–04, 179;
men's hegemony 14, 51, 71, 81, 87–90,
105, 116, 124, 135, 141, 144–46, 149,
158, 190, 212; *see also* Anglo-Celtic/
male middle class privilege; chauvinism;
class; frame; privileged; ruling class
masculinity
hereditary: elitism 3, 12–13, 45; monarch/
monarchism 192, 210; privilege 23, 46,
49, 51, 208, 212; *see also* Monarchy;
privileged
hierarchical: anti- 68, 172–79;
bureaucracies 179; cultural-structures
13; elites 4, 48, 105; less 10, 56, 84, 106,
174; males 103–06, 192; non- 178–80;
organisations 179; structured/structures
39, 55, 156, 174–75
hierarchy 172–80; executive hierarchy
21, 25, 90, 118, 194; leadership
hierarchy 57, 163; 'less hierarchy'
5, 12–14, 26; rigid hierarchy 15, 27,
66, 172
human/nonhuman 123–26

IeNGOs (International environmental
nongovernmental organisations) 5, 7–8,
21, 29, 38, 55, 78, 103, 177–79, 189–90;
see also My research project
identity: activist 12; agentic 21, 155;
Australian 4; CALD 9; civic 22, 41;
Indigenous cultural 182; men's 80–81;
national 43, 48–49; of the subject 21;
women's 16, 37, 74, 91; work 81, 114;
see also subjectivity

imperialism 17, 25, 35, 41–43, 61;
see also Arendt's critique of imperial
chauvinism; Red Vienna
incompetence (gender): age/ageism,
tags of technical incompetence 158;
assumptions of female incompetence
152; assumptions, women's technical
and physical incompetence 96;
assumptions, women's technical-
scientific incompetence 105; labels of
10; labels, female technical-scientific
incompetence 174, 190–91; labels,
scientific-intellectual incompetence
159; labels, technical incompetence
169; stereotypes, female technical-
intellectual incompetence 18, 62;
stereotypes, women's technical and
scientific incompetence 95; stigmas, age,
gender and incompetence 159; stigmas,
female intellectual incompetence 111;
stigmas, female scientific-technical
incompetence 158; tags of female
technical incompetence in science
113–15; women's resistance to labels/
stereotypes/stigmas/tags 190, 204
Indigenous: identity 181–84;
reconciliation 5–6, 33, 185, 214;
rights 9–10, 33, 181–83; sovereignty
4–6, 33, 185, 191, 214; Stolen
Generation 185, 214–15; Tasmanian
9, 181, 185; Treaty 4–6, 31–34, 49, 52,
181–85, 191, 200, 213–15; women's
justice 181, 185; women's leadership
31, 181–85, 214; women's multiple
performative agentic competencies
19; women's rights 181; *see also*
Initiatives, my
industrial elites 22, 37, 49, 83, 108, 138,
149, 200; *see also* empirical; gendered;
hierarchical; masculinist; military;
patriarchy; patriarchal; ruling
elites
inequality *see* gender equality/
inequality
(in)equity/(in)justice: Bill of Rights Act
201; career (in)equity 27; feminist aims
of 84; frames/framing of 77, 96–97,
100, 171, 184–85; gender (in)equity
35, 70–71, 214; Initiatives 32–33; key
frame, of 190–92; male hegemony 61;
sub-frames, of 5–12, 17, 177, 190–92;
women's (in)equity 48–49, 101, 106,
160, 192, 199–200; women's leadership
struggle 28, 33
IeNGOs *see* eNGOs

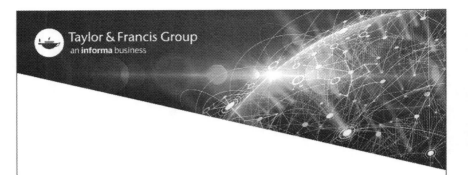

Printed in the United States
by Baker & Taylor Publisher Services